JOHN HUME
THE PERSUADER

JOHN HUME
THE PERSUADER

Stephen Walker

GILL BOOKS

Gill Books
Hume Avenue
Park West
Dublin 12
www.gillbooks.ie

Gill Books is an imprint of M.H. Gill and Co.

© Stephen Walker 2023

9780717196081

Designed by Liz White Designs
Proofread by Emma Dunne
Indexed by Eileen O'Neill
Printed and bound in Great Britain by Clays Ltd, Elcograf S.p.A.
This book is typeset in Minion Pro and FreightBig Pro

The paper used in this book comes from the wood pulp of sustainably managed forests.

All rights reserved.
No part of this publication may be copied, reproduced or transmitted in any form or by any means, without written permission of the publishers.

A CIP catalogue record for this book is available from the British Library.

5 4 3 2 1

For Katrin, Grace, Jack and Gabriel.

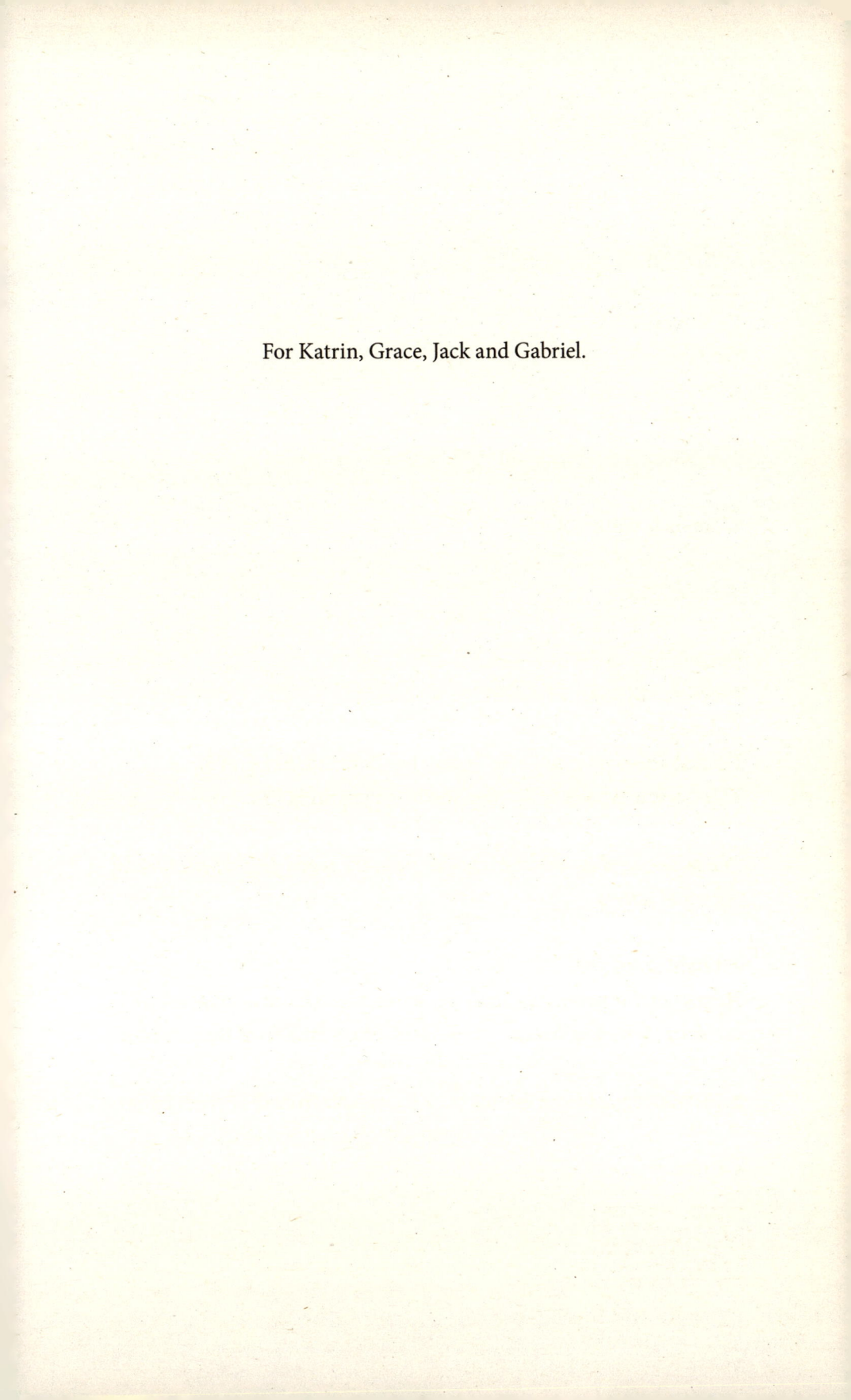

CONTENTS

Prologue ix
1. Wee Johnny Hume 1
2. Maynooth man 14
3. Pat and parcel 24
4. The faceless men 36
5. Ulster at the crossroads 47
6. We shall overcome 66
7. Party time 80
8. Bloody Sunday 98
9. Writing on the wall 114
10. Yes Minister 129
11. Follow the leader 144
12. Ourselves alone 161
13. The monkey and the organ grinder 177
14. Let's talk 193
15. Peace in a week 213
16. Thumbs up 231
17. President Hume 248
18. Down at the Waterfront 266
19. A night in Oslo 282
20. Doctor's orders 296
21. Stepping down 307
22. Ireland's Greatest 322
23. Thank you John 333
24. The Persuader 344
    Acknowledgements 365
    Sources 367
    Bibliography 372
    Endnotes 375
    Index 405

PROLOGUE

Derry, February 1992

On a Saturday morning in February 1992, John Hume was at home in Derry with his wife, Pat. The Humes would often begin their weekends there and then would travel in the afternoon to their holiday home in Greencastle in County Donegal. On this winter day, the MP and MEP needed a break more than ever. He was exhausted, fed up and highly stressed. Exasperated by the lack of political progress and the endless cycle of violence, his frustration was at boiling point.

As leader of the SDLP, he was particularly annoyed with the backbiting and criticism that was coming from within his own party. The latest talks process initiated by the British government had failed to make any headway, and his colleagues seemed split on whether or not to enter another round of negotiations. Hume wanted to make another attempt. Others, notably his fellow MPs Seamus Mallon and Eddie McGrady, felt the conditions being placed on further discussions would not work.

Hume was hurt and thought his authority was being questioned. He was fed up with being criticised by some colleagues who, in his view, were not prepared to be bold or imaginative. He had always believed that dialogue was the answer to creating political stability in Northern Ireland, so, if his party rejected this new round of talks he wanted to know what the alternative was.

He felt isolated and lonely and, not for the first time, he was depressed. He had read in the press how his leadership was being questioned, and he was convinced that it was time for a fresh start. He had put his thoughts down on paper, and it was now time to follow through with his plan. Someone else could take the flak. His stewardship of the party that he had helped to found was coming to an end. Hume was in a dark place. He felt that he had tried everything to try and advance politics in Northern Ireland. He had talked to Sinn Féin but there was little sign that there would be a permanent IRA ceasefire. He had had numerous discussions with the other parties, but a political agreement was elusive. He was worn out, and it was time to step down.

In another part of Derry, Mark Durkan had finished breakfast and was getting ready to make the 70-mile journey to Belfast. Headhunted by Hume in 1983, he was his assistant, speechwriter and confidante. A former student leader, Durkan was bright, articulate and fiercely loyal to his boss. He was seen by many as a future party leader. In his role as SDLP chairman, he was due to travel to West Belfast to spend the day canvassing. A general election was expected in the coming weeks, and the party had high hopes of taking the seat from the Sinn Féin president, Gerry Adams.

As he prepared to leave his house, Durkan's home phone rang, and when he answered it he heard a familiar voice. Pat Hume told Mark to come over to the house immediately and speak to John. It was clearly urgent.

Pat, normally the voice of quiet calmness, sounded agitated. In the background, Durkan could hear John wanting to know who she was talking to.

When Durkan arrived at the Humes's home minutes later, it was clear all was not well. Pat ushered him in and John unburdened himself. He had simply had enough of being SDLP leader. He was battered by the constant criticism, and he was convinced some of his colleagues would not support him in another round of inter-party talks. He felt undermined, he was cross with the press coverage, and he believed resignation was the only way out. He told Durkan that his 13-year reign as leader was over.

Durkan listened and then responded by using 'John Hume tactics' on John Hume. He reminded him that he always said 'you don't react to reaction'. Durkan argued that he should pause and think. He urged his friend to simply work through the consequences. It was role reversal – the apprentice was advising the master. Hume, so often the dispenser of logic and wisdom to colleagues, was now being urged to heed his own advice. With every response from Durkan, there came another dramatic Hume revelation of what he believed had to happen.

Hume informed his assistant that, as well as quitting the party leadership, he also wanted to give up his Westminster seat. He candidly told Durkan that he needed to be ready to fill his shoes and become the new Foyle MP. Durkan countered this argument by telling Hume that this was not the time for him to step away from parliament. Hume had been having secret conversations with the Sinn Féin president, Gerry Adams, with the hope that the talks could lead to a permanent IRA ceasefire. Durkan made it clear to Hume that, if he quit parliament and walked away from the leadership, 'this will wreck everything'.[1] It was a powerful argument for peace.

Hume then offered a document to Durkan who started to read it. It was a two-page statement about to be issued to the Press Association announcing his departure as SDLP leader. For Durkan, it was a devastating read. The press release was incendiary and Hume's guest knew it must not be issued under any circumstances. The two men then talked some more and the atmosphere improved.

Finally, it was agreed that John and Pat would think about things over the weekend and would not say anything publicly. They agreed to go to their holiday home in Donegal, relax and unwind and take time to 'get their breath'.

Durkan had achieved what Pat Hume hoped he would. He had talked her husband back from the brink. As he headed for the door, he still had the document detailing Hume's intention to quit.

Outside the house, he said his goodbyes and Pat Hume mouthed a 'thank you' to him and held up crossed fingers. She was relieved that the crisis had been averted. Before his guest could drive off, John Hume raised his arm and told him to stop. He then asked for the return of his resignation statement. Durkan's sleight of hand had not been clever enough.

The Humes headed for Donegal. Mark Durkan went in the opposite direction and drove to Belfast. He had already done a day's work. A good day's work – convincing his friend and mentor to stay the course and finish the job.

Sometimes persuaders need to be persuaded too.

THE PERSUADER

1

WEE JOHNNY HUME

'I was the lucky one, I passed the 11 plus.'
John Hume

Derry's most famous politician was not always known as John Hume. For years he was called Johnny and, to this day, old school friends still refer to him affectionately by that name. It captures a boyish sense of mischief when his world was dominated by a love of soccer, cricket and comics. Even at his funeral in August 2020, when his life was being replayed, there were stories of how Johnny the schoolboy would eventually become John the statesman.

Hume and his home city are entwined. To understand him as a political leader it is necessary to examine his roots and his experience. His childhood and family life shaped his thought process, his language and ultimately his ideas. His upbringing gave him an understanding of history and a sense of place. As a child of the 1930s, he grew up in a recently divided Ireland and, as a young Catholic boy, he was well aware of life in a religiously mixed society. The border was in plain sight and he could see it and experience it. The political consequences of partition were all around. Donegal and Derry, once part of the same equation, were now apart.

As he grew up, he was also surrounded by a list of social ills. The streets were home to bad housing, unemployment, poverty and gerrymandering by unionist politicians. These were all local issues, yet they would eventually gain national importance. Hume saw the world from a Derry perspective – a place that reflected the competing identities of

Britishness and Irishness. It was a city that historically was overshadowed by conflict and division. Even the very name of his birthplace is contested to this day.

Unionists generally call the city Londonderry, which was the title it was given by the trades guilds from London after the Plantation of Ulster. A new walled development was built by the River Foyle and named Londonderry by royal charter of King James I in 1613. The surrounding land was given to companies which encouraged English and Scottish settlers, and at the same time, limited land was made available to Irish tenants. Unionists have always seen the name 'Londonderry' as a reminder of their Britishness and their ties to Britain.

History hangs over Hume's homeplace. The city is central to Orange folklore, and it is revered as the sacred place where Protestants held out between 1688 and 1689 against an advancing Catholic army. This is the ground within the shadow of the walls where the battle cry of 'no surrender' was coined. For loyalists, unionists and members of the Orange Order and the Royal Black Institution, the city has a special place in their history. Every year the Apprentice Boys of Derry commemorate the actions of the 13 apprentices who shut the city gates in 1688 and set in train the Great Siege.

For nationalists, the city is equally significant. They feel Derry is as Irish as Dublin and insist that it is ultimately governed by the wrong country. They see the 'London' prefix as colonial appropriation. In their eyes, it is a reminder of a past best forgotten. When John Hume was growing up, Derry's split identity was very evident. The city had a shared history but two very different outlooks – just like Northern Ireland itself.

Born on 18 January 1937, life began for John Hume in a small terraced house on 20 Lower Nassau Street in Derry. His parents were Sam Hume and Annie Doherty, and the couple had married a year earlier. At 32, Annie was some 14 years younger than Sam. He was born in 1890, the youngest of his family who originated in the Scottish Lowlands. Although the Humes were Catholic, one side of the family had Protestant roots.

Sam's grandfather William Hume, a Presbyterian, arrived in Ireland from Scotland in the mid-nineteenth century. A skilled stonemason, he came to County Donegal looking for a job and would eventually end up in the village of Burt at the base of the Inishowen peninsula. He built station houses for the new railway, and his handiwork has stood the test of time, as some of his stone bridges still survive. He married a young Catholic woman and left behind his Presbyterianism as he experienced his new life in Ireland.

His grandson, Sam Hume, had little formal education. He left school aged 12 and, like many of his generation, he had to leave Ireland to find employment. He initially moved to Scotland to stay with family members where he worked in the shipyards of Glasgow.

When the First World War broke out in 1914, he, like thousands of young Irish men, joined the British Army and in the uniform of the Royal Irish Rifles saw service in France. He survived unscathed but, like many of those who witnessed the bloody horrors of the Great War, the experience left a mark. John recalled one conversation with his father:

> I remember saying to him late in life about it, why do you not talk? And he said the terrible memories. He said he was in a trench and a shell knocked his belt off, but it killed his colleagues ... and he'd never forgotten it. And as a result, he was very much against war because of what it means in practice.[1]

Sam Hume eventually came back to Ireland and later got a job in the civil service where he worked in the Ministry of Food. When the Second World War broke out he switched back to his old work and joined Harland and Wolff shipbuilders, working as a riveter along the banks of the Foyle and helping to service the vessels from the Atlantic fleet. The city was a strategic port and was used as a safe haven for Allied ships and submarines.

Life was economically tough so the cash from the wartime work was much needed by Sam and Annie Hume. They started living in one room in the Bogside area of the city and had to wait several years before they could find a bigger property. Soon John was joined by brothers and sisters. There were four boys, John, Harry, Patrick and Jim, and three girls, Annie, Sally and Agnes.

Family life was very busy at 10 Glenbrook Terrace, which was the first home the Humes could call their own. It was rented accommodation and was a very cramped two-up, two-down terraced house. It was simple and functional but, for a large family like the Humes, it meant there was little space or privacy. There were two bedrooms upstairs, with Sam and the boys sleeping in one room and Annie and the girls sleeping in the other. On the ground floor, there was a living room and a kitchen. There was no indoor bathroom; the family used an outside toilet in the yard.

When the war ended in 1945 so too did Sam Hume's work as a riveter. The timing could not have been worse as he was now in his mid-fifties and had seven children to feed. He would not work again, though others in the community had a need for his talents.

He had a way with words and was particularly talented at letter writing and administrative work, so neighbours and friends would often call at the Hume house for help with filling in official documents. John Hume's son Aidan recalls how his grandfather Sam helped people: 'He was unemployed for years but he was very gifted. There would be a line of people outside the door. He was never involved in politics, but it was almost like he ran a constituency clinic. You would have a line of people out the door looking for him to write a letter.'[2]

With his exquisite handwriting, Sam Hume became a man in demand. His years in the civil service had given him an understanding of bureaucracy and a head for figures, so friends with financial problems very often made a beeline for his door.

There was no payment for his assistance; occasionally a packet of cigarettes would be left behind by a grateful caller. Sometimes the small Hume house would be full of people seeking help. As John recalled:

> Our main room was where we ate and did everything at the wooden table. I'd be sitting doing my homework every night and my father would be sitting at the table writing letters. And the people would be queuing up and

coming in to get him to write letters for them about their problems to government departments ... because not only was he a first-class letter-writer, but he knew the inside of the whole government system. So what I always say about that, is that from when I was no age the problems of our people were normality to me and I think that shaped a lot of my thinking because ... it's childhood that makes you what you are.[3]

Sam Hume was a supporter of trade unions, and his politics would have been rooted in helping the community. John says his father was not interested in the constitutional question: 'My father was fundamentally, I think, a Labour man, which in those days in Derry didn't exist as a political party. His view was that politics should be about people's living standards.'[4]

It is clear Sam Hume had an enormous influence on how his eldest son John would come to view the world. He introduced him to the concept of public service, although Sam Hume would have passed it off as simply helping his neighbours. Hume's father is credited with passing on a series of anecdotes about life that John would quote in later years. He advised him to stay away from the flag-waving politics of nationalism. The much-told story goes that Sam and 10-year-old John happened upon an election meeting in the street where nationalists were waving flags and there was much talk about Irish unity. Hume Senior told his son that he should stay away from such things. When young John questioned this, his father said it was because 'you cannot eat a flag'.[5]

The phrase became part of John Hume's political vocabulary, and when he was being interviewed by journalists during his political career it was a tried and tested soundbite. In later years, Hume was often criticised by his political rivals and journalists for endlessly repeating phrases. The flag story became a well-worn anecdote and was often cited as an example of Hume's so-called 'single transferable speech', which was the nickname the media gave to his stock-in-trade answers. Hume said the advice from his father in 1947 was his first political lesson. He said it taught him that it does not matter what flag you identify with; the most important thing is giving people a decent home and food on their table. To Hume, politics had to be much more than national identity. It was about making people's lives better and giving citizens opportunities. Looking back at his childhood, Hume says his parents never talked about party politics: 'Politics of any description were never discussed in our family – they were not part of our world.'[6]

As a child, his relationship with his father was good. Sam Hume was very sociable and enjoyed reading and telling stories. John would also have witnessed his father holding court with his neighbours and friends, and he inherited his ability to tell stories. Life for the Humes in post-war Derry was difficult, as it was for many thousands of people in the city's working-class communities. Good housing and jobs were hard to come by. Money was not just tight – at times it was completely non-existent. Hume would later recall: 'Looking back on it, not only was it extreme poverty; I wondered how my mother actually succeeded in rearing us.'[7]

John Hume was eight years old when his father lost his job. It was a crushing blow to Sam Hume and the household. Reflecting on his father's unemployment, John felt he had been poorly treated: 'I found that incredible because given the job he had during the war, I would have thought someone like him would have got a job but it underlined the unionist control in this part of the world.'[8]

Like many other Derry women, Annie Hume became the main breadwinner when Sam lost his job. As Annie Doherty, she was born and lived in a street that became world-famous and was home to the iconic Free Derry Corner in the Bogside. With a limited education, she had begun her working life as a child. John recalled how her childhood and his were very different: 'My mother's life was very much like many in her time. She was obviously a very highly intelligent woman, but she never went to school because in those days people didn't.'[9]

Annie Hume brought extra money in by working as a seamstress from home and she prepared shirt collars at night for Derry's busy textile trade. John, as the eldest, would stay up with her and help: 'I remember I used to do her secretarial work for her. I used to tie [the collars] up and write the numbers and all the rest of it.'[10]

If Hume inherited his father's sense of public duty, he was also clearly influenced by his mother's work ethic and determination to survive in the most trying of circumstances. He also had a very good relationship with Annie's mother and was a frequent visitor to his grandmother Doherty's home:

> She always encouraged me with my schooling, and we were very fond of each other. Her house was nearer to my school than my own, so I went to her for lunch every school day. She was an excellent cook and, while she prepared the meal, I would run errands for her, such as buying her snuff for which she had a great fondness.[11]

Aware that the family finances were tight, young John contributed by doing a daily paper round and delivering newspapers round the streets in the early evening: 'I did my best to earn money because we were poor. I used to deliver newspapers every night.' The extra cash from delivering copies of the *Belfast Telegraph*, which amounted to a few shillings a week, all went into the Hume family coffers. The newspaper round did not just provide much-needed income, but it indirectly added to the young schoolboy's understanding of current affairs. Hume would read the papers as he delivered them and felt he was 'fully informed as to what was happening in the world'.[12]

At St Eugene's Primary School, he was regarded as a clever boy who worked hard in class. He got on well with a teacher who instilled a belief in him that schoolwork opened the door to opportunity. He started to excel academically and at eight years of age won a class prize which attracted the grand sum of half a crown. Hume was well aware that he was in possession of serious money which could help the family finances. However, others in the school had different plans for Hume's winnings.

A quick-thinking teacher soon appeared at his desk and rattled a charity collection box under his nose. He turned to Hume and said: 'I hear that somebody is carrying a lot of money here. I think the black babies will do well today.'[13]

The box was rattled and Hume remained still and looked ahead. The box was shaken vigorously again and young Johnny Hume stayed calm and stared into the distance. The standoff continued until the teacher gave up. Hume did not give way. He believed the cash would be much better in his mother's hand than in the collecting tin. He would later establish a reputation for kindness but, with an unemployed father and six siblings, he believed the charity donation would have to wait for another day. To Hume's watching classmates it was an early indication of his stubbornness and singlemindedness.

By now, he was also becoming increasingly fascinated by the workings of the Church, so much so that he became an altar boy at St Eugene's Cathedral, the large imposing nineteenth-century gothic church which towered over the Bogside. There were daily masses during the week and services at the weekend, so the young John was constantly making the short journey from the family home to the church grounds. There he would often be in the company of the Bishop of Derry, Neil Farren, who lived beside the cathedral.

Hume remembers the early starts: 'I would go to the cathedral every morning to serve mass. And, of course, when you become a sort of senior altar boy, the Bishop would choose you to be his permanent altar boy. I used to regularly go to Bishop Farren's mass at half eight every morning in the bishop's house.'[14]

The Humes lived in an area of Derry known as the Glen. The streets were mixed, with Catholics and Protestants living together. John Hume recalled: 'In our street, there were three Protestant families and we were extremely friendly. There was no question of any differences between us at all.'[15]

However, he added: 'There were other streets in the district that were totally Protestant and other streets that were totally Catholic. One became very aware of that.'[16] Hume said life as a child was great fun and he said the space outside his house was his playground:

> In my street, there was only one motor car. He was a taxi man, Johnny Bradley. He did not own it, but he was

employed. Nobody else could afford a car and, for that
reason, we were able to play football on the streets and
tie ropes on the lampposts and create swings. We created
our own games.[17]

John Hume captained the Glen Stars football team and in one memorable final they beat a team from Rosemount to win the Father Browne shield. As a football-mad boy, he was understandably thrilled and said it was 'one of the proudest days of my life'. His brother Patsy recalls how John was carried shoulder-high by his team mates. John enjoyed his childhood and said his days in the Glen were 'the best period of my life'.[18]

By 1947, a dramatic law change would alter the course of Hume's life. The Education Act, which had been introduced in the rest of the UK, was finally brought into Northern Ireland. It provided compulsory secondary education for all that would be funded by the state. It meant children could be lifted out of poverty and could be offered a grammar school education, and Hume was one of the first to benefit from this new legislation. He sat the 11 Plus examination and, not surprisingly, passed. That meant he had a scholarship to attend St Columb's, Derry's Catholic grammar school which had previously only been accessible to those children whose parents were able to pay fees.

Hume had to explain to his mother how the scholarship worked:

> I will never forget coming home and saying 'Mammy, I
> am going to college.' And she said, 'We can never afford
> to send you there.' I said, 'But you don't have to pay for
> me, I have got a scholarship.' And she said, 'What is that?'
> And that just underlined to me that ordinary people knew
> nothing about this whole area because they were never
> involved in any way.[19]

Education offered John Hume something many of his parents' generation could only dream of. He admits he was fortunate: 'I was the lucky one. I passed the 11 Plus in its first year and got educated. And then I got a university scholarship. And without those things, I would never have been educated, because before my time nobody in our community got educated unless you belonged to a family who had a business or were professional.'[20]

When he walked into his new school for the first time Hume had a sense of unease: 'I felt that inferiority complex because we were the first 11 Plus – the first generation to go to St Columb's College – and as we grew up that was the place that only the wealthy went to.'[21]

Founded in 1879, St Columb's, at its heart, had a strong Catholic ethos and a reputation for academic excellence and discipline. Many of the staff were priests and they often encouraged their best pupils to consider a future in the church. Faith was already an important part of Hume family life, as John recalled in an unpublished interview in 2003: 'In those days our religion was central to our lives. And, of course, in the evenings my mother would say the rosary with all the family. And that was very normal and almost all the families in the street would do the same thing.'[22]

As an altar boy and someone with a strong faith, John Hume was a prime candidate to go into the priesthood. It was what he wanted, and he felt comfortable in the company of priests. Although most of the St Columb's boys were encouraged to play Gaelic games, the young Hume, by now universally known as Johnny, was mad about soccer. At St Columb's, the boys would play matches at break time with the city boys pitched against the country boys. Seán McCool, from Carndonagh in County Donegal, was the same year as Hume and he also ended up studying for the priesthood at Maynooth, which was Ireland's major Catholic seminary. McCool says Hume was a 'very stylish' player and good with a ball at his feet.[23]

Jim McGonagle, who was two years his junior at St Columb's, remembers Hume playing soccer in the schoolyard and how he loved 'holding onto the ball'. Hume loved the game and 'he could talk soccer all day long'. He specifically remembers Hume getting excited about Derry City winning the Irish Cup in 1954.[24]

In the summer months, he would often spend all day playing cricket. His love of the sport, the most English of games, was quite unusual for a

Catholic schoolboy. He started to go to a place known as the 'Big Field' where he would mix with Protestant boys and they would form teams and play endless games. He loved cricket and he was a good bowler, coming to the attention of an umpire who had influence with one of the local clubs.

Hume later recalled: 'He spotted me bowling and he went to City of Derry, which was a senior cricket team, and told them he had found a great young bowler and they should take me on. And they approached me. I was astonished. I ended up playing senior cricket for City of Derry. Most people find that hard to believe, but that's true. I was the City of Derry's left-arm spin bowler.' In later life, Hume says people were often surprised that as a Catholic he was so good at cricket: 'When people remind me of that these days I just say to unionists, well, I was always good at playing you at your own game!'[25]

Away from the sports field, Hume excelled in the classroom. Throughout his time at school, his grades were good and, as he progressed through the years, his desire to be a priest remained undiminished. He discussed his career plans with his parents and they were fully behind him. His mother, Annie, who was a devout Catholic, was particularly thrilled at the prospect of having a priest in the family. Life for the teenage John Hume was very busy. His schoolwork was intense and with little opportunity at home to read books and write essays in peace he often had to wait until his siblings had gone to bed at night before he could seriously study. His days were long and hectic but very productive. The schoolboy Hume was introduced to a wide range of new subjects. He began a lifelong love affair with French and he excelled in History, two subjects he would later study together in detail at Maynooth. He was also taught Latin and Greek, as the school wanted to encourage boys to consider the priesthood and both subjects were seen as essential.

The young student particularly liked the English classes and enjoyed the way the subject was taught. The school is famous for producing several acclaimed writers, amongst them Brian Friel, Seamus Heaney and Seamus Deane. They got to know Hume and lifelong friendships developed among all four. Heaney remembered Hume from his time at

St Columb's and said that even in those early days Hume gave 'the impression of somebody with a very steady moral and intellectual keel under him, somebody reliable and consistent, who operated from a principled and definite moral centre'.[26]

Looking back, Hume did not gloss over his time at St Columb's. In the 1950s, school life was tough. Like at other institutions, staff at the college used physical punishment if boys underperformed or misbehaved. He recalled one occasion when his classmates were given six slaps for failing to remember the Greek alphabet. It was accepted at the time as standard practice: 'If you were wrong you got slapped. Being slapped was a very normal form, in those days of school, of ensuring that people were disciplined. It was the normal way of maintaining discipline in schools in those days and it was normally accepted by everyone, including parents.'[27]

As a pupil, John Hume continued with his afternoon paper round but was keen to keep it secret from the school authorities. He didn't want them to know that his family needed the cash:

> I remember one night my teacher, Rusty Gallagher, saw me and I tried to hide and he mentioned it to me the next day in school. But he obviously understood my sensitivity and he was praising me. He said, 'God, it's great to see you earning money for your parents.'[28]

Pupils at St Columb's were divided into two categories – day pupils and boarders. Jim McGonagle, who went on to have a long career as a priest, was a boarder and remembers Hume's kindness towards those boys who lived on the premises. He recalls John offering hungry boarders extra portions of food.

Away from studying and schoolwork, there was still time for fun and friendship, and Hume became good pals with Joe Coulter who lived close by. Joe, like John, had a strong Catholic faith and was interested in the priesthood. He was the older brother of Phil Coulter, who would go on to establish himself as a world-renowned songwriter and performer.

Phil Coulter also went to St Columb's, although he was several years behind Hume. He remembers him coming into his house:

> John and my brother, Joe, were big buddies. So John would have been knocking about our house quite a bit. Our house was one of those houses where there were three boys in the family. It was a kind of open-door house. So John probably spent as much time in our house as he could.[29]

Hume thought much of Joe Coulter, and they were model students who shared a love for education and had a strong desire to go into the Church. The expectation at St Columb's was that they would go off to Maynooth and become priests. Hume was not just a friend of Joe Coulter. He was also a close pal of Phil's, and in later life, the two men often performed in public singing the song 'The Town I Loved So Well'. It was written by Coulter in 1973 and became an unofficial anthem for Derry and John Hume. Phil Coulter says Hume had a good voice: 'The thing about people in Derry generally, John included, is everybody in Derry believes they can sing. Whether they can or not, it doesn't really matter, but they believe this with fervour. They have this kind of pact with God.'[30]

Hume's singing almost became as famous as his speeches. In correspondence with this author, Senator George Mitchell recalled how he met Hume at the US ambassador's residence in Dublin when he witnessed the Derry politician entertaining the crowd: 'As a politician myself I had often spoken before large gatherings, but I had never sung solo at one. I was pleasantly surprised that John's singing was as good as his speaking.'[31]

Over the years Hume and Phil Coulter formed quite a musical partnership. Their friendship would last a lifetime and the composer would perform when Hume was awarded the Nobel Peace Prize in Oslo in 1998.

When the time came for his final year at St Columb's, Hume sat a series of tests including the Bishop's Examination. He also had to sit a Latin examination, and not surprisingly he passed them all. That meant he had secured a prized place at St Patrick's College in Maynooth.

A new life was about to begin.

2

MAYNOOTH MAN

*'It takes a good man to go in but it
takes a better man to walk away.'*
Sam Hume

John Hume's new home was now some 16 miles west of Dublin. Maynooth was a world away from Derry and with his pal, Joe Coulter, he quickly had to adjust to this regimented world. Soon, life was made up of meditation, prayers, lectures and silent retreats. The freedom the two boys had enjoyed at home was now curtailed and they were soon on a fast learning-curve trying to absorb the countless rules and regulations.

At 17, Hume had rarely been far from the famous walls of his home city and now he was in unfamiliar surroundings mixing with people he hardly knew. He had signed up for a three-year undergraduate course in History and French, intending to do an additional four years of theological study. He would also be learning Logic and Philosophy in what was seen as a very intensive course. The expectation was that he would be in the seminary for a full seven years and then he would enter the priesthood.

Within days, as he settled into his spartan room, he began to experience a rather basic lifestyle. There were long periods of silent meditation and prayer beginning shortly after 6 a.m. Students were instructed to rise and get dressed in silence. After breakfast, most mornings were taken up by study periods and lectures. Lunch, which was generally small and uninspiring, was followed by more lectures, silent study and then a spiritual talk at around 7 p.m. After supper, there was some free time and then all students were expected to be in bed by 10 o'clock.

It was all controlled, as Hume recalled:

> You had to [go to] your room at a specific time to study. Unlike in university where you could not bother until you had to. Therefore, you did study. But in the between time was when you met with your colleagues and the habit there was you met at a particular point in the grounds and the groups of every district met together and you stood there chatting.[1]

Monsignor Brendan Devlin is well-placed to have a view of what life at Maynooth was like. He experienced days there as both a student training for the priesthood and as a teacher offering guidance to seminarians. He studied at St Patrick's from 1948 until 1952 and later returned to teach Modern Languages. He says there was a reason behind the timetabling: 'The general theory of the thing was that you never had a minute to yourself except the long period of recreation in the middle of the day was long enough to organise and play, let's say, a game of football.'[2]

The authorities at Maynooth were keen to impress on their young seminarians a strict moral code, and rules on behaviour were made clear as soon as the boys arrived. There was a ban on alcohol, and smoking was only allowed on the grounds. There was no access to newspapers, radio or even television, and contemporary current affairs magazines were prohibited. It seemed the outside world would stay just that – outside.

Some seminarians who had experienced boarding schools found the transition to Maynooth relatively straightforward. Seán Donlon, who was there from 1958 to 1961, was one of those.

Ultimately, he would not enter the priesthood but instead would spend thirty years in the Irish Civil Service, including a spell as Irish ambassador in the United States. He and Hume would become close friends in later life and he would play an important behind-the-scenes role in Anglo-Irish relations. As a young man, he enjoyed his time at Maynooth and learned a lot but says students lived life in a 'bubble' and college staff tried to shelter them from the outside world. For example, the authorities were keen to keep the young seminarians away from members of the opposite sex. Donlon recalls: 'You did not see a woman in the grounds.'[3]

If a pupil's sister was visiting, she would not be admitted to the building and instead would be confined to the fringes of the college grounds. Donlon remembers how pals who wanted to see a female sibling had to 'go and see her at the gate lodge'.[4] There were also rules that students were only allowed in each other's rooms if they were sharing the accommodation.

Hume settled in quickly and took to his studies with the same determination and application he had shown at St Columb's. His love of history was encouraged and developed by his tutor Tomás Ó Fiaich, a charismatic individual who would later go on to become a cardinal and serve as Catholic Primate of All Ireland.

Ó Fiaich would play a seminal role in the Catholic Church in the 1980s and he became a key figure in the political life of Northern Ireland during the Troubles, although he and Hume would often take conflicting positions. As a lecturer and role model, he would have an enormous personal impact on Hume's time at Maynooth. A fellow northerner from Cullyhanna in County Armagh, Ó Fiaich had been a brilliant student at St Patrick's a decade earlier. He graduated in 1944, with a first-class degree in Celtic Studies, and later went to St Peter's College in Wexford where he was ordained as a priest in 1945.

Ó Fiaich also studied at University College Dublin and Louvain University in Belgium. Appointed initially as a lecturer in Modern History at Maynooth, he later became a professor and eventually assumed the title of president of the college. A talented linguist who spoke Irish, French and German, he had a reputation as an innovative and enthusiastic lecturer.

Hume and Ó Fiaich got on well together and the young Derry scholar was one of his first students in Maynooth. The two men had much in common. They were both from the North and shared a passion for history, as well as a love of sport. Unlike other lecturers, Ó Fiaich was keen to seek out his charges away from the classroom and engage them in conversation as they walked around the grounds. Ó Fiaich was a smoker and although smoking was banned inside the building it was allowed outside, so he would often chat to students as he enjoyed a quick cigarette between lessons. Hume said he learned much from Ó Fiaich: 'He brought history alive by the very way he talked about it and I never forget taking notes all the time at his lectures.'[5] The admiration, it seems, was mutual.

Monsignor Brendan Devlin knew Tomás Ó Fiaich well. The two men were colleagues and shared a deep interest in the Irish language. They enjoyed history and Irish culture and spoke in Irish when they met. Devlin says Ó Fiaich had a high regard for his young protégé: 'One of the early things Ó Fiaich turned John towards was the local history of Ulster. Now, being a Derry man, John didn't need much pushing.'[6]

Hume was fascinated by history and embraced the course and, in particular, he relished Ó Fiaich's approachable teaching style. This was Hume's first detailed introduction to history and it opened up his mind to the study of different cultures and communities. He, like Ó Fiaich, was intrigued by the twists and turns of Irish history and he mastered the course quickly. He also made an impressive start by ending his first year with honours. Seán Donlon also had experience of Ó Fiaich and says he was brilliant at helping students who showed promise in history. He was taught by him after Hume left Maynooth and remembers that if you worked hard and engaged in the subject, 'Ó Fiaich almost adopted you if you wanted to learn.'[7]

The history lecturer was popular with students and often bent the rules. Donlon recalls how the GAA-mad teacher would love nothing more than talking about the latest All-Ireland results. He was particularly keen to discuss the performance of his home county of Armagh. Donlon remembers how he would regularly tear out a match report from a copy of the *Irish Independent* on a Monday and share it with the pupils. As newspapers were initially banned for pupils, this act of defiance naturally caused a stir around the classroom. Donlon recalls that Ó Fiaich was careful not to pass on the whole newspaper in case the boys would be distracted by 'adverts for women's underwear'.[8]

So what should we make of Ó Fiaich's influence on John Hume? Monsignor Brendan Devlin says it is clear Hume's thinking was influenced by Ó Fiaich, but he insists that the young student would have still questioned much of what he was being taught: 'I would not run away with the idea that it was Tomás Ó Fiaich who turned Hume onto politics. Hume was well able to make his mind up. Hume was not the kind of guy who was just influenced by an eloquent teacher.'[9]

Seán Donlon insists that whilst Ó Fiaich was influential and introduced his students to new ideas, Hume and his tutor had a very different political outlook. He says Hume was never on Ó Fiaich's 'wavelength' politically.[10]

As a student, John Hume had a reputation for being his own man and making his own decisions. As part of his course, he studied Logic under the tutelage of Professor Dermot O'Donoghue. For Hume, this part of his degree was revelatory: 'I was very interested in Logic because of its promotion of thinking … my Professor of Logic was Father O'Donoghue … a strange man but I found him very, very good because he promoted thinking, and good thinking and logical thinking'.[11]

Hume undoubtedly did a lot of deep moral and philosophical thinking in Maynooth and it laid the foundation for his political ideals. So how did this impact his growing political thoughts? Dan Keenan observed John Hume at close quarters, both from his time working as an SDLP press officer and as a journalist in Belfast and Dublin. He later wrote a PhD thesis examining Hume's Derry origins. Keenan believes Hume's time in County Kildare made an impact on his politics: 'I think a lot of the Hume worldview emanates from Maynooth.' He makes the point that Hume was, after all, at a Catholic seminary and hoping to become a priest so, 'he is going to reflect many of the aspects of the philosophy that the church has or had at the time'. Keenan also observes that Hume defined himself as a social democrat and he believes Hume's social democracy is 'steeped in a wider definition of Christianity as he practises it'.[12]

Whilst Hume spent much time studying and examining ideas he would continually return to his personal experiences, as Monsignor Brendan Devlin recalls: 'John Hume, in a sense, was the embodiment of Derry. He was a Derry man first, last and all the time. He talked like a Derry man and thought like a Derry man.'[13]

Devlin speculates that Hume's fascination with history and his study of the past may have started to provoke some rather personal and political queries. He suggests that it got Hume to think about his background and experience:

> You begin to ask questions … how did this come around? I grew up in a city surrounded by battlements. Everything inside the battlement was Protestant and everything in the slums was Catholic. Is this normal in the city? Is this a normal city? And if you have any brains at all you begin to find out it is not. You know, it's not normal and the government of the city is gerrymandered. My crowd is getting no show at all. There must be a reason for this. And, of course, John got into all that.[14]

Hume did not just perform well in History in his first year. He also excelled in French and was fortunate to have an impressive professor from the Lorraine region of France called Hubert Schild. Under Schild's guidance, he immersed himself in the French language and culture, and conversations in the classroom were rarely in English.

In the summer holidays, his language skills improved when he took a break from Maynooth and left Ireland for the first time and travelled to France, visiting Saint-Malo in Brittany. As a young man, he was now spreading his wings and experiencing a slice of life that could not be more different from the cloistered world of Maynooth. Yet, in one sense he may have felt at home when he walked down the streets of Saint-Malo. Like Derry, it is a famous walled city and as he gazed up at the tall granite stones it probably all looked very familiar.

As a budding 'Francophile' he also attended language classes in Paris. This was the beginning of Hume's love affair with France. It was a place he would relax and holiday in for the next five decades. Whilst at Maynooth, he became proficient in spoken and written French:

> Most of the students who came to Maynooth had done Greek because of their choice in earlier years … I was probably the only honours student or maybe there were

two or three, but what it meant in practice was that the honours conversations were in French, the result of which is that I became a very fluent French speaker.[15]

John's family took great pride in their eldest son's language skills as Hume recalled: 'Nobody on the parents' side would ever have spoken another language, you know, and they were amazed that I would be doing that.'[16] Hume's fluency in French was a life skill that turned out to be most useful, particularly when he became an MEP and regularly travelled to Strasbourg and Brussels. Such was his proficiency in the language, and love of it, that he also learned several French songs which he was able to perform, both word-perfect and in tune.

Away from the classroom, there were opportunities for other activities and he played sport and began to hone his debating skills in weekly competitions. There was much to occupy young minds at Maynooth. Hume was busy and found time to edit the college magazine and even persuaded his old St Columb's pal Seán McCool to become a contributor.

McCool says all the staff 'thought the world' of Hume and he and his old schoolmate spent many happy days strolling the grounds of St Patrick's. Whilst luxuries were limited for the seminarians, Hume did manage to get his hands occasionally on sweets or other treats. Renowned for his 'sweet tooth', Hume used to like nothing more than devouring a bar of chocolate. McCool recalls that Hume had a reputation for kindness, but when it came to sharing his chocolate things would be different. He jokingly remembers Hume telling him to 'get away on and get your own'.[17]

Hume seemed at home in the surroundings of Maynooth. He was popular, well-liked and progressing well. On the surface, it appeared that he was content with life in County Kildare, but as time moved on things started to change. He began to privately question whether he really wanted to be a priest and dedicate his life to the Catholic Church. Journalist Paul Routledge wonders if Hume's disillusionment 'may owe something to the prolonged glimpses of the outside world he experienced during the summers he spent in France'.[18]

The young Derry man may have started to find the world of Maynooth rather claustrophobic. With its detailed rules and regular timetabling, St Patrick's had the feel of a strict public school. Hume had never been a boarder, unlike some of his contemporaries, so may have found the move to Maynooth harder than most. In this closed world, Hume was beginning to find the regulations suffocating and was starting to wonder if he was on the right path. Fundamentally, he had to ask himself a question – did he want to be a priest? Was this how he wanted to spend the next 40 or 50 years of his life? There may also have been other reasons which made him start thinking about an alternative career. During his time at St Patrick's, John Hume had the reputation of being an industrious student, who was serious about his vocation. However, an incident in his final months may have helped him decide that a life in the priesthood was not what he wanted.

Bound by its long list of strict routines, St Patrick's College posed a challenge to any rebellious student. Hume was by nature not a rule breaker but in his third year he ended up being disciplined. He unwittingly allowed another student to come into his room. Regulations dictated that only roommates were allowed in shared accommodation and Hume was seen by the dean chatting with a visitor in his room.

Days later, he appeared before a disciplinary committee. He outlined why he felt he had not broken any rules but his explanation was not accepted. He was sanctioned by the college authorities. The reprimand meant he would not be awarded a 'tonsure'. This was the ritual shaving of a small part of the scalp which was done before students took holy orders. According to the journalist Barry White, Hume was 'sickened by the way he was treated'.[19]

A severe stomach complaint led to a period in hospital and he missed his final honours exams. He was laid up for several weeks so his graduation was indefinitely put on hold. The time away from the classroom also gave him an opportunity to reassess his future and he decided that he would not go into the priesthood but instead would leave Maynooth. It was undoubtedly a difficult decision. He agonised over it, but if he felt he was letting his parents down he need not have worried. His father was supportive and he told John, 'It takes a good man to go in but it takes a better man to walk away.'[20]

Jim McGonagle, who took the same path as Hume from St Columb's to Maynooth but who ultimately entered the priesthood, says in one sense it would have been 'easier to stay than to go'.[21] After three years inside a seminary, Hume was now stepping out into the unknown, and his future career was shrouded in uncertainty. It was a tough call but not an uncommon one. Some young men who entered Maynooth found the demands too much and wanted to get married and have a family. Others had a crisis of faith or preferred a career where the financial rewards were greater. Those who turned down the opportunity were often referred to in unflattering terms as 'spoiled priests'. Seán McCool and John Hume lived parallel lives for a while. Both ex-pupils of St Columb's and Maynooth they both ultimately rejected the priesthood and embraced teaching. McCool says he and Hume did not talk about their career choices but says he found the decision to reject the priesthood 'traumatic'. He remembers what it was like leaving Maynooth: 'You feel alienated when you go home.'[22]

At St Patrick's there were unwritten rules if students decided to leave. Seminarians were encouraged not to initially inform their classmates but instead to keep their decision private. The protocol was that a staff member should be informed and then a series of behind-the-scenes discussions would follow. This may have been an attempt to buy some thinking time and give students an opportunity to reconsider.

Tony Johnston, from Derry, was at Maynooth at the same time as John Hume and left after his degree. He says there was no pressure placed on students if they rejected a career as a priest. He recalls that the teaching staff accepted the decision and usually just 'shrugged their shoulders'.[23]

As a senior figure and good communicator, Tomás Ó Fiaich would often be tasked with meeting departing students to discover why they wanted to quit. Ó Fiaich's approachability and down-to-earth manner made him the ideal person to chat to seminarians who were thinking of leaving. In 1961 Seán Donlon's time at Maynooth came to an early end.

He decided to leave and met Ó Fiaich to have a conversation about his future. The pair travelled in the lecturer's Morris Minor to a Dublin hotel where they enjoyed a meal together and chatted about the future. The history tutor showed Donlon great kindness by helping him make the transition from St Patrick's to a course at University College Dublin where Ó Fiaich had studied. He drove him across the city to the UCD campus and he introduced him to many of his contacts. Donlon says he never fell out with Ó Fiaich and says the academic was always 'very generous'.[24] Hume had a similar experience. He also got a trip to a Dublin hotel and a meal courtesy of the authorities at St Patrick's. The good food and the warm words did not alter his final decision.

John Hume would never become Father Hume.

3

PAT AND PARCEL

'There would be no John Hume without Pat.'
Phil Coulter

John Hume was soon back home on the familiar streets of Derry and living once again in cramped conditions with his parents and siblings. At 20 years of age, his life had come full circle and he needed a job urgently. This was not how he imagined life would have turned out.

Despite the uncertainty of what lay ahead, he had at least come to some conclusions and had decided that his career lay in the world of teaching. However, he knew that this decision would not be straightforward. With no teaching experience or training qualifications, he knew it would be difficult to persuade any school principal to give him a start. With fortuitous timing, he secured a job at the Christian Brothers Technical College teaching French and Irish. It was an ideal opportunity, and since he was competent in both languages it suited him perfectly.

Hume took to teaching in the same way he approached studying at Maynooth, and he threw himself into this new role with enthusiasm and vigour. He was a natural communicator and quickly established a reputation as a popular teacher who was capable of getting the best out of students. He had no formal training, so his style and manner were based more on instinct than anything else. He tried to bring both languages alive for his pupils by getting them to talk before they began to concentrate on the niceties of grammar.

He returned to Maynooth briefly in 1958 to sit his finals. He then had the joy of graduating, and with a degree to his name, he hoped that other teaching posts might arise. When a new secondary school opened in Strabane in 1958, an ideal opportunity presented itself. Hume joined the staff at St Colman's and embraced the teaching of French with his trademark enthusiasm and creativity. The pupils at St Colman's were different to the scholarship boys Hume would have mixed with during his days at St Columb's in Derry. The new school was made up of those students who had failed the 11 Plus and whose career aspirations were often for manual or semi-skilled jobs. Hume faced quite a challenge teaching students whose knowledge of French was limited or, in some cases, non-existent.

Don McCrea was one of Hume's students at St Colman's and he would later become a close friend of his and work as his driver. He says unlike other teachers Hume had 'the common touch' and made his lessons 'captivating'.[1] From Sion Mills, McCrea, like many young men in the village, loved his cricket with a religious fervour and there was much rivalry with teams from surrounding towns and villages. McCrea says even though Hume regarded himself as a good seam bowler, the boys from Sion Mills thought their cricketing teacher was just 'average' and they had better players.[2]

Hume was always keen to encourage his pupils to stretch themselves and was always interested in fresh ideas that could enhance their learning. He decided to make contact with his alma mater, and soon he and Monsignor Brendan Devlin from Maynooth were talking:

> John would ring me up from time to time to discuss the problems of a secondary school teacher – not that I was an authority on teaching. I have no real experience of teaching French but we would chat about these things. And one of the things I suggested to him, I think, was to encourage his senior students to use French, not merely chatting to each other but above all to try and learn to write to express themselves. And for that reason, I encouraged him to start a school magazine in French for the French department, which John promptly did.[3]

Hume's bold decision to set up a magazine won him plaudits and recognition from many in the education world. The new publication was commended by the French Consul in Belfast and Hume's teaching methods started to grab the attention of school inspectors and teachers in other institutions. His academic results were impressive with most of his students passing French with distinction.

By now, he and Patricia Hone were dating after they met at a Legion of Mary dance at the Borderland dance hall in Muff in County Donegal. The pair got together during the Easter holidays of 1958 and, after a series of dates, their relationship became serious. At that stage, as Pat recalled, her future husband 'did not have any great interest in politics'.[4]

With five siblings, she lived in the Waterside area of the city across the river from where the Humes lived. She grew up in Cross Street, her father, Patrick, working in a small building business and her mother, Mary, running the family home. Pat and John discovered they had much in common. She had working-class roots and had been a grammar school girl. Rosemary Logue was a number of years behind her at the city's Thornhill College and remembers Pat being approachable and much admired when she was Head Girl: 'She was the loveliest person you could ever have met. Any youngster of any age she would have engaged with. She was a rising star and she was beautiful as well.'[5]

Pat had originally decided to go and study pharmacy but changed her mind and went off to St Mary's College in Belfast to train to be a teacher. She and John got married in 1960 and their nuptials even caught the attention of the local press. Hume would often say that his marriage proposal was one of his better decisions in life.

John Hume's story can't be fully told without chronicling his relationship with Pat and her influence on his life. During John's 40-year political career, she became his confidante, his organiser and, for thousands of constituents, she was the first point of contact. The couple would enjoy 60 years of married life together and would bring up five children, Therese, Áine, Aidan, John and Mo, and in later life, there would be grandchildren and great-grandchildren.

As a couple, they were a good mix and complemented each other in their personalities. Whereas John at times would be a little impatient, and sometimes could be seen as distant, Pat was more relaxed, as their daughter Áine recalls: 'Mum was very calm. I suppose she took things much more slowly than Dad and listened more carefully sometimes than Dad. Dad must have been a really good listener, but it didn't always feel like he was. He always seemed preoccupied.'[6]

Aidan Hume says his mother often kept his father right at key times:

> She would have been quietly influential, but I think he really respected her opinion and then she kept him grounded and made sure on the one side it didn't go to his head and then the other times that it didn't deflate him too much.[7]

Phil Coulter got to know the Humes very well and socialised with them over many decades. He says Pat Hume's importance can't be overstated: 'There would be no John Hume without Pat. You can take that to the bank. Right through all the highs and lows, John used to say he was the parcel and Pat delivered him.'[8]

The Humes's first home was a small terraced house on the Waterside close to where Pat was brought up, and then the young couple moved to a bungalow. By this time John was heavily involved in the credit union movement and much of his spare time was spent at meetings. As the inaugural treasurer of Derry Credit Union he was kept busy and he worked hard with the founding members to build the organisation up in its early years. This was his first foray into public life and it was a great apprenticeship for the political life that would follow.

Hume, it seems, spent little time relaxing, and he embarked on writing and researching an MA thesis, which became a labour of love. It was an examination of Derry's economic history entitled 'Social and Economic Aspects of the Growth of Derry, 1825-1850'. The young teacher chronicled the city's role as an important port and also tracked the birth of the shirt industry. In his research, he also analysed how the population almost doubled and he investigated how his homeplace had a role in Irish emigration.

Hume threw himself into his MA. He spent hours examining shipping records and poring over local newspaper reports and over time he was able to build up a detailed picture of what life was like in Derry during an important time in the middle of the nineteenth century. As he worked at night and during the school holidays, he was encouraged from afar by his old Maynooth tutor Tomás Ó Fiaich, who helped to supervise the final version.

Hume did return to St Patrick's at Maynooth occasionally and Monsignor Brendan Devlin remembers chatting with his former student about his job and the difficulties of teaching. He assumed Hume's career path was now set in stone: 'For me, he was just a recently graduated student, and I thought he was going to spend his life teaching French in Strabane.'[9]

However, Hume's days in Strabane were numbered when he was offered a job back at his old school in Derry. It meant an end to the 30-mile daily commute and resulted in him being reunited with some of the staff who remembered him as a pupil. He began teaching French and History at St Columb's and typically he embraced his new position with enthusiasm and fresh ideas.

He was not just focused on life at school. Away from the classroom, Hume was conscious that in his home city money was in short supply and life was tough for those without a job or with a limited income. He became increasingly interested in the idea of a community bank known as a credit union that could help people who were finding it difficult to get a traditional bank account.

In 1960, he was a founder member of the Derry Credit Union, establishing it along with several others including Father Anthony Mulvey, his friend Michael Canavan and Paddy Doherty who would later become better known as 'Paddy Bogside'. They all pooled their savings and the new initiative began life with the sum of £7.00. The system of banking was straightforward and it all worked under a cooperative ethos. People paid into a central pool which meant they could avail of low-interest loans and also get interest on their savings.

The idea was not just about managing money: it was aimed at giving people control of their finances. This was John Hume's first venture into public life, and as he toured the country encouraging people to set up credit unions he used straightforward language: 'My philosophy in those days was self-help. I used to say to people: our heads and hands are as good as the other side, why aren't we using them to build?' He regarded setting up the credit union movement as his finest achievement: 'It's the thing I am proudest of because no movement has done more good for the people of Ireland.'[10]

Hume threw himself enthusiastically into the group and thought nothing of driving hundreds of miles to deliver a talk or help a scheme become established. Derry Credit Union was the first in Northern Ireland and he later became the youngest ever president of the Credit Union League of Ireland. Mary McAleese remembers Hume visiting her local Catholic parish hall in Belfast when she was a teenager. He came to encourage parishioners to set up a credit union: 'I had never heard anyone speak, first of all with his dignity, but also with his understanding of human dignity with his vision and with his passion. I thought he is the man of our times.'[11]

Hume began to push himself physically and was in the classroom during the day in Derry and then he would travel long distances at night on credit union business. Denis Bradley was taught by Hume in St Columb's. Looking back, he says Hume was very different from the other teachers:

> He was a breath of fresh air in that first year but you could also begin to see that he would come in very tired because he would share the fact that he had perhaps been in Dungannon the night before, or on one or two occasions I think he had been in Cork and driven home from there because he had become very engaged with the Credit Union.[12]

Like Hume, Denis Bradley would go on to have a wide and varied career. He would enter the priesthood but would ultimately leave it and enjoy various roles including being a filmmaker and a journalist and vice-chairman of the Northern Ireland Policing Board. Like Hume, in later life, he would get involved in secret talks aimed at ending the violence of the Troubles.

As a schoolboy at St Columb's, Denis Bradley remembers Hume trying to get pupils to think differently: 'He set up a debate in which he made three or four of us argue that Northern Ireland should be changed by nationalists joining the Unionist Party, by changing it from within and making us argue that in a debate. And that would have been a rarefied moment.'[13]

Hume loved debating and saw the benefits of helping young minds develop by giving them the opportunity to construct arguments and deliver them in public. He set up a current affairs society while working on his public speaking style and got plenty of practice as a member of the Colmcille Debating Society. By this stage, he was driving hundreds of miles every week on credit union business and he thought nothing of coming back home in the small hours of the morning and then existing on a few hours of sleep before going into school. Pat got used to her husband's absences: 'It was like being married to a travelling salesman.'[14]

In his mid-twenties and full of ideas, John Hume was determined to make the credit union thrive in every corner of Ireland. It was unpaid work but he found it rewarding in the knowledge that it had the potential to change lives. If Hume saw 'self-help' as the way to improve community life, he viewed education as the key to unlocking his students' potential.

Professor Paul Arthur, who would become a respected academic and a close friend of Hume's, went to St Columb's and says his teaching style set him apart from other members of staff: 'He had a very good reputation and in a place like St Columb's, which was very stodgy. I mean some of the teachers were incredibly conservative, but Hume did not belong to that at all.'[15] He was popular with his pupils, who, behind his back, inevitably referred to him as 'Johnny Hume' just as he was known when he was a student at St Columb's.

The journalist Martin Cowley, who was at the school when Hume taught there, remembers how the teenage boys used to privately make fun of his fashion sense. He wore a suit with a jumper and his ties were always done up in a large Windsor knot. Cowley recalls that Hume's knot was so big that it 'would take up half his neck'.[16]

Away from the textbooks, Hume felt passionately that it was important his pupils knew what was happening in the streets outside the classroom. Northern Ireland had effectively been a one-party state since its formation in 1921. The Unionist Party dominated the political landscape and controlled the Stormont chamber and routinely sent a majority of MPs to Westminster. For decades, the party was seen as the natural party of government in Northern Ireland.

In 1963 there was a changing of the unionist guard when Lord Brookeborough resigned after twenty years as prime minister and Terence O'Neill took over. The former finance minister was seen as the natural successor and there were high hopes that he would be a reforming premier who would transform Northern Ireland. There was much that John Hume believed had to change.

Derry was home to many social injustices. He felt there were too many people out of work, forcing thousands to emigrate. He had witnessed gerrymandering when it came to the allocation of jobs and houses and he felt Catholics were not being given the respect and opportunities they were entitled to. Hume had a lot to say and soon he had a chance to say it. In 1963 he came to the attention of a wider public when the BBC commissioned him to write a script for a documentary about Derry. It was made on a shoestring budget of just under £100 and was filmed by Terry McDonald with help from Charlie Gallagher, who was a post office engineer, and it was narrated by Brian Hannon, who was a Church of Ireland curate.

Called 'A City Solitary', it was broadcast by both BBC and RTÉ and was shown as part of the arts festival in Derry's Guildhall. Hume's MA thesis proved to be most useful and it formed the basis of his script, as he tracked the development of the city. The documentary examined emigration and the different living conditions of Protestants and Catholics during the Victorian era, with Hume using the metaphor of the city's bridges to talk about uniting the two traditions. The film also looked at the city's name that traditionally divided unionists and nationalists, and he suggested that Londonderry and Derry should both be used as a title.

The film was viewed as a success and was seen by the *Irish Times* journalist Michael Viney. An English reporter, he had been tasked in the spring of 1964 by his editor, Douglas Gageby, to travel around Northern Ireland by bus and train and write a series of features. As an outsider, he hoped to capture a fresh view of what life north of the border was like. He later described the two-week assignment as 'one of the most depressing experiences I have known'.[17] However, his biggest joy and surprise came when he went to a showing of Hume's film and was impressed with the Derry man's 'outlook and vigour'.[18]

The journalist returned to Dublin and recommended that Hume be given a platform by the *Irish Times*. Hume was asked to write two articles about the political situation in Northern Ireland. He needed little persuasion and sat down and penned what in a sense became a manifesto for change. That work would become seminal, laying out Hume's analysis of what social injustices existed in Northern Irish society and what needed to be reformed. The features marked the public birth of Hume's political thinking and he did not hold back in his thoughts. On 18 May and 19 May 1964 under the headline 'The Northern Catholic', he took aim at a series of targets and set out a series of recommendations.

Using his script from his documentary and his experience of living in Derry, Hume wrote about the great social problems of housing, unemployment and emigration. He laid the inaction at the door of the unionist government but added that the 'present Nationalist Political Party must bear a share of it'. His withering criticism continued: 'Good government depends as much on the opposition as on the party in power. Weak opposition leads to corrupt government.'[19]

Hume added: 'Nationalists in opposition have been in no way constructive. They have quite rightly been loud in their demands for rights, but they have remained silent and inactive about their duties. In 40 years of opposition, they have not produced one constructive contribution on either the social or economic plane to the development of Northern

Ireland.' Hume went further in his critique of those in political life: 'Leadership has been the comfortable leadership of flags and slogans. Easy, no doubt, but irresponsible.' Hume argued many Catholics had been unwilling to speak their mind 'for fear of recrimination' and said terms of abuse like 'Castle Catholic' or 'West Briton' were often used if criticism was made of the traditional nationalist view.[20]

Hume then used his article to focus on community relations and argued that 'the Protestant tradition in the North is as strong and legitimate as our own.' He added that if a man wanted Northern Ireland to remain part of the UK that did not 'make him a bigot or a discriminator'. He also laid out his approach to the constitutional question and proclaimed that a united Ireland was only achievable with the 'will of the Northern majority'. He wrote:

> If one wishes to create a united Ireland by constitutional means, then one must accept the constitutional position. Such a change would involve what has been a great stumbling block to the development of normal politics in the North. Catholics could then throw themselves fully into the solution of Northern problems without fears of recrimination. Such an attitude too, admits the realistic fact, if it is to come, and if violence, rightly is to be discounted, it must come about by evolution, i.e., by the will of the Northern majority. It is clear that this is the only way in which a truly united Ireland (with the Northern Protestants integrated) can be achieved.[21]

These were Hume's first public words on the principle of consent. He knew by articulating these thoughts he was breaking with the past and publishing sentiments that ran counter to the standard nationalist argument. Consent was rarely talked about in nationalist circles when it came to the issue of ending partition and creating a united Ireland.

What Hume was saying was that the debate about a united Ireland had to be more than reuniting territory – it had to be about bringing people together. He argued that politics was more than a border. He wanted it to be about people and in particular their relationships with each other. This argument would become more pronounced throughout Hume's career, and as he developed his thoughts, this principle would be central to his political thinking on the issue of Irish unity. His argument was that the ending of partition was simply not enough and that the consequences of change had to be properly thought through. Other nationalists argued that it was the UK government that was the real barrier to unification, whereas Hume, in his articles, was making it clear that it was the relationship between nationalists and unionists in Northern Ireland that would be pivotal to any future constitutional change.

Hume's passing reference to violence is also worthy of examination. His two *Irish Times* articles were published in 1964 before the Troubles broke out in Northern Ireland, but Hume knew enough about history to know violence cast a long shadow over Irish political life. He was well aware that in his home city there were those who believed in physical force republicanism, and he knew that history had a nasty habit of repeating itself. His words were a warning and a hope that violence would not happen. With the luxury of hindsight, his remarks look prescient.

Hume's attack on the Nationalist Party was savage, and he made it clear that the current politicians who sought to represent the nationalist community were failing and a new movement was needed: 'The necessity for a fully organised democratic party which can freely attract and draw upon the talents of the nationally minded community is obvious.'[22]

This was a clarion call for action. In simple terms, Hume was making it clear that if people wanted to change society, they needed to make it happen through their own political actions. His strong words were not just reserved for those nationalist politicians who he felt were failing the electorate. He had striking opinions on what unionists needed to do. He argued forcefully that if the Unionist Party was sincere about creating a better society, they must accept that religious and political discrimination was unjust and had to be tackled and eradicated. Hume argued that Catholics should be encouraged to sit on public bodies, and unionists must accept that it was legitimate for people to want a united Ireland.

He also urged unionists to accept that the majority of Catholics simply wanted what Protestants wanted – a fairer, kinder society in which to 'live and rear their children'.[23]

Nearly sixty years on, Hume's two articles may at times read like an idealistic polemic, but in May 1964, his words were seen as ground-breaking. Hume was young and politically inexperienced. Yet, here he was, an unknown figure writing in one of Ireland's leading newspapers challenging old certainties, redefining political positions and mapping out a way that Northern Ireland could be reformed.

What people got to see were his first political utterances. This was his manifesto, and the positions he adopted would be arguments he would often return to. Hume insists they were not a signal that he was about to enter public life. He outlined his thoughts in an unpublished interview in 2003:

> When I was writing that article I had no intention of entering politics. It was just me giving my views that the people of the island were divided, not the territory. Therefore they could only be brought together by agreement, by the principle of consent.[24]

After the *Irish Times* printed his thoughts, the expectation was that he was now poised to run for office, but Hume was focused on other work.

4

THE FACELESS MEN

'I am not anxious to enter active politics.'
John Hume

Derry was experiencing a housing crisis. The city had the worst housing record in Northern Ireland and there was a desperate need for new homes to be constructed. The chronic shortage of public accommodation meant that families were crammed into two-up, two-down terraced houses. Many of the existing buildings were old and dilapidated and desperately needed renovation, with some having just primitive toilets and kitchens. The responsibility to build new homes lay with the unionist-controlled City Corporation, but in Hume's eyes, they showed little or no interest in building houses in Catholic areas. He could see what needed to change and, rather than waiting for politicians to act, he had his own ideas.

In 1965, along with a local priest, Father Anthony Mulvey, he helped to establish the Derry Housing Association. Mulvey and Hume had worked together on the establishment of the credit union. He and Hume were kindred spirits who both strongly believed that 'self-help' was the way forward. Hume became chairman and the group started to find accommodation for hundreds of people across Derry.

The association got to work and started to construct houses. Progress was slow, but the group did manage to build a number of dwellings and things started to look promising. The journalist and political activist Eamonn McCann knew Hume well. He lived close to him and like Hume attended St Columb's, although they were several years apart. McCann was left-wing and his politics were very different from Hume's. Where Hume wanted evolution, McCann wanted revolution. He felt Hume was too 'reformist', but admits that at the time his political rival did provide 'practical solutions in a way the old Nationalist Party had not been able to deliver'.[1] He remembers the work the association did in the city in the 1960s. He says to this day people of a certain generation still refer to them as 'Father Mulvey's houses'.[2]

When Hume's group wanted to increase their construction schedule and build 700 houses it applied for planning permission. However, it was stopped in its tracks by the unionist-controlled council which feared that this development could threaten their majorities in unionist-controlled areas. Housing was now a political issue and Derry was just the latest part of Northern Ireland to witness discrimination. A group called the Campaign for Social Justice had been established in Dungannon by Patricia McCluskey and her husband Conn, and the organisation was active in documenting abuses in employment, housing and local government. There was now a growing sense of frustration amongst the Catholic community that the much-promised reforms from Prime Minister O'Neill were just that – promises.

A big test for the unionist government at Stormont was where to site Northern Ireland's next university. The demand for university places was high and expected to rise dramatically – Queen's University in Belfast simply could not cope with the numbers. Derry seemed like the perfect location for Northern Ireland's second university. It already had Magee College, which had been operating for a century, and it all seemed to make geographical and logistical sense to place any new educational development in Northern Ireland's second city. (The existing college got its name from its founder, Martha Magee, who left £20,000 in her will to set up an institution for the training of Presbyterian ministers.)

Hume firmly believed that the Magee site in the heart of the city was the ideal home for a new university and he felt that a properly run campaign could bring together different sections of the community. Things moved quickly and he spoke at a meeting in the city's Guildhall and was elected chairman of the University for Derry campaign. Within weeks, he was making speeches and explaining how a new university could transform the landscape of Derry in political and economic terms. It was an initiative that had cross-party support and the campaign also had the backing of the main churches. It all fitted into Hume's approach of bringing people together from different sides of the community for what he saw as the common good.

By early 1965, there were some suggestions that things were beginning to change politically in Northern Ireland. In January, Prime Minister O'Neill sprang a surprise when he invited the taoiseach, Seán Lemass, for talks at Stormont. The move, which even caught O'Neill's cabinet colleagues unawares, was seen in the press as part of a new agenda. There was talk that the visit of Lemass signalled a change to North–South relations and suggestions in the press that O'Neill wanted to be a reforming prime minister and create a shared future for everyone in Northern Ireland.

However, O'Neill took a lot of flak from right-wing unionists for organising the visit and his critics included the Reverend Ian Paisley, a firebrand preacher who was becoming increasingly vocal in his opposition to the Unionist Party leader. O'Neill also faced discontent in his own party and it meant he had to tread lightly in the months ahead if he wanted to maintain their parliamentary support. Against this ongoing atmosphere, Hume continued to lobby for Derry to be chosen as the site for the new university. He had assembled a cross-community coalition with the nationalist MP for Foyle, Eddie McAteer, and the unionist mayor, Albert Anderson, both endorsing the idea.

Many other unionists did not back the move. At Stormont it quickly became clear there was an alternative plan in place and Derry was going to lose out. The unionist government had set up a group to consider the creation of a second university in Northern Ireland. The committee was chaired by the English academic Sir John Lockwood, the former vice-chancellor of the University of London, and even before his report was published there were strong rumours that Derry would lose out. It seemed politics was at play, and for all the talk of a new agenda, cynics suggested that the old one was still in place.

Two days before the recommendations were finally revealed John Hume spoke at a packed meeting at the city's Guildhall. Even if he had private fears about what was about to happen he did not show them. In an eloquent and powerful speech, he energised supporters by telling them of the great benefits that a new university could bring to Derry. Campaigners who had feared the worst were right to be pessimistic, as Lockwood's group recommended that Northern Ireland's second university should be built in the mainly Protestant town of Coleraine, some 30 miles east of Derry. Hume and his colleagues were furious but not entirely surprised.

On 18 February 1965, activists took their fight to the very heart of government and a cavalcade of cars turned up outside Northern Ireland's parliament at Stormont. Thousands of protestors made the 70-mile-long trip to East Belfast in an attempt to persuade the prime minister, Terence O'Neill, to ignore the Lockwood report and site the new university in Derry.

A sea of people greeted MPs and senators as they gazed out their windows and looked across the lawns of the Stormont estate towards the imposing statue of Sir Edward Carson. It was a noisy and crowded affair as cars and people mixed together and protestors quickly made their way to the steps of Parliament Buildings. There was a cross-community feel to the protest as the nationalist MP Eddie McAteer, who was now Stormont's leader of the opposition, stood alongside the unionist senator Albert Anderson. They were joined by campaign chairman John Hume, neatly dressed in a suit and tie, who was clutching a file of papers. Press photographers and camera crews jostled with each other as they captured the three men when they walked towards the building.

From the first floor, two MPs sympathetic to the protestors looked on. Gerry Fitt, who represented Belfast Dock, and Austin Currie, who was the MP for East Tyrone, stood together and watched the demonstration unfold. It was their first sighting of John Hume. Fitt, who had a sharp political sense, spotted Hume and turned to Austin Currie and prophetically said, 'Big Eddie needs to watch that boy.'[3] Whilst Eddie McAteer was the established MP for Foyle and nationalism's leading voice, Fitt and other acute observers all sensed that Hume was the coming man.

The university campaign brought an estimated 25,000 people onto the Stormont estate and the unionist-controlled administration certainly got the message of what people in Derry thought. Sadly for Hume and those that supported him, the minds of those in power were already made up.

As prime minister, O'Neill turned the Derry decision into a vote of confidence and unionist MPs at Stormont were put under a three-line whip to back the choice of Coleraine. In large numbers, they rubber-stamped Lockwood's decision. Hume hoped some unionists would break ranks and see the merits of his argument, but he had little success.

There were some unionists who rejected the argument for Coleraine. Desmond Boal, a unionist MP for Shankill, who was born in Derry, did back the move to site the university in his home city. His support was academic because the debate was lost, though he did state later that he felt his unionist colleagues had made a mistake.

The decision to site the new university at Coleraine and reject Derry devastated Hume. He felt hurt and let down. There was little time to rest and ponder what might have been. His new-found profile meant that he was now in demand and being tipped for a future in politics. In March 1965 that opportunity arose when Terence O'Neill surprisingly called an election and Hume's name was being suggested as a potential Stormont MP. The *Derry Journal* carried a report that there was speculation that he would stand for election. At 28 years of age, a married man with a family and a secure job, it was a big decision.

Credit union members and friends of Hume all suggested that he should put his name forward in the Foyle seat and challenge Eddie McAteer, the leader of the Nationalist Party. Hume did not dismiss the idea out of hand and, as his biographer Barry White chronicled, a meeting was organised with several supporters and Hume considered the merits of standing. He was naturally cautious of giving up his teaching job but he was also not convinced he could beat McAteer, who was a political veteran enjoying the support of Derry's Catholic establishment. The meeting went on for several hours as the conversation flowed back and forth, and arguments were made as to why Hume should put his name forward. The consensus was that the Nationalist Party needed to be challenged, and

Hume was the most obvious person to take on McAteer.

Hume stood his ground and despite the overtures and the personal pleas he could not be persuaded to run. Just as he did not want to become a priest, now it seemed he did not want to become a politician either. Finally, in the small hours of the morning, after hours of discussions, he announced definitively that he would not be a candidate. One of his supporters, Dr Jim Cosgrove, who would go on to play a role in the SDLP, took Hume's decision badly: 'I thought you had guts. You are not the man I thought you were.'[4]

The criticism must have hurt and Hume released a statement later saying: 'I have been approached by an independent group with a view to contesting the seat. I have given the matter a lot of thought, but I am not anxious to enter active politics, and I have decided not to let my name go forward.'[5]

The Hume versus McAteer showdown would have to wait for another day. Paul Arthur says, at that time in Derry, Hume was seen as the future and Eddie McAteer was viewed as the past: 'There was going to be a clash at some stage as to who was going to be top dog in Derry and clearly it was going to be Hume.'[6]

Eddie McAteer ran and retained the seat for the Nationalist Party, but electorally he was living on borrowed time. Hume may not have been an elected politician and did not have a mandate but he continued to be in demand for political rallies and meetings. McAteer may have been a representative at Stormont but it was Hume who many wanted to hear from.

In June 1965, he travelled to London to appear at a meeting organised by the Campaign for Democracy in Ulster. The group had been set up with the support of MPs, mainly from the Labour Party, and campaigned for changes to housing, employment and civil rights in Northern Ireland. Hume used the occasion at Fulham Town Hall to talk about the unionist government's decision to site the new university at Coleraine. Hume said the decision to reject Derry was not based on a 'single academic criterion'.[7]

Hume also criticised unionists and claimed that Terence O'Neill and his colleagues put party politics before anything else. He used the occasion to question whether the Treasury in London would scrutinise the cost of the new university in Coleraine which he said would cost £200 million. He then added:

> The tragedy is that this plan comes at a time when the Northern Ireland problem shows more hopeful signs of an internal solution than ever before. It is my belief that the problem can only be solved by the people of Northern Ireland themselves, and then only when the mental border that divides our community has been largely eradicated – when bigotry and intolerance have been driven from our shores.[8]

Hume's use of the phrase 'internal solution' is worth examining. This suggests that he believed back in 1965 that the political and social problems could be solved within the confines of the Northern Ireland state. He would argue later in his political career that an internal solution was not the answer and would not work. He would later see politicians in London, Dublin, Washington and Brussels as key players in the peace process. He would also come up with the three-stranded talks process formula involving the local parties, the British government and the Irish government.

Hume's Fulham speech largely concentrated on the decision to build the new university in Coleraine. His anger was palpable and his words reveal how he felt let down by the political system. He claimed some of his opponents were 'bigoted and influential Unionists from Derry'.[9]

The *Derry Journal* had earlier reported allegations that there were figures within unionist circles in Derry who had advised Prime Minister Terence O'Neill to choose Coleraine rather than their own city. The newspaper said the allegations, from the Unionist MP Robert Nixon, mentioned 'faceless men' who were concerned that Derry had a reputation as a 'papish city'.[10]

This suggestion that Derry unionists opposed the building of a university in their city depressed Hume, as Pat Hume recalled: 'He was clearly disillusioned after that, especially when it came to light that some people who had actually been pro-Coleraine were actually Derry people who didn't want the place to prosper.'[11]

Hume now concluded that unionists in his city would undermine Derry if they felt there was a threat to unionism's position of power and privilege across Northern Ireland. The Derry university campaign, which enjoyed cross-community support, was clearly seen by many unionists as a direct challenge to the political status quo. The outcome of the Lockwood report and Stormont's decision to endorse it left Hume battered and a little bruised: 'The unionist administration must be taught that they cannot run away from Derry and West Ulster, and if they seriously want to create a modern community they must treat all citizens with dignity and equality.'[12]

The reference to West Ulster needs some context. It reflected a growing feeling amongst nationalists that unionists at Stormont had a clear strategy of discriminating geographically. The feeling was that unionists wanted to keep prosperity and regeneration to areas east of the River Bann, which would largely favour unionists. That meant that Derry and other places where there was a nationalist majority would not benefit economically. Some saw the decision to site the university in Coleraine as part of that geographical discrimination. Hume saw the decision as part of an ongoing trend. In his eyes, Derry was suffering and had been left behind. Railway infrastructure had been scrapped and a new city had been established in County Armagh.

Whilst the campaign to bring the university to his home city ultimately failed, it did not deter Hume from continuing his community work. He was teaching at St Columb's and, away from the classroom, he continued to travel and develop the credit union movement across Ireland.

Although busy, it was clear the young teacher was unsettled and was prepared to consider a career change away from the classroom. He enjoyed filmmaking and when a job appeared at the BBC in Belfast he was very interested. There was a vacancy for a producer in the schools broadcasting unit and on Friday 2 July he made the journey to Broadcasting House in Belfast. Nine shortlisted candidates were all vying for the one job, two internal and seven who were external. Well prepared, with his teaching experience and his knowledge of filming and scripting, he must have impressed the five-strong interviewing panel, which included the then Head of Programmes. However, despite doing a good interview he did not get the job. It went to David Hammond, who was already working for the corporation. He would go on to have a very successful career as a filmmaker and singer. Hume did well in the interview, or 'board' as it was known in BBC circles, and he was considered 'also suitable for appointment'.[13] That meant he could be offered the next available job, but he had other plans.

For some time he had been thinking about entrepreneurial ideas that would take him away from his day job at St Columb's and change his life completely. For some time, he had considered setting up a business and at one stage had even toyed with the idea of bottling water and selling it. A local mineral water company in Derry had closed down, and having seen how bottled water was popular in France he thought the idea could take off in Northern Ireland. He approached a number of local businessmen but according to Pat Hume they were not impressed and told him 'he was mad in the head and scuppered the idea'.[14]

Hume was ahead of his time and in a 2003 interview Pat Hume said if her husband had persevered with the bottled water idea he 'could have been a very wealthy man'.[15] The proposal to bottle water was quickly shelved and instead, other ideas were investigated. Geographically he did not have to look too far and soon another opportunity presented itself.

During a speech to local business leaders, Hume talked about inward investment and how jobs could be created in Derry. He wondered why commercial opportunities were being missed and suggested that new thinking was needed to bring employment to the city. He used the example of the local salmon trade and wanted to know why fish were being sent to London to be smoked and why it could not happen in Derry. The River Foyle was one of the top salmon-producing rivers in Northern Ireland with the largest population of Atlantic salmon. To Hume, this was an economic resource on the city's doorstep that needed to be maximised. After his speech ended, he was approached by his friend Michael Canavan, who was a local bookmaker and businessman. Canavan made

Hume an intriguing offer: 'John, if you want to set up a smoked salmon plant, I'll finance it.'[16]

Canavan was used to making the odd gamble, though this looked like a safe bet. Hume was a workaholic who believed in self-help and had bags of energy. He knew that if he funded the project Hume would give it his all. Within days, the schoolteacher and the bookmaker started a crash course in the world of fish. They found some premises in an old bakery in Corporation Street and Hume travelled to England to learn how salmon was smoked:

> We called it Atlantic Harvest but I knew nothing about smoking salmon – I discovered that how you smoked the salmon was a very secret thing. So I took myself off to London and wandered around a smoked salmon plant watching how they did it and came back and taught some people here and we got the smoked salmon plant set up.[17]

Hume gave notice to St Columb's and quit his teaching post. It was a bold decision and raised some eyebrows, but he felt it was the right move and, with a degree of uncertainty, his new career with Atlantic Harvest began in earnest. The two entrepreneurs decided that they would source fish from Derry and Donegal and Hume's working day would begin at first light, as Pat Hume recalled:

> He used to go off very early in the morning to buy the salmon as the fishermen came in and he would go to the various fishing ports like Moville and Malin and Buncrana ... and I think he would have gone even down as far as Killybegs.[18]

Aidan Hume was a small boy when Atlantic Harvest began to operate and recalls his father taking him on road trips to pick up fish: 'I just remember he had an old blue van for the business and there were a couple of ovens basically in a large shed off Bishop Street in Derry. So I think I was attached to him for about a year. We would go everywhere.'[19]

As the business began to take shape, Hume travelled to London seeking orders for his niche product: 'We had to get a market for it because in those days only the very well-off people ate smoked salmon.'[20] He made contact with his old pal Phil Coulter, who was now in London creating a name for himself in the music business. Coulter recalls the visit: 'John came over on a sales trip and he didn't know his arse from his elbow really in terms of selling smoked salmon.'[21]

The budding businessman wanted some advice from his old friend and asked Coulter where he should go in the English capital:

> Now, I wasn't so sophisticated that I would be eating smoked salmon seven days a week, but I knew enough from being in the music business for a couple of years at that stage. I tell you there's one community who eat a lot of smoked salmon, that's what I learned in London, and that's the Jewish community. There's a couple of big Jewish delicatessens that you should definitely hit.[22]

Approaches were made to businesses in London, and other orders followed to keep the smoking ovens busy back in Derry. Meanwhile, a political contact also helped Atlantic Harvest secure a deal on the cruise ships that left Southampton. Robin Chichester-Clark, the Unionist MP for Londonderry, was at a social event and heard how the catering staff who supplied food to passengers on liners were keen on sourcing smoked salmon. The MP informed Michael Canavan, so Hume was duly despatched to Southampton where a deal was done to regularly send fish from Derry to the south of England. Hume and Canavan were now cleverly targeting their customers and adverts placed in quality English broadsheets brought more business their way.

From trainee priest to school teacher, from community activist to fish salesman, John Hume's career was going in unpredictable directions. As Northern Ireland headed towards the 1970s, he faced more unexpected twists.

5

ULSTER AT THE CROSSROADS

'I felt it was time for a new generation.'
John Hume

An October day in 1968 changed the course of Irish history. It started peacefully in Derry but ended in chaos and bloodshed. By nightfall, the world had heard of Duke Street and watched television pictures of policemen batoning protestors. Life in John Hume's home city would never be the same again. To many observers, that autumn Saturday was the moment when Northern Ireland's Troubles began. It came to be viewed as the spark that lit the bonfire.

On a bright afternoon, around five hundred demonstrators gathered in the city centre as part of a march organised by local activists Eamonn McCann and Eamon Melaugh. The two men had rung the Northern Ireland Civil Rights Association (NICRA) from a phone box in Derry and asked the group to sponsor the march.

NICRA had successfully run a similar march between Coalisland and Dungannon in August and the feeling was that another demonstration in Derry would give the campaign momentum and good press coverage. NICRA was now at the forefront of the civil rights campaign and was attracting a lot of media attention. Set up in a Belfast hotel in 1967, it was part of the ongoing movement to highlight discrimination in housing and employment. The group wanted to protect the freedom of all citizens, highlight abuses of power and promote individual rights. They also demanded freedom of speech and assembly. NICRA specifically wanted 'one man, one vote' in council elections and an end to gerrymandered electoral boundaries to prevent discrimination.

The political situation in Derry was stark and the voting wards had been split to preserve a Protestant majority. Catholics were a majority of the voters across the city with around 14,000 on the electoral roll compared to nearly 9,000 for Protestants. Yet at election time, more unionists were regularly returned because the wards had been created and manipulated to give more seats to unionists. NICRA wanted this practice to end and demanded a redrawing of electoral boundaries.

The group was a broad coalition of political opinion and included the non-aligned and others in local parties as well as trade unionists and students. The group aimed to be cross-community and deliberately avoided taking a stance on the 'national question' and, whilst there were members who were nationalist or republican, there were other supporters who came from the unionist tradition.

Hume was wary of NICRA and had concerns about the Derry march. He had been invited to set up a NICRA branch in his home city but had refused as he was worried that the group had been infiltrated by what he regarded as left-wing activists. Hume was particularly concerned about people like Eamonn McCann. He was a street-wise socialist activist who was making a name for himself in Derry. McCann vividly recalls Hume's concern: 'I was one of the organisers and he [Hume] played no part in organising that first march. He was always a bit wary, you know, of marches which involved in any prominent way radicals or what he would have seen as extremist militants.'[1]

McCann says Hume took issue with those who saw the civil rights campaign as part of the class struggle: 'He was against introducing socialist ideas. He was quite explicit about that, you know. This was not about class; this was about democracy.'[2] Hume was conflicted. Even though he had concerns about the makeup of NICRA, he fully supported the aims of the group. He also had fears that the Derry protest could get out of hand and possibly lead to violence. He knew he could not ignore what was happening nor stay away from the event.

NICRA officials came to Derry days before the march and agreed on the route but, unaware of the geography of Derry, missed the significance of where the protest would go. It was to begin in Duke Street in the Waterside area and then go across the Craigavon Bridge and through the city walls and then end up in the Diamond, which was the commercial centre of Derry.

The RUC had major concerns that if the march went ahead there would be disorder on the streets. The Apprentice Boys, one of the Protestant 'loyal orders', which commemorates the 13 apprentice boys who slammed the gates of the city shut in 1688, had also planned an event on the same day. It wanted to parade along the same route. It was all a potential recipe for chaos and disruption. The RUC feared that violence would break out and the unionist home affairs minister Bill Craig banned all parades and marches in Derry. The RUC made it clear that demonstrators would not be allowed to proceed. Craig was deeply suspicious of NICRA and saw it as an anti-unionist grouping and claimed it was being used by nationalists and republicans. NICRA tried to call the demonstration off but went ahead when it became clear several Derry activists were going to march anyway.

Although the Stormont ban put off some potential protestors, a series of high-profile politicians travelled to the city to take part. Gerry Fitt, the republican Labour MP for West Belfast who had been in Blackpool at the Labour Party conference, turned up with three Labour MPs from England. As well as the Westminster MPs there were Stormont representatives including Austin Currie and Eddie McAteer.

Currie was seen as part of the new wave of politicians, and he had become the youngest-ever MP returned to Stormont when he was elected in East Tyrone in 1964 as a nationalist. He was now becoming very active in civil rights protests and made headlines in June 1968 when he staged a sit-in at a house in County Tyrone. A single Protestant girl had been allocated a house in preference to Catholic families in greater need, so Currie and other activists took over the house in protest. The squat caused a blaze of publicity and put the issue of housing on the front pages. By organising a march in Derry, activists hoped to put the focus on the Londonderry Corporation's housing policy, which was under attack for favouring Protestants.

There was a nervousness in Derry in the days leading up to the October parade. As a junior reporter on the *Derry Journal*, Martin Cowley was just starting out on his journalistic career. He says the talk on the streets was about one thing: 'There was an atmosphere coming up to it of tension. Was this march going to be allowed? Was there going to be trouble? Was there going to be a confrontation? And there was an expectation there was going to be some sort of confrontation.'[3]

By mid-afternoon on Saturday 5 October, Austin Currie, Eddie McAteer, Gerry Fitt and other leading figures were at the head of the parade as the march assembled outside the old railway station on the Waterside. Using a megaphone and standing in front of a group of men and children, RUC Inspector William Meharg informed the crowd that they could protest but could not proceed into prohibited areas. Ivan Cooper, a close friend of John Hume, stood nearby listening. A Protestant, from a unionist background, he had once been a Unionist Party member but was now in the Northern Ireland Labour Party. A shirt factory manager, he was dressed in a suit and tie and looked more like a businessman than a protestor.

He borrowed the police megaphone and, just like Inspector Meharg, he spoke to the crowd and explained that they were on the streets in a bid to end discrimination in housing and employment. He added that the march was about freedom of speech and freedom of assembly. Cooper was articulate and direct. He called on the crowd to 'act in a responsible manner' and made it clear there was no wish for 'bloodshed or violence'.[4] The crowd cheered his peaceful sentiments and moments later the marchers moved forward, watched by police officers, journalists and photographers. At Duke Street, lines of RUC officers linked arms and blocked the road. Inspector Meharg again used his megaphone to repeat his warning to marchers not to proceed any further. They were instructed that they were about to break the law. As the front of the march edged forwards under the Civil Rights Association banner, protestors and police officers came face to face. There was shoving and pushing and RUC officers began to assault the marchers with their wooden batons. Placards and banners were ripped from the hands of marchers as policemen tried to push the protestors back down the street. People screamed as officers lashed out at anyone in their way.

Austin Currie, who was at the front of the march, said it was chaotic: 'It was like the "Charge of the Light Brigade", really. Policemen to the front of us, policemen to the back of us, no way out.' Eamonn McCann says the police had the marchers penned in: 'If you are trying to disperse a march, you don't block it off at the front and the back. Looking back on it, this wasn't a crowd dispersal operation, this was a punishment operation.'[5]

Senior figures at the front of the procession were in the RUC's sights and both Eddie McAteer and Gerry Fitt were injured. Fitt was struck by a police baton and was bleeding from his head. There were pleas from the crowd to officers to stop using their wooden truncheons but the calls were ignored. Paddy Douglas, from Donaghmore in County Tyrone, who was a former St Columb's pupil, held out his hands and pleaded for the violence to stop.

Captured by the television cameras he turned to the officers and shouted, 'Gentlemen, please, for God's sake'.[6] Instantly, he was hit in the stomach with a baton and doubled over in pain. Other policemen chased protestors across the street, striking them as they tried to run away.

The *Derry Journal*'s Martin Cowley was on the pavement at the front of the march and was dressed in a three-piece grey suit. Looking back, he jokes that he was 'the best-dressed protestor you have ever seen'.[7] He knew there was 'going to be a momentous story' and wanted to be there.[8] Standing on the footpath, he had taken shorthand notes of some of the earlier speeches and hoped that the police officers would see that he was a journalist. When the trouble began he was just yards from the advancing RUC men:

> I remember feeling a thud in my head. I thought, what was that? I was really stunned. I thought it must be a baton and then another came and then there must have been another one. I remember struggling and I fell to the ground and I was surrounded and looked up and there were three

policemen around me and I was shouting, 'Press, Press' and holding my press card.[9]

Cowley got up, battered and groggy, and tried to walk on. He spotted District Inspector Ross McGimpsey and felt slightly relieved, thinking he would recognise him as a reporter and come to the rescue. Cowley was well used to seeing him at close quarters from his reporting duties at the courthouse in Derry. However, McGimpsey simply made matters worse. He shouted at Cowley, 'That's the boy,' and he charged after the young reporter and hit him several times with his blackthorn stick on the head, drawing blood and knocking him to the ground.[10]

The young reporter was initially detained by the police and only released after NICRA officials intervened, pointing out that he was a journalist. Only then was he taken by ambulance to Altnagelvin Hospital for treatment. When he finally arrived at casualty, he said there were so many people seeking treatment it looked like 'a war zone'. Still in his three-piece grey suit, now soaked with blood, he was given an X-ray and received stitches in his head.

Amidst the noise and the chaos in Duke Street, one key observer was concentrating hard on capturing exactly what was happening. Gay O'Brien, an RTÉ cameraman, recorded iconic images that day that would go around the world and put Northern Ireland on the global news agenda. His footage of a bleeding Gerry Fitt and his film of Paddy Douglas being assaulted by a police officer placed the RUC and the unionist government under an international spotlight.

The black-and-white images from an innocuous Derry street would change the established narrative and convince many that Northern Ireland needed fundamental reform. Others would go further, believing that the Duke Street footage showed that partition had created a violent unionist state and the only way forward was an 'armed struggle'. Hume's home city was now a tinderbox.

Over the years, Hume's exact role on that fateful October day has often been examined. He had no hand in organising the event, nor was he at the head of the protest like Gerry Fitt, Eddie McAteer or Austin

Currie. It is well documented that Hume had concerns about the parade itself and he had political differences with those who organised it:

> Like anyone else in the city I just marched in it. But I was deeply shocked by the treatment of the marchers in Duke Street on that day. And of course that led to a huge public reaction because of what happened in Duke Street when we were literally baton-charged off the street by the police, and it was a totally non-violent march.[11]

However, some have questioned whether John Hume was there at all. Some years later, Gerry Fitt told Hume's biographer Paul Routledge that Hume was not present.[12] Fitt and Hume would part company politically in 1979 and there was friction between the two men, so Fitt's comments may have been mischievous. Austin Currie says the suggestion that Hume was not actually at the march was made in an attempt to discredit him: 'It was alleged by political opponents that he did not become involved in the demonstration, but John confirmed it and I believe him.'[13]

Others saw Hume at the October 5 protest. Rosemary Logue was standing with her husband Jimmy at Duke Street just before the march began. Rosemary is the sister of Martin Cowley, the *Derry Journal* reporter who was attacked by police officers during the parade. She arrived early and recalls hearing the warning issued by County Inspector Meharg, which she found 'breathtaking'. She then remembers John Hume coming over to speak to them. He turned to her husband and said: 'Jimmy, I would not have Rosemary here today. You should get Rosemary home. There is going to be bother. I wouldn't have wanted Pat here today.' Rosemary Logue took Hume's advice and went home while her husband joined the march.[14]

Eamonn McCann, one of the march organisers, says Gerry Fitt's comments about Hume and the march should be taken with the proverbial 'pinch of salt'. However, McCann says Hume was hesitant about the march and was unsure what to do. He says Hume 'walked on the pavement alongside the march'. McCann argues that by not actually walking in the march but yet accompanying the parade, Hume was 'half there and half not'.[15]

The violence in Derry did not end in Duke Street that weekend. Trouble broke out in the Bogside and the Creggan and crowds clashed with police officers. The political fallout began immediately with Bill Craig, the home affairs minister, praising the police and attacking the demonstrators' behaviour. Naturally, others in Derry saw things very differently. John Hume was angry about the weekend violence and also worried about the direction the civil rights campaign in the city might take. He felt it needed leadership and he started working on a plan. Within days it was ready. At the City Hotel, activists gathered to discuss a second march and talk about how the campaign would go forward. Dozens of people packed into the room in the hotel and a new group called the 'Derry Citizens Action Committee' was formed with Ivan Cooper as chairman and Hume as vice-chairman.

For Hume, this was a huge personal moment, as it marked another step on the road towards political involvement after the university campaign. The new body fitted his personal philosophy as it endorsed non-violence, was well-organised and had support from across the community with Protestants in leadership roles. The aims were straightforward as the group wanted civil rights for all in areas of housing and employment and demanded fair elections. Hume was the guiding light in setting out the committee's objectives as he recalled in an unpublished interview in 2002:

> It was non-party-political. We were seeking equality of treatment for all sections of our people, one person, one vote and you know, who would be against that? People forget in those days you only had a vote in local government if you were a ratepayer so growing up in our family, my father and mother had votes, but I didn't have a vote. And of course that was part of the whole gerrymandered system.[16]

The new grouping organised a series of protests including a mass sit-down at the city's Guildhall Square on 19 October. Hume's rival, Eamonn

McCann, saw things differently, not just politically but strategically. He wanted a more radical approach to the civil rights campaign. McCann had established a reputation for direct action and was involved with the Derry Housing Action Committee, which had highlighted poor living conditions by dragging a caravan into the road and blocking traffic. He thought Hume's new group was too cautious and conservative in its approach, but he accepts that Hume accurately captured the mood at the time:

> Looking back on it, people were able to come out and march behind John without feeling that they were being led into danger – physical danger or political danger. And that was very strong. A very important thing and I think it's important for the way John emerged.[17]

A sit-in took place at Guildhall Square and an estimated 5,000 people turned up. The event concluded with the singing of 'We Shall Overcome', an anthem which was associated with the civil rights campaign in the United States. Hume was inspired by the work of Martin Luther King, an American Baptist minister, who was a civil rights campaigner and who supported non-violence. King was a political hero of Hume's and he had admired his fight against racial segregation. 'We Shall Overcome' was made famous by the singer Pete Seeger, and after it was heard at American protests and seen on television reports it was quickly adopted by activists in Northern Ireland.

In early November, Hume's group took to the streets again and this time the route was familiar. The Action Committee decided to retrace the October march that they had not been allowed to complete but this time the approach was different. Only 15 committee members symbolically took part in the procession from Duke Street across Craigavon Bridge and into the city centre. With Hume, Michael Canavan and Ivan Cooper at the front of the march, it passed off peacefully and ended with the now traditional rendition of 'We Shall Overcome'.

Derry was now becoming the protest capital of Northern Ireland, and demonstrations and protests became part and parcel of normal life in the city. Civil rights supporters were still being viewed with suspicion by many unionists, but it was clear the calls for change were being listened to. In London, there was real concern about the situation and the prime minister, Harold Wilson, was personally worried about recent events. He had watched television footage of the Duke Street violence and politically he had much sympathy for the demands of the civil rights activists. He wanted to see reform and he wanted it to happen quickly.

On Wednesday 4 November, Wilson had talks with Northern Ireland's prime minister Terence O'Neill, who travelled to London with fellow ministers Bill Craig and Brian Faulkner. They went to Downing Street and the protests and the civil rights demands were top of Wilson's agenda. Wilson made it clear in plain terms that change had to happen. He called for immediate moves in the way public housing was allocated and he wanted a fairer voting system, changes to security legislation and the appointment of an ombudsman to examine complaints.

Fresh from the success of their most recent protest, John Hume and his colleagues planned another event for the city. The Action Committee proposed another march on 16 November, which would take the route of the controversial protest from 5 October when trouble broke out in Duke Street. This new march was promptly banned from entering the old walled city by Bill Craig, Stormont's home affairs minister, who was now well versed in trying to stop protests in Hume's home city.

On the eve of the march, the Church of Ireland bishop Dr Charles Tyndall and the Catholic bishop Dr Neil Farren both agreed to open their churches overnight so prayers could be said. The move by the two religious leaders was seen by Hume as critical and underlined his desire that the civil rights protest should be non-sectarian, with support from both communities.

In the bright November air, Hume and his colleagues defied the ban and an estimated 15,000 people turned up to protest. They gathered on the Waterside and crossed the River Foyle by going over Craigavon Bridge. On the city side, there was a line of police officers blocking the route. It all looked ominous and there was a sense that history was about to repeat itself. Protestors and police officers stood opposite each other as they had done in Duke Street. Hume and his colleagues did not want any trouble and they planned their next few steps.

At the police lines, several Action Committee members, including Hume and Michael Canavan, stepped over the barriers and breached the order. It was a token gesture and the police did not intervene. Protestors were then told by the parade organisers to make their way into the city not in procession but as if they were simply walking into town like day-to-day shoppers.

Hume said the move worked.

> What I did was I went up to the front. I was at the front of the march of course. And I got marchers to march on the footpaths and the police could not stop them at all from doing that. So they marched on the footpaths right up to the Diamond Square where we had our major meeting.[18]

It was a masterstroke and, apart from some stones and bottles being thrown from the Fountain area, it was largely trouble-free. Hume and his colleagues were delighted. They had made their point and there was no violence. Less than a week later there was dramatic news. On 22 November Terence O'Neill announced that a series of reforms would be introduced – the very changes that had been called for by Harold Wilson during the meeting in Downing Street. A five-point plan was revealed including the introduction of a points system to allocate council houses. This was aimed at making the system fairer and less open to abuse. The Londonderry Corporation, which was seen by many protestors as completely unaccountable, was to be replaced by a Development Commission. Some sections of the 1922 Special Powers Act which allowed arrest and detention would be removed. The right of business owners to have additional votes would be scrapped to make the voting system fairer and an ombudsman would be established to examine grievances. It marked a dramatic shift from the unionist government, and whilst the measures did not satisfy every demand of the civil rights campaign, it was acknowledged by Hume and others as a step in the right direction.

The reforms were not universally welcomed, and the move faced opposition from many unionists. In particular, there was fierce criticism from the firebrand preacher the Reverend Ian Paisley, who was now building a reputation as O'Neill's arch-nemesis. Paisley and his colleague Major Ronald Bunting were to figure prominently in counter-demonstrations during the civil rights campaign. Paisley regarded Terence O'Neill as treacherous and saw the civil rights campaign as a vehicle for a united Ireland.

Politically, Terence O'Neill felt Northern Ireland was now at a defining moment and on 9 December he made a televised address. He said important choices lay ahead and warned that 'Ulster stands at the crossroads.' O'Neill's use of that phrase, which would become much quoted, made many viewers sit up and take notice, as he was not a man prone to exaggeration. He told them, 'I am not a man given to extravagant language.' He asked people: 'What kind of Ulster do you want? A happy and respected province in good standing with the rest of the United Kingdom, or a place continually torn apart by riots and demonstrations and regarded by the rest of Britain as a political outcast? As always, in a democracy, the choice is yours.'[19]

O'Neill's broadcast was a gamble. It was an attempt to restore calm and chart a peaceful way forward. Two days after his 'crossroads' address he made another political move and sacked Bill Craig, the controversial home affairs minister, who had been on a collision course with the civil rights movement for months. As 1968 came to an end, the streets around Derry were relatively quiet as activists in the Action Committee wanted to give the reforms some time to work. If Hume and his colleagues were prepared to show patience and wait, others were not so generous. Seventy miles down the road at Queen's University, a radical group called People's Democracy announced plans for a long march from Belfast to Derry to begin on New Year's Day in 1969. The group was a radical left-wing organisation and one of its best-known members was Bernadette Devlin, who would later go on to become the youngest woman ever to sit as an MP at Westminster. Devlin was now a veteran of civil rights marches and had been at NICRA events and the now infamous Duke Street march in Derry in October.

She and her colleagues wanted to walk from Belfast to Derry over a four-day period to highlight their demands for a fairer voting system, the ending of discrimination in employment and housing and a repeal of what they saw as repressive security legislation. The march from Belfast to Derry was modelled on a similar protest in the United States when civil rights activists who wanted an end to racial discrimination walked from Selma to Montgomery in Alabama in 1965.

Hume and others in Derry's Action Committee did not approve of the People's Democracy plan and thought the event was provocative. He met some of the organisers including his Derry neighbour Paul Arthur. Hume told them he was against the idea of a march: 'I was strongly opposed to it because I felt that civil rights marches should only take place in areas where they would not provoke sectarian conflict and I was worried about a march coming all the way from Belfast and passing through certain loyalist areas that would lead to attacks on the march and would lead to violence.'[20]

Nonetheless, despite the concerns and worries marchers left Belfast on the first day of 1969 and headed north. They faced blockades along the way, particularly at Antrim and Randalstown, though there was no major trouble at that stage.

However, the most serious incidents happened on Saturday 4 January when loyalists with clubs attacked the protest at Burntollet Bridge just outside Derry. A number of the marchers were struck by stones and sticks and some were driven into a nearby river. The RUC was accused of failing to give the travelling protestors proper protection. When the march finally arrived in Derry it was obvious for all to see what they had experienced. Bloodstained protestors began to recount the details of the attack at Burntollet and the mood in Derry began to change. Locals clashed with the RUC and rioting went on for hours. Barricades were erected and local youths repeatedly clashed with RUC officers who often took the law into their own hands and lashed out indiscriminately. A pirate radio station was established and the iconic slogan 'You Are Now

Entering Free Derry' was painted on a gable wall close to Hume's grandparents' home. He hoped for calm but that was all he could do because the atmosphere was now toxic. With the help of colleagues, however, he managed to remove some barricades. It was clear that the broad civil rights movement was now split and arguments over tactics and strategy looked set to continue.

Hume took time away from Derry and attended a march in Newry on Saturday 11 January. If he was hoping for some comfort he would have been bitterly disappointed about what he witnessed. The events of that foggy day were captured for an edition of the prestigious ITV programme *World in Action*. The pictures that were beamed across the UK made tough viewing for Hume. The RUC wanted to keep the demonstrators away from a largely Protestant area so the march was to be rerouted. Tensions flared at the police barrier when the procession was diverted, much to the annoyance and anger of many in the crowd. Sensing the real possibility of an outbreak of violence a series of speakers appealed for calm. One told the crowd he did not want to see the town of Newry 'disgraced' and said: 'We in Newry are not bloodthirsty people.' [21]

Next, it was the turn of John Hume. He took the megaphone and politely advised marchers to follow the route agreed with the authorities. He appealed to the crowd and pointed in the direction they should take. Many heeded his advice but later, when darkness descended, a riot broke out and a series of vehicles were burnt. Hume knew that the Newry riot and the subsequent headlines would damage the cause of civil rights. He spoke out two days later, making it clear that it was not the purpose of civil rights marchers to attack either the police or 'Paisleyites'. He also warned civil rights activists about their behaviour: 'If, however, we loot, burn and attack, we lose all sympathy.'[22]

By now, Hume had established himself as a thoughtful speaker who was much in demand at rallies and marches. He had a profile and a platform and was seen as one of the most articulate voices arguing for civil rights. Then an unexpected personal and political opportunity arrived. Terence O'Neill called a snap election, and polling day for the new Stormont parliament would be on 24 February. It became billed as the 'crossroads election' after O'Neill's television broadcast back in December.

For Hume, it was decision time. What way would he go? Was this the time to enter the political world? It was not a new dilemma since he had considered this question in the past. He had been encouraged to run before in Foyle and he was also approached to run as a Westminster candidate in Mid Ulster.

The death of the Unionist MP George Forrest had caused a by-election in Mid Ulster and civil rights activists like Denis Haughey felt that an agreed nationalist candidate could take the seat. Haughey and a number of others from the area felt Hume was the ideal candidate, so they invited him to a meeting in Magherafelt. Hume made the journey from Derry and listened to a series of passionate approaches. As Haughey recalls: 'Each of us made our case as to why he should agree to be nominated by us as a unity candidate and he listened to us all politely and then shook his head politely and said, "I can't do that".'[23]

With a Stormont election about to be held, Hume had a different plan. He wanted to be a candidate closer to home. It meant that the Hume versus McAteer battle would finally happen, and for good measure, they would be challenged by another Derry character, Eamonn McCann of the Northern Ireland Labour Party. Hume issued a manifesto that talked about how a new party would allow people full involvement in the decision-making process. He said the as-yet-unnamed movement must be non-sectarian and must root out sectarianism. He called for the need for radical social and economic policies that challenged conservatism. On the future of Northern Ireland, he said there must be no constitutional change without the consent of its people. The last point on consent was a repetition of the argument he first developed in his *Irish Times* article back in 1964.

Campaigning on the streets that he was so familiar with, Hume presented himself as the new voice of Foyle. His supporters portrayed him as the future and as they canvassed they made it clear that Eddie McAteer was a man of the past.

Despite the rivalry, Hume says he thought well of his main opponent, but in 1969, he felt compelled to challenge him:

> I have always had a high regard for him but I felt it was time for a new generation. I think he felt the same himself because he had asked me to stand for an election previous to that, for a Westminster election and I knew that he didn't want to stand for election again, that he wanted a new generation to come forward.[24]

There was some reluctance from Hume to allow his name to go forward but inevitably he felt it was the right thing to do. Eamon Hanna was in Derry at the time and was training to be an accountant. He says Hume hated having to challenge McAteer but the feeling was that the Nationalist MP was 'past his sell-by date' and Hume was seen as his natural successor: 'I know people had been encouraging him to go into politics, but Derry is very small scale. He liked Eddie even if he thought maybe he could be more effective. Eddie didn't really believe in the principle of organisation.'[25]

Although Hanna was not involved in politics then, he did witness the electoral fight between McAteer and Hume: 'I used to go out at night. I wasn't canvassing or anything, but I was able to observe. Derry at that stage was so small and claustrophobic, but it had a camaraderie, a joy about it that Belfast did not have.'[26]

To help with the organisation, Michael Canavan, Hume's business partner in Atlantic Harvest, switched temporarily from selling fish to promoting a new brand of politics. He became the campaign manager, and a large team of activists were put in place to deliver leaflets and knock on doors. Hume was 32 years old and another career change was on the horizon. It seemed his time was about to come. There was an energy to his campaign that McAteer's push for votes lacked. People wanted to see Hume and engage with him.

The future SDLP leader Mark Durkan was a schoolboy at the time and remembers that Hume was regarded as a bit of a celebrity. The campaign had created a bit of energy and Hume's supporters knew they had to persuade McAteer voters to switch. Public events were seen as critical to getting people to rethink their traditional vote. Mark Durkan remembers his mother going out to where John Hume was canvassing so she could hear him speak: 'It was part of her way of making her mind up, you know, seeing and giving everybody a hearing'.[27]

Lifelong friend Phil Coulter says his childhood pal personified a very different approach, not seen by voters before: 'For somebody to come from our community who had a much more imaginative and more forward-thinking view of where this whole scenario should go was, for us, exciting. And I thought John should carry that torch. And it was a transition from the old Nationalist Party.'[28]

The February election highlighted a fundamental difference between McAteer and Hume when it came to the issue of the border. McAteer, the elder statesman, felt the civil rights movement had underplayed the importance of the 'national question' and had essentially airbrushed away the issue of partition. Hume, the young energetic challenger, insisted that the civil rights movement had to be separate from party politics. He argued that the Nationalist Party's analysis was wrong:

> Their basic attitude was simply anti-partition, get rid of the border and it will solve our problems. The civil rights movement was of the view that whilst those problems were still in existence, at least we should all be living with equality and with equality of treatment and that's why the civil rights movement, in a sense, was separate from the political situation at the time.[29]

McAteer, who had been a Stormont MP for 22 years, had originally intended to step down from politics, but he changed his mind at the last minute and said supporters encouraged him to stand again. Eamonn McCann, running as the Northern Ireland Labour Party candidate, also had his eyes on winning the seat, but it was not to be. The radical socialist says that, in the final days of the campaign, it became clear that Hume was going to win: 'It was just the way the people of the Bogside were talking. The number of people who said to me, sorry we can't vote for you. We have to get John in.'[30]

Hume's message appeared to be striking a chord as he argued that politics could no longer be about 'flag waving' and instead should concentrate on economic and social issues. As polling day approached, support was moving away from McAteer, as some felt he had misjudged the public mood some months earlier. The MP had originally welcomed Terence O'Neill's civil rights reform package in 1968 and said: 'I would like to give it a chance. It is half a loaf.'[31]

The remark went down badly as Denis Bradley remembers: 'Eddie was a lovely man but he was now being associated with the past, you know, half a loaf is better than no bread. Hume was saying, well, actually I don't think we should settle for that. We have the right to eat all the bread like everybody else.'[32]

Hume stormed to victory polling 8,920 votes, compared to McAteer who came second with 5,267. McCann ran in last with 1,993 votes and lost his deposit. He could have made some money out of this financial misfortune as two separate Derry benefactors approached him the next day and said they would pay his £150 lost deposit, which in 1969 was a tidy sum. McCann declined their generosity. Looking back at the result of 1969, he insists that people in Foyle saw Hume as the perfect choice: 'John represented the careful, Catholic, moderate voice that was not going to frighten the horses. People in Derry wanted the unionists out, they certainly did. But they did not want a troublemaker, and I was seen as a troublemaker.'[33]

Hume's victory grabbed the headlines. After all, he had toppled the leader of the Nationalist Party and ended the career of a veteran political heavyweight. He had been elected on his first foray into politics with an impressive majority of 3,653. The turnout of 84 per cent was one of the highest in Northern Ireland and Hume's team had run a textbook operation.

When all the results were declared from the 'crossroads election', it became clear that the political map was changing. Terence O'Neill just about hung onto his Bannside seat after a strong challenge from the Reverend Ian Paisley, who like Hume was fighting his first election. Paisley was beaten but he and his brand of politics were on the rise. The strains within grass-roots unionism were obvious and during the campaign, there was much tension between official and unofficial unionist candidates who were split on whether or not O'Neill was the right leader and if it was right to endorse the civil rights reforms. Thirty-nine unionist MPs were returned to Stormont and, although the majority backed O'Neill, his long-term future still looked uncertain. The Nationalist Party lost three seats to Independents, who were Hume and his friends Ivan Cooper and Paddy O'Hanlon. The Northern Ireland Labour Party and Republican Labour both ended up with two seats each. John Hume resigned from his job with Atlantic Harvest. In the final week of February 1969, he got ready for a new career.

6

WE SHALL OVERCOME

'I began to think this guy is special.'
Paul Arthur, talking about John Hume

Sitting proudly at the top of a mile-long drive, behind the imposing statue of Sir Edward Carson, a handsome Portland stone building was John Hume's new place of work. This part of East Belfast was where he had been sent to stand up for the people of Foyle, to argue, to lobby and to speak about what he saw as the evils of injustice. Many nationalists saw Parliament Buildings as a place of privilege, a seat of power where the majority governed at the minority's expense. On the first Wednesday of March in 1969, John Hume took his seat in the chamber and when he got up to speak it marked his transition from street protestor to parliamentarian. Debating skills honed in the halls of Derry kicked in and he wasted little time in attacking those sitting on the unionist benches. He accused them of ignoring people's grievances for years.

Not surprisingly, the theme of civil rights featured in his opening remarks:

> I would say that if we are to have a just society it can only be brought about by keeping certain fundamental attitudes and principles in view. It can only be achieved if we believe in the equality of rights of every citizen in our community.[1]

Weeks later the divisions between the parties were laid bare during a debate on the Public Order Bill, which nationalists argued was too draconian. Unionists voted to close the debate while Hume was speaking. The new member for Foyle and seven others sat on the floor and refused to resume their seats. They began singing 'We Shall Overcome', their favourite anthem of protest, and the sitting was eventually suspended with the demonstrating MPs each banned for a week. Hume may have been expected to play by the rules of the house but it was pretty clear he was going to do things on his terms.

He was now forming alliances with other parliamentarians and coming to informal agreements on how non-unionists should behave at Stormont. He was conscious that he had been elected on a promise of establishing a social democratic party and discussions on a new movement were continuing. He was already working closely with Ivan Cooper and Paddy O'Hanlon. They were friends and civil rights activists who had won seats in February's election at the expense of the Nationalist Party. Hume wanted to reach out to others like Austin Currie, Paddy Devlin and Gerry Fitt. Currie was currently a Nationalist Party MP and Devlin was in the Northern Ireland Labour Party and Fitt had been elected under the Republican Labour banner. In the early days, Hume and his like-minded colleagues worked together as a loose coalition and, although they talked both formally and informally about forming a new party, it was a very slow process which would ultimately take months to come to fruition.

Away from Stormont, there was no change in the demands from civil rights activists and there was a growing sense of impatience in some quarters. Protestors planned to march from the infamous Burntollet Bridge to Derry on Saturday 19 April. Not surprisingly, Home Affairs Minister Robert Porter banned the protest with concerns that there could be violence directed at the marchers. The ban prompted protestors to gather in Derry city centre and trouble broke out between some members of the crowd and the RUC. Stones were thrown and the police used batons on protestors. John Hume pleaded with a group of teenagers to leave the scene and go home, but his attempts failed. They sat down in the street and the violence continued with more stone-throwing and petrol bombs.

A violent game of cat and mouse developed, with the RUC chasing the young men and attacking them with batons once they caught up with them. The events of that April Saturday would have tragic consequences. The RUC pursued a group of young men into a house on William Street where Sammy Devenney and his family lived. Nine officers attacked the 42-year-old and other family members after they broke down the front door. The attack was so severe that there was blood all over the house and it was sprayed on walls and chairs. Devenney received serious injuries to his skull, eyes and mouth and he suffered a heart attack. He was hospitalised, released and re-admitted in May. He died on 16 July.

For Hume, the attack on William Street was distressing:

> I knew the Devenneys very well, both Sammy and his wife Phyllis. I had been very friendly with them particularly in our Credit Union days, and of course, they were people who were totally and absolutely non-violent and would have had no connection of any description to any paramilitary organisation.[2]

The vicious assault on the Devenney family shocked the community and left John Hume 'very emotional'.[3] The fact that this happened at the hands of the RUC inside a family home added to the horror. That night and into the small hours violence continued, and it now seemed that Derry was witnessing trouble that was out of control. The next day the situation looked ominous, as dozens of police officers stood close to the entrance of the Bogside and it seemed as if they were getting ready to raid houses and make arrests. Hume sensed this was a moment of enormous danger that could lead to bloodshed. He helped to organise an evacuation of residents to other parts of the city and many were taken to the Creggan, an estate that looked down on the houses of the Bogside. He knew he had to stop the RUC from going any further.

Contact was made with Robert Porter, Stormont's home affairs minister, and along with Church and civic representatives, a request was made that the police should withdraw. It was made clear that the residents would be returning by five o'clock that evening. If the police had not gone Hume said he could not be responsible for their actions. It was a bold statement – perhaps seen as a threat – but an honest assessment of how Hume viewed the situation.

Shortly before the deadline expired, the RUC withdrew and Hume was able to escort the Bogside residents back home. The threat of trouble was not over completely as dozens of angry residents then marched towards the city centre and congregated close to Butcher's Gate. Stones were thrown and Hume knew matters could escalate very quickly. He met up with his friend Father Anthony Mulvey, who was at the front of the crowd. Mulvey, like Hume, wanted to avoid violence and knew time was of the essence. He allowed Hume to climb on his shoulders so the crowd could see him and the Foyle MP then delivered an appeal for peace.

Hume's address was powerful and he urged his constituents to go home and let political arguments take the place of stones and petrol bombs. He said he understood their anger but argued that violence would not help their cause. Cool heads prevailed and further trouble was averted. Hume was now getting used to intervening on the streets and having to use his negotiation skills to prevent trouble. It was dangerous work and required much bravery, as Paul Arthur recalls from his days in Derry:

> I always remember Hume going out afterwards to try and break up the riots, to try and persuade the young people that they should not be doing this. And, you know, that took a huge amount of effort and you are going to get a lot of abuse. So that's when I began to think, this guy is special.[4]

His work on the streets was even acknowledged in an official report by Lord Cameron which would be published later in 1969. The Cameron Commission was set up to investigate violence since October 1968 and trace its causes. Hume was praised as a peacekeeper and his efforts were regarded as 'outstanding'.[5]

Days after the Derry trouble, Northern Ireland's prime minister became a political casualty of the ongoing tension and violence. Terence O'Neill's gamble of going to the polls for the 'crossroads election' had failed and he had been unable to maintain support within the Unionist Party. His critics felt he had offered too many concessions to the civil rights campaign and had made changes too quickly. Some felt he was acquiescing to the threat of violence and suggested his plans were helping those who wanted a united Ireland.

O'Neill's unionist credentials had been under attack for some time, and he was also getting little support from London, which viewed the television pictures from Northern Ireland with increasing alarm. In April 1969 he resigned, bringing his six-year premiership to an end. The contest to replace O'Neill came down to two men whom he had worked closely with. Major James Chichester-Clark and Brian Faulkner battled it out for the leadership amongst their unionist colleagues. Chichester-Clark triumphed in the narrowest of margins by 17 votes to 16 and on 1 May he became the party's leader and Northern Ireland's fifth prime minister.

There would be no honeymoon period for the new premier and little time to take stock of what was happening. As the summer took hold it seemed that Northern Ireland was becoming more and more fractious and violence was almost part of daily life. On Saturday 12 July, there was serious rioting in Derry, Dungiven and Belfast. The next day in Dungiven, 67-year-old Francis McCloskey was hit on the head with a baton by an RUC officer and died 24 hours later. In August the situation remained tense and there were real fears that an Apprentice Boys parade in Derry could lead to serious violence.

The annual event was scheduled for Saturday 12 August. The prospect of street disorder was raised by the Irish government during discussions with London, but their concerns were dismissed. Hume also had major reservations about the planned event and was worried that serious violence would break out. He wanted the march banned, which led to calls that he was being a hypocrite since he had often been on the streets to argue for greater civil rights. Hume felt the timing of this parade and the route would simply inflame tensions: 'I felt that to hold a march through the centre of the city given the tensions that already existed could be very dangerous and therefore I appealed to the Apprentice Boys not to march through the city centre.'[6]

Hume decided that he had to tell the authorities in Dublin and London in person how he felt. He held talks south of the border with Taoiseach Jack Lynch and then travelled to London in the hope of seeing Jim Callaghan, the Home Secretary. He could not get an appointment with the cabinet minister and instead had to make do with his deputy, Lord Stonham. The brief talks did not change anything and there would be no last-minute ban by Stormont.

The atmosphere in the Bogside was tense ever since the death of Sammy Devenney. There was animosity at the way the RUC had behaved towards the Devenney family and there was a real fear from Bogside residents that on the day of the parade they would soon be under siege.

With that in mind, a group called Derry Citizens' Defence Association was set up which was more militant than Hume's Action Committee. The influence of the original group now appeared to be dwindling. Attitudes were hardening and there were genuine concerns that Bogside residents would be attacked by either the police or, potentially, loyalists. The new grouping planned to seal off the area with the erection of barricades, and as the weekend approached, materials started to be gathered to prepare street barriers. What unfolded next would ultimately change the history of Northern Ireland.

With his fellow Stormont colleague Ivan Cooper and Eddie McAteer, Hume took to the streets on Saturday 12 August to plead with residents not to engage in violence. Time and again they linked arms and formed a human barrier to stop youths from getting close to the procession and the police lines. At street corners, Hume had animated conversations with young men begging them to stand back or simply go home. It was an impossible task. Derry was a city of contrasts, divided by geography and now fractured by politics.

In the city centre, close to the historic walls and around the main shopping area, the bands played and the Apprentice Boys paraded, cheered on by supporters. To outsiders, the event looked like a community pageant with colourful banners and bands playing music. To loyalists and unionists, this was about maintaining tradition. It was, in their eyes, a celebration of culture and they were simply doing what their fathers and grandfathers had done. In the Bogside and across other mainly Catholic areas there was an air of angry apprehension. This was no ordinary Saturday. Hundreds of policemen were on duty and in front of metal barriers RUC officers stood at flashpoints to keep the marchers and the residents apart. At the Littlewoods store at the junction of William Street and Waterloo Place, the two sides came within yards of each other. Insults and stones were thrown and the atmosphere at times was hostile.

As the afternoon wore on and the parade finished, the anger did not disappear. There were battles between the police and local Catholic and Protestant youths and there was serious rioting. The parade was over but the trouble was not. Early in the evening, the RUC decided to try and quell the trouble. Hundreds of officers with armoured vehicles and water cannon entered the Bogside. The police were met with resistance and stones and petrol bombs rained down on them. Some youths took to the roof of Rossville Flats, which meant they were able to look down on the police and attack them from above. The RUC officers were poorly equipped and had very small riot shields which offered little protection from petrol bombs. Some officers took to throwing stones back into the crowd.

As the street battles continued, police chiefs realised that the situation was showing little sign of coming to an end. Just before midnight, after some nine hours of rioting, the RUC used CS gas for the first time in its history. It was a momentous decision. A police armoured car smashed through a barricade at Rossville Street and the CS gas canisters were let off by the officers. Also known as tear gas, it was used as a crowd control measure and caused pain in the eyes, coughing, sneezing and skin irritation. Those youths that stayed on the streets quickly learned that they could deal with the latest RUC tactic if they placed vinegar-soaked handkerchiefs over their noses and mouths. The police action simply hardened the resolve of the Bogsiders, and local residents fought back at what they saw as an invasion. There was a feeling of revolution in the air and the rioting continued in what would later be called 'The Battle of the Bogside'.

Bernadette Devlin, now the new Westminster MP for Mid Ulster, was on the scene helping locals build barricades from material left by construction workers. She and others in the Citizens' Defence Association had planned where the street barriers should go. Hume had no say with this group who saw him as too conservative.

Hume and Bernadette Devlin were two very different characters with contrasting political approaches. Whereas Devlin was seen as a socialist firebrand out to take on the establishment, Hume was viewed by many as a moderate. Devlin's politics were on the far left whilst Hume regarded himself as a social democrat and would have been seen as a centrist. He was a pacifist. Devlin was sentenced to six months in jail for her part in the Bogside riots. At the time she stood by her actions: 'If the same circumstances rose again [I] would have no problems helping them again.'[7] Hume often criticised Devlin for her political approach and later on one occasion told Irish government officials: 'Devlin was a disaster. She had gone wholly over to the International Socialists in Britain.'[8] Whilst Hume and Devlin shared much common ground in the civil rights campaign regarding the need for social change, they often differed over tactics, particularly when it came to bringing people out onto the streets.

Even though his authority as the Foyle MP was being challenged during the disturbances in Derry, Hume was determined to try and stop the violence. Throughout the day he stayed on the streets talking, arguing and trying to dissuade youths from getting involved in trouble. He was effectively working as a quasi-fireman and a peacekeeper, going from street corner to street corner to keep the violence at bay.

At one stage he got word that there was going to be trouble at Rosemount RUC Station, which local youths had surrounded, and there was talk it might be petrol-bombed, potentially trapping the officers inside. Hume went to the scene:

> A big crowd gathered outside and I was worried about the trouble and I went up and addressed the crowd and calmed them down and persuaded them to leave and I went up to talk to the police at the station to tell them that the people were going to leave, but as I was walking towards them they opened fire with gas.[9]

Hume was hit in the chest by a CS gas canister and he passed out. He recovered quickly and when he came round he went back to resume his conversation with the police, telling them that the crowd was about to depart. By 13 August, the Bogside resembled a scene from a Second World War movie. There were burnt-out cars in the streets, and barrels and wood blocked some roads. Windows were boarded up. There were small fires still burning and the roads were strewn with rocks and glass. Northern Ireland's second city looked unrecognisable. The damage was not just to property, as dozens of residents and police officers were injured. Many were taken to Altnagelvin Hospital in the city, whilst others preferred to be treated across the border in Letterkenny. In Dublin, there was great alarm at the unfolding situation in Derry. Taoiseach Jack Lynch made a television broadcast expressing his fears over what he had witnessed on the news bulletins. He announced that Irish Army field hospitals would be set up near the border to assist those injured in the Derry trouble. He said: 'It is clear now that the present situation can not be allowed to continue. It is evident that the Stormont Government is no longer in control of the situation.'[10]

Lynch also said a UN peacekeeper force should be brought in and there should be talks with the London government about the constitutional position of Northern Ireland. He also made this memorable remark: 'It is clear also that the Irish government can no longer stand by and see innocent people injured and perhaps worse.'[11] The taoiseach's intervention was understandably welcomed by nationalists and a rumour went round the Bogside that the Irish Army was going to cross the border into Northern Ireland – a claim that was simply not true. Predictably, unionists reacted with anger to Lynch's remarks and they saw his broadcast as unwelcome and unhelpful.

As the rioting continued in Derry, violence spread to other parts of Northern Ireland. Belfast, in particular, was ablaze and the news bulletins were now filled with stories of attacks and shootings. It looked like Northern Ireland was on the brink of civil war. Hume left the battered streets of the Bogside on Monday 14 August and travelled to Stormont where MPs had gathered to sit in an emergency session and discuss a government motion condemning the recent violence and praising the work of the police force. The prime minister, James Chichester-Clark, said the decision to allow the Apprentice Boys to march had been the correct one. He praised the role of the police and attacked the taoiseach's intervention. He said the Irish government was not being helpful and accused it of being unfriendly.

Unionist MP John Taylor declared that 11,000 members of the B Specials would be deployed to assist the RUC. The B Specials were an armed part-time police auxiliary unit who were almost entirely Protestant and were much hated in Catholic communities that viewed them as partisan. Taylor's announcement, seen as an attempt to crush dissent on the streets, caused alarm in the ranks of non-unionists. Hume made a short address and it was clear he was emotional. He was not in great shape to deliver a speech. He had spent the last two days walking the streets of Derry. He had been injured with CS gas and knocked unconscious and he had had little sleep. Undeterred, he addressed the chamber by talking about his own experiences:

> Probably more than any other member of this House I know what the last few days have meant to people. I had hoped that crisis could perhaps bring out the best in some people in this House but I regret to say that the sterility of this house was never more in evidence than it is today.[12]

Hume described John Taylor's contribution as a 'jackboot speech' and then he ended his comments: 'We are quite firm, we shall not be moved. My colleagues and I, Mr Speaker, will say goodbye.'[13]

With that, Hume and six of his like-minded colleagues walked out of the chamber. They then missed a most dramatic announcement. Robert Porter, the home affairs minister, got to his feet and told the house that, after discussions involving the RUC and the UK government, British troops would be deployed into Northern Ireland. The move had been approved by Prime Minister Harold Wilson, who had agreed in principle that if the unionist government at Stormont wanted military support it would get it.

When the official request came, Jim Callaghan, the Home Secretary was in mid-air. He was on an RAF plane and was handed a note outlining the appeal. He read it quickly and scribbled a response which was handed back to the navigator. Within minutes the troops were on their way.

At 5 p.m. members of the 1st Battalion, the Prince Of Wales Own Yorkshire Regiment, marched into the Bogside. Residents initially reacted with joy and there was a feeling that things were about to change. The 'Battle of the Bogside' had lasted for two days and the area had effectively become a 'state within a state'. It was now seen as 'Free Derry' and it was in the control of the Defence Association where the writ of the unionist government did not run. The trouble across Northern Ireland had resulted in deaths and hundreds of injuries. Many houses had been destroyed in days of attacks. An estimated 1,500 Catholic families had been forced to leave their homes with around 300 Protestant families suffering a similar fate. Mixed streets where families from different backgrounds once lived were changing and more areas were becoming colour-coded in a map dominated by green and orange.

Bombay Street in Belfast, a predominantly Catholic area, was attacked and burnt by loyalists. Residents say they received little or no protection from the police and had to defend themselves with stones and guns. The attack in the heart of West Belfast became a defining moment for many republicans. For years the IRA had been dormant after its failed border campaign had been wound up in 1962. The outbreak of the August violence caught many republicans by surprise and in 1969 the IRA was disorganised with limited access to weapons. Unable to defend streets from loyalist attacks, the IRA was seen by many republicans as useless and ineffectual. The criticism prompted graffiti which declared 'IRA = I Ran Away'. The Bombay Street attack was one of the incidents that changed the debate in republican circles and in the days that followed the IRA began to reorganise and source weapons.

Hume was well aware of the discussions going on in the background and knew further violence was being talked about. He desperately wanted to concentrate on finding political solutions and continued talking to those who carried influence in London and Dublin. When the Home Secretary, Jim Callaghan, arrived in Northern Ireland for a three-day visit, Hume invited the cabinet minister to Derry. Amidst an enormous crowd, the Foyle MP and his colleague, Ivan Cooper, met him outside the Littlewoods store close to the Bogside. Hume outstretched his hand and in front of the cameras told his visitor that his constituents represented 'the living symbols of injustice in Northern Ireland'. He informed the Home Secretary that in the Bogside he would find 'the worst housing, the highest unemployment and the heaviest emigration and I hope you are bringing a solution with you'.[14]

Callaghan knew one visit could never realistically deliver that demand but, ever the politician, he smiled for the crowd and remarked: 'I am very glad to come, very glad indeed to be here and to see everybody.'[15]

The problem was it seemed that everybody in the Bogside wanted to see him and Callaghan was mobbed by the crowd like a visiting film star. Hume was understandably keen that the visit would go well and he knew it was essential that it passed off trouble-free. The atmosphere was boisterous but good-natured. There were shouts of welcome from the crowd but also demands to abolish Stormont and release prisoners held under the Special Powers Act. Some residents broke into song and, to the now traditional strains of 'We Shall Overcome', the political delegation tried to inch its way down the street. It was an impossible task. Such was the size of the gathering that the Home Secretary was only able to walk 50 yards in 30 minutes.

Hume used the opportunity to tell his visitor about the huge problems faced by Bogside residents. He told Callaghan that there had been widespread discrimination against Catholics in the allocation of public housing. Hume argued for a centralised authority and his guest replied that he should leave it with him and he would follow that idea up. Ultimately, Hume's suggestion would come to pass and housing allocation would be reformed.

As the visit continued, the three politicians, Cooper, Hume and Callaghan, were now almost being crushed by the crowd. It was starting to get quite dangerous and it was clear that the Home Secretary's planned walkabout was going to have to be abandoned. His hosts suggested he take refuge in a two-up two-down terraced house near Free Derry Corner which was home to a Mrs Doherty. Inside, over a cup of tea, one of the most important men in British politics met representatives of the Derry Citizens' Defence Association and listened to their concerns. Callaghan then declared: 'I must speak to the people before I leave.'[16]

He climbed the stairs to the small front bedroom and leant out the window and with a megaphone in his hand he delivered an impromptu speech. He told the crowd that he had received a courteous and enthusiastic welcome and said he was told he was perceived as neutral but declared: 'I am not neutral. I am on the side of those, whoever they may be and in whatever community they live, who are deprived of justice and freedom.'[17]

Those words got the biggest cheer of the day. Callaghan had hit the spot. Before he left the Bogside he asked the crowd to give their political representatives some time and space to come up with solutions. The speech could have been written by Hume and it delivered the message that the local politician felt his constituents needed to hear. Change could happen and it could come politically.

Hume knew amongst the crowd that day there were some influential figures who had little time for politics and who favoured military action. He knew their arguments inside out, as he had heard them many times. They were sympathetic to the IRA and they believed that to beat force you needed to use force. Hume knew how persuasive that brand of thinking was. It was part of Irish history and ingrained in the republican psyche, and he knew the demand for an armed response to discrimination and loyalist attacks was being openly discussed. He was also conscious of talks going on in republican circles about the future direction of the IRA. As the year ended, those divisions boiled to the surface and the IRA split. The organisation had two camps with one that became known as the 'Officials' and the other referred to as the 'Provisionals'.

The Provisionals accused the Officials of failing to protect communities during the August violence and said the current leadership had become obsessed with politics rather than seeking a military role. A younger more militant brand of republican was emerging, one which advocated violent confrontation. Hume knew this was a dangerous time. He understood that politics had to be seen to work. Earlier in the year, after he was elected to Stormont, he had promised to seek social change through a new political party.

The time had come to deliver.

7

PARTY TIME

'I had misgivings about his motives and doubted the strength of his loyalty to us as a group.'
Paddy Devlin on John Hume

John Hume adored being in Donegal. It was his special place. Ever since he and Pat had got married in 1960 the couple would cross the border for long weekends and holidays. He particularly enjoyed going to the Irish-speaking area, the Gaeltacht, and loved spending time close to Gweedore, which was sandwiched between the Derryveagh mountains and the Atlantic Ocean. For Hume, this was a place apart. Over time Pat and John and their growing family would be a familiar sight on the beaches and in the local hostelries. It was not long before they had a network of friends they could socialise with.

Bríd Rodgers, who was from Gweedore and who would go on to become an SDLP Stormont minister, recalls the early days of holidaying with the Humes: 'The kids all played together and had a great time because there were quite a few families there from the North, and we used to go out in the evenings and have dinner and sing-songs.'[1]

The Humes would often rent the same house over the summer. Mo, John's daughter, was too young to remember the early Donegal holidays but recalls the later ones: 'We would go every year for the month of July to Bunbeg, as my mum was a teacher. So, as soon as she finished teaching, she would pack the car and we would head off.'[2]

The Humes quickly established a wide group of friends who would regularly head for Donegal in the summer. Political contacts would also be encouraged to book time off and join the family. Seán Donlon also holidayed with the Humes in Bunbeg:

> It was the sort of place where you could have some semblance of family life in the sense that the adults would stay up very late drinking and singing and telling stories. The children would be dragged out to the beach to play and eventually given some food and it was all very relaxed.[3]

As well as fun on the beach and singing in the pubs at night, there were big days out with other families. Every year there was an organised trip to Gola, a small island off the coast of Bunbeg. Hume's son, also called John, recalls how the trip was often the highlight of the holiday:

> You would start talking about it eleven months in advance. We would all go out to Gola on this boat. It would have been a fishing boat and they would pile ten families on. You would not do it today. Ten families – not a life jacket amongst us – you know 25 or 30 kids, 20 adults, and off we would go to Gola for the day. That was the biggest day of the year.[4]

Hume also took the opportunity whilst on holiday to cook, which was something he rarely did when he was back in Derry. His daughter Therese remembers how her father would annually prepare a big family meal:

> Because he had worked in the smoked salmon business he had contacts in Burtonport and he used to be able to land himself a salmon or a lobster or something like that from various people. And he would cook them up. He would also cook a salmon once a year when we were down in Bunbeg. He would cook the salmon and new spuds and it always tasted very good.[5]

Being in Bunbeg also gave Hume the opportunity to speak Irish more frequently, although, in the early days, he felt his language skills needed some work. Bríd Rodgers recalls how Hume was asked to interview with the Irish language station Raidió na Gaeltachta. He was worried that his Irish would not be up to scratch, since he had not really practised it since his school days at St Columb's. Rodgers, who was a native speaker, gave him a quick crash course with key phrases. She remembers tuning into the broadcast: 'He sounded like a native speaker. That evening I met the interviewer who told me she never realised John was such a fluent Irish speaker.'[6]

Donegal offered Hume respite from the pressure cooker world of politics. During his entire political career, it was where he went if he needed to think through ideas or recharge his batteries. It was also the backdrop to key discussions during Hume's time as a party leader and different parts of the peace process. Bunbeg and the surrounding area were also where crucial conversations were held about the formation of a new party. Hume and Ivan Cooper and Paddy O'Hanlon had all been elected to Stormont as Independents and knew each other well from the civil rights campaign. They were keen to set up a new party and were politically close to Hume. The Foyle MP then started to have discussions with Austin Currie, a Nationalist MP for East Tyrone. Currie believed in the idea of a modern party and had been arguing within the Nationalist Party for some time for change. He recalls: 'In my first election campaign in the by-election in 1964 the time for a modern political organisation was central to my campaign. The real change that was made was that Hume, Cooper and O'Hanlon were of like mind.'[7]

Bringing Gerry Fitt and Paddy Devlin on board was always going to be the trickiest part for Hume. He and the two Belfast representatives were very different, both in personality and in aspects of their politics. Devlin and Fitt saw themselves in the socialist tradition and both had strong Labour views. Hume regarded himself as a social democrat and not a socialist. Devlin was currently in the Northern Ireland Labour Party and Fitt had been elected as a Republican Labour candidate. Fitt was very outgoing, with a quick wit and a reputation for one-liners. He was not a product of grammar school and unlike Hume he was self-taught. He liked his independence and was wary of joining a party.

Eamonn McCann recalls a conversation with Fitt when talk of a new political grouping was being discussed: 'Gerry did not want the party at all. Gerry told me at that time, "If you form a party there will be wee men on bicycles going round the constituency storing up trouble." He was a great man for one man, one vote, but not within his party.'[8]

Devlin was regarded by some as a big-hearted maverick with a quick temper and, sometimes, a coarse tongue. Like Fitt, he had an outgoing personality and a colourful CV. He joined the IRA and was interned and went on to become involved in trade union work and was elected to Belfast City Council representing the Irish Labour Party. He later got involved in the Northern Ireland Labour Party and became its chairman.

Devlin got to know Hume through their work together on civil rights issues and their time at Stormont. Yet the Belfast man was always wary of his Derry counterpart:

> From the outset of our relationship I had misgivings about his motives and doubted the strength of his loyalty to us as a group. He had a tendency to identify the most powerful and influential people amongst those we encountered and go off into corner huddles with those pace-setters and opinion-formers.[9]

If the new party was to have a wide appeal it was felt it needed a strong presence in Belfast, so talks involving Fitt and Devlin, who both represented seats in the city, were seen as crucial. In order to get to know each other better, Hume organised a series of weekend meetings in Bunbeg where ideas could be discussed and people could socialise in the evening. He invited Fitt and Devlin and they joined him, as well as Ivan Cooper, Austin Currie and Paddy O'Hanlon. Hume handled the discussions with his colleagues well and sought out points and areas of common interest. Even though there were differences, they all had experience working together as they had recently formed a loose coalition at Stormont and had taken on shadow portfolios. Hume was confident the talks would result in an agreement to form a party.

To many political watchers, he was Stormont's rising star, and as an Independent MP, he was courted by several political groupings who were interested in recruiting him. In March 1970, Jim Hendron made contact with him. Hendron was in the New Ulster Movement, a group of Catholics and Protestants who were liberal in their political outlook and who wanted to develop cross-community politics. Hendron was chairman of the New Ulster Movement's Bloomfield branch in East Belfast and had been tasked by his colleagues to invite Hume to speak at their monthly meeting. After a series of conversations and many questions, the Foyle MP agreed.

Hume arrived at Hendron's house one evening in his Vauxhall car, which was littered with newspapers, and the two men travelled together to the Glenmachan Hotel. Normally branch meetings attracted around forty people, but Hume drew a crowd of well over a hundred. Hendron was taken aback by the numbers as he arrived in the packed car park, and he was approached by one of the hotel staff who said they should have been informed about the size of the crowd. Hendron brought Hume into the building and the MP asked for a few minutes to gather his thoughts. Hume had clearly not prepared a speech. Instead, he took out his pen and wrote a few lines; as Hendron recalled: 'He just put a few bullet points on a fag packet.'[10]

The Derry man's ad-libbed address was brilliantly received. He was given a six-minute standing ovation. Afterwards, Hume confessed to Hendron that he had addressed many political meetings, but that was the first 'non-nationalist' political gathering. Hume impressed his audience and he seemed exactly the type of person they wanted to represent them. For months, a collection of activists known as 'the group of 16' had been working behind the scenes to prepare the launch of a new party, which was to be called the Alliance Party.

After the meeting at the Glenmachan Hotel, Hume went for a drink in North Belfast. It was there he met Joe Hendron, Jim's brother. Joe joined the Alliance Party briefly but would later become the SDLP MP for West Belfast. He remembers their first meeting: 'I was very impressed by him. You could not be anything else but impressed by John. He had a very clear mind and he felt strongly about matters.'[11]

With the launch date approaching, Jim Hendron made a bold move and asked Hume to join the group, which would include Catholics, Protestants and people from a mixed background. Hendron made it clear that if Hume joined he would have enormous influence in the party's direction and would be in the leadership. Jim Hendron thinks Hume 'might have ended up as leader'.[12]

Hume was non-committal to the approach but wished Hendron well and wanted to stay in touch. The two men talked again when Hume called at Hendron's house, which was not far from the Stormont estate. Hendron sensed Hume was intrigued but not inclined to take it any further.

On Monday 20 August, the day before the Alliance Party was launched, Jim Hendron made a final attempt to recruit Hume, but he declined, saying he was about to form his own grouping with five other Stormont MPs. However, Hume desperately wanted to know what name Hendron's party was going to take. Hendron said he could not tell him, as the title was embargoed until the next day, but Hume particularly wanted to discover if the new group was using the words 'social', 'democratic' or 'labour'. Hendron did not reveal the party's name but confirmed that it did not include any of the words Hume was interested in.

On 21 April 1970, the Alliance Party of Northern Ireland came into being, and Oliver Napier and Bob Cooper became co-leaders with Jim Hendron as one of the founding members. So why did Hume refuse Jim Hendron's offer, when much of his politics seemed to be close to the Alliance Party? Hume talked about creating a party that was non-sectarian. So was this not a perfect opportunity?

Jim Hendron says geography and circumstance played a part: 'He had been a successful Independent MP for Foyle. He was publicly identified with Foyle, therefore he was publicly identified with nationalism, even though at that stage he did not call himself a nationalist.'

Hendron says if Hume had joined this new group he would not have become a nationalist leader as the new grouping was aiming to be cross-community: 'We were from the beginning appealing right across the board to unionists and nationalists.'[13]

In reality, joining the Alliance Party would have been a much bigger political risk for Hume than setting up a group with Ivan Cooper and others. He already had working relationships with five other Stormont MPs and he had established a good constituency setup in Foyle where the overriding political mood was nationalist. Jim Hendron accepts that Hume did not have any close friendships with the founders of the Alliance Party so it would have represented a big step into the 'unknown'.[14]

Looking back, Hume had no regrets about his decision:

> At the time I was not in favour of the Alliance Party being set up. I felt there was a mood in the community for new politics. That mood was reflected in our election results that led to our situation. That led some people to think of creating the Alliance Party, although none of them had any mandates about doing that. And of course, it ended up what it was from the beginning, basically a middle-class group, and the liberals on the unionist side from the Protestant community joined up with it and the sort of people that maybe would have joined our party at the time.[15]

Reflecting on those early days he thinks some people from the Protestant tradition were probably put off joining the SDLP:

> But I suppose one of the reasons they would not have joined us was because of the past parties that other members of our party had been in, like the Nationalist Party and Republican Labour members etc. I assumed that. But if the Alliance Party hadn't been formed at the time – this is only an opinion – I believe that we would have had a stronger non-sectarian membership and support.[16]

In 1970 John Hume and his Stormont colleagues continued their talks about forming a new party. He recalled how the discussions gathered pace in Donegal: 'Knowing the place and the hotels there, I arranged that our meetings would take place down there in a more relaxed atmosphere over weekends. And the dialogue we had down there of course was very positive and very constructive.'[17]

Central to the new party was a series of aims and values, and Hume's handiwork was evident: 'We were drafting policy papers and of course, in particular, a constitution for the party, and the central issue of course, which I was heavily involved in, was the approach to Irish unity.'[18]

Hume insisted that his view on consent, first articulated in his *Irish Times* features in 1964, was central; he insisted that the unity of Ireland could only come about with the consent of the majority of people in Northern Ireland.

As the meetings continued, they were interrupted by a Westminster election in June which returned a Conservative government with Ted Heath as prime minister. The Ulster Unionists took 8 of the 12 seats, with Ian Paisley winning in North Antrim and Bernadette Devlin and Gerry Fitt both retaining their seats. In the Londonderry constituency, Hume acted as election agent for his old rival Eddie McAteer, who stood under the Nationalist Party banner. His decision to work with McAteer did not go down well with others who thought it was a missed opportunity to break with the past. Paddy Devlin thought it made more sense for Hume to back Claude Wilton as a candidate. Wilton was a civil rights campaigner, a Protestant who had run as a liberal candidate before. Paddy Devlin thought Wilton's nomination would send out a non-sectarian cross-community message which could help their new party in the weeks to come. Instead, Hume threw his weight and that of many of his supporters behind McAteer. It was a conservative choice for Hume, but in the end, it did not result in victory. McAteer failed to take the seat and it was won by Robin Chichester-Clark, the sitting unionist and brother to James, the Northern Ireland prime minister.

Hume's decision to back McAteer was not the only issue that threatened to derail the talks around a new party. Paddy Devlin claims Hume had embarked on separate discussions in Donegal about the possibility of setting up a new Catholic political party. If Devlin's intelligence is correct then what was Hume up to? Was he keeping his options open and perhaps having second thoughts about forming an official alliance with the likes of Devlin and Fitt whose brands of socialism he did not share?

Hume's friends were now getting impatient about the delay in forming a party. Denis Haughey, who would later become one of Hume's trusted allies, told Hume the new party would be built around him, but he detected that Hume was being cautious. He felt the indecision was 'paralysing him'.[19]

Haughey and a number of others who had met in the civil rights movement had been badgering Hume for months to get on with setting up the new movement. He recalls a blunt phone call with Hume in 1970 when he said: 'If you are not prepared to move, some of us will move anyway because we need a political structure to cope with this problem. He said to me, "Denis, don't move, there are moves afoot."'[20]

The pace quickened in July and Hume was back fully engaged with forming a party with his Stormont colleagues. The six Stormont MPs met at a hotel in Bunbeg and drafted a document that would be the principles of the new party. Now things were moving quickly, but there were still two remaining pieces of business. Firstly, who would lead this new movement and, secondly, what would it be called? The leadership appeared to come down to a choice between Fitt and Hume. It seemed that if it came to a vote, Gerry Fitt would have the upper hand. The Belfast man was seen as the more experienced political operator and as a Westminster MP there was a feeling that he had the contacts who could give the party much-needed profile and influence. Denis Haughey insists that Gerry Fitt and Paddy Devlin would not have joined the new party had they not been promised jobs.

He was advised by Austin Currie that the two Belfast representatives had to be offered something:

> It was Austin who convinced us that unless we make Gerry the leader he is not going to cooperate with us. Paddy Devlin was an explosive, volatile character and it was thought we need to give him some kind of blandishments to take part in this experiment. So he was made Chief Whip.[21]

After months of protracted talks, matters began to speed up when the story of the new party was leaked to the press. The question of who should lead it was naturally posed by journalists, and when Fitt was asked in an RTÉ interview if he was going to be the leader, he confirmed he would be. Hume would take the role of deputy leader. Now all that remained was the name of the party. Not surprisingly, opinions were divided on what it should be. Hume had always said that he wanted the new movement to be a 'social democratic' party, so he wanted those terms in the title. Fitt and Devlin, who came from the socialist tradition, wanted the new name to include the word 'Labour' to reflect the party's left-of-centre credentials. The MPs met to resolve the issue at a hotel in Toomebridge in County Antrim. To throw inquisitive journalists off the scent they pretended that they had come to the village to discuss eel fishing, which was the area's most famous export. When the discussion came to the name of the party the traditional positions remained. Fitt and Devlin wanted 'Labour' and argued that without it the title of the party would not be acceptable in working-class areas of Belfast. Hume and others insisted on the words 'Social Democratic' because they wanted the party to have a European dimension.

It was crucial to Hume that those words were in the title. Paul Bew, who cut his political teeth in People's Democracy and later became a member of the House of Lords, remembers observing Hume at that time. Bew was politically close to Paddy Devlin and says Hume's politics were very different from Devlin's: 'When I think about this, the ghost of Paddy Devlin is in my ear. Hume was always more of a social democrat than a socialist.'[22]

Austin Currie recalls the meeting where the name was discussed. It was quite a lengthy session and eventually it was agreed that the new movement would be named the 'Labour and Social Democratic Party':

> I remember we had ended the discussion and moved on to something else. Devlin was sitting back in his chair and then suddenly he sat up ... the Labour and Social Democratic Party ... The LSD party ... no way. We can't

have it tied to money and drugs. Almost immediately Hume and I said right ... it's the Social Democratic and Labour Party. And that is what it became.[23]

Three months after the Alliance Party was launched, the SDLP was unveiled at the Grand Central Hotel in Belfast on 21 August 1970. In front of journalists and camera crews, Gerry Fitt took centre stage as leader with John Hume as his deputy. The leadership team could not have been more different, and from the start, it was clear there was tension between Fitt's brand of street socialism and Hume's more academic approach. As well as the launch, other practicalities were in hand to turn the idea of a party into a functioning political movement.

Party offices were secured at College Square North in Belfast, a bank loan was organised and adverts were placed in local newspapers offering party membership for ten shillings. Recruits came into the new movement from a variety of places. There were applications from those who had never been in a party before but who were simply impressed with Fitt and Hume's brand of politics. Some new members joined after leaving the Nationalist Party, feeling that the SDLP had a more modern approach. Fitt and Devlin also encouraged members of the Northern Ireland Labour Party and Republican Labour to join and many also crossed over from the NDP, which had been set up in 1965. It was a nationalist party that believed that partition should be ended but only by democratic means. Two of its candidates had included Alasdair McDonnell and Eddie McGrady, who would later go on to become SDLP MPs. Sensing there was little point in continuing as a party, the NDP folded in October 1970.

From those early days, the SDLP said it was a 'non-sectarian' party and wanted to attract moderate unionists and Protestants who shared their centre-left politics. The hope was that disadvantaged Protestant voters who felt let down by successive unionist governments would feel they had much in common with their Catholic neighbours. Denis Haughey says in those early days more should have been done to recruit Protestants. He says he encouraged John Hume to reach out to

Protestants and get a number to join the party and publicise their membership in unionist supporting newspapers: 'Several times I said to him and each time he said that's a great idea. He never got round to it.'[24]

Haughey insists that Hume should have done more in those early days to appeal to people from traditional unionist backgrounds:

> My view was that was more important than some of the things that he devoted so much to. That would really have been a radical change of direction both for the SDLP, for the movement for civil rights, for political progress. If John had set about doing what I wanted him to do, I think that would have been a very, very important, transforming event in the history of Northern Ireland.[25]

As the party came into being, the streets were still filled with tension. Belfast was experiencing a summer of discontent and violent unrest. In June, there was serious rioting across Belfast. Provisional IRA snipers opened fire during clashes by the Short Strand. During rioting five Protestants and a Catholic were shot dead. Groups of loyalist paramilitaries were starting to become active all over Northern Ireland.

In July, there were British Army searches for weapons in the Lower Falls in Belfast which led to a two-day curfew and a gun battle with the Official IRA. This was a key moment. The initial warm reception for the troops evaporated after four men were killed by soldiers. Three were shot and one was knocked down by a military vehicle. Whilst 100 firearms were discovered during the raids, the entire operation would have devastating long-term consequences for the relationship between the Catholic community and the British Army. It led many to believe the Army was not an impartial body but instead a hostile force. The honeymoon was over.

The shootings by the British Army helped to swell the ranks of the Provisional and Official IRA, who were now two quite separate groups. The Provisionals were fine-tuning their bomb-making capabilities and there was a series of explosions in Belfast and Derry. Two RUC constables were killed in a booby-trap car bomb in Crossmaglen. 1970 ended with some bleak statistics. There were 28 Troubles deaths – 19 civilians, 6 members of the IRA, 2 RUC officers and Richard Fallon, who was the first member of An Garda Síochána to be killed in the conflict.

The new year brought little relief. In January there was rioting in the Catholic Ballymurphy estate, Ardoyne and the Protestant Shankill estate. In February 1971, the IRA shot Gunner Robert Curtis during a gun battle in the New Lodge area of Belfast. He was the first serving soldier to be killed by the IRA during the Troubles. A month later, three off-duty Scottish soldiers were lured from a pub by members of the IRA in Belfast and shot. The killing of the three soldiers prompted a political crisis. Unionists believed that the security situation was getting out of control and they looked to Westminster for help. There were calls for internment without trial and demands for thousands of additional troops to go into areas where the IRA was seen as active. James Chichester-Clark flew to London for discussions with the prime minister, Edward Heath. The unionist leader was under intense pressure from his colleagues who desperately wanted to see a greater security presence on the streets. Heath sanctioned an extra 1,300 troops, but when Chichester-Clark got back to Belfast he was told by his party colleagues that this number was derisory. Two days later, the pressure became too much and he stood down: 'I have decided to resign because I see no other way of bringing home to all concerned the realities of the present constitutional political and security situation.'[26]

His premiership had lasted less than two years. Once again, the Unionist Party faced a leadership battle. In a vote amongst Unionist MPs at Stormont, Brian Faulkner easily saw off the challenge of Bill Craig to become prime minister. A former minister of commerce, he had failed by just one vote to take the leadership at the previous contest in 1969 when Chichester-Clark triumphed. This time Faulkner was seen as the natural successor and won by 26 votes to 4. Northern Ireland had seen three prime ministers at Stormont in two years and the new premier began life in an atmosphere of fear and political instability. The nature of his task was summed up in a headline in the *Daily Mirror* which declared that he was 'The Man with the Worst Job in the World'. Faulkner was shrewd enough to know that things had to change and he had to do things very differently to the previous unionist prime minister. He knew his cabinet had to be more widely representative of Northern Ireland. He appointed David Bleakley, former chairman of the Northern Ireland Labour Party, to the post of minister for community relations. Bleakley was the first non-unionist minister to be appointed to a Stormont government and it was seen as a significant step. Faulkner also wanted to change the way committees scrutinised Stormont and he proposed all-party involvement.

As Northern Ireland marked its fiftieth anniversary, not everyone was in a celebratory mood. Hume told party activists in June that partition had failed and he felt unionists were incapable of governing. He said it was time for new thinking and he called for the scrapping of the 1920 Government of Ireland Act. In its place, he argued for a new form of government where there would be representatives from each section of society – one of the first times he had articulated this model which would become more popularly known as power-sharing. As MPs gathered at Parliament Buildings in June, John Hume turned his remarks to Faulkner's early days in office and accepted that changes had been made though he felt there needed to be more. He said political change takes time and told the house: 'Progress is not in a straight line, but progress is taking place. The choice we face today is a very serious one and it can be expressed very simply – chaos or community.'[27]

Across the chamber, Faulkner was listening very intently to the words of the SDLP deputy leader: 'Although he went on to talk about the failure of partition, I was generally pleased with this response from a person regarded at the time by unionists as one of the most intransigent opponents of the State.'[28] This spirit of goodwill was evident when Faulkner hosted private talks between the Ulster Unionists, the SDLP and the Northern Ireland Labour Party. The groups issued a joint statement saying the talks were helpful and constructive and that they would meet again. The positive atmosphere was shattered within days.

On Thursday 8 July, less than 48 hours after the Stormont discussions ended, two Derry men, Seamus Cusack and Desmond Beattie, were shot dead by the army. The accounts from local people and the army differed, with the soldiers saying that, in the case of Desmond Beattie, he was about to throw a bomb. He was unarmed and not carrying any weapons. Seamus Cusack was also not armed, despite army claims that he had been carrying a rifle. There had been rioting in the area and the army had come under attack. The deaths of the two men angered the local community and John Hume demanded an official inquiry by the Westminster government into the shootings. At Parliament Buildings he went further than simply asking for an official investigation and said if an inquiry was not forthcoming the SDLP would leave Stormont. When no official inquiry was set up, Hume and his colleagues carried out their threat to walk out. The move on 16 July was dramatic and bold.

Hume believed he and his colleagues could no longer support a system of government that in their eyes was corrupt and was not prepared to investigate and challenge lawbreakers. Yet Hume's move did not have universal support in the party. Paddy Devlin thought the walk-out was wrong: 'Gerry and I were livid with anger. Just at the time when there were signs that we might be getting somewhere, the old nationalist knee-jerk of abstention was brought into play.'[29]

Hume's view held sway. He believed Stormont had lost all credibility, and the SDLP announced they would set up an 'alternative assembly' which would meet at Dungiven Castle. Now, just as the dust was settling on Northern Ireland's fiftieth-anniversary celebrations, the very existence of Stormont as a political institution was at stake. Faulkner was saddened and surprised by the SDLP decision to walk out, but he had other political problems to contend with. As the security situation worsened, he faced constant calls for the introduction of internment from unionist quarters.

By mid-July nearly 80 people had died in the Troubles, and there had been hundreds of explosions and shootings. Faulkner and his cabinet discussed the idea of internment many times and for weeks the internal debate raged. Unionist hardliners were convinced it was the answer to quelling trouble and breaking up the various paramilitary groupings. Faulkner had previously argued against its introduction when James

Chichester-Clark was in office. Faulkner felt back then it should only be used 'in extremity by a democratic government'.[30]

The bombings in July made the new premier feel that the time to use it again had arrived. In early August, Brian Faulkner flew to London to have talks with Prime Minister Heath. By now, the principle of internment had been agreed by the unionist administration and what was being discussed was the mechanics of how it would work in practice. On 9 August, 'Operation Demetrius' swung into action and 342 men were arrested. Nationalists, republicans, civil rights supporters and suspected members of the IRA were all detained. The intervention was flawed from the start, as much of the information that the arrests were based on was either wrong or simply out of date. Within 48 hours dozens of men were freed and allowed to return home. No loyalists were arrested, which added to the belief that this was simply aimed at the Catholic community. The arrests prompted political condemnation and riots broke across Northern Ireland.

If internment was meant to quell violence, then it failed from the word go. It became the number one political issue and it dominated Hume's time. Constituents contacted him in large numbers to ask about their loved ones. As the city's only nationalist MP, he was the man in demand. Soon he was able to visit some prisoners in custody and report back on what their conditions were like. It was constituency work – but 24 hours a day.

In those unpredictable and violent August days, the introduction of internment changed the political dynamic. Stormont as a political institution now seemed in greater peril than ever before and the SDLP's withdrawal further undermined the institution's credibility. Politicians in London and Dublin were watching their television sets with horror as the conflict continued on the streets. Hume stood by his party's decision to leave Stormont. In an interview with the *Irish Times*, he explained the rationale: 'The system of government cannot continue. That is the reality. We want peace in Northern Ireland, we want justice, we want stability.' Hume said the boycott of Parliament Buildings was 'an act of political judgement'.[31]

It was a majority decision within the SDLP Stormont group. Although it was driven by Hume, the move was not supported by Fitt and Devlin, who had opposed the walk-out over the Derry shootings. The two Belfast MPs believed the party 'had fallen for a Provo trap'.[32] Paddy Devlin also felt the walk-out created a vacuum and put the Provisional IRA 'into the driving seat'.[33]

Hume was not party leader but, on this occasion, his influence reigned supreme. It was an early indication of his power and thinking. He was not the leader, but he could direct party policy.

The Stormont walk-out by the SDLP signified the control that Hume now had on the fledgling party. Denis Haughey says his friend may have held the title of deputy leader, but in reality, he was running the organisation and that brought him into conflict with Gerry Fitt:

> Gerry realised that the media, the press, the general population and all the other people involved apart from Devlin – all the other people involved in the operation, looked to John as the natural leader. And when the press phoned up to know what this new party was doing it was John Hume they wanted to talk to.[34]

The SDLP's withdrawal prompted much political analysis. It was quite the turnaround for a party that promised to take the fight for political reform to Parliament Buildings and hold unionism to account. Now the SDLP had adopted the traditional nationalist policy of abstentionism. The party also called for a ban on anyone taking public office as a protest over internment. Having left the benches of Stormont, the SDLP was now committed to taking their brand of politics to an alternative assembly.

In reality, Dungiven was hardly a carbon copy of Parliament Buildings and some commentators viewed the 'alternative assembly' as simply a stunt and irrelevant. Instead of cross-party debates, the party was effectively talking to itself. It was a non-unionist talking shop but there were other parts to the campaign, as SDLP MPs began to take part in sit-downs and demonstrations.

Hume and his Stormont colleague Ivan Cooper now found themselves on Derry's streets every day. On one occasion with Hugh Logue, another SDLP member, the three men sat down and blocked British Army vehicles from proceeding. The street was cleared by the use of water cannon and Hume was drenched and promptly arrested. Logue, Cooper and Hume were frogmarched along Derry's Lone Moor Road in an arrest operation led by Paddy Ashdown who later went on to lead the Liberal Democrats.

Despite the seriousness of the occasion, there was a fair bit of gallows humour. Logue, who had long hair and a beard, was alongside Hume, with Cooper on the other side. Hume then remarked: 'Logue, you look so much like Jesus and I am on the wrong side.' Cooper chipped in: 'Once a priest always a priest.'[35]

Later, a crowd marched to a local RUC station and demanded their release. When Hume was freed, he was given a rousing homecoming. Approaching his mid-thirties, this former teacher's life was now unpredictable. In March 1969 he had begun his parliamentary career with much promise. He was billed as the man who would take on the Stormont establishment. Eighteen months on, he was back where it all started – protesting on the streets.

8

BLOODY SUNDAY

*'Many people down there feel it is a
United Ireland or nothing.'*
John Hume

John Hume stood on the sand; across from him was a uniformed British Army officer. They were within touching distance. The politician was in his trademark suit and tie, his mop of black hair tousled. He looked concerned. He and the soldier were separated by barbed wire, and behind the barrier, a line of troops stood pensively clutching their riot shields and batons. They had already fired rubber bullets at the protestors in an attempt to push them down the strand away from the army line. It was a bright Saturday afternoon in January 1972, and as he stood amongst thousands of demonstrators, Hume was in no mood to be fobbed off with excuses. He demanded answers from the man who was now blocking his path: 'Could you tell me on what authority you are holding us back here from walking along?' The officer told Hume he was in a prohibited area. Hume then demanded a ceasefire: 'Ask those men to stop firing rubber bullets at women please.' He was told: 'They will not. They will stop it, provided you keep away from the wire and don't try to enter this prohibited area.'[1]

Hume insisted that he and his colleagues be allowed to go further. He and around 2,000 others wanted to get close to the internment camp to demonstrate the ongoing detention of hundreds of men without trial. In front of the television cameras, the commanding officer told Hume the march was being stopped from getting any closer because it had been 'prohibited by the government of Northern Ireland'. Hume was defiant:

'It is not our government and that is why you are here, because it is not our government.'[2]

Fundamentally, that was at the heart of the situation. Hume and his followers were citizens in search of a state – politically homeless and feeling abandoned – whilst their MP was now a parliamentarian without a parliament.

Around 30 miles from Derry, Hume and hundreds of his constituents had come to Magilligan, a small peninsula at the entrance to Lough Foyle. The site once housed a British Army base and was now home to one of the controversial new internment centres. Across the water was the shoreline of Donegal and the village of Greencastle, close to where Hume would later own a holiday home.

For some, this was all very personal, as their loved ones had been taken to Magilligan some months earlier. Singing the now traditional civil rights anthem 'We Shall Overcome', the march began in an upbeat mood. As the crowd walked down a small lane, they were soon on the spacious golden sand, which stretched out in front of them. Balloons were released by the marchers and, overhead, army helicopters monitored the procession. For five miles the protestors walked across the strand – their aim was to get as close to the internment camp as possible. When the crowds finally arrived at the camp their path was blocked by armed soldiers and barbed wire.

At the army lines words were exchanged and some protestors tried to get around the barriers. The troops, members of the Parachute Regiment, opened fire with CS gas and rubber bullets at close range. Other soldiers attacked the crowd using batons and hit protestors on their heads as they turned to run. It was pandemonium and the marchers scattered in all directions with some ending up in the sea. As some protestors fell into the sand, soldiers kicked out at them and others in the crowd were treated to a range of anti-Irish insults.

There were many injuries, and as the light faded, the bedraggled and bruised marchers walked back down the beach and returned to Derry by bus. Hume spoke to the press about the day's events, making it clear that in his view the British Army were guilty of 'beating, brutalising and terrorising the demonstrators'.[3]

Hume was desperately disappointed the Magilligan protest had ended in that way. In an unpublished interview he recorded in 2002, he said the beach was deliberately chosen as a venue in an attempt to avoid any trouble:

> There is no way there could be violence on a beach of any description. If people wanted to throw stones, there were no stones on a beach. And if there were, how could they escape other than running into the sea – so it was a guarantee of total non-violence. And for that reason, I was totally shocked and deeply shocked when we were marching on the beach, that the British Army for the first time appeared at a civil rights march and put barbed wire across the beach to stop us marching. And there was no trouble of any description from the marchers, but they fired gas at us as well.[4]

Monica McWilliams was a young teenage protestor on the beach that day. She had travelled with her family to take part in the demonstration:

> Magilligan was like a family day out. There were young people, older people, parents with children. So, there was never a notion that John Hume was calling people out that day to come on that march to oppose internment and that it was ever going to be a violent protest.[5]

She says it became a 'shocking day' and the tactics used by the British Army were 'incredibly oppressive'. She witnessed Hume's conversation with the officer on the sand and says the Foyle MP set 'a standard of how people should behave'.[6] McWilliams would later go on to become a university professor, set up the Northern Ireland Women's Coalition and serve as an MLA at Stormont and as a human rights commissioner.

In the early 1970s, the Parachute Regiment, whose members were on duty in the Derry area for the first time, was no stranger to controversy. Back in August 1971, ten people were killed in an army operation in Ballymurphy in Belfast. Those who died included a Catholic priest and a mother of eight, who were all killed over a three-day period. An inquest in 2021 would conclude that nine of the ten victims were killed by soldiers, and the coroner could not say who shot the tenth victim. The Parachute Regiment had a reputation for being aggressive and had plenty of wartime experience. It was seen as an elite force within the British Army with a ruthless fighting mentality. Questions started to be asked within the Catholic community as to whether it was the right type of regiment to be deployed to deal with civilian protests. John Hume was in no doubt about their unsuitability and said their aggression was to blame for the trouble on the beach at Magilligan. It would not be his last brush with members of the regiment.

The issue of internment and the rise of protests had given NICRA a new lease of life and the group organised an anti-internment rally for Sunday 30 January in Derry. After his experience at Magilligan, John Hume had serious concerns about what was going to unfold in his home city: 'I was very worried about what would happen on the streets if there were troops on the streets stopping the march or dealing with the march. Because if they stopped a march on the beach, what were they going to do in the city? And, therefore, I strongly opposed the march. Unfortunately, the organisers disagreed with me.'[7]

John Hume's daughter Therese remembers the planned NICRA march in Derry being discussed in the family home. She recalls how her father's experience at Magilligan beach had convinced him that the atmosphere was becoming dangerous: 'He sort of worried there was a change in the way the army was behaving.'[8]

As a public figure and a campaigner for change, Hume found himself in a difficult position. He was the Foyle MP and was naturally viewed as a champion for civil rights, yet he was planning to stay away from an anti-internment protest in his constituency that many of his voters were planning to attend. It was a tough call, one which he knew he would be criticised for, but he had serious reservations about what would happen.

On a dry winter's day, marchers gathered in the Creggan estate and, after a short delay, began to walk behind a lorry carrying the Civil Rights Association banner. As they made their way towards the Bogside the crowd swelled in number and as they marched there were occasional bursts of song. As the protest began, John Hume was at home in West End Park watching the crowds walk past his window. The march wound its way to Rossville Street by Free Derry Corner, which was where police officers and soldiers had gathered. Disturbances broke out when stones were thrown and soldiers responded with rubber bullets, tear gas and water cannon. Members of the Parachute Regiment then moved forward to try to detain some of the marchers. Minutes later soldiers began to open fire.

The shots were so loud they were heard at the back of the march but also by John Hume:

> I was sitting in my own home and shortly afterwards I heard the shots and I was really shattered. And people started running up my street into the house to find out who was dead and telling me what had happened. And I had to go to the hospital to find out who was dead. And it was one of the most shocking days of my life.[9]

Therese Hume was also in the family home that day. The 10-year-old was at the top of the house when the firing began: 'You could actually hear the shooting from out the window, and I was looking out to see if I could actually see anything from that top window ... and I remember Ivan Cooper coming up to the house at one point because everybody was in a very panicked state.'[10]

Hume's Stormont colleague, Paddy Devlin, had travelled from Belfast but had arrived late after being held up by the security forces on his way. When the MP finally got to the march the shooting had finished, and he went straight to Hume's house where he found his deputy leader 'in great shock'.[11]

Journalists were using the Hume house to file their stories about the shooting, and Devlin told his friend that the reporters needed to leave so they could talk about what to do. Hume agreed and told him: 'Get our own people in here to the parlour and let's agree a strategy on this.'[12]

Understandably, the situation was confusing and frightening. The initial reports suggested that 11 people had died. That figure would rise to 14. In the turmoil, there were differing accounts of exactly what had happened. The British Army insisted it had been fired on first and had responded. Those on the march at Rossville Street were adamant that the troops opened fire without warning.

A fresh inquiry conducted by Lord Saville would later conclude in 2010 that those who died posed no threat to the soldiers and did not do anything to justify the shooting. He reported that whilst there was 'some firing by republican paramilitaries', on balance the army fired first.[13]

The dead were all male and included teenagers. Most of those who died were killed instantly on the streets, whilst others were transported to hospital, where they could not be saved. Hume was being informed by the hospital authorities who was dead and who was injured, and families were coming to him for information:

> I will never forget telling one family – the McDaids – that wherever their son was he was not in hospital and therefore he wasn't dead. And they were pleased, and they left my house to go down home. And after they left my phone rang, and it was a surgeon in the hospital and he said, 'I am sorry, I made one mistake, there's another young man dead here, Michael McDaid.' And I had to leave my house and walk down and tell the family. It is one of the worst experiences of my life.[14]

For the next few hours, Hume spent time visiting the families of the injured and the dead. The grief was raw. He knew many of them well. These were his constituents, and some were people he had helped in his role as an MP. There were members of the credit union, neighbours and friends and in one case a schoolmate. It seemed everybody knew somebody who was either injured or who had died. The footage of what had happened was now being broadcast across the world and that day in Derry would forever be known as 'Bloody Sunday'. The shootings would change the city and the history of the Troubles.

Seán Donlon, who was working for the Department of Foreign Affairs in Dublin, had built up a strong relationship with Hume and he remembers receiving a phone call from him hours after the killings:

> It was a panic call and the main purpose of it was to find out from me how he could immediately talk to Jack Lynch. The phone call between John and Jack happened. I don't know exactly, probably seven or eight on the Sunday evening. I don't remember, frankly, other than that John was in something of a panic mode which was unusual for him.[15]

Donlon's conversation with Hume helped Taoiseach Jack Lynch to get a clear understanding of what was happening on the ground. There was a great deal of misinformation, rumour and counter-rumour, and Donlon says Hume was regarded as 'a reliable source of information'.[16]

Hume was in demand as an interviewee from the many journalists who were now in Derry. He gave countless interviews to the press and the broadcast media and compared the killings to the Sharpeville massacre in South Africa in 1960 when police officers killed 69 protestors in a black township. Speaking to a reporter from the *Irish Times*, he made it clear where the blame lay for Bloody Sunday: 'The British Army opened fire indiscriminately on the civilian population attending a peaceful protest in the Bogside today. Their action was nothing short of cold-blooded murder – another Sharpeville and another Bloody Sunday. Their action has left this city numb with shock, horror, revulsion and bitterness.'[17]

It was another interview that Hume gave, this time to RTÉ, that caught the most attention. On the city's famous walls, he was asked by an interviewer to sum up the feelings of the people of the Bogside. His answer would be analysed for years to come. Referring to the houses below him, he remarked: 'Many people down there feel now that it's a united Ireland or nothing. Alienation is pretty total and we are all going to have to work very hard to deal with the situation.'[18]

Hume's opponents wasted little time to make political capital out of the 'united Ireland or nothing' line, even though Hume was attributing the remark to people in the Bogside. Those were not the thoughts of Hume himself but in the binary world of Northern Ireland politics, where perception is often what matters most, that did not matter. Brian Faulkner was one of those who criticised the remarks and, in his memoirs, published in 1978, he said the SDLP MP was caught up in 'the emotional aftermath' of the shootings.[19]

A darkness descended over Hume's home city and in those February days of 1972 there was little conversation about political reform and lots of talk of revenge. Eamonn McCann, who had been on the Bloody Sunday march, recalls the feelings of anger and the desire to strike back at the British Army:

> In the week after Bloody Sunday I would say that a substantial majority of Catholics in Derry were in favour of armed struggle of some sort. They may not have formulated it in the way republicans did, but they were for taking it to the Brits as the only fucking language they understand. Shoot the fuckers. That was very common amongst middle-class Catholics. That is what we have to do. There is no solution here. We will have to shoot the fuckers. John, I remember, stood against that and that was not a popular thing to do. It was not popular with me or anyone else.[20]

The killings of 30 January pushed many young men in Derry into the ranks of the IRA. Denis Bradley, who was working as a priest in the city, recalls the hours after the shootings: 'I remember that night walking the streets with a young priest friend of mine and both of us saying, we have lost the young people; this is a whole change.'[21]

The Dublin-based newspaper the *Irish Press* speculated that there would be plenty of willing recruits: 'If there was an able-bodied man with republican sympathies within the Derry area who was not in the IRA before yesterday's butchery, there will be none tonight.'[22]

Across Ireland there were anti-British demonstrations and in Dublin the British Embassy was attacked and burnt. At Westminster, Bernadette Devlin ran across the Commons chamber and slapped a shocked Home Secretary, Reginald Maudling, in the face after she accused him of lying about Bloody Sunday. Stormont was now on borrowed time and the prime minister, Edward Heath, was coming under increasing pressure to introduce direct rule. He had already established a tribunal to investigate the shootings on Bloody Sunday, which would be chaired by Lord Chief Justice Widgery. The move was greeted initially with scepticism by many in the Bogside who doubted whether it would deliver a true and accurate finding – and they were proved right.

In February, the Official IRA struck back with a vengeance and bombed the home of the 16 Parachute Brigade in Aldershot. Seven people were killed, including five women who worked as civilian cleaners at the base. A male gardener and a Catholic chaplain also died. The Official IRA said the bombing was retaliation for the shootings by the Parachute Regiment on Bloody Sunday.

In March, the bombings continued, when two women were killed in Belfast city centre in an explosion at the Abercorn Bar which saw some 70 people injured. A car bomb in Donegall Street in Belfast, later in the month, killed 7 people and injured 150 people. As the security situation worsened Edward Heath was running out of patience. He had a series of discussions with Brian Faulkner, making it clear that the authorities in London needed to take control of law-and-order powers in Northern Ireland.

In March the dialogue reached a dramatic climax when unionist politicians travelled to London for nine hours of talks. Heath told his visitors that as well as taking over security issues he wanted to end internment, appoint a Secretary of State for Northern Ireland, hold a constitutional referendum and he hoped to see local talks with the SDLP with a view to reaching a cross-community government. Faulkner and his cabinet met and decided they could not accept Heath's plans. They felt it would be impossible to carry on without law-and-order powers. Ministers in Belfast argued that the move undermined their authority and was not justifiable. The unionists were boxed in and knew London had the upper hand. Brian Faulkner resigned as prime minister. Stormont fell and would never sit again in that form. Direct Rule was introduced, and as the month came to an end, Willie Whitelaw made political history by becoming the first-ever Secretary of State for Northern Ireland.

For the first time in half a century, Northern Ireland did not have a government. Fifty years of unionist rule had come to an end, not by the hand of republicans or nationalists, but through the actions of a Conservative prime minister.

Unionists felt betrayed by Heath and inevitably took to the streets. Bill Craig's Vanguard movement organised a series of protests and there was a two-day stoppage to oppose the abolition of Stormont. The days of action resulted in public transport being halted, power supplies being shut off and most large industries closing. The shutdown was a reminder that unionists may have lost influence at Westminster but they still had enough muscle to bring Northern Ireland to a standstill.

Understandably, nationalists and republicans saw Stormont's demise very differently. There was a view that this was now an opportunity for fresh thinking. For many in the minority Catholic community, there was a sense that constitutional change was in the air. After five decades of partition, the issue of the border was now back on the agenda. To Hume and his supporters, this felt like a watershed moment: 'I was very pleased to see the end of Stormont, and I think I have always regretted that unionists would never look objectively at the whole nature of Stormont. It was one-party rule.'[23]

The Foyle politician and his party had some big decisions to make. Was this the moment to begin talking about new political arrangements? In a statement, the party called for an end to the violence, saying that would help end internment, and called on the British Army and the RUC to stop political arrests. The SDLP had not only been boycotting

Stormont but had been staying away from discussions with the British government. Willie Whitelaw, as the Secretary of State, was keen to make a mark in his new role. He desperately wanted to see an improvement in the political atmosphere. He knew that engaging with the local parties was the key and overturning the SDLP ban on talking to government ministers was crucial.

The wooing of John Hume and his colleagues began in earnest, but as ever, the political atmosphere was linked to external events. The Widgery Report into the killings of Bloody Sunday was published in April and did nothing to improve relations with the Catholic community. Lord Widgery concluded that the soldiers had been fired on first, although he stated the soldiers' firing 'bordered on the reckless'. He concluded that there would have been no deaths had there not been an illegal march which created a 'highly dangerous situation'.[24]

Widgery's report was considered a whitewash by the families of the dead and injured. The relatives felt vindicated since many had already predicted what the outcome would be.

Hume believed the investigation by Widgery was flawed from the start: 'I said at the time that I had been opposed to the Widgery Tribunal because it was not an objective tribunal of any description and therefore the results of his report proved that I was correct.' On the streets, there was no let-up in the violence whilst Stormont lay empty. In April, 11-year-old Francis Rowntree became the first person to die as a result of being hit by a plastic bullet. In May, the Official IRA kidnapped and shot a soldier on leave in the Creggan estate in Derry: 19-year-old William Best from the Royal Irish Rangers was shot in the back of the head and was left on waste ground. His death prompted a protest march by Derry women. It also led to the SDLP calling off its ban on people taking public office.

The summer of 1972 brought several fresh initiatives aimed at halting the violence, and Hume was heavily involved in the moves behind the scenes. Through personal friendships and contacts, he and Paddy Devlin got word that the leadership of the Provisional IRA might consider a ceasefire if the conditions were right. This would lead to Hume's first experience of negotiating with the Provisional IRA and the government at the same time.

On 13 June, Seán Mac Stíofáin, the chief of staff of the IRA, said there could be a seven-day ceasefire if the British agreed to stop arresting people, halted searches and allowed Irish citizens to decide how they should be governed. The Provisional IRA invited Willie Whitelaw to meet them in Derry for talks, but the Secretary of State declined. The minister said he would not respond to an ultimatum and there needed to be a ceasefire first. Sensing there was an opportunity, Hume felt it was now time his party dropped the ban on meeting the government. Devlin and Hume travelled to London and met the Secretary of State with two officials. Essentially this was a meeting to discuss 'talks about talks'. It was a chance to lay out the ground rules if full-blown discussions happened. The meeting went well, and Whitelaw made it clear that he was willing to act and respond positively if the violence ceased and that internment could be ended if the conditions were right.

Hume and Devlin were heartened and flew to Dublin to meet the other SDLP MPs to brief them on what had happened and seek approval to take matters further. The others backed the initiative, so the plan was able to proceed. Hume returned to Derry where a meeting was arranged with senior IRA leaders and he and Devlin met Seán Mac Stíofáin and Dáithí Ó Conaill. The two IRA men listened intently as Hume and Devlin outlined what they were trying to achieve and explained what they had been told by the British government. In response the IRA agreed to hold discussions with British officials and a ceasefire became operational from midnight on 26 June.

Then, dramatically, in July Willie Whitelaw made a bold move. He held secret talks in London with the Provisional IRA at the Cheyne Walk home of Northern Ireland Office Minister Paul Channon. The IRA delegation included two young men who would become key figures in the Troubles and the peace process – twenty-two-year-old Martin McGuinness, who was an IRA figure in Derry, and Gerry Adams, who had come to the fore in republican circles in Belfast. Adams was an internee and had been given special dispensation to attend the discussions. He had been released into the custody of Paddy Devlin and the politician had to make sure the young republican did not abscond.

After the meeting, the ceasefire remained intact but only for a handful of days and on 13 July it came to an end with the deaths of three soldiers and a civilian. Hume was bitterly disappointed and felt the ending of the ceasefire marked a missed opportunity. He believed the IRA had mishandled the situation. However, the whole experience of being involved in talks gave him an insight into negotiating with the IRA and the government. The ceasefire was a welcome lull from the daily reports of violence but what followed would turn out to be some of the worst days of the Troubles.

On 21 July, which became known as 'Bloody Friday', the IRA set off 21 bombs across Belfast killing 9 people and injuring 130 people. Some of the dead had their remains swept up and placed in plastic bags. At the end of the month, 3 IRA car bombs exploded in the village of Claudy within 15 minutes. The explosions killed 9 people including an 8-year-old girl and two boys aged 15 and 16.

On the same day as the Claudy attacks, 'Operation Motorman' swung into action as the British Army began to dismantle 'no-go' areas in Belfast and Derry in an attempt to restore control. In total, 4,000 extra troops were brought in and in the middle of the night in pouring rain the operation, involving soldiers in armoured personnel carriers, began. There was some shooting and two people were shot dead in Derry. Hume was not impressed that the British troops only went into Catholic areas and he appealed for calm: 'Listen, the choice is a grave one. Whatever your emotions, there is only one way for us and that is to go down the road to a political settlement, whatever the difficulties. And we will see to it as political representatives that the solution will satisfy you.'[25]

Hume sensed that an agreement had to be found quickly before violence became the accepted norm. He continued to speak at SDLP branch meetings although, according to Eamon Hanna, sometimes he was under so much pressure 'he did not turn up'.[26]

However, Eamon Hanna and his wife, Carmel, who later went on to be a Stormont minister, remember one occasion when the Foyle MP arrived at a meeting of the North Belfast SDLP branch. Eamon recalls how Hume warned of the need to make an urgent political agreement and said: 'If we don't solve this problem now it will go on for 50 years.'[27]

The Hannas say Hume's remarks were scoffed at by some in the audience. A long-term political solution remained Hume's focus and in September 1972, after a bloody summer of violence, the SDLP published a policy document entitled 'Towards a New Ireland'. For Hume, this was a chance to map out what needed to happen to restore faith in the democratic process, secure justice and detail how constitutional change could occur. The party called for a declaration from the British government that there should be a united Ireland. The proposal said British ministers had to be persuaders for unity. The document proposed joint sovereignty of Northern Ireland between the UK and the Republic of Ireland, both sharing powers in areas like defence, security and policing. It was a novel idea and its aim was to take account of 'both sections of the North'. However, such a move was planned to be a temporary solution with a united Ireland still the long-term goal. The document talked about 'Protestant fears' but did not refer to 'unionist fears', which is not necessarily the same thing.[28]

There was also a plan for an 84-seat Assembly, elected by proportional representation, and there was a proposal for an Executive of 15 members. The document suggested that the Union flag and the Irish tricolour would have equal status. The party also argued that the people of Northern Ireland should have the right to claim either Irish or British citizenship. There would also be a constitutional court, a community relations board and a national senate of Ireland. The party also wanted to see two commissioners from the UK and Ireland who would act jointly and must sign all legislation to make sure the Assembly would not exceed its powers. There was also a call for a new unarmed police force.

The SDLP document clearly illustrates much of John Hume's thinking and, when compared to the Good Friday Agreement of 1998, it is possible to see the similarities in terms of the Assembly, an Executive and a reform of policing. The proposal for joint sovereignty understandably got much criticism at the time, particularly from unionists. Brian Faulkner thought the idea was 'silly' and would later write that it was an indication that the SDLP were unable to 'recognise Northern Ireland as an entity'.[29]

The proposal was also rejected by the British government, which was busy with plans of its own for Northern Ireland.

On 24 September, Willie Whitelaw invited the local parties to a conference in Darlington in County Durham. The SDLP was still boycotting government ministers as internment had not ended, so Hume and his colleagues stayed away. They were not the only absentees – the Reverend Ian Paisley did not make the journey either. In the end, the Ulster Unionists were joined by the Alliance Party and the Northern Ireland Labour Party. With only three groups becoming involved in the Darlington trip, the credibility of the process was questioned.

However, for Whitelaw, it was an opportunity to listen and continue a somewhat limited political dialogue. He and the prime minister, Edward Heath, both wanted to quicken the political pace, so in October proposals were published aimed at making some progress. A border poll was pencilled in for 1973 and the UK government said there would be further talks about establishing an Assembly back at Stormont.

Hume and his colleagues did not like the idea of a border poll but the mood in the party was in favour of engaging in political discussions with the UK government once again. At the party's annual conference in November, Hume argued that the SDLP should be involved in the forthcoming talks, and activists endorsed this position. By now, Hume's reputation as a politician stretched far beyond the shores of Britain and Ireland. He had gained international coverage through his interviews with foreign media, and his analysis was often sought by visiting dignitaries.

In November 1972, Senator Ted Kennedy, from one of the most famous and influential political families in America, sought Hume's advice. When the approach was initially made, Hume thought he was being pranked: 'I got a phone call and the voice said this is Ted Kennedy and I said pull my other leg. He said he was going on a visit to Europe and he had been told that he should meet with me to get fully briefed on the Northern Ireland situation – he was actually going to Bonn in

Germany.'[30]

Hume agreed to fly out to meet the senator, whom he had first met back in 1969. Practically, there was the small matter of how his unexpected trip would be funded. Pat Hume remembers the conversation with her husband:

> It was when he put the phone down that he remembered he was unemployed, Stormont having been prorogued in March. My salary was inadequate even for running the house – it didn't permit luxuries like a trip to Germany. So, being a member of a credit union was so useful. It was for unexpected expenses like this. With a loan in place, what was to be the first of many important meetings took place between Edward Kennedy and John.[31]

The Bonn meeting would start a relationship with Ted Kennedy that would last for decades and would help Hume build up a network of allies and friends in the United States. Kennedy had previously taken a strong interest in Irish affairs and had spoken at Trinity College in Dublin. He had also told the US Senate that 'Ulster is becoming Britain's Vietnam'. Those remarks drew much adverse reaction from unionists and politicians in London.[32]

For Hume, the trip to Germany proved some light relief after a depressing and upsetting few months. When 1972 came to a close, it marked the bloodiest year of the Troubles, with nearly five hundred people dead. The new year would present the SDLP with its first electoral test, and there would be intensive political talks. For the party, there was much work to be done.

For the Hume family, it would also prove to be a worrying time.

9

WRITING ON THE WALL

*'They attempted to kill John,
they attempted to kill his family.'*
Eamonn McCann

By 1973, the IRA had hatched a daring plan to hurt John Hume. In their eyes, he was a traitor to the cause – someone who was betraying the old ideals of nationalism and acquiescing in the partition of Ireland. The decision was taken to strike where he was most vulnerable – at his home.

John, Pat and their five children, Therese, Áine, Aidan, John and Mo, lived close to the Bogside. Everyone in the area knew the family home, since it doubled up as a constituency office. Every day there would be a constant stream of people coming to the door looking for help or advice. Often mothers and fathers would call seeking information on which police station their sons had been taken to after being arrested. To the Hume children, this was all normal. In those early days, the house had no security measures and John Hume operated an open-door policy. Therese remembers that their home was rarely quiet: 'People would come to the door the whole time. The house never emptied.'[1]

In keeping with his beliefs in pacifism, John Hume refused to carry a personal protection weapon. His children played in the street and walked to school – often past walls daubed with graffiti insulting their father. The family home was regularly attacked with paint and stones and, understandably, Hume's children often worried about their father's safety.

Áine, one of the Humes's daughters, says she remembers praying to God that if her father was attacked, he would not suffer:

> I remember bargaining a lot with God. Which is crazy, you know. Because I used to worry about Dad getting killed. So I remember saying please can it be sudden, and please can it be that he does not have to suffer. And trying to make it as un-traumatic as possible, you know.[2]

Áine may have worried and prayed about her father but she too had become a target. She attended St Anne's Primary School in the Rosemount area, was well-known as one of the Hume children and walked home every day. Aware of who she was and the route she took, the IRA decided to kidnap her. On the day in question, the kidnappers arrived at the school and spotted their target as she left the premises. She was bundled quickly into a car and driven towards the border. Her captors may have thought the operation had gone well until they realised they had snatched the wrong child. They had, in fact, picked up a girl who closely resembled Áine.

It was a case of mistaken identity, and the girl was released unharmed, as Áine recalled: 'They let her go once they looked at her schoolbooks. And I am just hugely grateful that it wasn't me.'[3]

What the IRA planned to do with Áine Hume had its members successfully kidnapped her is not clear. Was it an attempt to get her father to leave politics? What is clear is that the IRA had a deep loathing for John Hume and his politics. Eamonn McCann recalls how he was viewed by them: 'They hated him – that is not too strong a word to say. The people who would become the Provos – Provisional Sinn Féin or the Provisionals at the time – hated John Hume.'[4]

McCann says the IRA were serious about hurting Hume:

> I mean the Provos don't like to be reminded of this. They attempted to kill John – they attempted to kill his family. There was one occasion they threw petrol bombs at John's house in West End Park. The entire front of the house was engulfed in flames, the entire front of the house. It was a serious attempt to kill the Hume family.[5]

Hume was not just a target of republicans; he was also a hate figure to loyalist paramilitary groups. Now a well-known face through his many television appearances, he experienced abuse out in the streets. Aidan Hume remembers being out with his father when he was pelted with eggs and another occasion when a dog was set on him. He also recalls being with his father in a van when he was surrounded by an angry mob: 'There were probably about fifteen people who attacked the van and tried to pull him out by the hair.'[6]

Politics was a dangerous world, and John Hume's children had to try and learn to deal with the consequences of being in the public eye. There would be demonstrations and protests outside the family home, fake bombs were left in the street and there were abusive phone calls, as Therese Hume recalls: 'There would have been a lot of threatening letters, threatening phone calls, bullets sent in the post one time, a couple of bullets sent at different times. That kind of thing was going on for quite a while and there was an undercurrent of nastiness.'[7]

Therese's sister, Áine, says many families had similar experiences:

> Everybody growing up in Northern Ireland developed a kind of antennae where you could walk into a room and almost before anybody said a word you could sense the level of hostility. It was just I suppose we had to learn in a way to kind of manage that.[8]

Mo Hume, John's youngest daughter, says in later years she used to have to pass a wall on her way to school that bore the slogan 'Hume Traitor'. She says before the peace process there was no cachet in being John Hume's daughter: 'It was not cool. He was not cool. He was vilified, you know, so it wasn't cool having John Hume as your dad.'[9]

Back in 1973, Hume and his colleagues needed lots of backroom help as the party faced its first electoral test. They needed members, potential candidates and staff to run the party office on a daily basis. One day Geraldine Cosgrove, who was better known as Gerry, happened to be walking past the SDLP headquarters in College Square North and came across a host of familiar faces. Out in the Belfast street, she spotted John Hume, Ivan Cooper, Paddy Devlin and Austin Currie. The party's big hitters were all household names from their nightly appearances on the teatime news. Cosgrove watched the men chatting and she was intrigued and slightly star-struck. She knew a little bit about the personalities involved.

The 20-year-old had been to secretarial college and was a trained typist and had experience working in an office. She was keen to move on from her current job and when she heard the party was recruiting an assistant to the general secretary she applied. She thought the position was ideal. After all, she had the background and the skills, and coincidentally she lived just a short walk from headquarters. She got the job and began working for the party. With elections on the horizon, there was much to do: 'We had to get structures in place, select candidates, organise training sessions for them and generally get ready.'[10]

Party membership had grown since the early days of August 1970, and it was important to attract people from rural and urban areas and different backgrounds. Many signed up from the NDP, the Nationalist Party, the Republican Labour Party and the Northern Ireland Labour Party, whilst other recruits arrived with no previous political experience. Paddy Devlin, whose power base was in the working-class streets of Belfast, remembers how some newly joined members had different views: 'We had a lot to do to instil Labour values into our new recruits. It was a hard job. Some of the teachers were particularly strident and most of the members were far too nationalist for my taste.'[11]

John Hume and Paddy Devlin took on the role of preparing training materials and writing briefing notes for their candidates. As a former teacher, this was second nature to Hume, and he and Devlin went off to a Dublin hotel and worked around the clock to come up with a set of documents. Candidates were then put through their paces in Donegal over a series of days in preparation for the campaign that lay ahead.

The first visit to the polling stations in 1973 for voters was the border poll which Ted Heath had called some months earlier, and it was one that the SDLP made it clear it could not support. Hume felt the initiative was doomed and the result was predictable. He had problems with the questions that were being posed. The first asked: 'Do you want Northern Ireland to remain part of the United Kingdom?' The second question posed the alternative, which was: 'Do you want Northern Ireland to be joined with the Republic of Ireland outside the United Kingdom?' Hume thought there should be a third question which should have asked voters if they would agree to a united Ireland if the terms were agreeable to the people of Northern Ireland. Without a third question, Hume thought the exercise was pointless, so the SDLP and other nationalists boycotted the vote.

Five days before the poll he met a representative of the new Irish government to brief him on how he thought the vote should be handled. The fresh administration in Dublin was a Fine Gael–Labour coalition which had been ushered in after 16 years of Fianna Fáil rule. Hume was keen to stress that the new taoiseach, Liam Cosgrave, needed to show sensitivity and be careful when issuing public statements about the border referendum. Hume declared that it was important not to stoke tensions in the days leading up to the vote. He made it clear that he wanted to 'keep the situation cool for the voting so as not to evoke a large poll on the unionist side'. Hume said he hoped that less than 50 per cent of the electorate would vote in favour of the link with Britain.[12]

Ultimately, Hume's desired outcome did not come to pass, and the turnout reached close to 58 per cent with nearly 600,000 people taking part. Of those, nearly 99 per cent backed the link with Britain with 1 per cent backing the prospect of a united Ireland. Political reaction was predictable with unionists welcoming the result and the SDLP claiming the results proved nothing.

There was barely time to digest the border poll results when Willie Whitelaw announced plans to put in place a 78-seat Assembly at Stormont elected by proportional representation. He announced voting for the new forum would take place in June. London wanted politicians in Belfast to once again run their own affairs, but it would not be a return to the old ways. Westminster made it clear that there had to be a power-sharing government and the days of one-party rule were confined to the history books.

There would be a new Executive which would have powers currently held by the UK administration in areas like education, agriculture and industry. For unionists, it meant they could control some of the powers they had previously exercised but it had to be within a power-sharing administration and there would have to be a new relationship with Dublin. This new arrangement would be called a Council of Ireland. The Secretary of State believed this move would help Catholics in Northern Ireland address their Irish identity.

It was this part of the government's plans that would cause some unionists the most anxiety. How exactly would this new understanding with the Irish government work? What would it entail? What would North–South relations look like? The governing body of the Ulster Unionist Party voted to accept the government's proposals. However, strong opposition caused a split. Bill Craig was part of the defeated minority and went off to form the Vanguard Unionist Progressive Party. Hume felt the British government's inclusion of a new North–South relationship was welcome but was not specific enough. He wanted the Council of Ireland to be given much greater powers.

There was a welcome for the size of the Assembly and the use of proportional representation as a voting method – two moves the SDLP had repeatedly called for. In fact, such proposals were contained in the SDLP's document 'Towards a New Ireland'. However, John Hume felt the plans from London still fell short in terms of police reform.

In the round, there was enough in the plans to get the SDLP to commit to going into a new Assembly. Before that poll could take place there were the council elections for the 26 new district areas. This was a massive undertaking for the party that included members who had never fought an election before. Denis Haughey says resources were tight and he remembers it was a 'hand to mouth' existence. He recalls he and his colleagues felt 'completely unprepared'.[13]

As this was the SDLP's first electoral test, it meant the party had a lot of new faces on show. One political debutant was a teacher from Markethill called Seamus Mallon. He had been impressed with many activists in the civil rights campaign and had attended anti-internment marches. He became a politician by accident rather than by design. When his local SDLP candidate pulled out of the contest hours before the deadline closed, Mallon tried in vain to find a replacement. He rang some party members and asked them to stand but his search proved unsuccessful, so he then decided to put his money where his mouth was. The problem was he had no money. So with the clock ticking, desperate measures were called for: 'I discovered I needed a deposit of £25, no small sum in those days. I went into a shop, where I knew the owner and said, "Could you lend me £25? I'll not tell you what it is for and I'll let you have it back tomorrow." That was the beginning of a 32-year treadmill of politics for me.'[14]

Mallon's unconventional loan paid off and he won a seat on Armagh District Council and began a lifetime of public service. He joined dozens of other SDLP candidates who were successful and on its first electoral outing the party secured a respectable 13 per cent of the first preference vote. For a party barely three years old it was an impressive entry into the crowded world of electoral politics. Other parties were also making their first appearance on the ballot paper including the Alliance Party, the DUP and the new Vanguard movement.

The council elections were seen as a dry run for the Assembly poll in June, and in the weeks leading up to the vote, campaigning took place against a backdrop of violence. An IRA bomb in Coleraine killed six pensioners and in Belfast, there were killings by loyalist paramilitaries, including a new organisation calling itself the Ulster Freedom Fighters, a wing of the Ulster Defence Association.

In 1973 the UFF killed SDLP Senator Paddy Wilson and Irene Andrews on a road in East Belfast. Senator Wilson, who was one of the party's original members, was Gerry Fitt's election agent. A Belfast City councillor, as well as a Stormont senator, he became one of the first political figures to be killed in the Troubles. Wilson was shot and stabbed 32 times and his fellow passenger, Irene Andrews, was stabbed 19 times. In 1978, John White received a life sentence for their murders and following his release became involved in politics. As a member of the Ulster Democratic Party, White would take part in talks with the prime minister, Tony Blair, in 1996.

The brutal killings of Paddy Wilson and Irene Andrews caused widespread anger and condemnation. The SDLP spent the final days of the election campaign in mourning. When the ballot papers were finally counted the party had surpassed its performance at the local election, securing a 22 per cent share of the first preference votes which gave it 19 seats in the new Assembly. Denis Haughey, who was now vice-chairman of the party, was delighted:

> I thought if we got eight or nine seats in the new Assembly that would be grand, that would be credible, but to win 19 was way beyond what I had hoped for. It swept all of the other little opposition groups off the table. They became quite meaningless really.[15]

Brian Faulkner's unionists triumphed, but there was a price to pay for the idea of power-sharing. The unionist vote was split several ways and the election result meant the parliamentary arithmetic was much tighter than the former prime minister would have liked. Twenty-four unionists backed the government's proposals for a power-sharing Executive and 26 unionists made up of DUP, Vanguard and other unionist MPs opposed it. Faulkner knew that if he was to proceed with a cross-community government he would face opposition at every step and he understood that many in the unionist community would need constant reassurances. However, if the pro-power-sharing unionists joined forces with SDLP representatives and the Alliance Assembly members then a working majority was possible.

Armed with the Stormont voting strengths, Willie Whitelaw moved fast. On the Monday after the election, he called the party leaders to Parliament Buildings for a meeting to try and map out how an Executive could be formed. What followed were months of political wrangling. Hume and Devlin took the lead within the SDLP in terms of preparing talks and papers and finessing ideas and proposals. The two men spent much time together in Dublin and they also went off to Donegal to write and research documents. During the inter-party discussions, Brian

Faulkner could see that the SDLP were serious about power-sharing and was impressed with the effort Hume and others were putting in. He ended up negotiating and dealing more with John Hume than Gerry Fitt, even though Fitt was the more senior figure. Hume was across the detail of the talks in a way that Fitt wasn't. Fitt also had to travel to London regularly as a Westminster MP which meant his days were split between London and Belfast. Hume might not have been the SDLP leader but he was effectively the party's chief negotiator.

Brian Faulkner thought he was an able opponent, though he clearly found him irritating at times, and described him as 'a formidable political thinker with great personal integrity but sometimes exasperating dogmatism'.[16]

The unionist leader's relationship with Hume was good and they were professional and cordial with one another. Robert Ramsay, who was Faulkner's private secretary, saw both politicians at close quarters and says Faulkner actually got on better with Fitt than Hume: 'I think he personally liked Gerry Fitt. He would have preferred Gerry Fitt over Hume. He always said to me, in terms of the power-sharing executive, that Hume played a straightforward game.'[17]

Even though the politics of Fitt and Faulkner were poles apart, it seems the unionist found Fitt's nationalism a little more palatable than Hume's. Ramsay says Fitt was seen as less strident than his SDLP colleague:

> His greenness was a lighter shade. He was sort of the 'Labour man' type of thing. A lot was his personality and certainly ... Hume was slightly aloof. I think even from his buddies. There was a shyness about him in a way, while he could have a few drinks with the boys he wasn't as gregarious and clubbable as Gerry was.[18]

Hume's aloofness was picked up by others who spent time with him. Michael Lillis began meeting him when he worked with the Irish Department of Foreign Affairs. Their relationship started when Lillis travelled to Derry in 1972 to discuss the ill-treatment of detainees. He and Hume would have discussions regularly and they became friends. The civil servant soon discovered the MP's idiosyncrasies: 'I would often spend a whole day with him, and he would go silent on you for up to two hours. He would say nothing as he was working his way through something and thinking.'[19]

The Hume silent treatment was not just reserved for work matters. Even at home in Derry, when he was away from political meetings and negotiations, he would come across as preoccupied. His son John says his father often seemed distracted: 'He would almost go into a trance.'[20]

Often family life would be happening around him and he would be oblivious: 'He would be sitting in the kitchen with loads of people sort of killing each other around him. But he would be on a different planet.'[21] Sometimes the political pressure got to Hume. Gerry Cosgrove says she noticed it around party headquarters: 'John would get really stressed. We used to laugh about it. We used to say, "Don't ask John how he is because he will tell you." He was always, "Oh I don't feel well."'[22]

Talking about his health was John Hume's obsession. Tim Attwood began working with him in the late 1980s and says it was a running joke in the party that John seemed to be permanently unwell and was obsessed about what was wrong with him: 'John was a hypochondriac, so people didn't believe he was ill. Now I had many, many conversations with him. If you had a cold, he had a cold. If you had a sore leg, he had a sore leg.'[23]

Bertie Ahern, the former taoiseach, was another individual who was on the receiving end of stories about Hume's health woes. Ahern developed a great respect for Hume, became good friends with him and got to quickly know about his obsession with all things medical:

> John could be quite depressive as you know – 500 times I got the story about the consultant in America who told him that this anxiety in his stomach was coming from the stress of his job. And he would look at me, especially when I was taoiseach, and he would say, 'Do you know that

this famous consultant who was meant to be the world's number one said there are two professions that suffered this? And you had better be careful. He said it was astronauts and politicians.'[24]

Hume probably had good reason to be constantly preoccupied with his health. He smoked and drank and travelled extensively and often worked long hours. Stress and tiredness and the pressure of complex negotiations often took their toll. During the latter part of 1973, he was carrying a particularly heavy burden. He was working around the clock and was routinely travelling from Derry to Belfast and also going to Dublin to keep the Fine Gael–Labour coalition updated on what was being discussed. Much rested on getting the position papers ready in time for the talks with the Irish and British governments and the Stormont parties.

The strains finally caught up with him. He was exhausted and not surprisingly ended up in hospital. It would not be the last time that Hume would need rest and recuperation from the pressures of seven-day working. On this occasion, he recovered well and the discussions continued with the SDLP pushing for cross-party agreement on reforming policing, ending internment and setting up a Council of Ireland. The council was very much Hume's baby and he naturally took the lead in discussing it on behalf of the party. Over October and November, the talks continued. Away from the discussions, it was clear that amongst unionists the opposition to power-sharing and greater North–South cooperation was growing.

By 22 November 1973, the negotiations on forming a cross-community administration were not complete, but there was agreement in certain areas and the makeup of the Executive was revealed. Brian Faulkner would become chief executive with Gerry Fitt taking on the role of deputy chief executive. Amongst the other appointments, Hume was to be the new minister for commerce, with Austin Currie on housing, development and local government and Paddy Devlin as the social security minister.

The new Executive was expected to begin work in January 1974. It was a landmark moment marking the start of Northern Ireland's first-ever cross-community government. For Hume, the commerce brief seemed ideal. He was passionate about the creation of jobs and he wanted to lift up local communities where unemployment was high by offering new opportunities. He knew the importance of work to people's lives and well-being, having studied the economic history of his home city. His practical experience with the credit union movement and a personal understanding of business from his days at the Atlantic Harvest salmon operation also helped.

Before he accepted the role, Hume was lobbied by the Irish government, which suggested he could have greater influence at Stormont as finance minister. That role was seen as the second most powerful in the executive after the job of chief executive. Hume's decision raised some eyebrows and Seán Donlon, who was with the Irish Department of Foreign Affairs, remembers how politicians tried to get Hume to change his mind: 'We tried to persuade him to become minister for finance. He wasn't going to be prime minister, obviously, that was going to be Brian Faulkner, but he felt he wanted to get directly involved in the industrial development of Northern Ireland.'[25]

Looking back at the situation in 1973, Austin Currie says Hume made the right choice: 'His thinking was he could achieve jobs, particularly west of the Bann. He also saw the implications and the international possibilities to create employment, so that was his objective.'[26]

Hume was also politically savvy enough to know that the sight of a politician opening factories or unveiling new products would be good PR for the SDLP, so there could be party-political benefits to heading up the commerce department.

However, before Hume could step into the ministerial car there were still some major hurdles to overcome. At the Civil Service College at Sunningdale in Berkshire, a conference was organised to finalise the remaining sticking points. The British and Irish governments were there, led by Edward Heath and Liam Cosgrave respectively, and there was a delegation of unionists, the SDLP and the Alliance Party. The main talking point was to resolve matters surrounding the Council of Ireland.

The Sunningdale talks were aimed at agreeing on what precise functions this body would have and how it would operate. In general terms, the plan was to have a Council of Ministers made up of ministers from Dublin and Stormont. There would also be a Consultative Assembly made up of 30 members from the Northern Ireland Assembly and the same number from the Dáil.

There was an immediate and obvious pinch point between the unionist and SDLP delegations. Brian Faulkner knew this was the issue that would be the hardest sell to his electorate and would be seized upon by the supporters of Ian Paisley and other critics of power-sharing. Faulkner wanted the proposed body to be more symbolic rather than one with real authority. Hume wanted the Council of Ireland to be able to harmonise laws across the border and be a real symbol of Irish identity on an all-island basis.

Hume faced pressure on a series of fronts to make sure that the Council of Ireland was more than a talking shop and had real power. Party members wanted to see an Irish dimension to the new power-sharing arrangements. Hume also insisted that the Council of Ireland was influenced by the ethos of the European Economic Community, a body which he had long believed was a force for good and had a peace-building role. There were other matters on Hume's 'shopping list' and he was also mindful that the twin issues of policing and internment were key and any new administration at Stormont must tackle these areas in a satisfactory and just way.

He had experienced the trauma and pain caused by Bloody Sunday, the march at Magilligan and Operation Motorman, where the RUC attempted to reclaim 'no-go' areas in Belfast and Derry. Hume insisted that political progress and policing went hand in hand and he wanted the practice of internment scrapped immediately. He knew that if the SDLP agreed to a new form of government with internment still in place, his party would be open to fierce criticism from republicans.

Over the weekend at Sunningdale, the discussions over security were not straightforward and hit a brick wall over policing and the future of the RUC. Hume wanted a new force that could be supported by all sections of the community and would be seen as impartial, but he privately knew that wholesale change was not going to be supported by the British government or by the unionists. In the meantime, he wanted the RUC to be accountable to the Council of Ireland. The unionists demanded that the Northern Ireland Executive control the police whilst London wanted a say too. The talks reached an impasse and it looked like the problems over policing would prevent a final agreement. The negotiations had gone long into the night and the teams were tired and there was a sense after hours of talks and endless meetings that a breakthrough wasn't going to happen. At breakfast time on Sunday 9 December, it looked like Brian Faulkner was preparing to leave and return to Belfast. In an attempt to keep the talks alive, Paddy Devlin went to have a word with him and the two men left the building for an early morning walk. Outside, Paddy Devlin cut to the chase. Used to trade union negotiations, he went straight to the sticking point. He bluntly asked what it would take to get an agreement and Faulkner said he needed Devlin's party, as his potential partners in government, to publicly support the RUC.

Devlin returned to see Hume and other colleagues, and after much discussion, a new policing draft was agreed which stated that the Police Authority would be appointed by the Secretary of State after consulting the Executive which would have consulted the Council of Ireland. Faulkner insisted privately this arrangement was 'meaningless' and he would later write that he agreed to the move because Edward Heath had pledged to devolve policing powers as soon as the 'security emergency came to an end'.[27]

Hume also sought assurances from the prime minister that internment would be phased out and the release of detainees would begin.

It was agreed that the Council of Ireland would have powers to coordinate economic measures and look at cross-border matters like tourism, transport and electricity. Its inclusion was largely down to Hume's negotiation skills. He was the architect of the plan and he saw it as a prerequisite to any wider deal. On the other hand, Brian Faulkner saw the council as an advisory body rather than something with real power. He did believe that there would be a new spirit of cooperation between police forces north and south of the border which would assist in the fight against republican and loyalist paramilitaries. He was also heartened that there was a commitment by the Irish government to respect the wishes of the majority of people in Northern Ireland, which he insisted settled the constitutional integrity of Northern Ireland. He thought Sunningdale was a good deal and a member of his negotiating team believed the agreement would 'go down in history as a unionist victory'.[28]

On the evening of Sunday 9 December, the parties and the British and Irish governments reached an historic agreement, and Northern Ireland's first power-sharing government was agreed in principle. Hume, with support from the Irish government, had managed to pull off quite a coup to get unionists to agree to the Council of Ireland and to secure commitments over internment. As ever with Northern Ireland politics, there were two critical audiences. Faulkner had to promote the deal to a very sceptical unionist community which sensed a sell-out. He knew he had a tough task on his hands. Hume knew that there had to be real delivery on the Council of Ireland and an end to internment. Otherwise, there would be little for SDLP voters to support.

As the old year ended, a new era was about to begin.

10

YES MINISTER

*'With his linguistic skills and earnest eloquence,
John Hume made a natural Minister of Commerce.'*
Ken Bloomfield

On the last day of 1973, John Hume was in East Belfast and making his way to Stormont Castle. Situated close to Parliament Buildings, the impressive Scottish baronial building with its turrets and towers had once been owned by the rector of Newtownards. For half a century it was home to unionist prime ministers who determined how Northern Ireland would be ruled.

In the crisp December air, Hume walked up the steps and made his way to the old cabinet room where he took his place with his unionist and Alliance colleagues. There he was greeted by the new Secretary of State Francis Pym, who had replaced Willie Whitelaw some weeks earlier, and they were joined by the Lord Chief Justice, Sir Robert Lowry. The two figures were present to hand the seals of office to the new members of the Executive. After a swearing-in ceremony and a few words, the freshly appointed ministers took a break for a buffet lunch. Suitably refreshed, Northern Ireland's first-ever power-sharing government assembled for its first meeting. Around the room were notepads, carafes of water and ashtrays and on the walls hung a series of portraits including one of Benjamin Disraeli, Queen Victoria's favourite prime minister. With light streaming through the windows, ministers could see the manicured lawns outside, the glass house and the conservatory, where the castle's former residents once relaxed.

In a place once the exclusive preserve of unionists, this cross-community coalition set about the task of governing. In mid-afternoon, the chief executive, Brian Faulkner, began proceedings and as he looked around he sensed there 'was a feeling of comradeship and trust' between those assembled.[1]

For weeks, Hume and Faulkner and others had been arguing hard about how this new form of government would work. They had tested each other's patience and at times the discussions seemed never-ending. The talks at Sunningdale had been heated and were often at the point of collapse. Now the negotiators were partners who wanted to make Northern Ireland's first cross-community administration work. With that in mind, the Executive's press team released a statement stating: 'We want the new year to see the beginning, not just of a new system of government, but of a new spirit. Let 1974 be the year of reconciliation.'[2]

Those optimistic sentiments were not shared by everyone. Away from the corridors of Stormont Castle the opposition to this novel form of political arrangement was being stepped up with menacing undertones. Loyalist paramilitaries, including the UVF and the UDA, formed an umbrella group called the Ulster Army Council, and they threatened to bring the Sunningdale Agreement down. The deal was denounced by Ian Paisley, members of the Vanguard group and anti-Sunningdale unionists in Faulkner's party.

His critics decided to bring matters to a head just days after he and Hume sat around the same table to unveil the new administration. On 4 January, the Ulster Unionist Council, the party's governing body, rejected the Council of Ireland. The move was backed by 427 votes to 374 and Faulkner's fate as party leader was sealed. He had hoped for a slim majority, but it was not to be. He believed many activists had misrepresented the Sunningdale deal and out of fear 'the party was rejecting the greatest opportunity it had ever faced'.[3]

What one of his party colleagues had earlier described as a victory was now seen as a unionist capitulation. Faulkner had a decision to make. He concluded that he could either lead the Ulster Unionist Party or the Executive, but he could not do both. So after much thought and speaking to friends and family he took the dramatic decision and ended his 28-year party membership. His resignation heartened the anti-Sunningdale unionists, who now sensed that the power-sharing experiment was damaged. Faulkner and his Executive colleagues were now on borrowed time. Faulkner's critics received another boost in mid-January when SDLP assemblyman Hugh Logue issued a speech at Trinity College in Dublin where he said that the Council of Ireland 'is the vehicle that will trundle through to deliver a United Ireland. The speed that vehicle moves at depends on the unionist population.'[4]

The remarks caused a predictable furore. Opponents of the Council of Ireland seized on the comments, and it was another blow to the Faulkner unionists. Logue went to see Hume, who was in hospital at the time, and the two men discussed the speech: 'Being the typical teacher, John said to me your mistake was putting a full stop after a United Ireland – you should have put a comma.'[5]

There was further trouble on the horizon for the Executive and it would come from all directions. In Dublin, Kevin Boland, a former Fianna Fáil cabinet minister, began legal proceedings to have the Sunningdale Agreement deemed unconstitutional. He objected to a paragraph in the deal which stated: 'The Irish government fully accepted and solemnly declared that there could be no change in the status of Northern Ireland until a majority of the people in Northern Ireland desired a change of status.'[6]

For the Executive, the Boland case was an unnecessary distraction and it was seen by some as a mischievous legal manoeuvre. Brian Faulkner was particularly worried that if the case went Boland's way it would mean that the Irish government would change its position regarding consent. The taoiseach, Liam Cosgrave, assured him that Dublin stood by the Sunningdale deal, but the move simply added to Faulkner's woes which were at this stage mounting by the week. In Britain, there was a political crisis after the prime minister, Edward Heath, introduced a three-day working week in an attempt to preserve fuel supplies. Electricity was restricted due to industrial action by coal miners and railway workers. Schools and factories were closed and employees had to work by torchlight. As Edward Heath and the unions locked horns it seemed likely that the prime minister would call a snap general election to break the deadlock.

With a Westminster poll expected within weeks, anti-agreement unionists came together and formed the United Ulster Unionist Council (UUUC). The grouping involved the Ulster Unionist leader, Harry West, who had succeeded Brian Faulkner, the Reverend Ian Paisley of the DUP and Bill Craig of Vanguard. They wanted the abolition of the power-sharing Executive and an end to the Council of Ireland. The UUUC sensed the forthcoming poll was their chance to galvanise their supporters and attack the new arrangement at Stormont. Against this backdrop of opposition, the new ministers pushed ahead with their jobs. Hume threw himself enthusiastically into his role as commerce minister. Even Faulkner noted that his power-sharing colleague had 'an enormous amount of energy'.[7]

Ken Bloomfield, who was permanent secretary to the Executive, also praised his work ethic: 'with his linguistic skills and earnest eloquence John Hume made a natural Minister of Commerce.'[8]

Hume was keen to travel overseas and promote Northern Ireland as a place to invest in and create badly needed employment. A bureau had been established in Brussels to attract investment and in 1974 it was being run by Robert Ramsay, who was a familiar face to Hume, as he had been Brian Faulkner's principal private secretary. As the appropriate minister, Hume travelled out to the office to speak to politicians, journalists and opinion-formers about the prospect of Northern Ireland becoming a venue for investment. Robert Ramsay says the Derry man was very well received: 'John Hume started very well, particularly because he could make a speech in French and answer questions in French ... I suppose that was the very pinnacle of his career in many ways ... It was a very good visit.'[9]

Speculation continued that a general election would be called, and Hume knew that a campaign and then a poll would be fraught with difficulty. He sensed the already fragile Executive would come under great strain. He pleaded with the prime minister not to go to the country as he feared the anti-Sunningdale parties would turn it into a referendum on power-sharing and the Council of Ireland. Faulkner and Fitt made a similar appeal to Francis Pym, the Secretary of State. Faulkner was blunt and said an election at this time would 'do immense damage to the Executive'.[10]

The overtures from Stormont to Downing Street were rejected, as Heath was convinced a fresh mandate at Westminster would prove he was in charge and solve his dispute with the unions. Northern Ireland was not his priority and Sunningdale and its out-workings would have to wait. Heath called the election for Thursday 28 February, urging voters to speak with their vote. 'This time,' he said, 'the strife has got to stop.'[11]

In Northern Ireland, there was conflict of a different kind as the campaign got underway. It became, as Hume had predicted, a referendum on power-sharing. The anti-agreement unionists used a clever slogan: 'Dublin is just a Sunningdale away'. It struck a chord with large sections of the unionist electorate who sensed they were being betrayed and pushed into a united Ireland. The UUUC agreed on a single candidate for each constituency and when the ballots were counted 11 of the 12 Westminster seats were held by anti-Sunningdale MPs. Gerry Fitt held West Belfast and was the only pro-Executive candidate to be elected. It was a disaster for the power-sharing parties and their opponents now declared that the people of Northern Ireland had no confidence in the new Stormont administration.

Edward Heath's gamble failed and he failed to win enough seats to return to Downing Street. Instead, Harold Wilson took office leading a minority Labour government. The new Northern Ireland Secretary was Merlyn Rees and when he arrived in Belfast the anti-Sunningdale campaigners were feeling confident that power-sharing was entering its final days. The Ulster Workers' Council was formed, made up of Harry West of the Official Unionist Party, the DUP's Ian Paisley and Bill Craig of Vanguard.

One of those attracted to Vanguard was a shy academic from Queen's University called David Trimble. With his knowledge of the law and his ability for quick and clear thinking, he quickly rose up Vanguard's ranks.

The UWC did not just attract politicians and the politically active: the group also included representatives of loyalist paramilitaries, including the UDA and UVF. Mindful of how the miners in England had confronted the government in London, militant loyalists decided they too could use their industrial power.

Faulkner sensed that without changes to the Council of Ireland the entire power-sharing administration would be short-lived. He raised his desire for modifications at an Executive meeting in April, but the SDLP insisted that the Sunningdale deal should not be altered. Paddy Devlin says his party did not understand the level of political difficulty Faulkner was in: 'We paid little heed to his fears at first, for we judged he had enough support to carry the day inside and outside the Assembly.'[12]

The SDLP was debating how to proceed. Many party activists insisted that large parts of the Sunningdale deal were not being honoured. The policy of internment was continuing despite pledges from the UK government that it would be phased out. This was causing much angst in nationalist communities, as was the idea that there would be changes to the Council of Ireland, which the SDLP saw as a breach of faith.

As the debate about the Executive's future rumbled on, Hume flew off to the United States as part of a trip aimed at promoting Northern Ireland as a destination for investment. He used the trip to meet his old friend Ted Kennedy and his visit was well received by the media, which now viewed him as the voice of the Catholic minority in Northern Ireland. Back in Belfast, the future of power-sharing reached a pivotal point in May. When the issue reached the floor of the Assembly chamber, it was at times a brutal and rancorous debate. The anti-agreement unionists portrayed Faulkner as a traitor, and there were warnings that if the Council of Ireland was endorsed at Stormont, loyalists would bring Northern Ireland to a standstill. The Executive groupings largely stood firm, even though there were a number of dissenting voices.

When the Assembly finally voted on the issue it was to support Faulkner's amendment, which called for Sunningdale to be supported provided it was backed in letter and spirit by both governments. The amendment went through by 48 votes to 28. When the result was made known and the house rose for the day, William Beattie, one of Ian Paisley's closest supporters, shouted 'No surrender'. Outside, the UWC announced that a strike would begin and the fight against Sunningdale would enter a new phase.

The early hours of the stoppage seemed low-key, but then matters took a sinister turn when masked men turned up at factories and offices ordering them to close. Soon roads were being blocked by men wearing balaclavas standing by barriers and hijacked cars. Supplies and deliveries to shops were stopped. The atmosphere was menacing, and intimidation was rife. Soon the ferry port of Larne, a key shipping route to Britain, was cut off. The strike had taken hold and there was not a part of Northern Ireland that was not affected.

John Hume found himself at the centre of the Executive's battle to keep the lights on. As minister of commerce, he had the responsibility of maintaining electricity and if the situation became critical it would be his job to limit supplies. Having watched the miners' strike in Britain the UWC knew that access to electricity was a powerful political tool. Plans were discussed by Hume's department about bringing in army engineers who would work alongside members of staff who refused to strike and together they could keep the power stations functioning and organise the distribution of oil. Hume was now under enormous pressure both professionally and personally.

Bizarrely, his ministerial driver was on strike, which meant that his means of transport became limited. Over the months since taking office, Hume had formed a friendship with his driver:

> He was a very decent man. I remember I got on very well with him and you know he used to leave me here (in Derry) ... into the middle of the Bogside in those days and in that way, he became part of the community ... because he got to know people in the area.[13]

With tensions across Northern Ireland being raised and roadblocks in most towns, driving became precarious and Hume had to be careful where he travelled. He was instantly recognisable and had become a hate figure for the strikers and other loyalists as well as the IRA who regarded him as a sell-out. He was often driven by others and never wore a seatbelt in case he needed to get out of the car quickly. For some time he was unable to return to the family home in Derry, so he was living out of a suitcase and staying with friends and supportive civil servants. He stayed one evening in the home of Maurice Hayes, who was a senior civil servant in the office of the Executive. Hayes brought Hume to his home in Strangford and recalls being with him as he worked on contingency plans: 'I reflected on the irony of sitting in the dark with the Minister for light, waiting for the indulgence of the strikers to provide us with a brief period of illumination to work on the oil plan.'[14]

As Hume worked on his energy proposals, other party-political problems needed close attention. The SDLP and Faulkner were still at odds over the Council of Ireland with both sides showing little sign of compromise. A proposal to water down the council was put forward which would see it with fewer trappings, and this was agreed by the Executive. However, it was rejected by the SDLP Assembly group despite pleas from Hume. This prompted Brain Faulkner to say he would be resigning as chief executive.

Gerry Fitt then asked the NIO minister Stan Orme to meet the SDLP Assembly group. Some backbenchers had a change of heart. They reversed their original decision and endorsed plans for a slimmed-down Council of Ireland. Power-sharing was saved, but not for long. With the strike in full swing, the situation was becoming critical and, as part of his plan, John Hume suggested that officials should run petrol stations and distribute fuel supplies with support from the security forces. His proposal was backed by the Executive.

To coordinate matters across various departments and deal with the effects of the strike, a Joint Ministerial Steering Group was set up. It involved Hume, Bob Cooper and Leslie Morrell from the Executive, representatives from the NIO including Stan Orme and others from the RUC, the British Army and other civil servants. Ken Bloomfield remembers attending one of the meetings and hearing Hume's analysis of what lay ahead: 'Hume presented the situation in the starkest of terms. Disintegration was almost complete; they must decide whether to govern or not; they must act now or not at all. The Executive needed backing for its oil plan, but this would only be a first step.'[15]

Bloomfield also recalls that Hume was fearful of what might happen on the streets if the strikers were allowed to control essential services:

> Hume clearly feared that the Catholic community, which had so far been passive in the face of these dramatic events, might not remain so indefinitely. People in his native Derry were now cut off from gas and electricity, and he feared serious community trouble if nothing could be done.[16]

Hume was becoming increasingly frustrated at the slowness of London's response. He felt the prime minister and the Secretary of State, Merlyn Rees, were dithering at a time when speed was crucial. He believed there was little time to act and without swift movement from London and the introduction of military personnel, the strike would continue to cripple Northern Ireland. His plan to use troops at petrol stations and in the power stations was referred to Downing Street and the matter was discussed at Chequers on 24 May when Harold Wilson held talks with Brian Faulkner, Gerry Fitt and Oliver Napier. Hume's energy plan was discussed as Ken Bloomfield recalled: 'The reception of arguments for the oil plan was not unfriendly but, rather typically, Wilson seemed as much if not more preoccupied with presentation as with substance.'[17]

When the meeting ended, the Executive parties came away with the impression that London was about to act, that the strikers would be faced down and the Hume plan would be put into operation. It was also agreed that both Harold Wilson and Brian Faulkner would make televised statements the next day. The prime minister used his address to attack the loyalist strikers and said that the stoppages were being run by 'thugs and bullies'. He highlighted the cost of financing Northern Ireland – saying that British parents and British taxpayers had seen their 'sons vilified, spat upon and murdered'. He claimed those who purport to act as if they were an elected government spend their lives 'sponging on Westminster and British democracy and then systematically assault democratic methods. Who do these people think they are?'[18]

Wilson talked tough but did not detail how he was going to break the strike. Paddy Devlin watched it and concluded that the broadcast was a 'massive anti-climax'.[19]

Ken Bloomfield also watched the speech and thought Wilson's words were 'catastrophically unhelpful'.[20] The prime minister was being advised behind the scenes by Sir Frank King, who was the General Officer Commanding in Northern Ireland. King had concerns that by involving the security forces in John Hume's plan, the situation would get worse. Aware of this debate going on in the background, senior SDLP figures met in Gerry Fitt's house and decided to contact the administration in Dublin to get politicians there to support their calls for military action. Paddy Devlin and Ivan Cooper then left to tell the taoiseach, Liam Cosgrave, what was happening.

Finally, it was agreed that 21 petrol stations would be taken over by the security forces. As the minister responsible, John Hume was in charge of liaising with the army, but somehow his plans were leaked to the strikers and they disrupted the operation by mixing fuel tanks at the stations. This ironically led to less petrol being available rather than more, so the long-delayed military action proved worthless.

It was all now too late, and the Executive was entering its final hours. It was reported that Northern Ireland's hospitals might have to stop operating. The power cuts were also getting longer and there were interruptions to the water supply alongside health concerns about the treatment of sewerage. Hume continued his nomadic existence of staying away from home and on the evening of 27 May slept in Markethill, in the County Armagh home of Seamus Mallon. The next day Mallon became Hume's driver, and along with Tom Daly, Frank Feely and Paddy O'Hanlon, they all squeezed into Mallon's Volkswagen Beetle and set out for Stormont.

In Portadown, Mallon was worried about loyalist roadblocks, so he stopped at a nearby British Army base and asked for a secure escort. He explained he was travelling with a member of the Executive, but he was refused assistance. Muttering swear words under his breath, he returned to his car and began the journey to Belfast along a series of country backroads. Hume was characteristically quiet in the car but occasionally would pipe up with a question, 'Where are we now?', to which O'Hanlon replied: 'For Christ's sake Hume, don't you know that we are on our way to our political funeral?'[21]

The car journey got dramatic when they were stopped close to Lisburn and blocked by a police car in front of them and one behind them. John Hume had been spotted in the car and, thinking he was being kidnapped, the police officers intervened. Apologetic, the officers then agreed to escort the four men to Stormont. Once they said their goodbyes at the gates of the Stormont estate, John Hume broke his silence: 'Those policemen knew who I was, isn't that right?' O'Hanlon did not miss a beat: 'Yes, minister.'[22]

Hume would only have that title for a few hours. Power was ebbing away from the Sunningdale experiment by the hour. Sensing that the battle was lost, Faulkner made one last attempt to save his administration. He did a political U-turn and said he was prepared to mediate with the strikers despite initially saying he would not engage. His decision was supported by the Alliance Party, but Hume and his colleagues would not back the idea. Neither would the Secretary of State, Merlyn Rees, and once it became clear that London would not support mediation it was essentially the end of Northern Ireland's first cross-community government.

Brian Faulkner and the other Executive members met in the cabinet room, and he informed his colleagues that he would be resigning as chief executive. It was not a surprise. Faulkner signed off with some words of hope: 'After five months of being able to work together, Catholic and Protestant, I hope that one thing can remain – that we do not attack each other on a sectarian basis ever again.'[23]

Over the green baize table, there was small talk and a series of handshakes, as Gerry Fitt recalled: 'There was no recrimination or bitterness, only emotion, respect, and a sense of friendship.'[24] There was one final turn of events after Faulkner resigned. Fitt, Currie and Hume refused to step down, bizarrely remaining in post. Within hours, however, their warrants of authority were withdrawn by Merlyn Rees and it was time to finally say goodbye. Power-sharing came to an end, as did John Hume's brief ministerial career. The strikers had won and London was back in charge. So what are the lessons from the failure of power-sharing in 1974?

Hume always insisted that the deal at Sunningdale could have succeeded if Harold Wilson and Merlyn Rees had taken a tougher stand against the UWC and the strikers. In an unpublished interview he gave in 2003, he maintained that the decisions of 1974 influenced what happened afterwards: 'The fact that the Ulster Workers Council strike was allowed to bring down the power-sharing Executive strengthened violence. Because it encouraged the loyalists to realise that their violence was winning, by bringing down the power-sharing Executive.'[25]

He believed it strengthened the IRA as well because they felt the only argument 'the British understand is force, and that made the 70s an extremely difficult period indeed'. Hume also felt the British authorities capitulated to the UWC strikers and that 'was one of the biggest mistakes of the last 20 years'.[26]

In the early days of the UWC protest the strikers were poorly organised, so had the security forces moved decisively against them and cleared barricades, it is possible the campaign of disruption would not have developed. Others say there were party-political decisions taken that if handled differently could have kept the power-sharing project alive. Gerry Fitt argued that the SDLP was too wedded to the Council of Ireland and should have shown greater sensitivities to the wider unionist community: 'Blind to everything but their precious Irish dimension, they stoked up the anger of hardline loyalists by pressing uncompromisingly for the Council of Ireland.'[27]

He thinks the council should have been delayed and phased in later, although a similar move was finally agreed by the SDLP. Fitt says it was too late, adding that: 'As a result, they lost everything, not only the prospect of a Council of Ireland but power-sharing as well.'[28]

So, was it a negotiating mistake by Hume to initially press for the full implementation of the Council of Ireland? He admitted during the latter stages of power-sharing that the council would have to be delayed. So should he have done that much earlier? The civil servant Robin Ramsay watched the fall of Stormont from France. He was returning with his family to Belfast having agreed to come home from his Brussels job to once again assist Brian Faulkner. He thinks Hume and others in the SDLP overplayed their hand:

> I think they rather overdid the running to and from Dublin and their emphasis on the Irish Council. I mean, literally everybody settled down on that. I don't think they needed to do it. I know some of the people involved. We needed to do it, to show to our people that we had won something in terms of strengthening links with Dublin, but I think they overdid it. They didn't really need to do it. It did a lot of harm in terms of how they were viewed by the ordinary unionist community who didn't appreciate all the subtleties of the needs of the SDLP.[29]

Hume has always rejected any suggestion that it was his stance on the Council of Ireland that caused the Executive to collapse: 'The Council of Ireland didn't actually come into existence; the opposition was totally to the Sunningdale Agreement and to power-sharing in any shape or form. There's absolutely no doubt that that was very strong in the unionist community.'[30]

Hume's assessment was shared by others who personally witnessed the final days of the power-sharing experiment. Maurice Hayes, who was Assistant Secretary in the Office of the Executive, insisted that it was the concept of a cross-community government that provoked strong unionist opposition: 'I have never subscribed to the commonly held view that it was the Council of Ireland that brought down Sunningdale. This, I believe was the presenting issue used to cloak the very deep-seated aversion amongst unionists to sharing power with Catholics and nationalists.'[31]

Although power-sharing was short-lived and Hume's ministerial career lasted just short of 150 days, some think he enjoyed the experience. Hume's son Aidan says his father was bitterly disappointed when the Executive collapsed: 'The sad thing was that things didn't survive in 1974, but he really loved it. That might have been when he was happiest in politics. He loved working together and he actually built a close working relationship with Brian Faulkner back then.'[32]

Others think the fall of the Executive changed Hume's thinking. Reg Empey was a member of Vanguard in 1973 and opposed the Sunningdale Agreement. He later went on to join the Ulster Unionist Party and became a power-sharing minister and acting first minister in 2001. He thinks the experience of 1974 convinced Hume that a purely internal solution to Northern Ireland would not work: 'I think it seared him; that is probably the word I would use. I think he came to the conclusion that fixing Stormont as he would have seen it on its own wouldn't do. Unless it was part of the wider direction of travel.'[33]

So were mistakes made before power-sharing was established that could have helped to cement the deal and garner community support? Hume believed there was an obvious one. He argued that the agreement that established the Executive should have been the subject of a referendum: 'Our mistake at Sunningdale was that in having reached agreement, we should have put it to the people, because that became a strong point of mine for future agreement.'[34]

The failure to hold a referendum after the Sunningdale talks stayed with Hume all his political life and it became an issue during the Good Friday negotiations in 1998. Ultimately, at the SDLP's insistence, the agreement negotiated on Good Friday was put out to public vote north and south of the border with referenda on the same day. Critics of the Sunningdale deal argue that it was put to a public vote of sorts at the general election of February 1974. That poll, just weeks into the life of the Executive, effectively became a referendum on power-sharing and anti-Sunningdale candidates triumphed.

For Edward Heath, it was a disaster on several fronts. The election resulted in the Conservatives losing power at Westminster and ushered in a minority Labour administration led by Harold Wilson.

Heath's electoral gamble also signalled the death knell of power-sharing, which had not had time to bed in. The final collapse of the Executive on 28 May was greeted with celebrations in loyalist areas and there were bonfires and street parades. The strike came to an end and workers returned to work, barricades were lifted and there were no more power shortages. Paisley and the other members of the UUUC were jubilant whilst senior politicians from London found themselves in very familiar territory. They stepped in once again and the Assembly was prorogued, and direct rule became the order of the day.

However, within weeks, there was talk of trying again.

11

FOLLOW THE LEADER

*'We are going to have different opinions,
but never mistake that for a lack of respect.'*
Seamus Mallon on John Hume

In the summer of 1974, John Hume arrived at Downing Street to hear what the new prime minister had to say about life after Sunningdale. The British government was taking soundings on what could be done to fill the political void after the UWC strike. The SDLP position remained unchanged, and Hume reminded Harold Wilson that any new plan without a North–South dimension simply would not wash. He insisted that there had to be an Irish dimension to any cross-party agreement aimed at creating a political settlement.

When the government's plans were finally unveiled in July, Hume was underwhelmed by what was being proposed. It was planned that there would be a newly elected Assembly, but it would be called a Convention, which would meet and decide the best way forward for Northern Ireland. Hume was not satisfied that the plans were clear enough and he thought they lacked clarity regarding power-sharing and the Irish dimension. He wanted a legal guarantee that any new deal would have both these areas underwritten into new legislation.

There would be elections to the Convention in 1975, but before they took place Hume had another campaign to consider. Harold Wilson wanted a stronger electoral mandate at Westminster and called an election for October – the second of 1974. Hume contested the Londonderry seat and tried to unseat Willie Ross but the anti-Sunningdale unionist triumphed. The only change to the electoral map was in Fermanagh and South Tyrone where the OUP leader Harry West lost out to Frank Maguire, who stood as an agreed anti-unionist candidate.

The SDLP leader Gerry Fitt was returned to Westminster, but for Brian Faulkner's new party, the Unionist Party of Northern Ireland (UPNI), the result was a disaster as its candidates could only register around 3 per cent of the vote. Five months after the collapse of the Executive, the overall feeling in the unionist community had not changed: 10 of the 12 MPs sent to the House of Commons from Northern Ireland were all part of the coalition against power-sharing. The mood for a revamped Executive based on a cross-community government did not exist and the election result suggested that a future Convention poll would produce a similar outcome.

As questions were posed about what a future administration might look like, there was a series of secret talks taking place aimed at halting the violence. In December 1974, Protestant church leaders met the Provisional IRA and, over Christmas, a temporary ceasefire was called. The talks in Feakle, in County Clare, were followed by secret discussions between the NIO and the Provisionals. These contacts resulted in the ceasefire stretching to mid-January. The Secretary of State, Merlyn Rees, controversially set up a series of incident centres so the Provisionals could liaise with the government and the ceasefire could be controlled. Rees said there could be talks if there was a long cessation but by April any trust that had been established had broken down and the violence returned.

Hume was doing his own quiet work behind the scenes in Derry to reduce tension and stop the violence. Robin Eames came across him in his role as the Church of Ireland Bishop of Derry and Raphoe. The two men were first introduced in a house in the Bogside where the newly installed Eames had gone to meet local residents and hear about their fears and worries:

> As the conversation went on there was a hush and I did not know what had happened – what had I said wrong? And then I was conscious that the door had opened and

a little man had walked into the meeting. And he walked straight through the crowd, put his hand out and said to me, 'Welcome, I'm John Hume.'[1]

Hume and Eames got to know each other, and it was useful for both men to use their list of contacts from different parts of the city. Together with Edward Daly, the Catholic Bishop of Derry, the three men often helped to stop violence taking place by holding quiet meetings or having discreet conversations. Eames says Hume was well-connected and was always prepared to step forward: 'John was able, where it was possible, to put me in touch with people or mention names or give messages through Edward Daly to me and others which would turn out to be significant.'[2]

Eames would later become Primate of All Ireland and, with Denis Bradley, would go on to chair a group which would investigate the legacy of the Troubles. Back in the 1970s, he says John Hume's behind-the-scenes work was impressive: 'John Hume had a respect for life and yet was able to formulate contacts that in turn saved lives.'[3]

Politics took centre stage in May 1975 when the elections for the Convention were finally held. The contest was along familiar lines. The UUUC was the umbrella body taking on board the OUP, DUP and Vanguard groups which opposed power-sharing and wanted majority rule. Those who argued for partnership government were the SDLP, the Alliance Party and Brian Faulkner's UPNI.

Hume stood in the Londonderry constituency and, with colleagues Hugh Logue and Michael Canavan, took three of the seven seats. When the overall votes were counted the picture was clear. Anti-Sunningdale unionists were in the majority, securing 47 of the 78 seats. The SDLP managed to win 17 seats in an election that saw turnout fall. It was the seventh poll in Northern Ireland in just over two years, so the electorate was becoming somewhat election-weary.

Despite the election results, the British government optimistically pressed on with the Convention idea in the hope that the discussions might generate a way forward. There were public debates and a series of inter-party meetings, but over weeks of talks, there was little sign of common ground. The UUUC insisted that law-and-order powers needed to be restored to Stormont. Whilst they agreed to minority representation on committees, there was no movement on a cross-party Executive. The SDLP, the Alliance Party and the Faulkner unionists continued to press for full power-sharing.

Even though the UUUC-supporting unionists continued to press for majority rule, there was one idea that sparked Hume's imagination, when Bill Craig of Vanguard proposed a voluntary coalition that would have included the SDLP. Craig was essentially flying solo, but Hume thought the remarks were a step in the right direction:

> While he was not arguing for fixed and permanent power-sharing he was talking about a voluntary coalition and given the right-wing he was coming from, to me that looked like a beginning in the change of opinion on the unionist side and a beginning of new thinking and thinking that was going in our direction.[4]

Craig got little support for his suggestion, and he was deserted and criticised by his unionist colleagues. Interestingly, his idea was backed by a certain David Trimble. However, the notion of unionism joining forces with nationalism disappeared quickly, and Craig's career never recovered. As talk of a voluntary coalition died, so too did the prospect of success. Finally, after months of trying, the UK government conceded defeat and the Convention met for the last time in March 1976.

It was a depressing time for the SDLP, and for figures like Austin Currie, it felt like the collapse of Sunningdale all over again: 'We were very dispirited and frustrated. We had to try and pick up the bits again. This was at a time when there was no possibility of any agreement with unionists.'[5]

After the Convention wound up, Hume, like other politicians, found himself without an income, and the family relied on Pat's earnings as a teacher. As the sole breadwinner, Pat was working at St Anne's Primary School not far from where John had spent his early life. In Derry, Hume continued to work as a constituency representative and deal with all the inquiries and complaints that he had been dealing with as a paid politician. He was trying to solve housing problems and employment issues, and he was often called upon to find out where detainees were being held by the police. Yet, he was doing all this casework for no salary and he knew that ultimately he had to look for paid work. He did not want to leave politics completely and was always interested in academia so when an opportunity arose to go to Harvard University he jumped at it.

He was offered a fellowship where he would lecture and study conflict studies. It was a perfect fit for him in many ways. It gave him a chance to earn some money, created some thinking time and it also meant he could renew old political acquaintances:

> The value of it was that I was in the Boston area, of course, in Massachusetts and that strengthened my contacts which I had with Ted Kennedy and Tip O'Neill, both of whom were from Massachusetts. I was in regular contact with them at the time and spent quite a bit of time, too, talking to the Irish community in Boston, and of course, my major message in those days was totally anti-violence because of the support that there was in the United States for the IRA's type of approach.[6]

Hume now believed that, after the failure of the Convention, fresh thinking was required, and new players needed to be brought into the political equation. He wanted to see the US administration take a greater role in helping to find a political settlement in Northern Ireland. Hume also believed that politicians in the United States could help to influence opinion makers in London and could even change current thinking.

In Boston, he used his time well and he got to know Senator Pat Moynihan and the governor of New York, Hugh Carey. Hume brought Moynihan and Carey together with his old friends Ted Kennedy and Tip O'Neill and managed to persuade the quartet to take a greater interest in Northern Ireland.

They became known as the 'Four Horsemen' and in 1977, on St Patrick's Day, which was the biggest day in Irish-American circles, they issued a joint statement promoting peace and rejecting any action that encouraged or supported violence. Hume viewed the move as highly significant, and he now had the White House in his sights. Previous US administrations had often shied away from commenting on Northern Ireland, and when they did, they often took their lead from London. Hume wanted President Jimmy Carter to make a statement on Northern Ireland and he felt such an intervention could change the political atmosphere. After the failure of Sunningdale and the Convention, he believed that there could be no political settlement without the backing of Dublin, London and Washington.

Hume wanted more than just political words of support. He also hoped for a commitment to financial aid and he wanted a denunciation of those Americans who offered money to the IRA. Carter had already made comments about Northern Ireland during his presidential campaign of 1976 when he highlighted human rights issues and talked about America becoming involved in the political debate. Hume felt he was pushing at an open door but knew it would take a great deal of lobbying to secure a detailed statement. He had been to the United States back in 1969 and quickly learned who were the best people to talk to. Diplomat Seán Donlon helped Hume during that initial visit:

> I brought John to meet Speaker John McCormack and the one thing I remember vividly from that meeting was that McCormack told us the way to influence what happened in America was not through the massive 40 million Irish-American community, but through people in Congress in Washington.[7]

Hume adopted this formula and sought out those individuals in Washington who had power and influence. In 1977, along with the Irish diplomat Michael Lillis, who was based in the United States, he began working on drafting the Carter statement. Lillis had first encountered

Hume back in Derry in the early 1970s and viewed him as someone who took a logical approach to problem-solving: 'I have never met a man who is as serious and who thought his way through every single issue in terms of the possible consequences of what he was saying.'[8]

Like Hume, Lillis was also friendly with Tip O'Neill, who was the Speaker of the House of Representatives and regarded as one of the most influential politicians in Washington. Lillis knew that the O'Neill link to Carter would be crucial in ultimately delivering a presidential statement on Northern Ireland:

> Jimmy Carter had no Irish connection of any sort. He was a peanut farmer from Georgia. But he desperately needed the support of Tip O'Neill to get his various priorities through Congress and the arrangement was that O'Neill met Carter once a week and O'Neill was enormously influenced by Hume.[9]

Lillis and O'Neill got on well and often socialised together:

> He was an extraordinarily powerful figure and very accessible. He and I became great friends and he became a frequent visitor to my house in Washington, partly because I had lived in Spain where you could buy Cuban cigars for about a penny each. I had become, I won't say addicted, but I had become a fan.[10]

Amidst the cigar smoke around the Lillis dinner table, there was much talk of how politics in Northern Ireland could move on and what role President Carter could play. With this axis in place linking Carter, O'Neill, Hume and Lillis, work began on drafting a statement that would get White House approval. Lillis and Hume worked on it for weeks, drafting and redrafting the paragraphs until they were content.

On 30 August 1977 President Carter's thoughts on Northern Ireland were finally made public and he examined a series of issues. He issued a strong call for the use of peaceful means in the bid to find a political solution which he said must involve both sides of the community and that 'protects human rights and guarantees freedom from discrimination'.[11] He made a direct criticism of those in the United States who funded the IRA or other groups which advocated violence. He then said he wanted to see a new administration in Northern Ireland which would command widespread acceptance, and he pledged direct financial help in the event of a settlement.

For Hume, the statement was a triumph and, in his eyes, it marked a new beginning. Whilst President Carter did not mention that there should be an 'Irish dimension' to any future settlement, his call for a future cross-community administration and his attack on those Americans who funded violence all originated from ideas presented by Hume. The commitment to offer a substantial financial investment in the aftermath of a political settlement was also another Hume idea.

The move by Carter broke with tradition, as previous US presidents rarely said anything about Northern Ireland. Seán Ó hUiginn, who served as Irish consul-general in New York and was later Irish ambassador in Washington, thinks it was a defining moment: 'The Carter initiative was so significant because although the text seems rather anodyne and banal – you are tempted to say what is the big deal – it was a very big deal in that it broke the convention that Washington did not comment on Northern Ireland at presidential level.'[12]

He believes the statement changed British–American relations when it came to the issue of Northern Ireland:

> The Carter initiative was the start of the American involvement and frankly it was the single most important factor in keeping the British reasonably focused and reasonably concerned about Northern Ireland. Their default positions otherwise would have been either neglect or indeed contempt at some point.[13]

The Carter breakthrough marked a moment of personal satisfaction for Hume when there was little cheer at home on the domestic political front. There was a stalemate in Northern Ireland with no sign of political progress or fresh initiatives. A strike similar to the one called during power-sharing in 1974 was organised by loyalists in May 1977 and those behind it demanded a return to majority rule. Unlike the previous one, this stoppage failed when the strikers could not get the backing of power workers. Hume had little confidence in the British government at this stage. There were plans to increase the number of Northern Ireland MPs at Westminster which Hume saw as a sop to unionists at a time when Labour's fragile government needed parliamentary support.

Matters were not helped by the fact that there was no personal chemistry between Hume and the Northern Ireland Secretary, Roy Mason: 'We regarded him as probably the worst Secretary of State we had. He had no sensitivity of any description to the discrimination and injustices that existed in Northern Ireland, and he was a very hardline right winger in his approach to the Northern Ireland problem.'[14]

Still on the lookout for paid work, an opportunity arose in the summer of 1977 which Hume jumped at. He was offered a job as political adviser to Richard Burke, who was an EEC commissioner who looked after consumer affairs.

The posting abroad opened up fresh opportunities and introduced him to officials and power brokers within the world of European politics. A committed Europhile, the job satisfied his growing interest in the workings and politics of the EEC and he was able to make many fresh personal contacts. It also fitted into his political philosophy as he was a firm believer in the European models of peace-building through social and economic ties. The job took him temporarily away from Derry and from the day-to-day world of Northern Ireland politics. With no locally elected Assembly and only one Westminster MP, the SDLP was struggling to function. Seamus Mallon recalled the difficulties: 'Organisation was a huge challenge. We had no resources, no money, no backup. Very often my branch met in the living room of my house because nobody would rent us a room, worried that a bomb might be planted in it.'[15]

All was not well within the party. Former minister Paddy Devlin was disillusioned with the way the SDLP was being organised. He claimed power was becoming centralised: 'More and more, the party was being autocratically run by John Hume and his cronies.' Devlin says he was left out of delegations and felt the party had betrayed its origins: 'I was openly furious at the way the party was being stripped of its socialism and being taken over by unadulterated nationalists.'[16]

Devlin issued a savage attack on the party, criticising what he said was indifference towards those without a job or in poor housing, and he denounced the party's decision to back EEC membership. In a dig aimed at John Hume, he also claimed the party had issued pro-EEC adverts which were not paid for. The SDLP executive hit back and within days he was expelled. One of the party's original founders was now out in the cold.

Devlin's departure meant that Gerry Fitt was the only member of the SDLP leadership who had a Belfast support base. It also resulted in Fitt becoming more and more isolated. From the Labour tradition, Fitt found himself ideologically outnumbered by those in the party who viewed themselves first and foremost as nationalists: 'It did cross my mind to sever my own links, but on reflection, I felt for the time being anyway it was better to stay.'[17]

For some time, much had rested on Fitt's shoulders both politically and personally. A constant critic of the IRA, his Belfast home had often been the target of stone throwers and petrol bombers. A violent crowd broke into his house in August 1976 and Fitt defended himself and his wife and family by scaring them off with his handgun. It was a frightening moment that impacted Fitt's health and that of his wife, Ann.

Like Hume, Fitt had little time for the Secretary of State, Roy Mason, who had replaced Merlyn Rees and was seen by the SDLP as someone who was fixated on military answers rather than political ones. Fitt was also critical of Callaghan's plans to grant more Westminster seats to Northern Ireland which, like Hume, he saw as a way of currying favour with unionists.

Fitt's unease with his party was not new. He had long felt that the movement's Labour origins were being ignored, and it was beginning to look like the old-style Nationalist Party under Eddie McAteer. The SDLP conference of December 1976 was a defining moment. It was an angry and divisive affair as activists debated a motion that the British government should declare its intention to leave Northern Ireland. There were strong emotions on display as the motion was defeated by 158 votes to 111. To Fitt, it was an indication of his party taking a more strident nationalist outlook: 'The atmosphere at party meetings in the latter part of 1976 became greener and greener.'[18]

Fitt, like Hume, opposed the motion, but it did get the support of a large number of public representatives including Seamus Mallon, who was now being seen as one of the party's rising stars and leadership material. He was also viewed as the torch-bearer of the party's nationalist soul. Away from the internal machinations of party politics, Hume had other matters on his mind. He had a plan and used his experience and time with EEC Commissioner Burke well. With European-wide elections due in 1979 it soon became clear that he wanted to be the party's candidate. He secured the nomination with some ease and started to put his energy into winning one of Northern Ireland's three seats.

In the political bubble of Westminster, Fitt found himself at the centre of much attention, as the Labour administration limped along with a wafer-thin majority. After a series of damaging strikes that affected public services and poor opinion polls, Callaghan faced a motion of censure and Fitt's support was seen as crucial. It was clear that the Labour administration was in office but not in power and a buoyant and confident Margaret Thatcher was seen as the prime-minister-in-waiting.

Overtures were repeatedly made from the Labour hierarchy to Fitt to secure his endorsement, but they were to no avail. Despite his long track record of supporting Labour, the West Belfast MP refused to back Callaghan, and his government dramatically fell by one vote which resulted in a general election. Callaghan's days in power came to a crushing end in the early hours of Friday 4 May. The Conservative Party leader Margaret Thatcher made history and became the first female occupant of Downing Street. Announcing her first cabinet some hours later, Thatcher named her chief whip, Humphrey Atkins, as Secretary of

State. His appointment raised a few eyebrows and the *Belfast Telegraph* greeted his arrival with the words 'Humphrey Who?'

In Northern Ireland, Gerry Fitt successfully retained his West Belfast seat and he and Frank Maguire were the only two non-unionists to be elected. The remaining 10 seats were taken up by the Official Unionists, the DUP, Jim Kilfedder and John Dunlop. As Westminster got used to the new political landscape, Hume was on the campaign trail for a seat in Europe. He put together a team to canvass and organise the vote and, as ever, friends were contacted for help. Phil Coulter, who was now a successful musician and a Eurovision-winning songwriter, agreed to compose a jingle.

With Coulter's dulcet tones filling the air, the Hume bandwagon took to the streets. This was a different campaign for the candidate as he was no longer confined to the familiar constituency of Foyle or Londonderry. He needed to take his message to every part of Northern Ireland in the hope of winning one of the three seats up for grabs. Using a proportional representation voting system, the three who emerged victorious were the DUP leader, the Reverend Ian Paisley, Hume and John Taylor of the Official Unionists. Hume secured an impressive first preference vote of 140,622, almost a quarter of the total vote, in a crowded field of some 13 candidates, including his former colleague Paddy Devlin. Hume had campaigned strongly and felt his pro-European message had struck a chord with voters.

The election had put him back in the media limelight and increased his profile and his authority in the party. He had effectively served an apprenticeship with EEC Commissioner Richard Burke, and now he was able to embrace life in Brussels and Strasbourg as a fully fledged MEP and build on the contacts he had made. Hume loved being an MEP and culturally and politically he felt at home in Europe. He wanted European political influencers to have a direct role in the affairs of Northern Ireland and play a key part in peace-building. Hume loved the political ideals of the European community and saw the body as a vehicle that could offer financial and political support but also could influence British policy in Northern Ireland. It was something he had tried before – notably in the United States, where he had built up a network of supporters and influencers in Washington and New York. He believed that Northern Ireland could not solve its problems on its own.

As a newly elected MEP, he got to work with a plan, and as a member of the socialist grouping he was able to sit with the most powerful bloc of politicians in Strasbourg. He argued that social deprivation played into the violence in Northern Ireland and he convinced his new political colleagues that there should be economic help. His lobbying proved successful and he secured agreement for special financial assistance. It was the start of many financial aid packages aimed at promoting economic and social development in Northern Ireland.

Hume's new role naturally brought him into greater contact with Ian Paisley, the leader of the DUP. The two men had obvious differences and a track record of clashing in television and radio studios over decades. However, Mark Durkan who worked alongside Hume for decades said they were able to establish a rapport:

> I always thought he had a good relationship with Paisley. I mean John used to always joke that there were two Paisleys. And he always knew which one it was by seeing where the glasses were on his nose. That told you which Paisley you were getting. Glasses down is angry, that is raging Paisley. Glasses up is more measured Paisley.[19]

There were other lighter moments too between Hume and Paisley. Don McCrea, who was Hume's driver, remembers an occasion when he drove to East Belfast for a meeting with Paisley. After the meeting finished it became clear to McCrea that the battery in the car was flat. Paisley then got his son Ian Junior involved. He remembers the conversation outside the house with his father and his guests: 'I said, what is wrong? They said the battery is flat. So I got some jump leads from the garage and attached them to my car and within seconds we got Hume's car started.'[20]

With the car now sounding healthy, Don McCrea was able to rev the engine. He remembers Ian Paisley Senior looking pleased that he had been able to help: 'There was Ian beaming away and in his best clerical voice he said, "Well young Hume, that is real power," and John just leaned over and in a quiet voice said, "No Ian, that is power-sharing."'[21]

Pat and John Hume would often find themselves at events in London or Brussels with Paisley and his wife, Eileen. She says they all got on well socially despite their obvious political differences. In an interview for this book, she explained that they shared many similarities:

> Pat was very nice. She was a great supporter of John of course, just as I was of Ian. We had that in common, we both had a family. We could talk quite openly. You know people get the wrong idea that because we belong to a different party you are always calling at one another or fighting with one another. But they had their differences and opinions about certain things as everybody knows but it didn't keep us apart. It didn't stop our friendship.[22]

Back in 1979, as Hume adapted to his new role in Europe, Margaret Thatcher's man at the NIO was also getting used to his new job as Northern Ireland Secretary. Humphrey Atkins began an initiative aimed at finding a fresh political settlement and announced a round of inter-party talks. Atkins made it clear that the discussion would not include talks about an 'Irish dimension', which was not what Hume wanted to hear. Hume insisted that without this on the table the talks were worthless and argued that unless this was placed on the agenda the SDLP should stay away. Hume's argument angered Fitt, who believed that the SDLP were copying the tactics of republicans and old-style nationalists by becoming abstentionists. He wanted the party to sit down at the talks table. The strains between him and other party members continued for a number of weeks. There was much arguing behind the scenes and Fitt increasingly found himself outnumbered in party meetings.

When the party executive rejected the invitation from Humphrey Atkins to take part in the talks process it was a defining moment. Fitt called a press conference and resigned: 'I have a feeling of unutterable sadness to see at this time the party which I helped to create turning so violently on the concepts on which it was founded. We have come to the end of a very hard road.'[23]

Fitt's departure was not a complete surprise, but it did mean that Hume now became acting leader. To many political observers, he had technically been in charge of the party for years. Bríd Rodgers says many in the party saw Hume as the driving force and Fitt as the figurehead: 'Gerry was a gut politician, he was not a strategic leader. So John really, in many ways, was the one that we always looked to even when he was deputy.'[24]

As MEP and the party's leading figure, he was now without question the spokesperson for Northern Ireland's nationalists. When party activists gathered in November to decide who should lead them it was an academic exercise. Hume was endorsed as leader with Seamus Mallon elected as deputy leader. It was the start of a relationship that would last for decades, and at times it would be tested almost to breaking point. Aidan Hume remembers Seamus Mallon acknowledging that he and his father often saw things differently:

> Seamus pulled me aside at the first European election count. Everybody went out and he said, 'I want you to understand one thing. Your father and I are going to argue. We are going to have different opinions. But never mistake that for a lack of respect. We are politicians. That is what we do.' And to me they were more like an old married couple.[25]

Gerry Cosgrove observed the relationship between Mallon and Hume at close quarters when she worked at party headquarters. She says John's secrecy would often annoy Seamus:

> Sometimes Seamus would say, 'Where is he? What is he doing?' And I would say, 'I don't know Seamus.' So there was friction. But they always came together in the end if

they disagreed. And then they had to go and do something – they did it together and no one would have known they had had a disagreement.[26]

With Mallon as his able deputy, 1979 marked a dramatic year for Hume. His personal circumstances changed, and as well as having the new titles of MEP and leader, he also had to forge relationships with freshly elected administrations in Dublin and London. The arrival of Margaret Thatcher as prime minister and the election of Charles Haughey as taoiseach changed the dynamic in Anglo-Irish relations. As far as Hume was concerned it did not alter his analysis when it came to finding a political settlement to Northern Ireland. Hume wanted both the British and Irish governments to work together and recognise the need for a North–South dimension to any potential solution. The SDLP finally agreed to enter the talks organised by Humphrey Atkins but the constitutional conference which began in January 1980 was boycotted by the Official Unionists. Hume found himself sitting opposite his MEP colleague the Reverend Ian Paisley, and from the start, there was little common ground.

The new SDLP leader raised the UK's constitutional guarantee to unionists, which he viewed as one-sided, and he stressed that London must recognise that Dublin was a joint partner in ultimately finding a political accommodation in Northern Ireland. He also used the discussions to highlight the need for a reformed police service that had the support of the whole community and argued that could only happen when there was political consensus. The talks were doomed to fail and on 24 March they were wound up without any agreement.

Two days later, Humphrey Atkins had other matters on his mind when he announced there would be no special status for those prisoners who had been convicted of terrorist offences. The move was part of the ongoing battle between the UK government and paramilitary prisoners. Several IRA inmates inside the H block at the Maze prison had for some time been involved in a 'dirty protest' where they smeared their cells with excrement as part of their campaign to wear their own clothing and be excused from prison work. They saw themselves as political prisoners and wanted to be granted special category status, which would distinguish them from other inmates, but Margaret Thatcher was adamant that was not going to happen. For months there had been a series of protests inside the jails, and outside there had been demonstrations and H Block support groups had been formed. However, these moves made little impact and soon there was talk of a fresh campaign, one that would change Irish politics forever.

12

OURSELVES ALONE

'As for unionists they have become a petty people.'
John Hume

Around the breakfast table in a house in Chelsea, John Hume was characteristically quiet. He had stayed overnight at the home of Dáithí Ó Ceallaigh, an Irish diplomat. The Foyle MP seemed preoccupied and may well have been going through in his head what he was about to do that morning. Ó Ceallaigh was well used to the silences and knew not to disturb his guest: 'It was as if he wasn't at the table, you know. He was thinking of the next move.'[1]

The two men finished eating and then Ó Ceallaigh said goodbye to his wife and children and drove Hume the short distance to the Palace of Westminster. Hume then went off to meet the prime minister in her room at the House of Commons. In the spring of 1981, his mission with Margaret Thatcher was a simple one but an incredibly tough one. He had come to try and get her to change her stance on the republican hunger strike taking place in the Maze. Afterwards, he met Ó Ceallaigh. Hume was furious and briefed the civil servant in blunt terms, 'She just doesn't fucking understand.'[2]

Hume's appeal to Downing Street fell on deaf ears. He had suggested a compromise which would allow the prisoners to wear their own clothes. Mrs Thatcher made it clear she would not intervene and Hume became angry and insisted that she was not taking the situation seriously enough. He asked her to consider what the political ramifications would be of prisoners dying in the Maze. Hume knew the arguments well as he had been down this particular road some six months earlier when republican prisoners had launched their first hunger strike under the guidance of IRA commander Brendan Hughes.

Brendan 'The Dark' Hughes was a powerful man. The long-time friend of Gerry Adams, he had been responsible for some of the worst violence witnessed in the Troubles. Hughes had been in charge of the IRA in Belfast and had commanded the 'Bloody Friday' operation in July 1972 when nine people were killed in a series of no-warning bombs across the city. For some time, he had been thinking about how the prisoners could make their campaign for political status more effective. Hughes felt the dirty protest inside the jail and the street demonstrations outside were having limited effect. So he began looking for fellow prisoners who were prepared to go on hunger strike.

The use of this tactic was part of republican folklore. Thomas Ashe, a veteran of the 1916 Easter Rising, refused to wear a prison uniform and went on hunger strike. Terence MacSwiney, who was the lord mayor of Cork, died on hunger strike in 1920 in Brixton Jail. Both men were seen as martyrs and if a hunger strike was embarked upon Hughes knew it would strike an emotional chord within the republican family, and put great pressure on the prison authorities. Along with Bobby Sands, who was serving a sentence for firearms offences, Hughes asked for volunteers to come forward if they were prepared to join the hunger strike in the full knowledge that they could die.

Dozens of prisoners said they wanted to be considered and it was a slow task for Hughes to sift through the names and consider who would be the best men to go forward. Finally, after much thought, a shortlist of seven was drawn up. There were six men – one from each county in Northern Ireland – and the seventh was an INLA prisoner. Hughes joined the list, but Sands did not: his opportunity would come later. On the morning of 27 October 1980, all seven republican prisoners refused to eat their breakfast and the hunger strike began. Hume quickly got involved in discussions with Secretary of State Humphrey Atkins, as did leading figures in the Catholic Church including Hume's old Maynooth tutor Tomás Ó Fiaich, who was now a cardinal and the head of the Catholic Church in Ireland.

Hume sensed that the prison protest could lead to violence across Northern Ireland and warned that there could be a serious escalation of trouble if the prisoners died. Not surprisingly, as he arrived at his first annual conference as leader in November 1980, the hunger strike dominated events. The issue was hard to avoid as supporters of the national Smash H-Block campaign gathered outside the Slieve Donard Hotel in Newcastle to hand out leaflets and lobby party members.

On the opening evening of the conference, delegates debated an emergency motion proposed by deputy leader Seamus Mallon. He criticised the UK government for the way the dispute was being handled and urged the prison authorities to let inmates wear their own clothing. He wanted the hunger strikers to give up their fast in the interest of saving lives. He also warned of the repercussions of the strike and urged fellow speakers to choose their words carefully.

When Hume took to the platform the next day for his keynote address it was impossible to avoid the presence of the noisy demonstrators in front of the hotel. Throughout his speech, he was heckled and slogans were chanted repeatedly – there was even one protestor with a megaphone – but as the shouts got louder outside so did the applause inside the hall. The next day, Hume continued his behind-the-scenes dialogue to see if a resolution could be found when he met for lunch with an official from the Northern Ireland Office. Whilst he had some ideas about how the strike could be ended, Hume was cautious and made it clear that any plans needed to get the backing of the prisoners. For the SDLP there was a need to approach the strike with sensitivity and care. Party activists did not want to see the strike continue and felt the British government needed to show greater flexibility. Seamus Mallon had already identified that there were political ramifications if prisoners started to die. There was real alarm that a series of deaths could inflame the republican community and boost the IRA.

As the strike continued, so too did the attempts by the Northern Ireland Office to engage with the nationalist and Catholic community. Hume used his influence as an MEP and had meetings with officials and met the prison chaplains and started to work on a proposal that he believed could bring the dispute to an end. The proposal would involve prisoners wearing their own clothes and would grant them concessions regarding freedom of association. Bríd Rodgers remembers Hume contacting her because he wanted to speak to one of the prison chaplains.

> I remember him ringing me one night at one o'clock in the morning, I was in bed. He was in Brussels and he wanted to talk to a chaplain in Long Kesh, Tom Toner, who was a great friend of mine, and he wanted his number because he wanted to get in touch with the people involved in the hunger strike to see if he could do something about it.[3]

Hume worked with Father Toner and tried to put together the makings of an agreement. As Hume's work continued, officials at the NIO were writing their own document which they were planning to present to a priest who would in turn brief the prisoners. As the discussions went on between civil servants, politicians, priests and prison staff, the hunger strikers were starting to get weaker. The health of one of the seven, Seán McKenna, was causing the most concern as he was deteriorating badly and there were real fears that he could die soon. As his condition worsened, Father Meagher, a Catholic priest, was handed a document from the British government and told to share it with the hunger strikers.

Before that happened, Brendan Hughes was informed by a prison doctor that Seán McKenna had only hours to live, and he wanted permission to take him to hospital. Hughes had given McKenna a guarantee that he would not let him die. He turned to the doctor and told him to feed his friend and he was taken away on a stretcher and given medical help.

Hughes recalled: 'The hunger strike was called off before the British document arrived. It was only later that night that Father Meagher and Bobby [Sands] arrived at my cell with the document.'[4]

Hughes's decision caused angst among a number of republican prisoners. Both Tom McFeely, who was on hunger strike, and Bobby Sands, who had watched the strike collapse, were against the decision to bring it to an end. Sands in particular was shaken by what had happened and felt the prisoners had been hoodwinked by the British government because their document in his view did not present any concessions. Sands began a series of conversations with prisoners about what their next move should be and he exchanged messages with Gerry Adams. He told Adams: 'I am prepared to die, and no one will call this hunger strike off, comrade.'[5]

The 26-year-old Sands now became the driving force for a second hunger strike and in February 1981 a statement was reported in the republican newspaper *An Phoblacht* that the previous hunger strikers had been 'morally blackmailed by a number of people and politicians who called upon them to end the fast and allow the resolution of the protest'. In their press statement, republicans singled out Hume and others in the Catholic Church: 'It needs to be asked openly of the Irish Bishops, of Cardinal Ó Fiaich and of politicians like John Hume, what did your recommending ending of the last hunger strike gain for us?'[6]

On 1 March 1981, Bobby Sands began his hunger strike and wrote in his diary: 'I am standing on the threshold of another trembling world. May God have mercy on my soul.'[7] The second hunger strike was organised very differently than the first. This time prisoners joined the fast in stages rather than all being on hunger strike together. Sands was the first to begin fasting and he was joined later by Francis Hughes and then others followed. Sands was determined to begin the fast and as he had declared to Gerry Adams he was prepared to die, which meant that in his eyes he was leading by example.

Within days of the strike beginning, politics intervened and an unexpected opportunity arose for the prisoners' campaign. Frank Maguire, the Independent republican MP for Fermanagh and South Tyrone, died suddenly, creating a vacancy at Westminster. It also opened up a golden opportunity for those who wanted to give the prisoners' campaign worldwide publicity, and it presented republicans with a political alternative to the IRA's campaign of violence. For republicanism, this marked a defining moment.

The move was backed by Gerry Adams, and after a series of discussions inside and outside the prison, Bobby Sands was nominated as a candidate to stand in the forthcoming by-election. For the SDLP this caused a dilemma. If the party put up a candidate, it knew it would be accused of betrayal in some quarters. An SDLP nominee would split the anti-unionist vote and in a marginal constituency it would almost certainly mean a nationalist would not take the seat. If John Hume's party decided not to run against Sands, the SDLP would be accused of political cowardice. It was a tough call, particularly in a constituency that was so evenly divided between unionists and nationalists. The SDLP decided to fight the by-election and selected Austin Currie. However, when the party discovered that Noel Maguire, Frank's brother, was going to stand it decided to withdraw. It seemed that a compromise had been struck. For a few hours, the issue seemed settled. However, the story of the by-election had a further twist when Noel Maguire pulled out at the last minute amidst rumours that he had received death threats. There was much debate within SDLP ranks about the lack of a party candidate. Activists were divided over whether they should run or opt out. Austin Currie was furious about the move and he and Hume had endless rows about the party's position. Years later Hume told the journalist Paul Routledge that it had been a very difficult decision: 'Sometimes in politics you are faced with two wrong choices and you take the lesser. The atmosphere was so emotional at the time, the danger was that we would have been wiped out.'[8]

Political observers felt that republicans had outflanked Hume and the SDLP, and the withdrawal of Noel Maguire meant the contest was now down to two candidates. It would be a straight fight between Bobby Sands, as the Anti H Block candidate, and Harry West, from the Official Unionist Party.

So was the decision by the SDLP and by Hume a strategic error? John Cushnahan feels the move sent out the wrong signals and had massive political repercussions. He was general secretary of the Alliance Party at the time and later became a Fine Gael MEP. He recalls talking to the SDLP's Eddie McGrady: 'Eddie said to me, "Every good leader is entitled to one mistake and this was John's."'[9]

Cushnahan was not alone in his view.

Even Hume loyalists think the party should have run a candidate against Bobby Sands in 1981. Alban Maginness, who would serve as party chair in the 1980s, thinks it was an error but feels it is wrong to pin the blame on Hume: 'I think the party did make a mistake, but I don't think you can put it at the feet of John Hume.'[10]

There was worldwide attention on the United Kingdom's most westerly constituency when voters went to the polls on 9 April. With a turnout of nearly 87 per cent, Bobby Sands received 30,492 votes, some 1,446 ahead of Harry West, who polled 29,046. The result changed the political dynamic on the island of Ireland and moved the prison dispute onto the world stage.

The victory for Sands put the focus on London, with continuing questions as to whether Mrs Thatcher was willing to compromise. The election of Northern Ireland's newest MP also reinforced the view in some republican circles that it was now time for Sinn Féin to formally enter the political fray after years of abstentionism. Hume knew that the politicisation of the prisoners' campaign would transform the atmosphere and sensed it would also put pressure on his party.

Looking back, John Cushnahan says the election of Bobby Sands was a watershed moment for Northern Ireland and the SDLP: 'It set back the cause of reconciliation for many years. More importantly, it was directly responsible for the launch of the IRA's political wing, Sinn Féin, as a major force which would eventually eclipse the SDLP.'[11]

Bobby Sands died on 5 May 1981, after he had gone 66 days without food. The funeral attracted tens of thousands of mourners and pictures were broadcast around the world. Bobby Sands, who began life on a Belfast housing estate, was now known the world over, and his death was mourned by politicians and presidents alike. The summer of 1981 was dominated by the deaths of more hunger strikers and street violence across Northern Ireland. The political outlook was bleak and the mood was fearful. As ever, the political analysis differed. Unionists were shocked that so many people would support Bobby Sands and felt Margaret Thatcher's approach was right. Nationalists felt the UK government was behaving in an intransigent way towards the hunger strikers and believed a solution could be found. In August, voters again went to the polls in Fermanagh and South Tyrone to find a successor to Bobby Sands. Republicans selected Owen Carron, who was heavily involved in the Anti H Block committee and had been the election agent for Bobby Sands back in May. The election re-run caused another dilemma for Hume and his party.

SDLP activists gathered in Dungannon in early August and after much discussion the selection convention decided against entering the race, and the decision was brought to the party executive later that week. For three hours senior figures considered what to do and decided to back what the local association had agreed. Afterwards, Hume declared: 'We had no alternative, for there was nothing for us to ratify. No nomination had been made. I think this decision by the constituency body reflected circumstances in Fermanagh–South Tyrone.'[12]

SDLP activists on the ground sensed there was little public appetite amongst nationalists for a candidate to rival Owen Carron. Once again Hume was accused of lacking political courage and he received much public criticism, particularly from unionists who felt he was again handing the seat to republicans. There was a feeling amongst SDLP activists that Carron would simply repeat what had been achieved back in May. Their prediction proved correct.

Carron succeeded Sands in the by-election, polling 31,278 votes, some 2,230 votes more than Ken Maginnis who received a tally of 29,048 votes. The move to electoral politics for republicans was not just confined to Northern Ireland. In the Irish general election in June, under the Anti H Block banner, Kieran Doherty, who was on hunger strike, and Paddy Agnew, who was an IRA man, were both elected. With a new administration in place in Dublin, Hume used his time to cultivate contacts and press for greater Anglo-Irish diplomacy. Charlie Haughey was replaced as taoiseach by Garret FitzGerald and he now led a Fine Gael government that was in coalition with Labour.

Hume got into a routine of flying back from Brussels or Strasbourg and then going to spend time with politicians in Dublin. He made a point of seeing people from across the parties and one of those he regularly met was Bertie Ahern from Fianna Fáil, who was just beginning his political career: 'Every time the SDLP came to town I was in at the meetings. So I might have been the boy taking the notes, or serving the tea but I was at the meetings, so I got to know all the delegations and I got to know John and through that got very friendly with John.'[13]

Ahern's relationship with Hume would last a lifetime, and the two men would be part of some of the big moments in Irish political history, particularly when Ahern became taoiseach in 1997. Their friendship would later stretch into their retired days and they would visit each other in their respective homes.

Hume's charm offensive with politicians in the Dáil and his flying visits to Dublin started to pay off. Although the hunger strikes had placed great strains on Anglo-Irish relations, there were signs that diplomacy between London and Dublin was starting to improve. The Northern Ireland Office had some ideas to break the political log-jam.

Like his predecessors, Secretary of State Jim Prior, had plans to try and revive Stormont, and he came up with an initiative that was dubbed 'rolling devolution'. Prior's idea was to set up the Assembly, which would work towards agreement on how devolution could function. Hume and the SDLP had major doubts about this move as it did not include an Irish dimension and there were concerns that the move did not embrace Executive-style power-sharing. The party had to consider how best to approach Prior's plan and amidst the SDLP hierarchy, including Seamus Mallon, there was a call to ignore the new initiative. There was a feeling that it was simply a talking shop with no power and it was offering no acknowledgement of Dublin's role. There was another consideration for party strategists – the rise of Sinn Féin. Republicans were now organised electorally and posed a threat in traditional SDLP areas. If the SDLP were abstentionists would they be distinguishable from the other abstentionists, notably Sinn Féin?

Hume came up with a plan that he hoped would keep his critics within the party on board. He wanted the SDLP to fight the elections to Prior's new Assembly but not take their seats if elected. In a sense, it was like the policy of the old Nationalist Party under the leadership of

Hume's old rival Eddie McAteer, a tactic Hume had once been very critical of. Hume won the day despite facing some opposition from the party executive. The move was agreed and the party began to think about contesting the election, selecting candidates and organising campaigning. In an election address, Hume made it clear that he felt the Prior plan offered little: 'The Prior Assembly has nothing to offer except the same political wrangling that has disfigured our politics.'[14] He also warned voters who might be tempted to vote Sinn Féin: 'I ask you to reject unequivocally those who would advocate or use violence to solve our problems.'[15]

The SDLP was clearly worried that Sinn Féin would poll well and eat into its traditional vote. This was the first time the party faced such strong opposition from within the nationalist community. For Sinn Féin this was a watershed moment, as hundreds of volunteers took to the streets to distribute leaflets and canvass for votes. The Sinn Féin machine was particularly well-organised in several seats, notably West Belfast, where Gerry Adams was the first to be elected, and in Fermanagh–South Tyrone, where Owen Carron topped the poll.

When the final figures were declared the landscape had changed. There were 49 unionists in total out of the 78 seats. The SDLP had secured a total of 14, which was down 3 from the Convention. The Alliance won 10, whilst Sinn Féin secured 5. It was an impressive achievement by Sinn Féin, who secured nearly 65,000 votes, a creditable 10 per cent of the vote. Republicans were well and truly on the electoral map and the nationalist community now had very different voices. The electoral support for Gerry Adams and his colleagues sent shock waves through the corridors of Westminster and Leinster House, and there were worries that the constitutional nationalism of John Hume was eventually going to be overtaken by the more radical republicanism of Sinn Féin.

In the closing weeks of 1982, John Hume was on a mission and would spend much time in Dublin. He wanted to create an all-Ireland forum, which he dubbed 'The Council for a New Ireland'. Hume planned to set up a body that would discuss what a new Ireland would look like. He wanted it to incorporate all traditions on the island and examine how Anglo-Irish relations could develop. He saw it as a vehicle to change

British policy in Northern Ireland and he hoped it could influence international opinion-formers. It was an idea Hume had been harbouring for some time.

The move had the support of the taoiseach, Garret FitzGerald, but Hume wanted the backing of the Fianna Fáil leader, Charlie Haughey. Haughey's endorsement was crucial. Having recently been deposed as taoiseach, Hume knew it was essential that Haughey agreed to participate but knew he had to handle the conversation carefully. Haughey's approach to Northern Ireland was different to FitzGerald's. He supported Irish unity, like FitzGerald, but was seen as much 'greener' than his Fine Gael counterpart, and often his remarks were not as diplomatic.

Hume did not have the personal chemistry with Haughey that he had with FitzGerald, but he felt there was enough common ground to convince the former taoiseach that an all-Ireland forum was worth backing. Hume travelled to Dublin to see him and was joined on the trip by Seán Farren. A party member since 1972, he was a friend and trusted confidante of Hume's and he had recently become party chairman. A lecturer at the University of Ulster, he had just been elected to Prior's Assembly. Hume was very nervous about his discussion with Haughey, which was to take place in his office in the Dáil. Farren and Hume had been doing meetings together in Dublin, but on this occasion, the party leader wanted to handle things differently, so he told his colleague: 'I am going to tackle this one on my own.'[16]

Hume walked away and left Farren to seek out a drink in Leinster House and wait:

> I was sitting nursing a pint in the bar. After about half an hour, the door burst open and in came John dancing a jig. Charlie Haughey had agreed to support the establishment of the New Ireland Forum. So John celebrated with a jig in the Dáil bar. His apprehensions about Haughey's approach had been allayed and off we went and set it up.[17]

Hume's impromptu victory dance illustrated how much had been riding on Haughey's decision. The SDLP leader now had the backing of the Republic's three main parties. Without the support of all three, Hume knew the initiative was doomed and would be criticised. He was delighted that he had received cross-party backing but there was some administration to do first. Garret FitzGerald thought the title of 'The Council for a New Ireland' invoked too many reminders of the failed Sunningdale experiment back in 1974 and would be viewed with immediate hostility by unionists. He persuaded Hume to accept his title of 'the New Ireland Forum', which was agreed upon by Charlie Haughey and the Labour leader, Dick Spring. Whilst things were going well in Dublin for Hume, in Belfast it was a very different story.

Hume's relationship with unionists in 1983 was not good. He had not endeared himself to them in his party conference speech at the Europa Hotel in Belfast. In his address, he was scathing of their approach to politics:

> As for unionists themselves, they have become a petty people. They represent themselves as the defenders and protectors of Protestant heritage in Ireland. No one has done more to destroy it. 'Ourselves Alone' is their motto. Let us hold all power in our hands. Exclusivism. That is a deeply violent attitude and it is no wonder that one can no longer find in such a philosophy any trace of the civil and religious liberty that is their proud heritage and that is such a necessary first principle for any solution to the problems of Ireland.[18]

The *Belfast Telegraph* seized on Hume's remarks and on Saturday 29 January its front-page headline declared 'Hume says Unionists a Petty People'. Understandably, the political representatives of unionism did not take kindly to the SDLP leader's comments. Hume's words were seen as confrontational rather than diplomatic and to some observers showed that he had little hope in developing political relationships within Northern Ireland. It underlined the fact that he was looking to develop relationships in Dublin rather than with his fellow politicians in Northern Ireland.

Dan Keenan, who worked for the SDLP and later became a journalist with the *Irish Times*, says the 'petty people' remark from 1983 stands out. He says it was 'counter-productive' and is 'evidence of the dysfunctionality of the relationship between Hume and unionism and unionists'.[19]

In 2019 Keenan wrote a PhD examining Hume's origins. He looked at his relationship with unionism and concluded that there was no suggestion 'that Hume disliked unionists simply because of their political beliefs or any other marker. Nor does it suggest he was anti-Protestant.' However, Keenan argues that the 'petty people' remark is an example of where Hume was 'culpable of sending mixed political messages to unionists – at once conciliatory and yet apparently hostile – and that he was habitually seen by them as talking out of both corners of his mouth'.[20]

Back in 1983, unionists and the Alliance Party were formally asked to take part in the New Ireland Forum. However, Sinn Féin was not invited. So when the Forum officially opened for business in May 1983 there were just four main party leaders in attendance – Hume, Spring, FitzGerald and Haughey. It was a historic occasion in the grandeur of Dublin Castle when Hume made his opening address. He made it clear what he saw was the Forum's purpose: 'The common goal of which I speak is and has to be reconciliation of seemingly irreconcilable problems on this island. Let that reconciliation start today in this room – between ourselves.'[21]

Hume said there were two audiences that the Forum must address, which were the unionist people and the UK government. He added that: 'The Forum is not a nationalist conspiracy, neither is it a nationalist revival mission.'[22] Naturally, Hume's analysis was not shared by those of a unionist or conservative tradition. Unionists saw the Forum as a nationalist talking shop determined to rubber stamp a united Ireland. Mrs Thatcher was not convinced that Hume's initiative was necessary and she saw it as a distraction. However, in the summer of 1983, after the Falklands War, she had other more pressing matters on her mind.

She called a general election for June and, for John Hume, this presented a fresh opportunity. New parliamentary seats had been created in Northern Ireland, which would now return 17 MPs instead of 12, and the change looked like it could benefit the SDLP.

Hume would be a candidate in the revamped seat of Foyle, and the party hoped it could make gains in other places. The contest in West Belfast had particular significance and the ensuing battle was an intriguing prospect. The sitting MP was Gerry Fitt, who had resigned from the SDLP in 1979 and sat in the House of Commons as an Independent. He was being challenged by Gerry Adams and the feeling amongst a number of political observers was that Adams would take the seat.

Hume desperately wanted to take the seat off Fitt and he knew he needed to stop Sinn Féin, who were becoming an electoral force. He thought Fitt would not beat Adams so he began to consider who the SDLP should run and who was capable of winning. Behind the scenes, an unlikely and rather unconventional plan was hatched.

Hume felt there was one person with good local connections who could beat both Fitt and Adams. The problem was that Hume's choice was not in the SDLP. In fact, it was even more complicated, as his ideal candidate was a leading figure in a rival party. The man Hume had in mind was John Cushnahan, who was the Alliance Party's general secretary.

There was some logic to Hume's plan. Cushnahan was from West Belfast, so this was his home patch, and he was well known. A Catholic, he had gone to school with Gerry Adams, and he had an appeal that crossed the traditional political boundaries. He was a good organiser and media performer and would most likely run an effective campaign.

Cushnahan has never spoken publicly about this bold approach from John Hume and, in an interview for this book, detailed what occurred:

> He sent a mutual friend of both of us to persuade me. The argument was put to me as follows. West Belfast, following the recent constituency revision, was now overwhelmingly a nationalist constituency. He believed I would beat both Gerry Fitt and Gerry Adams. The following argument was also put to me. As I was originally from West Belfast,

I would get a personal vote. On top of this, I would get a significant vote from the Protestant community because I had earned their respect as an Alliance politician and that the SDLP would deliver the rest. It was also put to me that the proven skills I had shown as the General Secretary of the Alliance Party would enable the SDLP to reverse the SDLP decline in their vote in the battle with Sinn Féin in the greater Belfast area.[23]

Cushnahan thought highly of Hume and would later judge him to be the most outstanding politician of his generation. However, back in 1983, he believed his offer to switch parties was politically 'opportunistic' and he did not want to unseat Gerry Fitt, whom he admired. Had Cushnahan defected and run as an SDLP candidate it would have been a big political story in 1983. It would also have dealt a blow to the Alliance Party and robbed them of one of their leading figures. Ultimately, Cushnahan was a candidate in the 1983 election but it was under Alliance colours in north Down where he failed to get elected.

The SDLP selected Dr Joe Hendron to run in West Belfast. He came second and Gerry Adams, as many had predicted, won and took the seat off Gerry Fitt (although he would not sit in Westminster in line with party's policy of abstentionism). The result ended Fitt's career in the House of Commons and he entered the House of Lords.

Across Northern Ireland, the Official Unionists took the lion's share of the seats with 11 MPs and the DUP won 3.

Hume ran in the revamped seat of Foyle and took it with an impressive majority of just over 8,000 votes. He had hoped he would have company on the trip to Westminster. Seamus Mallon was only 1,554 votes away from taking the seat of Newry and Armagh and Eddie McGrady was even unluckier. He was narrowly beaten by Enoch Powell in South Down who scraped home with a majority of just 548 votes. As Sinn Féin refused to take its place in Westminster because of its abstentionist policy, Hume became the lone voice of Irish nationalism on the Commons benches. He made his maiden speech in June 1983 and talked, as is tradition, about his constituency. However, the new MP went further than simply extolling the wonderful virtues of his Foyle seat. He gave a devastating critique of the UK government's policy in Northern Ireland. He argued that solutions were needed to solve 'some of the most serious human issues facing the House'.[24]

He also claimed that parliamentarians did not take the problems of Northern Ireland seriously and ignored much of what happened on a daily basis. He queried Mrs Thatcher's famous quote that Northern Ireland was as 'British as Finchley' and he boldly claimed: 'The truth is that Britain has psychologically withdrawn from Northern Ireland. Britain and Northern Ireland would be healthier places if that psychological reality were translated into political reality.'[25]

Hume now had three arenas to work in. He was an MEP, a member of the New Ireland Forum and now an MP. He was constantly travelling and was carrying the burden of leadership and the aspirations of thousands of constitutional nationalists. He knew there was an enormous job of work to be done, and he also realised he desperately needed help.

13

THE MONKEY AND THE ORGAN GRINDER

'I am going to confront these people face to face.'
John Hume on the IRA

Joe Duffy, Ireland's student leader, answered the phone in his Dublin office and within seconds recognised the voice at the other end. It was John Hume. He was looking for Duffy's colleague and housemate. 'Is he there?' inquired the politician. Duffy put the phone down and went in search of his friend.[1]

It was November 1983 and Mark Durkan remembers what happened next:

> He came and said to me (I thought he was joking), John Hume is on the phone for you or whatever. And so I took the call. John told me he was in Dublin Castle where the Forum for a New Ireland was meeting, and could I come and see him? If I can go to Dublin Castle in the afternoon and give his name to the security people and tell the security people who I am, that I would get in.[2]

Durkan knew the Hume family from his days in Derry and got to know John better when he was deputy president of Queen's University Students Union. Durkan went on to become deputy president of the Union of Students in Ireland (USI) and had campaigned in 1982 for the SDLP and for Hume in 1983 when he won the Foyle seat.

After receiving the phone call, Mark Durkan made the journey to Dublin Castle as Hume had requested and presented himself at the security gates. Built in the thirteenth century as a medieval fortress, it was an impressive building and had once been the headquarters of British rule in Ireland. Over the decades it had played host to many historical figures, such as the Duke of Wellington, Queen Victoria and Charles Dickens.

Durkan got through security by mentioning his MP's name and remembers meeting Hume and being given an impromptu tour. After the historical walkabout, his host cut to the chase. He offered Durkan a job as his Westminster assistant working in the Derry office. The SDLP leader had obviously spoken to others about offering the position to his fellow Derry man, as Durkan recalls:

> I remember one of the people he introduced me to was Austin Currie and I remember Austin talking to me as though it was already decided in those terms. So I told John I would think about it, because obviously I had commitments in USI at the time.[3]

Durkan agreed to the job offer and left USI and began working for Hume in February 1984, much to Joe Duffy's disappointment. The USI president, who would later go on to become a successful RTÉ broadcaster, rated Durkan highly and the two were great friends. The Hume–Durkan bond would become a defining relationship within the SDLP. Durkan would eventually follow Hume into electoral politics, become a Stormont minister, succeed him as Foyle MP and lead the party. The two men would become inseparable and over decades Durkan was Hume's closest political confidante. They understood each other, shared a similar political analysis and had the same attitude to public service.

Durkan began working in the Derry office alongside Pat Hume and Denis Haughey, who assisted John on European matters in his role as an MEP. Durkan's job move changed his life on a professional and personal level. He met Jackie Green, who also worked in the office and had been recruited by Pat Hume in the summer of 1983. Mark and Jackie started dating and later married. Durkan, who had a wry sense of humour, would later tease John Hume: 'You know this ambition you have about creating relationships. Me and Jackie is the only one.'[4]

Durkan took to his new life within the SDLP with enthusiasm. He began to draft press releases and write policy submissions, and he was a sounding board for Hume when he wanted to discuss proposals. The MP also started to trust his new assistant with his private thoughts and Durkan was soon regarded as a loyal aide who could be discreet and diplomatic when required. They became quite a team and Durkan quickly worked out when his boss wanted to chat and when he preferred to be left alone: 'You kind of knew when he was talking or when he wasn't talking. You just got that sense as to whether he wanted conversation or not. But I found him very open in that sense.'[5]

With the party still abstaining from the Assembly, Hume and his colleagues invested much time and effort in the deliberations of the New Ireland Forum. Dozens of submissions were taken and Hume was determined that ultimately there would be an agreed nationalist approach to Northern Ireland. There was a lot of focus in their deliberations on how unionist concerns could be accommodated and how unionists could have a sense of security in a new Ireland. The Protestant churches gave evidence to the Forum and, although the unionist parties boycotted the deliberations, both Michael and Christopher McGimpsey, who were UUP members, did attend. Between May 1983 and the spring of 1984, the Forum met 40 times under the chairmanship of Professor Colm Ó hEocha, who was a distinguished academic from Galway.

Inevitably there were tensions and differences behind the scenes as the final report was being drafted. Understandably, as the leader of Fianna Fáil, Charlie Haughey wanted the document to outline traditional nationalist thinking and fully endorse a unitary state model as the only way Ireland could be united. He wanted this idea to be given priority and insisted the words needed to be unambiguous. Haughey saw himself as the 'keeper of the flame' for nationalism. After all, he was leading a movement that billed itself 'The Republican Party'. When it came to seeing a unitary state as the most viable option, Haughey had support from Seamus Mallon on that issue whereas Dick Spring, Garret FitzGerald and John Hume were a little more circumspect. They wanted a general endorsement of Irish unity but preferred a more open-ended approach. The divisions delayed matters and raised the real possibility of two very different conclusions – a minority report and a majority report – which was an outcome Hume was desperate to avoid. He wanted agreement across the four parties and knew it was crucial to present a united front.

Whilst Hume personally got on well with Spring and FitzGerald, his relationship with Haughey was often fraught, as Dick Spring recalled:

> They had quite a tense relationship. I don't think Haughey liked John. John was getting a lot of limelight in relation to Northern politics. You know, Charlie didn't particularly like sharing the limelight with anybody for that matter. So their relationship was quite tense. Whereas I think Garret and I were much easier. You know, I think we were on the same plane.[6]

Haughey's tetchiness with Hume extended to other parts of their relationship. Eamon Hanna recalls how, as SDLP general secretary, he was often tasked by Hume to contact political leaders before the annual party conference. It was traditional that messages of goodwill and solidarity from other party leaders would be read out at the conference. Hanna recalls how on one occasion Haughey had repeatedly failed to respond to a request for a supportive message. With the deadline just minutes away, Hanna was asked by an anxious Hume to ring Haughey at his Abbeville home in Kinsealy in Dublin. Hanna recalls how he did not want to make the call but was pressured by Hume, who was getting more and more stressed, to do it.

With the conference about to start, Hanna lifted the phone and dialled the Dublin number. Hume had put him in a difficult position: 'I knew I was getting a hospital pass.' Hanna recalls what Haughey said: 'Who are you, you little fucker?' Hanna remembers faltering slightly ('I have a bit of a stammer'): 'I am the General Secretary of the SDLP and Mr Hume was wondering if you have a message.' Haughey then gave Hanna a brutal one-line answer: 'There will be no fucking message.'[7]

With no endorsement from the Fianna Fáil leader, Eamon Hanna improvised and invented a message purporting to come from Haughey. It was an anodyne statement of support which spared Hume's blushes. It was read out to the party faithful, who were oblivious to Eamon Hanna's work of fiction. It did not go completely unnoticed though, as one watching journalist wanted to read the statement afterwards. Hanna simply told the reporter it was not available and the conversation ended.

When the Forum Report was finally published in 1984, it detailed a number of possible options for how a future Ireland could look. One possibility was the creation of a united Ireland with one government. Another option was a federal solution where the North retained a regional government within an all-island structure. The third option was the idea of joint authority in Northern Ireland, where responsibility for governing would rest jointly with the Irish and British governments. The Forum participants also agreed to be open to other views which may contribute to 'political development'. This was a brief line in the report but a significant one.[8]

Hume knew that how the Forum's conclusions were reported in the press and interpreted by the wider public would be crucial. In his press remarks Charlie Haughey emphasised the 'unitary state' option and made it clear that this was his preferred way forward. It meant that Hume, Spring and FitzGerald had to mitigate this position and constantly state that there were other options on the table. Predictably unionists rejected the report. They saw it as one-sided and a direct threat to their Britishness. In their eyes, this was just a group of nationalist-inclined parties predictably calling for a united Ireland. In his comments, Hume insisted that the British and Irish governments needed to come together and have an open discussion on where political solutions could be found. Hume then underwent a punishing schedule touring television and radio studios to sell the Forum's message.

Sinn Féin's Danny Morrison remembers sparring with him:

> I debated Hume on television. It's funny the things you notice. He had dandruff on his shoulders and had a seven o'clock shadow not having had time to shave, his shoes were scuffed and he looked exhausted. I think he had been doing lots of meetings about the Forum Report all over the country and I felt some sympathy for him – although I didn't show it.[9]

Morrison and Hume saw a lot of each other in 1984 as they were candidates in the European election. As expected, Hume was re-elected as an MEP along with Ian Paisley and John Taylor. Paisley topped the poll and once again proved he was the main voice of unionism. Hume polled an extra 11,000 votes but his share of the poll dropped, undoubtedly due to the performance of Danny Morrison.

As republicans worked on their political strategy, the IRA was planning an audacious attack for later in the year. In October, the prime minister, Margaret Thatcher, was attending the Conservative Party conference and narrowly escaped injury when the IRA bombed the Grand Hotel in Brighton. She had been in her bathroom two minutes before it was wrecked by the blast which killed five people and injured dozens.

The next day, speaking at the party conference, the new Northern Ireland Secretary, Douglas Hurd, rejected the Forum's proposals and said the plans were unacceptable, including the idea of joint authority. Hurd's position was reiterated bluntly by Margaret Thatcher after she had talks with Taoiseach Garret FitzGerald at Chequers.

The prime minister, whose view was most likely hardened by the bombing in Brighton, said she could not support any of the Forum's conclusions: 'A united Ireland was one solution. That is out. A second solution was confederation of the two states. That is out. A third solution was joint authority. That is out. That is a derogation from sovereignty.'[10]

This became known as Thatcher's 'Out, Out, Out' speech and her comments, not surprisingly, angered the signatories to the Forum Report. Garret FitzGerald was furious and found the remarks 'gratuitously offensive'.[11]

Hume was also angered by Thatcher's dismissal of the report. He had come up with the idea, he had nurtured it and worked at it and felt Mrs Thatcher had rubbished the Forum's work in seconds. Hume could not contain his rage: 'The intransigence and extremism of Margaret Thatcher has fuelled the anger and bitterness upon which violence in Ireland feeds. There is now no credible political force on the unionist side in Northern Ireland which will accept anything short of majority rule, or which will agree to any form of political recognition of the Irish identity of the minority.'[12]

Even though the Forum's recommendations had been completely rejected by the British government, Hume was not completely despondent. He felt the initiative had still brought a degree of positivity to a debate that had become sterile. Hume was delighted the Forum had brought a series of parties together; he felt it had crystallised thinking and had hopefully reinforced the view in Dublin and London that further dialogue was needed to improve Anglo-Irish relations.

Although London had ruled out any prospect of joint authority, it was clear that there were at least signs of understanding in Downing Street that Dublin needed a greater say in the affairs of Northern Ireland. Hume continued to articulate the view that politicians in the Dáil and Westminster had a degree of responsibility to Northern Ireland and needed to be more proactive. The SDLP leader also turned his attention to the United States and through his allies known as the 'Four Horsemen' began to try to influence the White House. President Reagan, who came to power in 1981, had previously said very little about Northern Ireland, but through the work of the 'Four Horsemen'– Tip O'Neill, Ted Kennedy, Hugh Carey and Daniel Moynihan – the issue was now moving up the presidential agenda. Reagan had a close relationship with Mrs Thatcher and when the two met in December 1984, he raised the matter of Anglo-Irish relations and it seems his discussion had some influence.

In January 1985, things started to change in a way that heartened John Hume. He met the taoiseach, Garret FitzGerald, and after their discussions, he was invited to meet Mrs Thatcher in Downing Street. Hume found a very different Mrs Thatcher to the one who had so bluntly dismissed the Forum's recommendations some months earlier. The prime minister listened to the SDLP leader and appeared to be genuinely conciliatory and have a better understanding of some of the issues Hume was raising.

Some days later, London revealed a series of proposals aimed at improving British–Irish relations. A body known as the Anglo-Irish Conference would be established, which would look at issues of mutual interest such as human rights, policing and security. This was the first time the UK had publicly committed to an Irish government having a say in the affairs of Northern Ireland.

Behind the scenes much was changing, and there was dialogue between senior civil servants in Dublin and London. Hume was trusted by the Irish government and kept informed of how contacts were developing. Michael Lillis, who worked for the Irish Department of Foreign Affairs, spoke to John Hume regularly:

> The only individual or party or anything of that sort that was briefed constantly by the Irish government over those two years was John Hume. And he was briefed on a confidential basis and never once, by the way, betrayed that confidence, which created great problems between himself and other members of the party at that time like Seamus Mallon who was a very wonderful guy. But he found it difficult that he wasn't being included in the briefing we were providing.[13]

Seán Donlon was another Irish diplomat who was heavily involved in the behind-the-scenes discussions: 'At the beginning of those talks we told John Hume what we were trying to do. I got the impression that about that time he entered into some sort of contact, either direct or indirect, with Gerry Adams.' Donlon's sense was right. He had known Hume for years and spent many days and nights in his company. He knew how he operated and what he was interested in: 'I think there was no phase in John's political life when he didn't keep his eyes and ears open for the possibility of talking to the IRA.'[14]

Hume wanted to talk directly to the IRA. He used an interview with BBC Radio Ulster to make his approach, whilst he was appearing on air with the Sinn Féin president, Gerry Adams. The SDLP and Sinn Féin were about to lock horns in electoral battle later in the year during the local elections and Adams wanted to have talks about political cooperation. Hume used the opportunity to ask for talks with the IRA Army Council rather than its political wing.

Later, speaking on RTÉ radio, Hume made it clear why he wanted to meet the IRA: 'I am going to them as the leader of the majority of the nationalist community in Northern Ireland to ask them to end their campaign of violence and say that violence is destroying the communities both north and south. I am going to confront these people face to face.' Hume was later quoted as saying that he wanted to meet the IRA rather than Sinn Féin – because the IRA run the show: 'Why meet the monkey when you can meet the organ grinder?'[15]

Even though Hume thought a direct approach to the IRA was worth exploring, others believed he was being foolhardy and would be used by the armed group for publicity purposes. His offer to meet the IRA angered both the Irish and British governments. The taoiseach, Garret FitzGerald, and the Northern Ireland secretary, Douglas Hurd, made their opposition public. Hurd was particularly concerned that Hume's intervention could jeopardise inter-party talks, although Charlie Haughey, the Fianna Fáil leader, was supportive and expressed backing for the move.

Hume knew he was taking a risk, but he believed he had nothing to lose. Despite the criticism, he persevered with his offer to meet with IRA figures and he was contacted in late February 1985 with a view to setting up a conversation. Denis Bradley was involved in organising this meeting along with Brendan Duddy, who was a businessman from Derry. Duddy had previously acted as an intermediary between the IRA and the UK government, and he was keen to advance discussions.

Denis Bradley remembers what happened back in 1985: 'I actually drove Hume across the border. Duddy then drove him further, and he was picked up and driven around for an hour or two and then brought to a house and kept in a house for a day.'[16]

Hume met three representatives of the IRA, including one person who had escaped from the Maze prison in 1983. There was a delay to proceedings and, finally, the IRA said they were ready to talk to him but wanted to film the encounter. The proposal to film proceedings came out of the blue and had not been discussed beforehand. Hume objected and made it clear that he did not want the encounter recorded: 'I said no, I didn't come for that; I came for a private meeting and left. I didn't know why they were wanting to do that. I presume their reason was that they would want to then show it to all their individual members.'[17]

During Hume's absence from Derry, Denis Bradley visited the family home to see Pat and reassure her. He told her that John would be safe as he was convinced he would not come to any harm. He was furious when he heard how the meeting had gone: 'I was so angry with the IRA, the way they treated it. I thought it was atrocious.'[18]

Hume never got to meet the IRA Army Council. It was an embarrassing end to an initiative that he had high hopes for. He knew his political enemies would use the incident as a reason to not trust the IRA. It was a clumsy affair and badly handled by the IRA. The episode left Hume open to criticism even though he could still insist that he bravely tried to reach out, which is more than many other politicians were prepared to do. So was this a missed opportunity? Had Hume begun a proper dialogue with the IRA in 1985, how different would life have been in Northern Ireland in the 1990s? What we do know is that Hume was not put off by this false start and he remained determined to persevere with his attempts to end violence.

Looking back, the former Sinn Féin president Gerry Adams says the IRA made an error in wanting to film the Hume meeting. In an interview for this book, he said: 'I think that was unfortunate. That again was almost a clash of two cultures, you know, on the back of John saying, I would rather talk to the organ grinder. Well, who was going to speak for the organ grinder?' Adams can see why there was a desire to have the meeting recorded but thinks it was a mistake: 'It was probably ill-advised at the time.'[19]

As 1985 continued, diplomats in London and Dublin worked together in drawing up documents aimed at creating a new accord between the British government and the Irish administration. It was all done behind the scenes and in great secrecy. Hume was one of a handful of people who knew exactly what was being discussed. Even members of Mrs Thatcher's cabinet were kept in the dark. Hume, now trusted by Dublin and seen as a logical thinker, was central to the discussions and helped to advise Garret FitzGerald and the Irish civil service team. Away from the shuttle diplomacy, there was campaigning to be done in May 1985. On the ground, Hume saw his party's electoral share go up in the council elections, although the party lost two seats. Sinn Féin's rise continued with the party securing 59 seats.

Over the summer, the discussions between London and Dublin intensified and in November the political landscape changed utterly when the Anglo-Irish Agreement was unveiled. In the state drawing room of Hillsborough Castle in County Down, Margaret Thatcher and Garret FitzGerald endorsed a deal that would transform British–Irish relations. It was the most dramatic political development in Northern Ireland's history since its creation in 1921.

Both governments agreed to work together to promote peace and stability in a spirit of cooperation. There was agreement that there would be no change to the status of Northern Ireland without the consent of a majority. That was a key statement and one which Hume hoped would give unionists confidence and offer an incentive for them to negotiate with nationalists. The agreement also created a joint ministerial conference of British and Irish ministers to be set up, supported by a secretariat at Maryfield outside Belfast. Both administrations agreed to work together to combat terrorism and examine issues including human rights, policing and the administration of justice. The accord did not mean that Northern Ireland was now subject to joint authority, but it gave the Irish government an enormous say in areas of public life over which before it had little or no influence. It marked a dramatic change of attitude from Margaret Thatcher, who had bluntly rejected the Forum proposals just a year earlier.

As ever, in the world of Northern Ireland politics, the reactions were predictable and at very different ends of the scale. Nationalists generally welcomed the move whilst unionists were incandescent with rage, promising protests and mass demonstrations. Peter Robinson, the DUP deputy leader, accused the prime minister of signing away Northern Ireland's place in the UK, declaring that: 'We are on the window ledge of the union.'[20]

In contrast, Hume, whose handiwork was all over the agreement, praised the work of the two governments – he saw the Hillsborough Accord as a way to create a more peaceful society. He knew it was far from perfect and inevitably was full of aspirations but he felt it was important to have the premiers in London and Dublin working together. In a sense, Hume felt the deal was not a solution in itself but offered the framework for a solution: 'The Anglo-Irish Agreement was a major step, the first major step in the peace process because from that point onwards both governments remained very close in working together and the Joint Secretariat did the same.'[21]

Hume had succeeded in getting the two governments to work together and he had delivered what he believed was an 'Irish dimension', albeit one which had limited powers and influence. By having official Irish involvement in Northern Ireland, Hume believed the days of a 'unionist veto' were over and unionists would now be encouraged to negotiate with other parties: 'The Agreement has taken nothing away from the unionists. It has simply created a framework for equality for the first time.'[22]

Through his discussions with both London and Dublin, Hume believed he had helped to identify what was holding back political progress in Northern Ireland and now he had created a framework for finding a solution. His view was not shared by everybody within the broader nationalist family. Sinn Féin viewed it simply as a sell-out to the true ideals of Irish republicanism, and in Dublin, the Fianna Fáil leader Charlie Haughey condemned Garret FitzGerald's role in the deal and argued that he had sold nationalists short. He told the Dáil that the agreement gave 'legitimacy to a British administration'.[23]

It was a hasty move which he compounded by sending Brian Lenihan, a Fianna Fáil TD and trusted colleague, to Washington in an attempt to rally opposition to the agreement. Lenihan went to see important Irish Americans, including the 'Four Horsemen', with the aim of influencing the White House. Haughey's ill-fated plan to turn Irish America against the agreement failed at the first hurdle. Mark Durkan was in Hume's Derry office when the phone rang. It was a familiar voice on the line from Washington: 'I can remember in John's office getting the call from Teddy Kennedy saying what is going on here? Why is this man coming to see me against the agreement and all the rest of it? I was having to explain and promise to him that I would get word to John.'[24]

Hume made some transatlantic calls but there was nothing to worry about. Those who Lenihan went to see ignored his pitch and continued to take their advice from Hume. Lenihan had a wasted journey. The attempt by Haughey spectacularly backfired and Dick Spring says the Fianna Fáil leader's move was seen by many as treacherous: 'I personally think that was one of the biggest political betrayals in my lifetime. You know a lot of work had been done. We had made significant progress. And in fairness, I think the "Four Horsemen" in Washington gave Brian a fairly cold reception.'[25]

Haughey had tried to play the Foyle MP at his own game but he was no match for him. It was clear after years of work and lobbying that influential Irish Americans took their cue from the SDLP leader. The Lenihan trip simply highlighted the extent of Hume's influence and demonstrated how his relationship with power brokers in Washington was built on firm foundations. Back in Northern Ireland, unionists were trying to come to terms with the agreement, and their campaign of opposition and disobedience developed in a number of ways. Tens of thousands of protestors took to the streets of Belfast and unionist-controlled councils refused to strike rates. The slogan 'Ulster Says No' was launched. Banners were placed on council buildings where unionists were in the majority and cooperation with Northern Ireland Office ministers was withdrawn.

The unionist parties then decided that their MPs at Westminster should resign their seats. The by-elections would serve as a referendum on the agreement. In principle, it seemed like a clever tactic for unionists to galvanise opposition and create publicity, but in reality, the move proved costly. In January 1986, the SDLP deputy leader Seamus Mallon took the seat of Newry and Armagh and ousted Official Unionist MP Jim Nicholson. In South Down, Eddie McGrady nearly toppled the maverick unionist Enoch Powell.

Mallon's success delighted the SDLP. It gave the party another voice at Westminster and took some of the pressure off Hume, who had been the party's lone parliamentarian. The strength of McGrady's vote in South Down also gave supporters hope that at the next election he could outpoll Enoch Powell and they could gain another MP. Throughout 1986 unionists continued their opposition to the agreement and held a day of action. On the streets the atmosphere was tense and there was violence and extra troops were drafted in. Hume was steadfast in his support for the London–Dublin deal, insisting it was the right way forward. Despite unionist opposition, he believed he had helped to create a political space for future agreement between the Northern Ireland parties. He told the *Observer* newspaper that he 'always expected a furious unionist reaction to the agreement, but the Protestant boil had to be lanced. Mrs Thatcher is the right person in the right place at the right time and they are recognising that she will not be broken.'[26]

Hume's words are worthy of closer examination. He talked about the 'Protestant boil' being lanced. To some, that language will sound inflammatory and appears to jar with Hume's aims of reconciliation and agreement. Dan Keenan thinks it sent out the wrong message to unionists:

> Certainly on more than one occasion he refers to them in a pathological sense. That they needed to be educated, the boil needed to be lanced. They needed to be this or another, they needed to be taken down a peg or two and that's all done in very superior language.[27]

Keenan thinks Hume's remarks were sending out mixed messages:

> You know on the one hand, here is the guy making a single transferable speech for the need of cooperation and getting on together on this and the other. On separate occasions he would almost demonise them, to be quite honest with you, and talk about them in those terms. Which just does not make sense. You can't denigrate somebody and yet insist that you need their agreement.[28]

Was Hume speaking out of frustration when he suggested that the 'Protestant boil' needed to be lanced? It is interesting that rather than saying 'the unionist boil needs to be lanced', he uses the word Protestant, perhaps seeing it as interchangeable with the term unionist. Mark Durkan accepts that Hume's phraseology upset some people but he insists he was trying to convince unionists to change. He thinks his leader was saying to unionists that: 'If they want to have power again it is going to be on a different basis than they ever had it before. And they are going to have to agree to share that power.'[29]

In the mid-1980s, unionists were distrustful of Hume and were convinced he had little or no interest in reaching a settlement with them that involved devolution at Stormont. Lord Empey, who would go on to lead the Ulster Unionist Party, thinks Hume was not interested in a local assembly:

> I think many of us felt that into the 1980s and John basically was not interested in re-establishing some kind of institution in Belfast and he saw things moving well beyond. And, of course, at that particular stage, the violence was really terrible.[30]

Hume's analysis was that the violence from republicans was hampering the dream of a united Ireland and distorting the cause of nationalism. He was pleased that the two governments were now working together and he had backing from Europe and the United States. However, he saw that as only part of the solution. He felt that if the violence ended, political progress would flow. The key was a ceasefire and that required serious talking.

14

LET'S TALK

'What the fuck is going on?'
Journalist Denis Murray on being told
John Hume has met Gerry Adams

At his office in Derry, John Hume handed a letter to Mark Durkan and asked him to read the contents. The document was long and detailed. It had been sent by Father Alec Reid, who was part of the Redemptorist order at Clonard Monastery on the Falls Road. Brought up in County Tipperary, he had been working in Belfast since the 1960s and was a close contact of the Sinn Féin president, Gerry Adams. Reid had a track record as a peace broker and had intervened in the past to halt infighting amongst the different wings of the IRA. He wanted Hume and Adams to meet to discuss matters of mutual interest and to examine how they could advance the cause of nationalism and also work towards ending the violence.

Gerry Adams says the letter, sent in 1986, was about trying to find a solution:

> It was an argument for an alternative way forward. And also, although Father Reid might not have written this down, his strong view was that I was genuine and serious that if such an alternative could be developed that then it would be embraced by republicans.[1]

Father Reid had previously been to see Charlie Haughey at his home in

Kinsealy outside Dublin. He asked the Fianna Fáil leader to consider meeting Gerry Adams and after some thought Haughey had said no. However, he asked his adviser Martin Mansergh to keep in contact with Father Reid. Mansergh, a former civil servant who had worked for the Irish Department of Foreign Affairs, had been headhunted by Haughey to work for Fianna Fáil.

Disappointed by Haughey's response not to meet Adams, Father Reid then turned his attention to the SDLP. The Belfast priest had originally reached out to Seamus Mallon because he felt he would get a better reception from him than John Hume. Gerry Adams says there was a logic to first approaching the SDLP deputy leader: 'Seamus Mallon had the reputation of being greener than John Hume. So they pursued Seamus.'[2]

However, the attempts to get Mallon involved proved difficult, as Adams recalls:

> Seamus didn't respond positively, put it off. Said he would meet and so on and so forth. And in fact when Father Reid put it to him that he was thinking of meeting with John Hume. Seamus said look, don't be doing that yet. Leave me a bit of time. But anyway, eventually Seamus said no, he was not going to do the meeting.[3]

Father Alec Reid and Father Des Wilson went to see Seamus Mallon at his home in Markethill and asked him to have talks with Adams. The Sinn Féin president also wrote to him asking him for a meeting but Mallon thought this was a matter for John Hume and was not sure 'what use it would serve'.[4] Father Reid and Father Gerry Reynolds then sent a letter on Clonard Monastery headed notepaper to John Hume but the invitation got mislaid and never reached the SDLP leader. Another letter was drafted and this one, sent on 19 May 1986, found its way into John Hume's hands. Hume responded immediately and phoned the monastery, and on 21 May he met Father Alec Reid, Father Gerry Reynolds and Father Seamus Enright.[5]

After the meeting with Hume, Reid had discussions separately with

Adams to update him on how those discussions had gone and then wrote to Hume on 3 June summarising where he thought matters were. The tone of the letter to Hume was positive and said Adams was interested in continuing the dialogue 'but he would prefer to do so directly rather than indirectly because he is convinced that direct dialogue is crucial to real progress'.[6]

The two letter-writers then quoted Adams saying, 'It was wrong to say that Sinn Féin were identical with the IRA in their approach to the situation or that Sinn Féin as a political party were completely dependent on the IRA.'[7] Reid and Reynolds outlined the issues facing the leaders and made it clear how discussions could change the political and security climate: 'A meeting between you could open the way to a dialogue which could see the creation of a political alternative to the armed struggle.'[8]

It was suggested that the church could play a role in the discussions and could issue the invitation for face-to-face discussions. It was prepared to offer the Clonard Monastery in Belfast as a venue for talks. The other venue that was offered was Lourdes Hospital in Drogheda where church representatives had previously met Sinn Féin officials. Father Reid also told Hume that Adams felt positive about the contacts that had begun and that he rated the SDLP leader highly. Reid said he thinks Hume is 'head and shoulders above any constitutional politician, he knows of anywhere, especially in Ireland'.[9]

It was clear Hume was very interested in beginning a dialogue with Gerry Adams if the conditions were right. He discussed the approach with Durkan, who agreed in principle that Hume was right to meet and have talks with the Sinn Féin leader. However, Durkan told his boss that he was worried about the timing:

> You probably can't do this before an election. There is going to be a Westminster election this year. If you have talks before that, what if it was leaked, what if those talks turn into a demand for an electoral pact and all the rest of it?[10]

Hume had trained Durkan well, and the young assistant was able to pinpoint instantly what potential problems lay ahead if dialogue began immediately. Adams and Hume did meet in advance of the election and in September 1986 had discussions, which the Sinn Féin leader recalls were 'friendly and constructive'.[11] This was a private affair well away from the gaze of journalists and only known to a handful of people. Yet it was a seismic moment in Irish history. It marked the beginning of a new relationship between the two men – the start of a dialogue that would last many years and would lead to the Hume–Adams talks.

There was much political change in the air at this time in other quarters. The autumn of 1986 was an important time for republicans. In October it was reported that the IRA had held a convention and agreed to remove the ban on members taking seats in the Irish parliament or supporting candidates who wanted to sit in the Dáil. Sinn Féin held its Ard Fheis and voted to end the policy of abstentionism, which resulted in Ruairí Ó Brádaigh and others leaving the party to set up Republican Sinn Féin.

By 1987 the talk in the parliaments in Dublin and London was all about who would win power. In Dublin, Charlie Haughey was the new taoiseach and had replaced Garret FitzGerald whose coalition government had fallen. At Westminster all the parties were on an election footing, and with a June poll on the horizon, Sinn Féin unveiled a document entitled 'A Scenario for Peace'. The publication said the party wanted to 'create conditions which will lead to a permanent cessation of hostilities' and called for a date for a British withdrawal which would be supervised by the United Nations.

As the election drew closer, there was no let-up in the violence. One of Northern Ireland's top judges, Lord Justice Gibson, was killed along with his wife as they drove across the border. In May, the undercover battle between the security services and the IRA took a dramatic turn.

Eight IRA men were killed during an attack at Loughgall RUC station in County Armagh. The SAS knew of the operation in advance and were waiting for the men to arrive. The eight, who were members of the East Tyrone IRA, were shot and killed as they approached the station with a 200-pound bomb in the bucket of a hijacked digger. A civilian died after being caught in the crossfire. The attack marked the heaviest loss the IRA had ever suffered in one incident.

That same evening, Pat Hume and her daughter Mo were at the family home in West End Park in Derry when it was attacked by petrol bombers. Mo, who was a teenager, remembers looking out of the window and watching as petrol bombs started hitting the house. It was a frightening image. As the fire took hold, she recalled how neighbours came to help:

> Because we lived in a street without gardens, nobody had a hose. One guy up the street had a hose but it was like one of those water features, you know this kind of pathetic thing. So he is standing waiting for the fire brigade, with this kind of trickle of water to try and put out a fire in my mum's car and the whole of the house was in flames. And our next-door neighbour starts ringing up to try and get Martin McGuinness's phone number to complain and could not get it. In the middle of it all, Martin Cowley rings up. Martin was a journalist with the *Irish Times*.[12]

Cowley was unaware of the attack and had rung the Hume household to get a quote from John following the attack on Loughgall. He remembers Pat Hume answering the phone: 'Pat's voice was not the usual calm, restrained, soft voice. It was this controlled sort of panic, excited and her tone had changed completely. Martin, she said, either they are throwing petrol bombs at the house or they are throwing things at the house.'[13]

Cowley then drove to the house and recalls speaking to Pat Hume: 'It was terrifying for her. Normally Pat would be the essence of calm and elegance and propriety but she was very upset that night.' Mo remembers how the family were shocked and traumatised: 'I think that was probably the worst.'[14]

John Hume was nearly 200 miles away at an event in Waterford when he heard about the attack. He was upset and told the *Irish Times* of his 'distress'.[15] The petrol bombing was not an isolated event. In other incidents, John Hume's office was destroyed and his car was burnt. Mo Hume recalls another occasion when an angry crowd gathered outside the family home and they seemed intent on breaking in: 'So we locked the front door that night, the double doors. And I remember saying to my dad, "They are coming to get you. You know they are coming to get you." And he was very reassuring.'[16]

Understandably the attacks on the house made an impact on Hume and he confided in friends that he could be seriously injured or killed. Paul Arthur remembers one incident in Derry:

> He had a concern he was going to be shot. I remember driving with him from the Everglades Hotel to his home and there was a guy on a motorbike. You could see him tense up ... and he did say something to me when the motorbike passed but again, that was not uncommon.[17]

Monica McWilliams says the attacks on the Hume home and his worries about being shot must have impacted his health. She says those who took part in the attacks or threats against him should be held to account for what they did:

> Any husband or father feels they must protect their family, and what was happening to their family was a direct consequence of his actions and words. So it must have made him feel incredibly sad and must have worked on his mind at night. And so from my point of view, those who were breaking his windows and kicking his door and screaming derogatory names at him and his family – they have a lot to answer for.[18]

Dick Spring says many who had private conversations with Hume became aware of the difficulties he faced, and there were real concerns about his safety: 'There were times you definitely had to worry about his health, physical and mental health, because of the pressure he was under.'[19]

Hume was now facing massive personal and political strains. With the approach from Father Reid on hold, he took his party into the general election campaign with high hopes of winning some seats. The results went well and he saw the SDLP vote go up and Sinn Féin's go down. In South Down, Eddie McGrady finally toppled the Official Unionist veteran Enoch Powell and took the SDLP's number of MPs up to three. Powell was a political maverick and had been a Conservative MP in Wolverhampton before coming to Northern Ireland. In 1968 he earned notoriety when he made a controversial speech about immigration and warned that 'rivers of blood' would flow as a result.

Hume felt emboldened by the victory over Powell. With Mallon, McGrady and Hume now all sitting on the green benches at Westminster, the party looked in good shape. Despite polling well in West Belfast, Dr Joe Hendron was unable to defeat Gerry Adams, who remained Sinn Féin's sole MP.

In the summer of 1987, whilst he was on holiday, Hume met Paddy McGrory in Gweedore in Donegal and the two men got chatting about politics. McGrory was a well-known Belfast solicitor who was close to Gerry Adams, and he wanted to impress on the SDLP leader that Sinn Féin was serious about embarking on a peace process. Pat Hume remembers what McGrory said: 'I think he was trying to get through to John that Sinn Féin was anxious to get involved in politics. That would have been the first time that I heard that kind of conversation.'[20]

With the election over, Hume embarked on a series of discussions with Father Reid about a potential meeting with Gerry Adams. The two men met in a variety of locations including Derry and Belfast. Durkan also had contact with Father Reid and travelled to the Clonard Monastery in Belfast to get a sense of how the discussions would develop. As Hume contemplated his forthcoming discussions with Sinn Féin, the IRA's campaign of violence was continuing unchecked. In November, 11 people were killed in Enniskillen on Remembrance Sunday, in a bombing that drew condemnation from across the world. It was a horrific act and

Gerry Adams would later write that the bomb 'not only robbed 11 civilians of their lives, but it left the IRA open to accusations of callousness and indifference'.[21]

By the end of the year, a face-to-face encounter between Adams and Hume was agreed in principle. The Foyle MP then decided to inform his colleagues. Seán Farren remembers being at party headquarters in Belfast in late 1987 when Hume asked him to remain behind.

> He told me he was in discussion with Gerry Adams and that they had both agreed to widen out participation to include some other members of each party. And John was inviting me, Austin Currie and Seamus Mallon to be part of that. I agreed with it.[22]

In January 1988, Hume was ready to meet Gerry Adams. Before he travelled to see the Sinn Féin president, he called into SDLP headquarters in Belfast and chatted to party press officer Dan Keenan, who remembers their conversation:

> 'Listen,' he says, 'I am going off shortly and I have got a meeting with Gerry Adams.' And my jaw hit the floor. And he says, 'I am not telling you any more than that. But do nothing and whenever the meeting is over I will come back and we will have a statement.' We sort of nodded like goldfish you know and off he went.[23]

John Hume and Gerry Adams got on well in this encounter. Adams says there was a rapport: 'I think we both came to appreciate quite quickly that we were both serious about trying to sort this out.'[24]

Hume used the occasion to try to convince Adams that by signing the Anglo-Irish Agreement the UK government was now neutral on the future of Northern Ireland, which meant that the violence should end. That night, Hume dictated a statement to his colleague, Dan Keenan, and it was issued to the media. It was an announcement that declared the two political leaders had positive talks and would meet again. Within two minutes of sending out the statement, Keenan's phone rang. It was Denis Murray, from the BBC. Murray, a seasoned observer of Northern Ireland politics, was blunt: 'Dan, What the fuck is going on?' Keenan could tell Murray very little: 'This was the first anybody knew this was happening. It completely blindsided everybody.'[25]

This was a major story, even though this was not their first encounter, since the first set of discussions in 1986 initiated by Father Reid and Father Reynolds was private. The reaction from unionists was quick and damning. The discussions were condemned by both Ian Paisley and Jim Molyneaux and there was criticism from Tom King, the Northern Ireland Secretary. Hume was seen by unionists as a cheerleader for a 'pan-nationalist front'. He was cast as a dangerous bogeyman who wanted to push unionists into a united Ireland by joining forces with Sinn Féin. Hume knew his initiative with Adams needed support within the party and was able to get the backing of senior SDLP members when representatives from the constituencies endorsed the talks.

After Hume and Adams met, it was agreed to widen the discussions and there would be talks involving party delegations. Before the two parties got together each side exchanged letters summing up how the discussions between the two leaders had gone. Then it was time for the party delegations to sit down with each other, and in Belfast, under the watchful eye of Father Reid, that happened.

Sinn Féin's team included Danny Morrison, who had been an internee and was a former Assembly member. At the Sinn Féin Ard Fheis in 1981 he had famously talked about how republicans could achieve a political victory. He told activists: 'Who here really believes we can win a war through the ballot box? But will anyone object if, with a ballot paper in this hand and an Armalite in this hand, we will take power in Ireland?'[26]

At the talks, Morrison was joined by Derry republican Mitchel McLaughlin and Tom Hartley, who was a close friend of Adams and part of Sinn Féin's inner circle. The SDLP delegation included deputy leader Seamus Mallon and Seán Farren, who had served as party chairman.

Farren says Sinn Féin were clearly serious: 'The first thing that struck me was how well prepared they were. They had drawn up a document and they had obviously read through our policy papers. Publicly they were in the public domain anyway, but they were well prepared.'[27]

There was an understandable amount of apprehension on both sides during that first meeting. After all, the two parties were electoral rivals and the large personalities in the room had often traded barbed criticisms of each other. The SDLP team argued that since the signing of the Anglo-Irish Agreement Britain was now neutral on remaining in Ireland. Sinn Féin was not convinced of this argument and insisted that the 1985 accord had not altered London's view of Northern Ireland.

Gerry Adams says his analysis and Hume's were very different and he told him so:

> My first ask of him was that we have to have the right of self-determination. The people of the island should decide. The British were stopping that – the British had their self-interest. And they partitioned the island and they retained control. And that should be ended and people should decide what way they want to go.[28]

Seán Farren says they questioned the Sinn Féin team on whether or not the IRA's campaign of violence was achieving anything:

> We challenged them, with respect to that fundamental question. If you are running a war that goes on for 15/16 years with no sign of achieving, like, the most minimal of objectives that you might have had, surely, somebody must be asking the question, why should we continue with this? Now Adams, of course, had begun to ask those questions.[29]

The two parties exchanged a series of documents in 1988 and the communication started to get detailed and at times intense. Danny Morrison remembers the discussions and he watched John Hume closely:

> The meetings went on for hours except when we broke and had lunch together. There were papers being presented mostly, if I remember correctly, about the definition of national self-determination. We were political opposites but I began to admire his [Hume's] persistence because many times afterwards Gerry would talk to me about yet another incarnation of a discussion paper Hume submitted. Whereas I was not convinced we were going anywhere with these talks.[30]

Adams and Hume had endless discussions on the phone and in person, and Gerry Adams would sometimes ring the SDLP leader at his home. Keen to keep the discussions confidential, Adams was often coy with Hume's children when he rang the Hume household. Hume's daughter Mo remembers as a teenager answering the phone to the Sinn Féin president: 'He phoned up looking for my dad and asked to speak to him and I said, who is speaking and he said I prefer not to give my name. So I just said, "Dad, that is Gerry Adams on the phone for you."'[31]

Mo also recalls Adams calling at the family home in Derry to see her father and it remains the only occasion she has ever met him. Like her telephone call, their brief meeting was an amusing encounter: 'We had one of those telephone tables in the hall and I was kneeling looking up something when he came in our front door and said there is no need to kneel.'[32]

Mo wished at the time she could have struck back with a witty retort but her mouth was frozen from a visit to the dentist. Whilst Adams and Hume continued their discussions and Hume did so with support from colleagues, it was clear that not everyone in the SDLP was happy with the talks. One of the strongest critics was the South Down MP Eddie McGrady. He had been a long-standing opponent of Sinn Féin and was very concerned about what was being discussed and how it would reflect on the party. McGrady had a reputation for being calm and considered and was a strident critic of violence.

As the talks with Sinn Féin continued, Hume invited his colleagues to County Donegal for a get-together and a political discussion. When the issue of the ongoing discussions with Adams was raised, Hume said very little, except to add that when there was something to report he would tell his colleagues. Hume's response infuriated McGrady. Dan Keenan witnessed what happened next: 'McGrady stood up and said it is quite clear that Hume did not have the trust of his senior colleagues. And there was no further role he could have in this meeting and gathered his papers and walked off.' Keenan recalls how others responded: 'All I could see was people saying, Oh Eddie, stay on, stay on. And Eddie was incandescent. From somebody who was very mild-mannered.'[33]

The argument continued outside and then McGrady got into his car and made the long journey back to Downpatrick. Joe Hendron was also at the meeting and witnessed Eddie McGrady leaving: 'I knew Eddie was very annoyed all right, but I thought he was overdoing it a bit. Eddie was a man of great principle.'[34]

He says the McGrady walk-out seemed uncharacteristic. Hours later, Dan Keenan was despatched to go and talk to the South Down MP to see how matters with Hume could be repaired. According to Keenan, after the Donegal argument, their relationship was never the same: 'Hume would not have been very subtle in his dislike of what McGrady had said and done as a result of that and his lack of trust in him. And I don't think the two were particularly close after that.'[35]

Margaret Ritchie, who would later become an MP, Stormont minister and party leader, initially worked for Eddie McGrady as his constituency manager. She diplomatically recalled his relationship with Hume:

> There would have been probably tension and I do recall that. I suppose working for Eddie I could sense that. I was able to sense that tension at the time. But it was also managing, shall we say, a constituency workload and a parliamentary workload in such a way that didn't allow the other stuff to impinge.[36]

McGrady was not a lone voice; others within the party expressed doubts about the ongoing discussions with Gerry Adams, and the critics included the deputy leader, Seamus Mallon. Joe Hendron says Mallon made his feelings known at the meeting in Donegal with Hume. Mallon was worried about the effect the relationship with Sinn Féin would have on his own party:

> My strong view was that, as a political party, the SDLP would come out of this arrangement badly. I made it clear to John that I fully supported him in his efforts to get an end to violence but that, as a political party, we had to protect ourselves.[37]

In principle, Denis Haughey supported Hume's talks with Sinn Féin but like others he did have reservations about the discussions: 'I have to be honest and say that I did. But I thought it was the right way to go. But I did not trust the Provos. I thought, "They will betray us."'[38]

If some figures in the SDLP were at odds with Hume's strategy they did not keep their concerns private. John Alderdice, who became leader of the Alliance Party in 1987, also became aware of discontent amongst leading party figures including Seamus Mallon and Eddie McGrady: 'At various stages, they all intimated to me their profound difficulty with the whole process and the fact they were actually involved in it. It was a particularly John thing. It was very much a John-driven thing.'[39]

By late summer, it was clear that there would be no agreement between Sinn Féin and the SDLP and in September 1988 the formal discussions ended. Both party leaders said they were disappointed that there was not more common ground, but they vowed to carry on with the contacts they had made and talk again. In October, there was a fresh initiative aimed at breaking Northern Ireland's political log-jam which took place in unusual surroundings.

Representatives from four parties, the UUP, DUP, Alliance and the SDLP, met in Duisburg in West Germany to hold a series of behind-the-scenes discussions. The politicians were hosted by a Lutheran clergyman,

Eberhard Spiecker, and Father Alec Reid also attended the talks, which lasted for two days. Much of the private discussions examined the workings of the Anglo-Irish Agreement and the demands of unionists that it should be suspended. The SDLP took a very different approach, arguing that the agreement had to remain in place and that inter-party talks should take place with the agreement operational. The Duisburg discussions did not lead to a breakthrough and remained secret for some time until BBC correspondent Denis Murray broke the story in early 1989.

Politically in Northern Ireland, things remained stagnant and the IRA's campaign of violence continued, as did that of the loyalist groups. Despite the bombings and shootings, John Hume and Gerry Adams continued to meet. Hume's private conversations with Adams did not prevent him from publicly attacking the IRA. In November 1988, SDLP members gathered at the Europa Hotel in Belfast for their annual conference.

The city centre venue held the unenviable title of being the most bombed hotel in the world and, in his keynote speech, Hume was blunt and direct. He rounded on the IRA:

> They are more Irish than the rest of us, they believe. They are the pure master race of Irish. They are the keepers of the holy grail of the nation. That deep-seated attitude, married to their method, has all the hallmarks of undiluted fascism. They have all the other hallmarks of the fascist, the scapegoat. The Brits are to blame for everything, even their own atrocities. They know better than the rest of us.[40]

The SDLP leader also had words for his political rivals:

> Leaders of Sinn Féin have been saying recently that the nationalist nightmare has not ended. They are dead right because they and their military wing are the major part of the nightmare. There is not a single injustice in Northern Ireland today that justifies the taking of a single human life.[41]

The main political activity of 1989 focused on the district council elections and the elections to the European Parliament. Both polls were good results for the SDLP. In the council elections, the party's vote went up by just over 3 percentage points and in the European vote Hume was re-elected as MEP, with a personal vote that was higher than the party had ever achieved. He was returned along with the Reverend Ian Paisley, who topped the poll, and Jim Nicholson who replaced John Taylor.

Perhaps the most important political change came in July 1989, with the arrival of Peter Brooke as Northern Ireland secretary, when he succeeded Tom King. Brooke had an Irish background and his family was connected to Sir Basil Brooke, who was the first prime minister of Northern Ireland. These unionist links meant some in the nationalist community wondered if the new incumbent was coming to Northern Ireland with preconceived ideas and bias. It soon became clear that he was a thoughtful and well-read politician who understood the complexities of Irish history. With the political process in Northern Ireland at a standstill, his arrival managed to change the atmosphere. Hume met Brooke regularly and the two men got on well.

The SDLP leader thought he was unlike many of the previous politicians sent from London as he had an understanding of Northern Ireland and a desire to find a solution:

> He would be one of the Secretaries of State that I would single out as an outstanding Secretary of State and one that was committed to doing everything he could to solve the problem. And he was one who had very clear views and a clear understanding of the problem.[42]

Hume began to persuade Brooke that he should reach out to republicans and on 9 November 1990 he made a speech in London which was directly aimed at Sinn Féin and the IRA. The intervention was aimed at changing the narrative. Brooke used language that fitted Hume's analysis of the political situation. His words were aimed at convincing the IRA that the armed conflict should end and politics should prevail. Brooke's speech was thoughtful and carefully scripted and the most newsworthy line came at the end of his address when he said: 'The British government has no selfish, strategic, or economic interest in Northern Ireland.'[43]

Now Brooke was speaking Hume's language. He confirmed that Hume's analysis of the Anglo-Irish Agreement was correct. For his part, Hume hoped this was a game changer and republicans would now accept that the British government was serious about advancing the political process. As the local parties continued to digest Brooke's London speech, events at Westminster took a dramatic turn as Margaret Thatcher's leadership came under enormous strain. She faced a challenge to her premiership and failed to win an outright majority in the Conservative Party leadership contest. She resigned, ending 11 years in Downing Street, and John Major became Tory leader and prime minister. Much to Hume's relief, Brooke was kept on in Northern Ireland and the two men continued to have discussions about how the political process could develop. Hume now had good relations with the Northern Ireland Office and got on well with Richard Needham, who was a minister with responsibility for the economy and the environment.

He had been parliamentary private secretary to Jim Prior when he was Secretary of State and would go on to become the longest-serving minister under direct rule. Needham got to know Hume well, both socially, at functions, and on a political level during meetings and visits to his Foyle constituency. With high levels of unemployment in Northern Ireland, particularly in Derry, Needham and Hume had many conversations about securing much-needed investment.

Needham recalls how the SDLP leader would constantly pitch for new jobs for his Foyle constituency:

> He was a wonderful promoter. I mean, he sort of found this company called Fruit of the Loom, which was a huge American company making tee shirts. And they were going to set up in the south. And John and I, mainly John, single-handedly persuaded them to come north. So he was

a multi-faceted man because you could put him anywhere, in Brussels or London wherever.[44]

Needham and Hume became a bit of a double act when they met foreign investors who were interested in setting up businesses in Northern Ireland. The minister felt the MP was a great persuader and brilliant at selling Northern Ireland as a place to work but he got frustrated by Hume's personal appearance:

> I mean, he was such a scruffy bugger. I said to his wife, who was wonderful, I said, 'For God's sake Pat, kit him out before he comes.' So he had a newish suit. One tie and one suit which, you know, was mainly covered in tomato ketchup or whatever. But Pat had bought him a new pair of shoes but it didn't take a week for his ankles to expand around his shoes. And he couldn't tie the laces up. So we would see him with his laces undone. And the other problem was his hair. He was quite incapable of getting his hair into any sort of order. I had a wonderful private secretary and I said for God's sake get your comb out and give it to John. So she gets her comb out – a ladies' comb – and he sticks it in his head, we never find it again and it disappears.[45]

Hume was often reminded by family and friends to straighten his tie, fix his collar, or as Richard Needham remembers, simply brush his hair. They were comments motivated by concern. Hume's close circle simply wanted him to present himself in public in the best possible light. Garret FitzGerald observed: 'He has never been a fashion model. I am not one to talk but he is an even less cared-for-looking man than I am.'[46] Hume was well used to the comments about his appearance: 'People say, why don't you comb your hair? I tell them, it's me that's talking to people, not my hair.'[47]

Gerry Cosgrove recalls being in Washington with John, when she noticed, not for the first time, that his shoelaces were undone. She commented on the state of his footwear, which had seen better days. Hume simply said that he had little time to go shoe shopping and that when his shoes wore out he simply abandoned them wherever he happened to be. As a consequence, he confessed that over the years he had left dozens of pairs of shoes in hotel rooms all over the world.

Life for the SDLP leader was chaotic at times, and without the planning and organisation of his wife Pat, back in Derry, he would simply not have functioned as a politician. She organised his day, packed his clothes and booked his flights and accommodation as he continued to travel endlessly to Brussels, London and Dublin and the United States. He put on record his thoughts in a 1997 interview with RTÉ: 'I am a parcel and Pat delivers me and if we didn't work together, I couldn't have done what I have done.'[48]

Although there was still no political breakthrough in Northern Ireland, behind the scenes there were many conversations and discussions. Republicans were now having secret talks with both London and Dublin and Hume was continuing to work on finding a form of words the IRA could agree to that would end their violence. When documents emerged from his talks with republicans, Hume occasionally shared them with others to get a second opinion. The Labour leader Neil Kinnock became friends with Hume when the SDLP leader won the Foyle seat in 1983. He had a high regard for him and the two trusted each other. Kinnock remembers having a conversation with Hume in Westminster:

> He came to see me I think 1990, or early 1991, with a piece of paper. It was a draft of a possible calling of a ceasefire and negotiation of some kind of peace. And he showed it to me. I read it all in his presence in the office. It was not a very long document. And I said well this is the start, of a start, of a start. It is not really a signpost. It is certainly not a conclusion. 'No, I agree with that,' he said, 'but I just

wanted to know what your general attitude was.' And I said well, somebody is waking up.[49]

If the opinion polls were right, Neil Kinnock was on course to be the next prime minister, so Hume knew the Labour leader needed to be aware of what was being done behind the scenes to try and bring an end to the violence. In December 1990, the IRA announced a three-day truce over Christmas, which was their first in fifteen years. As the new year began, there were hopes that the political atmosphere was about to change and inter-party talks could get off the ground in the months ahead. Such optimism seemed misplaced as the IRA launched firebomb attacks in Belfast and carried out a daring mortar bomb attack in Downing Street in February. No one was injured in the explosion but the blast disrupted John Major's cabinet meeting and forced ministers to move elsewhere. It was a stark reminder to the political establishment that the IRA was still in business. In a sense, it was a blunt message from republicans. They wanted to talk, but they were still prepared to fight.

Keen to find a political consensus, Peter Brooke had been working for many months to try and get the parties around the table and in March it seemed his efforts had paid off. He unveiled a three-stranded talks process which, it was hoped, would lead ultimately to an agreement between the parties. Strand One would look at internal Northern Ireland matters which would aim to produce a stable devolved government. Strand Two would concentrate on North–South issues and look at cross-border matters. Strand Three would focus on British–Irish matters and the relationship between London and Dublin. The discussions were all linked and a new phrase entered Northern Ireland's political vocabulary: 'nothing is agreed until everything is agreed'. The talks would eventually run into difficulties, and by the summer of 1991, the process became bogged down in technical matters such as where certain talks would take place and who could chair proceedings. Hume and his SDLP colleagues took part in the discussions, but the Foyle MP privately knew that without any engagement with republicans the process could not succeed.

The Alliance leader, John Alderdice, remembers a meeting involving Hume, the DUP leader, the Reverend Ian Paisley and Ulster Unionist leader Jim Molyneaux:

> After a bit of discussion, John intimated to us that he felt he was going to have to engage with Sinn Féin. And I just looked around at John who was on my left-hand side. Jim was on the right-hand side. Ian was across, just the four of us, and I looked at him [Molyneaux] and he just went completely white. The blood drained from his face.[50]

Alderdice says it was a defining moment for Molyneaux:

> He was obviously very upset and said, 'Well, that's it. It is all over then.' Because from his perspective, and to be honest from mine too, if John went off to engage with Sinn Féin and were to reach any kind of understanding with them, however likely or unlikely that was, it made it impossible to engage with the rest of us.[51]

The Brooke talks did not produce any agreement and, not surprisingly, the formal discussions ended in July 1991. Once again, Northern Ireland was in limbo and it seemed that publicly there was little chance of finding a political solution. However, behind the scenes in London, Dublin and Belfast, there were other paths being followed. John Major's government was continuing with its secret talks with republicans and John Hume started a new initiative aimed at the two governments.

With his pen in his hand, the SDLP leader sat down and began to map out a series of ideas and principles. It was a text that would later form the Downing Street Declaration. Politics in Northern Ireland was about to enter a new chapter and John Hume was determined to help write it.

John Hume graduated from Maynooth in 1958.

At Maynooth. John Hume (left) with Brendan Devlin (seated) and his brother Ciaran.

John Hume married Pat Hone on 10 December 1960 in Derry.

Wedding party. From left: Annie Hume (mother), Pat, John, Sadie McCormack (Pat's sister) and Sam Hume (father). Front row: Maria and John McCormack.

John and Pat met during the Easter holidays in 1958.

On Derry's walls, filming with Terry McDonald.

Against the wall. John Hume (right), Hugh Logue (centre) and Ivan Cooper (left). This was when Hume turned to Hugh Logue and remarked that he looked like Jesus. (© *Mike Hollist/ANL/Shutterstock*)

An iconic image from the civil rights campaign, 16 November 1968. (© *images4media/Victor Patterson*)

Out with Dad. From left: Aidan, John Hume, Áine and Therese.
(© *Trinity Mirror/Mirrorpix/Alamy Stock Photo*)

Speaking at a protest at the Brandywell football ground in Derry, August 1971.
(© *PA Images/Alamy Stock Photo*)

Hume's home and office were routinely attacked. He was also a target of abuse from both loyalists and republicans. (© *Pacemaker Press*)

John Hume in action. The Persuader. (© *Mirrorpix*)

Protesting in Downing Street, 21 October 1971. From left: John Hume, Bernadette Devlin, Frank McManus and Austin Currie. (© *PA Images/Alamy Stock Photo*)

In an alternative to Stormont, the SDLP and other non-unionists met in Dungiven on 16 October 1971. John Hume getting ready for interview with journalist John McAleese of RTÉ. (© *Trinity Mirror/Mirrorpix/Alamy Stock Photo*)

Single transferable speech. Hume was often teased about delivering the same speech. He argued that by repeating the same words, his message would be understood. (© *Trinity Mirror/Mirrorpix/Alamy Stock Photo*)

Face to face. John Hume led an anti-internment protest on Magilligan Beach and famously confronted a British Army officer, 23 January 1972. (© *Jimmy McCormack/ The Irish Times*)

SDLP founding members. From left: Austin Currie, Gerry Fitt, John Hume and Paddy Devlin. (© *PA Images/Alamy Stock Photo*)

Marking the IRA ceasefire with Taoiseach Albert Reynolds and Sinn Féin President Gerry Adams in Dublin, 6 September 1994. (© *PA Images/Alamy Stock Photo*)

Three's company. David Trimble, Bono and John Hume campaigning for a Yes vote in the Good Friday Agreement referendum at Waterfront Hall, Belfast, 19 May 1998.
(© *PA Images/Alamy Stock Photo*)

The deal is done. John Hume and party colleagues at Castle Buildings in Belfast, 10 April 1998, minutes after the Good Friday Agreement was made public.
(© *Pacemaker Press*)

Thumbs Up! The trademark Hume gesture. (© *Peter Macdiarmid/Getty Images*)

John Hume and his old sparring partner Ian Paisley. (© *PA Images/Alamy Stock Photo*)

Pat Hume acted as John Hume's confidante and organiser. He often joked that he was a parcel and she delivered him. (© *NTB/Alamy Stock Photo*)

A night in Oslo. Celebrating with his fellow Nobel Laureate David Trimble, 10 December 1998. (© *BTB/Alamy Stock Photo*)

'The Town I Love So Well' – Hume travelled the world, but Derry was always home. (© *PA Images/Alamy Stock Photo*)

For decades Hume had the ear of numerous US Presidents. He first welcomed President Clinton to Derry in 1995. (© *Pacemaker Press*)

In the Great Hall at Stormont after quitting the Northern Ireland Assembly.
(© *PA Images/Alamy Stock Photo*)

Time's up! John Hume steps down as SDLP leader and enjoys a drink with Seamus Mallon and Northern Ireland Secretary John Reid, 10 November 2001.
(© *PA Images/Alamy Stock Photo*)

John with his sisters and brothers. From left: Sally, Annie, John, Jim and Patsy.

The Hume family. Back row from left: Aidan, Áine, Mo, Therese and John Junior. Front row: Pat and John. (© *Brian Spellman*)

Colin Davidson's portrait of John Hume was unveiled at the Palace of Westminster in November 2022. (John Hume, Painting by Colin Davidson © *UK Parliament WOA 7738*)

15

PEACE IN A WEEK

*'I don't give two balls of roasted snow, Jim,
what advice anybody gives me about those talks.'*
John Hume

Bríd Rodgers picked up a copy of the *Sunday Tribune* newspaper and could not believe what she was seeing. The journalist Ed Moloney was reporting that her party leader had been secretly meeting with Gerry Adams and the two men had been spotted at Hume's home in Derry. Rodgers was a senior SDLP figure, a former general secretary who had been a party member for over two decades. She was furious at what she had just read.

After finishing the article, she reached for the telephone and rang the Foyle MP: 'I said John, I can't believe you are doing this. We don't know anything about it. You know it is ridiculous. What are you at? And he started to say something, and I just … I was so angry. I put the phone down.'[1]

Rodgers and Hume were close and had holidayed and socialised on a regular basis. Her children and Hume's had enjoyed many summers on Donegal beaches, and she was a great friend of Pat Hume. She now felt John had let her down. For the next few minutes, she considered what she had read in the paper. She knew other party members would have the same question – what on earth was going on? Then the phone rang and it was John Hume. This time he got a chance to outline what he and the Sinn Féin president were talking about:

> He talked to me for maybe the guts of an hour, and he explained to me what he was trying to do. And I totally

agreed with him, and I said now that I know what you are doing I agree. But you know we were miffed that we didn't know what was happening.[2]

It was April 1993, and Gerry Adams had been spotted going into Hume's house in Derry by a neighbour who had passed this newsworthy piece of information on to the journalist Eamonn McCann. McCann in turn informed the reporter Ed Moloney who rang Hume and the story appeared the next day. Bríd Rodgers was not the only worried party member. Alasdair McDonnell, who would later become party leader, says activists had big concerns about what was happening: 'I think everybody had misgivings. I mean people were over a barrel in that they wanted the benefits but they didn't trust Adams to hold to his side of the bargain.'[3]

McDonnell says there were genuine fears within the SDLP that Sinn Féin would use them politically: 'We basically were worried that we were being taken for a ride ... We realised on the other hand that Adams probably wanted to move towards de-escalating the confrontation. But we weren't sure that he was not going to cannibalise the SDLP in the process, that he was not just going to use the SDLP as a platform.'[4]

As John Hume fielded calls from party members wanting to know what was going on, Gerry Adams was also trying to get in touch with the Foyle MP. Adams had been with Hume the day before but was now across the border, some 14 miles from Derry, on the Inishowen peninsula. The Sinn Féin president was staying with his cousin and had no mobile phone so had to find a call box to make contact:

> The only telephone access we had was in the Main Street in Buncrana and it was outside a pub and there was I making these frenzied calls trying to get John and find out what was happening and doing whatever else I was doing. Until I realised I had an audience of people with pints of Guinness and pints of beer all watching this going on.[5]

The revelation that Hume and Adams were in discussions again provoked predictable responses. Unionists were furious and criticised the talks, arguing that he should not be in discussions whilst the IRA's campaign continued. Despite the negative coverage, Hume was convinced that his meetings with Adams would bear fruit and was satisfied that eventually there would be a permanent ceasefire.

With concern amongst party members about his discussions with Gerry Adams, Hume knew he had to say something. He attended several party meetings and at one he offered to step away from politics if his initiative with Sinn Féin was not successful: 'I said to the party meeting, "Look my objective in this dialogue is to bring an end to the violence and if I fail, I will retire." I told that privately at a meeting and they accepted that.'[6]

The talks involving the two men weren't the only discussions taking place. A year earlier, Hume and the other party leaders, with the exception of Gerry Adams, had taken part in the latest round of talks under the new Secretary of State, Sir Patrick Mayhew. He had replaced Peter Brooke in a cabinet reshuffle after the Tories had won the general election and, against the odds, returned John Major to power.

The Mayhew talks, like the ones organised by Brooke, would not deliver an agreement, though some progress was made. As ever, the unionist parties and the SDLP approached the process from different positions. The unionists wanted to secure an agreement on devolution whilst the SDLP wanted to concentrate on North–South matters. Hume made it clear he was not interested in an internal settlement. He proposed a plan where a six-person executive would be established which would have three locally elected members and a representative each from the UK government, the Irish administration and the European Commission.

It was a novel idea and reflected Hume's view that neither power-sharing nor majority rule were long-term solutions. The proposal was rejected by the unionists and the British government who believed the idea was impractical and weakened the union. The Ulster Unionists did engage with the Irish government and Jim Molyneaux took part in talks, but Ian Paisley's DUP refused. Lord Empey, who travelled to

Dublin Castle, said the unionists did have some good discussions and also said there were some worthwhile talks with the SDLP but that he was critical of Hume.

He claimed the SDLP leader was often missing from discussions, which hindered the process. He thinks Hume was a stumbling block to an agreement, claiming that in his absence his colleagues would often agree to something only for John to block it later:

> It was very difficult to get anything agreed because what happened was clearly the SDLP colleagues contacted John, who would have been over in Brussels, and the minutes would have been pretty well trashed. And very large parts of the following day were always taken up by an argument over the minutes of what happened the previous day. So John, clearly, was very uncomfortable with the idea of his colleagues getting too comfortable with us on some form of re-establishing Stormont. He saw things in a much bigger picture.[7]

The claim that Hume was not interested in the Mayhew talks is rejected by Mark Durkan: 'You had this narrative developing that John did not want an agreement with the unionists. That he was obsessed with something, with Sinn Féin, you know. Which is just wrong.'[8]

Whilst there was some movement from the parties, and the engagement of unionists with the Irish government marked a sea change, ultimately the Mayhew talks ended in failure. Hume's idea of a six-person executive enjoyed little support. There was also no agreement on the issue of changing Articles 2 and 3 of the Irish Constitution which laid claim to the whole island as 'national territory'. Hume found himself the target of much criticism in the press and from rival politicians. One of the Alliance Party negotiators, Addie Morrow, claimed there was 'little chance' of agreement whilst Hume remained SDLP leader.[9]

Hume spent much of 1993 refining and reworking the document that he first began writing by hand in the autumn of 1991. He now faced a barrage of criticism from some newspaper columnists for his ongoing relationship with Adams. His fiercest critics came from the Dublin-based Independent newspaper group which published the *Irish Independent* and the *Sunday Independent.* Contributors to both papers repeatedly questioned whether his ongoing dialogue with the Sinn Féin president would lead anywhere. Regular headlines in the *Sunday Independent* were cutting and cartoons often derided the SDLP MP for associating with Adams. The criticism was relentless, and Hume's political judgement was often questioned.

Áine, John Hume's daughter, says her parents found the coverage 'profoundly disheartening'. She says they felt that the public was being given the wrong impression of what was going on: 'I think because it was such a distortion ... they were very disheartened by it.'[10]

Hume's son Aidan has a similar view. He says his father was thick-skinned when he came to being challenged, but the criticism from colleagues was particularly hard:

> I think within the party was probably the most difficult for him. That really hurt him and stressed him, but that was hard. In the press it is funny – people have commented that he did not like criticism. It depended where the criticism came from. If the criticism came from people he admired and respected it was pretty difficult. If that criticism came from others it was water off a duck's back.[11]

Mark Durkan remembers being in the office in Derry with John and Pat when the newspaper coverage was discussed and recalls how it affected the couple:

> It was just awful stuff. John found it hard to take. Pat was really distressed. Obviously, they were buoyed up by people who were also contacting them in support out of disgust. So in the office at the time, you were getting phone calls for and against the talks. You were getting letters for and

against, cards and all the rest of it. It ended up getting more for, than against.[12]

Colleagues of John Hume were acutely aware of how the press coverage was affecting him. Phil Coulter, who was now living in Dublin, was able to watch events from afar, with a good degree of inside knowledge. He believes his old friend was 'vilified' and says it was relentless, as every Sunday there was 'another slaughtering of John Hume'.[13]

More often than not, when the latest *Sunday Independent* edition appeared, the Humes would be across the border at their home in Greencastle on the Inishowen peninsula. The Irish diplomat and family friend Dáithí Ó Ceallaigh remembers one occasion being with John and Pat in Donegal:

> We were staying with them for the weekend. And on the Saturday evening, we went off with Brian Friel and his wife to have dinner. And then I got up early on the Sunday morning and I went off bird watching. And he [Hume] went off. He came back at about half past nine and he had the Irish papers with him. And he was mad. Absolutely mad. And Pat said to him, 'John, don't read that stuff.'[14]

Pat Hume was understandably protective. She could see what the press coverage and the political pressure were doing to her husband. It was all beginning to take a toll on him. He was smoking heavily and drinking and was suffering from stress. For much of 1993, Hume had been working on a document with Gerry Adams based on the text he had started two years earlier. Understandably, Hume was keen on privacy and discretion so work on the document was done at quiet times in his office in Derry. Mark Durkan would be there along with his colleague Jackie.

Durkan recalls the process of updating the latest Hume–Adams proposal:

> Jackie used to be brought into the office on a Saturday or Sunday afternoon to type up a new version where John was updating words from his point of view or whatever. And you know he would tell Jackie or if I was there, not to keep a copy. And then a couple of weeks later he would ask you for a copy.[15]

The final draft of the Hume–Adams document was completed in June 1993. It was given secretly to the British and Irish governments with a view that it would be turned into an Anglo-Irish declaration. Hume did not immediately reveal that the document had been handed to officials because he wanted to give both governments an opportunity to digest it and work on it. The impression was created that the Hume–Adams discussions were continuing apace, and no one in London and Dublin went public with the fact that they had sight of a document or that the substantive Hume–Adams talks were over.

As the weeks went by, with no sign of movement from John Major or Albert Reynolds, Hume started to get anxious. As Mark Durkan recalls: 'John was getting frustrated. While you were getting these constant attacks, particularly coming from the Dublin media and all the rest of it, he was left wondering, "What is happening here? I have been hung out to dry here."'[16]

Hume felt isolated and his family were worried about the pressure he was under. His son John remembers the time well:

> You would have to have been blind to have not noticed the change in his physical appearance, which was a direct result of the pressure he was under. He stopped eating really. I mean his appetite went. He was drinking outrageous amounts of coffee. He was smoking a lot of the time from what I can remember. And he was just very unhealthy and a lot of that was driven by the pressure.[17]

On 10 September 1993, Mark Durkan and Jackie Green got married and their reception was at a Derry hotel. Naturally, the guest list included SDLP figures and friends and family of the happy couple. It was not meant to be a day for politics but inevitably John Hume and the groom ended up discussing recent events. At the reception, Hume told Durkan that he was going to make a statement and announce that his talks with Adams had concluded, and their paper was with the two governments.

Durkan knew Hume was about to travel to America and was worried about a statement being released when Hume was out of the country. He warned his colleague:

> When this happens there is going to be a big reaction. You are going to have to own that and answer that. When this comes out and you are in America, Adams is going to be all over it. This is going to go everywhere. People in the party won't know what to say.[18]

Hume was becoming impatient with the two governments and his frustration was becoming obvious. Before his American trip, Hume travelled to London to see the prime minister in an attempt to get John Major to speed up his response to the document and sign up to a new Anglo-Irish declaration. Afterwards, standing in Downing Street, the SDLP leader was asked by reporters about his initiative with Gerry Adams. Pressed by BBC Northern Ireland's political editor, Jim Dougal, Hume was characteristically blunt: 'I don't give two balls of roasted snow, Jim, what advice anybody gives me about those talks because I will continue with them until they reach what I hope will be a positive conclusion.'[19]

Hume's frustration was now public. Back home, the political atmosphere remained tense. The loyalist paramilitaries saw Hume as part of a so-called 'pan-nationalist front' and the homes of SDLP members were regularly being attacked. Days after the Downing Street encounter, Hume and Adams issued a joint statement confirming that they had made 'considerable progress' in their discussions and that a document had been given to Dublin.[20]

What was not made clear was that a copy had also been given to London. Hume then jetted off to the United States as part of a drive to secure inward investment. There was much confusion about whether or not the document had been given to the authorities in Dublin. Some newspapers said it had and others said Hume was planning to hand it over. Officials in Dublin thought the SDLP leader had mishandled the situation and had added to the confusion. They were also worried that the Hume–Adams document now had so much prominence that it would frighten off the British government, therefore making a fresh Anglo-Irish declaration less likely.

When Hume returned from America, he met Albert Reynolds and Dick Spring. It was clear that both the taoiseach and the tánaiste were still unhappy with the way Hume had handled things before he went to the USA. Relations between Dublin and London at this stage were also tricky and the chances of a joint initiative looked unlikely. There was a coolness in London towards the Hume–Adams document and in some quarters of the UK establishment there was downright opposition to it.

What followed were seven of the darkest days in the history of Northern Ireland. An IRA bomb went off without warning on Belfast's Shankill Road killing ten people, including the bomber, Thomas Begley. Two children were among the dead and nearly 60 people were injured. The bomb was carried into Frizzell's fish shop by Begley, who was dressed in a fishmonger's white coat. He arrived at a time when the street was packed with Saturday afternoon shoppers. The IRA would later say that its intended target was an office above the shop where it claimed UDA members were meeting. There was no one in the office at the time and the IRA killed shoppers and shop workers. After rescue workers spent hours at the scene clearing away the rubble, the full horror of the explosion became clear. Two of the dead were girls aged seven and thirteen and another four were women. One woman lost both her parents in the explosion. The dead included the owner of the fish shop, Desmond Frizzell, and his daughter Sharon McBride.

The images of people digging in the wreckage shocked the world, and politicians from across the spectrum demanded answers from Gerry

Adams and the republican movement. Why was this done? How was this justified? How was this part of a peace strategy? Adams said the attack was wrong and said the IRA, which had been planning to kill senior UDA figures, had been blinded to 'the consequences of their actions if anything went wrong'. Hume found out about the bombing after he was phoned by his colleague Dr Joe Hendron, the MP for West Belfast who had dramatically defeated Gerry Adams the year before.

The Humes were shattered by the events on the Shankill Road and John came under intense pressure in the media to end his association with the Sinn Féin president. Pat Hume recalled the hours that followed: 'The phone started going, "John, the talks have to end. You can't continue to give credibility to these people." And so the pressure mounted and mounted.'[21]

Mark Durkan witnessed how upset Pat and John were: 'I remember Pat in tears saying, "How do they say they are interested in peace when they are still doing things like that?"'[22] The pressure on Hume and Adams intensified when the Sinn Féin leader carried the coffin of the bomber, Thomas Begley, at his funeral some days later. The image of the Sinn Féin president shouldering the coffin made world headlines and became a defining moment. Adams knew how his appearance would be reported but felt he had to go to the funeral and had to show his respect to the Begley family. He later acknowledged why those families who lost relatives in the IRA bombing would protest at his presence.

Yet, Adams, as Sinn Féin president, believed he could not disown Begley, who was part of the republican movement. If he had not gone to the funeral it would have probably ended his tenure as party leader. At his home in Derry, Hume watched the television footage of Adams carrying the coffin and started to cry. He was at breaking point both emotionally and physically. He had lost weight and since April, when his talks with Gerry Adams were revealed, he had shed two stone. Pat Hume says it was a dreadful time for her husband: 'He was not able to sleep. He was not eating properly. There were all sorts of vicious letters arriving in the post, vicious phone calls coming.'[23]

Around that time Hugh Logue remembers meeting John Hume in

Kitty O'Shea's bar in Brussels and the two old friends talked about events back home. Hume was deeply upset about the Shankill bombing. When the issue of Gerry Adams carrying Thomas Begley's coffin was raised Hume got very animated and said the Sinn Féin president had no choice. He told Logue: 'He had to – he needs to keep the movement together.'[24]

Like many times before, the Humes were in the line of fire. These were dark and frightening days in Northern Ireland and a new generation of people were being traumatised by violence. As the funerals were being organised and the injured continued to be treated, the very thought of a political breakthrough seemed fanciful and far-fetched. This was the moment that Pat Hume asked her husband to stop his discussions with Gerry Adams: 'It was the first time that I said to John, "John, do you not think the talks have to end?" And he was so intent on trying to get all violence to stop, I knew that he would continue.'[25]

Pat Hume was not the only family member who questioned the discussions with Gerry Adams. Áine said she considered what her father was doing but concluded that he had to carry on with the discussions: 'Everybody questioned that you know. But he was right. I think it was a lonely road at times, but, you know, you just had to keep believing.'[26]

Hume insisted to friends, family and journalists that he would carry on with his initiative with Adams. He told one interviewer that he would do 'everything in my power to bring this to an end'.[27] Sadly, the violence was far from over and loyalist paramilitaries were now planning revenge. In the days that followed, six Catholic men were killed by the UVF and the UFF in random shootings in Belfast, Lurgan and Glengormley. SDLP members and elected representatives were on the loyalists' hit list and Hume was right at the top. The SDLP leader was considered by loyalists to be most vulnerable at his Donegal holiday home in Greencastle, close to the shores of Lough Foyle. This was where he relaxed and where he probably felt the safest. Hume did not carry a personal protection weapon as he believed in non-violence, and he did not want bodyguards.

However, such was the level of threat, that eventually security measures were put in place. His son Aidan Hume remembers what was done:

I think there was a concern about somebody coming over in a boat from the other side. So there was actually a caravan of gardaí in the garden. Typically, when he was in Donegal, he wouldn't have had security, but I don't think he had a choice.[28]

A week after the Shankill bomb at Halloween, the UFF targeted Wilf White, a well-known character in Derry, who was an SDLP councillor and a postman in the city. Known as a 'Knocker' White, because of his job, he was originally from Yorkshire and had served in the navy before settling in Northern Ireland. He was a creature of habit and on Saturday afternoons would visit the same bar in the city. Thankfully, on this particular day, he unexpectedly changed his plans and went elsewhere. It was a decision that saved his life.

His would-be attackers went elsewhere and drove to the village of Greysteel, which is some nine miles to the east of Derry on the main A2 road. UDA gunmen arrived at the Rising Sun bar, a popular spot which was busy as it was a Saturday night and the evening before Halloween. As one of the gunmen walked in, he shouted 'trick or treat', before opening fire with an automatic weapon. One woman, Karen Thompson, who was the youngest victim at 19, said 'that's not funny'.[29] The bar was peppered with bullets and seven people were shot dead and another man died later from his injuries. Adrian McAuley, who was a paramedic, was one of the first emergency responders at the scene: 'We were stunned. We saw people shot and wounded and lying on the floor and slumped in their seats. The sound of crying and screaming was overwhelming.'[30]

Northern Ireland was now experiencing its worst violence in decades. The Humes were in London that weekend, where John was speaking at a conference about the healing process, when news of the Greysteel massacre came through. That night the couple watched the television pictures from Northern Ireland with absolute horror. The next morning they went to mass at a church in Kensington. Pat remembers that she found part of the service poignant: 'I remember the gospel was the Sermon on the Mount. Blessed are those who tried to make peace. And

I thought, maybe you should continue.'[31]

In the days that followed, the Greysteel victims were buried. At the funeral of 81-year-old James Moore, who was the oldest of the eight victims, Hume met his daughter Finuala Wyer. Outside the church, he offered his sympathies and put his arms around her to comfort her. She responded and told the Foyle MP: 'We were praying around the coffin last night. And we prayed that you would have the strength to continue with your talks because there is no other way.'[32]

John Hume burst into tears and his despair was captured on camera. It became an iconic image which summed up the pain and despair of the cycle of violence. Pat Hume was at John's side that day and remembers the raw emotion: 'Everybody was crying, but to see a very strong man, just the tears running down his cheeks, was so sad.'[33]

The photograph of John Hume crying and being comforted in the churchyard was picked up by the press and went round the world. It showed a broken man, yet the reality is that Hume's funeral conversation with Finuala Wyer gave him a sense of hope. It was just what he needed to hear, as he felt politically outnumbered and isolated. Pat Hume remembers how her husband felt: 'That was the thing that really strengthened him. He then was totally resolved.'[34]

Just 48 hours later, Hume was in Downing Street meeting John Major in an attempt to get him to breathe new life into the political process. Hume was so convinced that the document he worked on with Gerry Adams could transform the situation that he boldly declared there could be peace 'within a week'. Major and the Foyle MP got on well. There were occasions when matters got heated. The journalist David McKittrick reported one occasion when Hume grabbed the prime minister by the lapels. In correspondence with this author for this book, the former Conservative leader, now Sir John Major, says he cannot remember this incident:

> I cannot recall this occasion – unless it was when John Hume felt I was making progress and could reach a deal. This happened more than once, when John became excited

by a new opportunity or British initiative. He was an emotional and tactile politician.[35]

Major explained the political difficulties he had with Hume over his efforts for peace:

> The political problem with the Hume–Adams initiative was its source, which invariably ensured the suspicion and enmity of hardline Northern Irish unionist opinion and thus – in the House of Commons – right-of-centre Conservatives. Any initiative labelled 'Hume–Adams' was seen instinctively by a majority of unionists as hostile. This was frustrating since the same proposal from a different source – the churches for example – would have had a greater chance of being accepted. His presented a problem for the British government as we sought to bring opposing sides together.[36]

After his trip to London, Hume returned to Derry after one of the most gruelling weeks of his life. He was emotionally shattered and physically exhausted. He collapsed and was admitted to the Altnagelvin Hospital in Derry and staff there decided that he needed to be monitored for several days. Mark Durkan told the press that Hume had a high temperature and had been off-colour in recent days but there was 'no real cause for concern'.[37]

Hume's family were anxious. Áine remembers seeing her father: 'He had lost about three stones in weight, and he was absolutely exhausted. I remember really worrying for him.'[38] Hundreds of well-wishers sent cards and letters to Derry hoping that the SDLP leader would make a speedy recovery. Many praised Hume's peace efforts and urged him to continue with his discussions in the hope that the violence would end.

As he rested and convalesced in his hospital bed, the political rumour mill in Westminster and Belfast went into overdrive. There was speculation that the IRA had been in talks with the UK government. The

Secretary of State, Sir Patrick Mayhew, repeatedly denied that there was any such relationship and dismissed any suggestion that behind the scenes there had been conversations with the IRA.

The prime minister took a similar approach. He told the House of Commons that the idea of sitting down and talking to Gerry Adams and the IRA was sickening. Sitting beside Sir Patrick Mayhew in the chamber, John Major was questioned about suggestions that talks had been going on between government contacts and the IRA. The Conservative leader was clear: 'I can only say to the honourable gentleman that would turn my stomach over and most people in this House and we will not do it.'[39]

Yet it soon became apparent that John Major was playing a dangerous game and was not telling the full story. For some time, there had been detailed contacts between the IRA and the UK government. There was clearly a private position and a very public one, and the two things were not the same.

Major would later tell BBC Northern Ireland about those discussions: 'We were already engaged in private conversations and although one often despaired about where they would go, it was important we did that if we were going to create peace. If we hadn't had the secret channel to the IRA, if we hadn't had those talks and kept them secret, there would have been no peace process.'[40]

The conversations had been restricted to a small group but those ground-breaking discussions were about to be made public. On 28 November 1993, journalists Anthony Bevins, Mary Holland and Eamonn Mallie worked together and in the *Observer* revealed how the prime minister had established a secret communications link with the IRA. The dramatic revelations reported that a back-channel run by unofficial intermediaries had been in operation for some time and was so secret it had not even been disclosed to the taoiseach, Albert Reynolds. The talks between the IRA and the UK government involved two go-betweens, Denis Bradley and Brendan Duddy. The two Derry men had been involved in John Hume's aborted attempt to have talks with the IRA back in 1985.

Bradley and Duddy had been meeting in secret with senior

republicans and the British but John Hume was unaware of these conversations taking place. It was part of a channel of communication that had been set up in 1990 when Peter Brooke was Northern Ireland secretary. Bradley says he was told by the IRA not to inform Hume of the talks but eventually after numerous meetings and discussions he felt that position could not, and should not, be sustained. Bradley was also concerned that the UK government was ignoring the offer of a temporary IRA ceasefire which had been made through the secret channel. Bradley felt he had to act:

> A back-channel is a fine thing, but it has to come to an end. It cannot be the substitute for real politics, and the real politician in this was John Hume. He was the one with the in to the Irish government; he was the one who had the in to the English government.[41]

Bradley and Duddy decided to tell John Hume of their work in the background:

> I remember the night we met Hume and we met in Duddy's house. And he was in the house before I arrived and when I walked into the house, he said, 'Are you involved too?' That was his first reaction to me, and Brendan had already told him about this link. He may have had some suspicion that there was something going on, there was something happening, but he perhaps did not know fully. Anyway, we sat down and over a period of two to three hours filled him in completely. The reason I remember that so well is because we had already decided that we had reached the end of the road.[42]

Denis Bradley then told Martin McGuinness that John Hume was now aware of the discussions that had taken place between republicans and the British government. Republicans were not pleased with the decision to inform John Hume, although McGuinness had suspected that Denis Bradley would inform the SDLP leader about the talks. Republicans also believed that members of the back-channel were starting to make decisions on their behalf which, in the words of Gerry Adams, were 'breaking all the rules which go-betweens must adhere to'.[43]

It marked the end of this particular relationship. Bradley was informed that his services were no longer required: 'We knew that we were out in the cold. They sacked us. McGuinness brought me a letter saying we were more or less sacked. "You are gone."' The revelations surrounding the back-channel made world headlines and the UK government and the republican movement reacted in different ways. Sir Patrick Mayhew insisted that the IRA had passed on a message to the UK government stating that 'the conflict is over'.[44]

He said the government felt obliged to respond and contact was made earlier in the year. That version was challenged by republicans who insisted that no such message came from them. Sinn Féin said contacts with the UK government had been in place since 1990, not just a matter of months, as British officials were claiming. There were also discrepancies in documents that were subsequently released into the public domain, and Sinn Féin accused the UK government of tampering with notes of the meetings and details of the contacts. The war of words between republicans and British ministers continued for days.

Later, Sir Patrick Mayhew admitted that the British version of events, which had been placed in the House of Commons Library, contained numerous errors. In light of this, Sir Patrick Mayhew offered his resignation, but it was rejected by John Major who felt his cabinet colleague had an important role to play. On 3 December, the two men travelled to Dublin to meet Albert Reynolds and his colleagues for a crucial Anglo-Irish summit. Against the backdrop of the *Observer* story on the back-channel and the differences over the Hume–Adams document, the atmosphere was understandably feisty.

The opening exchanges in the grandeur of Dublin Castle did not go well. Albert Reynolds and John Major were in an argumentative mood, and to watching officials there seemed little chance of a meeting of minds. It was a very poor start and did not augur well. A break in the discussions helped to lighten the mood and soon progress was made on a range of issues, and the summit ended in better shape than it started. In the days that followed, British and Irish officials worked behind the scenes on the communique. The two prime ministers met again a week later and the atmosphere was good. Much progress was being made and the hope was a fresh declaration between London and Dublin could be revealed before Christmas.

Things were moving politically but as diplomacy went on in the background, the public pressure on John Hume continued. The *Irish Independent* published an attack on the SDLP leader written by Conor Cruise O'Brien, who had long been one of Hume's chief critics. With a sceptical eye, he questioned the Foyle MP's efforts and his column carried the headline 'How John Hume's halo gives a shine to the IRA godfathers'.[45]

As ever, for Hume, it was a hard read, though privately he could afford a wry smile. Better news was coming. On 15 December, John Major played host to Albert Reynolds and his cabinet colleagues in Downing Street. A joint British–Irish deal had been done.

16

THUMBS UP

'As of midnight, 31 August there will be a complete cessation of military operations.'
IRA statement.

At the famous Locke-Ober restaurant, one of the oldest dining establishments in Boston, Ted Kennedy and John Hume were in a talkative mood. There was a lot to catch up on. They had just come from the funeral mass of their good friend Tip O'Neill. The former Speaker of the House of Representatives had died some days earlier of a cardiac arrest in hospital. The 81-year-old was one of Hume's dearest friends in America and over the decades had opened many political doors for the Foyle MP.

O'Neill, like Ted Kennedy, was one of the 'Four Horsemen', who had regularly lobbied US presidents on Irish affairs and been an enthusiastic supporter of Hume's work. Forever associated with the phrase 'all politics is local', at six-foot-three, he was a larger-than-life figure. The Democrat, who was called Thomas Patrick but was better known as Tip, dominated the Irish-American political scene for years and was one of the most popular figures on Capitol Hill. Kennedy and Hume knew his passing marked the end of an era. They would miss his laughter amidst clouds of cigar smoke and his booming voice as he dispensed wise counsel.

In O'Neill's home city, hours after the funeral, Hume and Kennedy gathered to toast his life in the familiar surroundings of Winter Place. Their venue had a reputation for fine French cuisine and amidst the original paintings and Italian sculptures they reminisced. It was a favourite eating house of the Kennedy family, and in the early 1960s, JFK had dined there. The guest list over the years had included heads of state and the power brokers of Washington politics.

As Kennedy and Hume chatted, the senator wanted to know in detail what his guest thought about the Downing Street Declaration, which had been unveiled by the British and Irish governments the previous month. The December document was hailed by John Major and Albert Reynolds as 'an agreed framework for peace' and centred on a number of themes that Gerry Adams and Hume had spent months discussing.[1]

The deal addressed the issue of Irish self-determination, and this was a move in Hume's direction. There was an acknowledgement from London that nationalists had a right to pursue Irish unity, but any constitutional change had to have the consent of a majority in Northern Ireland. The statement declared that:

> The British government agree that it is for the people of Ireland alone, by agreement between the two parts respectively, to exercise their right of self-determination on the basis of consent, freely and concurrently given, North and South, to bring about a united Ireland, if that is their wish.[2]

Sir John Major says Hume influenced his thinking. In correspondence with this author, he outlined how he viewed the events of 1993:

> The Downing Street Declaration was the result of tough negotiation between myself and Albert Reynolds, and many others behind the scenes. But both sides were aware that the original idea of such an agreement could be traced back to the dialogue between John Hume and Gerry Adams. That is undoubtedly to John's credit. John Hume was therefore an important influence on how to proceed, but not upon the details of how to do so: his draft of the declaration would never have passed the 1992–97 Westminster Parliament.[3]

Sir John Major was referring to the fact that his Westminster majority was so small that he had to often rely on the support of Ulster Unionist MPs. He was also fighting battles in his own party over Europe, so he knew he had to tread a careful political line. He had a high regard for Hume's efforts:

> John was an ever-present 'good angel', appealing to the best instincts of those with fiercely opposing views to reach an agreement on Irish republicans and Westminster parliamentarians. He was unfettered by setbacks and indefatigable in lobbying for his ideas. Although his instincts and proposals were generally 'green' – and this was alien to hardline unionists' views – he welcomed engagement between London and Dublin as a great advance.[4]

Hume saw the declaration of December 1993 as a great advance. Major's instincts were unionist – after all, he was the leader of the Conservative and Unionist Party, to give it its full title. He made it clear that he would not be a persuader for a united Ireland but recognised that if there was consent to constitutional change he would not stop that move. The document also stated that the UK government had 'no selfish, strategic or economic interests in Northern Ireland', which was a repetition of the phrase first used by Peter Brooke when he was Northern Ireland secretary.[5]

To Hume, this was an essential statement. In a letter to the Sinn Féin president Gerry Adams, John Hume wrote that the document Reynolds and Major agreed to 'arose from our dialogue'.[6] The SDLP leader said the Anglo-Irish deal reaffirmed what was contained in the Hume–Adams document of June 1993. He posed a stark question to Gerry Adams: 'Is whatever difference there is between our June document and the joint declaration, and I see no difference in substance, worth the cost of a single human life?'[7]

Hume challenged Adams that there was enough in the Downing Street Declaration to convince the IRA to call a permanent ceasefire. The Anglo-Irish deal was the work of officials in London and Dublin, but in truth, Hume's fingerprints were all over it. Whilst the work of Hume influenced this version, the phraseology belonged to diplomats. Understandably, it contained much civil service language that was at times verbose and sometimes a little vague. This was because the agreement had to win over both nationalists and unionists. Sinn Féin seized on the wording and said the document contained 'confusions and contradictions' and the party wanted clarification.[8]

Whilst there was a welcome for the narrative surrounding the issue of self-determination, republicans still felt the declaration gave unionists a veto. Adams and his party colleagues wanted to know what would happen to prisoners once the peace process developed, and republicans also had other questions surrounding the British Army and policing. Sinn Féin set up a commission aimed at examining the declaration and said over the coming months they would consult their activists across the island of Ireland.

As 1994 began, Adams had another issue on his mind. He wanted to travel to the USA to go to a conference being organised by Bill Flynn, an Irish-American industrialist who took a deep interest in Irish affairs and was the CEO of Mutual of America. Flynn's event at the Waldorf Astoria Hotel in New York was in February and several Irish politicians had been invited to discuss the peace process. Adams had been unable to visit America in the past because of Sinn Féin's links to the IRA. He was officially 'persona non grata' and barred from travelling. The British government was against the idea of Adams being allowed into the United States and previously the American authorities had always taken guidance from London and refused the Sinn Féin president access.

However, this time it seemed that the circumstances were different. Both Albert Reynolds and John Hume felt the visa should be granted, arguing that such a move might help the IRA end its campaign of violence and influential Americans might use the opportunity to lobby Adams. Around the table in downtown Boston, after they had enjoyed a fine meal, Ted Kennedy asked John Hume about the visa for Adams. Kennedy recalled what his guest said:

> John told us there was a split in the IRA whether to accept the joint declaration and that a visa for Adams would help carry the internal debate. He made a very powerful case about the importance of moving the peace process forward and said this was a great opportunity to do that.[8]

Aidan, John's son, was also present in the restaurant: 'I think it was pivotal. Senator Kennedy wrote about it in his autobiography but he forgot I was there. But it was interesting just watching, watching things work.'[9]

Hume senior made a compelling case that the Sinn Féin leader should be granted a visa, and important decision-makers in the United States were beginning to take note of his appeal. One of the key players at this time was Nancy Soderberg, who worked in the White House as deputy national security advisor. Soderberg and Hume knew each other well and had a good relationship. She had also worked with Mark Durkan during his time in Washington in Ted Kennedy's office. An influential voice within the Clinton administration, Soderberg recalls that before the joint declaration was signed, Hume had flagged up the need to grant Adams a visa.

In an interview for this book, she remembered a lunch she had with Hume in the White House:

> I invited him to my office which was right off the situation room in the White House mess, which is a dark-panel, kind of a nautical-looking kind of room, a dining room. I did not know at the time but foreigners are not allowed in there. I had no idea. I invited him and found out later. I asked him [about the visa] and that was when he said it was time to engage Adams and we should give him a visa.[10]

Hume's position surprised Soderberg, because in the past he opposed such a move, as she did. She originally felt Gerry Adams was associated with violence and that the Sinn Féin president should stay out of America. Clearly, things had changed and events were moving fast. Soderberg considered Hume's view and in December they had another conversation about the granting of a visa. She was won over when she heard Ted Kennedy argue that Adams should be allowed entry into the USA: 'The clincher was Ted Kennedy getting on board. For Ted Kennedy, who had lost two brothers to violence, to advocate for Adams to come to the United States was a game changer.'[11]

There was a strong lobby advocating for the visa that also included Senator Chris Dodd, Senator Daniel Moynihan and the mayor of New York, David Dinkins. Former congressman Bruce Morrison was another influential figure who argued that Adams should be allowed to visit, as did Niall O'Dowd, who was an Irish-born journalist who worked in the United States. However, there were strong voices within the US administration who were opposed to the idea. The Justice Department and the State Department were against it and had concerns that if they allowed Adams to come in, the move would damage Anglo-US relations.

The British government had major objections to the visa being granted at a time when the IRA campaign of violence was still ongoing. Sir Patrick Mayhew met with the US ambassador to the UK and told him that: 'The fact was Adams had to renounce violence. Granting this favour before that would be completely wrong in Northern Ireland terms and also dangerous in terms of the US–UK relationship.'[12]

President Clinton was well aware of the UK opposition to the Adams visa and acutely conscious of the long list of powerful American voices who were against such a move. He faced criticism from Janet Reno, his attorney general, and also from the FBI. They were not the only critics. One of the strongest opponents was Warren Christopher, who was Secretary of State.

Soderberg remembers Warren Christopher's arguments:

> He was dead set against it, saying that the British will stop cooperating with us if we do this. We said, no they will not. They might get mad but it is in their own interest to cooperate with us on Bosnia and Iraq. They are not going to stop cooperating with that.[13]

President Clinton knew there was a risk to granting the visa to Adams but ultimately decided that the move would be beneficial. Nancy Soderberg also remembers a raft of calls from London urging the Clinton administration not to grant the visa. The Americans were reminded by the British officials of the IRA's long record of violence. In the end, Clinton boldly agreed to grant Adams a visa and in late January the Sinn Féin leader made the transatlantic trip. Soderberg says the prime minister was livid when he was informed that Adams was being allowed into America: 'Major did not actually talk to us for a week. They were absolutely furious.'[14]

In correspondence with this author, Sir John Major talked about his objection to the visa for Gerry Adams. He insisted that, at the time, London's opposition was correct: 'Because the British government believed we had been given the word of the US government that Gerry Adams would not be permitted to visit the United States to raise funds before violence was ended, and there was no doubt in our minds that is what he intended to do. Initially, a visa was indeed refused. However, following intense lobbying by the left wing of the US Democratic Party, it was later granted.'[15]

The granting of the visa was seen by many observers as a defining moment. It marked a key stage in the peace process. Adams, the outsider, was now becoming a key player on the inside. President Clinton, one of the world's most powerful men, was now prepared to trust Sinn Féin – a party once regarded as a political pariah. Clinton was also willing to risk a challenge to his country's oldest ally and ignore the strong warnings coming from John Major's administration. The US president knew there were dangers in what he was doing:

> And it was not just the risk of alienating the British, there was also the risk that I would stick my neck out, for example in the visa for Gerry Adams, and IRA violence would continue. Innocent civilians would continue to die and I would look like I had been played for a fool. And that, over the long run, had a bigger downside. But I trusted Hume's instincts and he amongst others encouraged the visa. He said, 'You know,

I can only take this so far. Someone with credibility with the harder-line republicans has got to be there.'[16]

Just as President Carter had ruffled diplomatic feathers in London back in 1977 with his statement on Northern Ireland, Clinton was now doing the same. The common denominator was John Hume. Clinton's decision reinforced the influence of the Foyle MP. The SDLP leader had again been a persuader and his line of argument had worked. When it came to Northern Ireland, it was clear that the White House took its lead from him. Hume's support for the visa sent Irish republicans a strong message. The SDLP leader was indicating to them that if they embraced non-violence there were opportunities ahead. Adams landed in the United States and his visit generated intense media coverage. He was granted a restricted visa for two days and on 1 February, with John Hume and John Alderdice, the leader of the Alliance Party, he attended the National Committee on Foreign Policy conference at the Waldorf Astoria in Manhattan. It was a whirlwind visit for Adams and a major publicity coup for his party. The Sinn Féin president told CNN's Larry King: 'I want to see an end to the Irish Republican Army. I want to see the IRA disbanded and the British army removed.'[17]

In the USA, Adams became the centre of attention for journalists and camera crews. Mike Nesbitt, who would later join the UUP and become its leader, was working as a television journalist at the time. He was reporting for UTV and was at the Waldorf Astoria and remembers how everyone wanted a word with the Sinn Féin president:

> When the conference was over I watched Mr Adams in the reception area of the ballroom. He was surrounded by television cameras. I counted upwards of 40 of them, encircling him like the rings of an onion. Then, in the corner, I spied John Hume. He stood alone, smoking a cigarette as he watched. Here was John, a man who had been flying back and forth to Washington since the 1960s, single-handedly cultivating interest in our affairs, effectively handing that

curiosity and commitment to a political rival. I thought it was a remarkable image. Clearly so did John, because when I started to interview him about how he felt about this apparent handover of influence, he became cross and terminated the interview, withdrawing permission to use what we already had on tape. I took it no more, no less, than a sign of the immense pressure he felt under. I also reflect that it was one of the greatest acts of leadership of the peace process.[18]

When Adams returned to Belfast, the argument over clarifying parts of the Downing Street Declaration was still rumbling on. In February, John Major and Albert Reynolds held talks in Downing Street, and John Hume said if clarification for December's declaration was needed, it should be given. Doubts were raised about the intentions of the republican movement in March when the IRA fired mortars at Heathrow Airport. It was a confusing picture and some commentators speculated that the peace process was at an end.

Yet, there was debate going on within republican circles and in April the IRA announced a three-day ceasefire which led to suggestions that a longer cessation was on the cards. The debate over the Major–Reynolds deal continued and the British government issued a 21-page commentary on questions Sinn Féin had about the declaration.

In June, republicans gathered in Letterkenny to assess the peace process and to consider what to do next. Both the British and Irish governments had been warned that the mood music from this conference in Donegal would not look good. Officials in London and Dublin were told not to be alarmed. Several speakers criticised the Downing Street Declaration and the press reported that Sinn Féin had rejected the December deal. That was not the complete picture, however.

A briefing paper was circulated to republicans which became known as the TUAS document. The initials were purported to stand for 'Totally Unarmed Strategy', although some commentators have suggested that it stood for 'Tactical Use of Armed Struggle'. Irrespective of the precise nature of the title, the document is worthy of examination. It summed up the debate and crystallised the thinking of the Sinn Féin leadership. The report concluded that if there was agreement with 'the Dublin government, the SDLP and the Irish-American lobby on basic republican principles which would be enough to create the dynamic that would considerably advance the struggle, then it would be prepared to use the TUAS option'.[19]

This signalled the end of the IRA's campaign, and the remarks made it clear that republicans wanted to work with Dublin, the SDLP and Irish America to bring about political change. There was also an assessment of John Hume's contribution. The report talked about the difficulties in advancing the political process and stated that: 'Hume is the only SDLP person on the horizon strong enough to face the challenge.'[20]

This was a recognition by republicans of Hume's work in creating a nationalist alliance which could change the political atmosphere. It was an acknowledgement that without Hume there would be no movement from politicians in London, Dublin and Washington. By joining the ranks of constitutional nationalism, republicans were saying that the 'armed struggle' was over.

As that moment moved closer, there was still some important business to be done. Republicans wanted an American visa for the veteran IRA man Joe Cahill, who was planning to travel to the United States to talk about the impending IRA ceasefire. Cahill had been linked to the IRA for most of his life. He was lauded by republicans as a folk hero and viewed by unionists and the British government as a paramilitary godfather. Born in 1920, he was given the death penalty for the murder of a policeman, a sentence that would be commuted. He went to prison and later he rejoined the IRA, becoming a senior commander in Belfast and a member of the Army Council. In the 1970s he went overseas to secure money and guns for the IRA.

The British government opposed the idea of giving Cahill a visa and the arguments offered by officials in London mirrored those that they presented when Gerry Adams applied to travel to America. The Sinn Féin president said the Cahill visa was a test of the bona fides of the White House: 'It was also an important indicator of how seriously the Clinton administration intended to take the issue of peace in Ireland.'[21]

President Clinton's office listened to the appeal from London and also took heed of the overtures from Dublin and Sinn Féin. Once again London lost the diplomatic battle and Clinton granted Cahill a visa, believing that the veteran IRA man's presence in the USA would help Adams deliver a ceasefire. Such a cessation was top of the agenda on 28 August, when John Hume and Gerry Adams met for talks. Adams briefed the Foyle MP on what was about to happen. Afterwards, the two men noted: 'We are indeed, optimistic that the situation can be tangibly moved forward.'[22] They both knew that a statement from the IRA was just hours away.

Three days later, on 31 August, Hume heard the announcement that he had been hoping to hear. As he sat in the studios of BBC Radio Foyle, he listened intently to Donna Traynor. Shortly after 11 a.m., the news presenter broadcast details of the IRA statement. She calmly informed listeners that the IRA had stated that as of 'midnight, 31 August, there will be a complete cessation of military operations'[23] Hume was being filmed and as he tuned in to the news he smiled for the camera. Characteristically, he gave the announcement a thumbs up. The IRA statement had his seal of approval.

In nationalist parts of Belfast and Derry, there were scenes of joy with cavalcades of cars and taxis flying the Irish tricolour. Outside Connolly House in Belfast, Gerry Adams clutched flowers and a bottle of champagne and spoke from a makeshift platform to crowds of supporters. The Sinn Féin president welcomed the news and praised the IRA for its statement. Other responses were not so generous. Unionists sensed betrayal was in the air and were sceptical about the IRA's motives. The move was criticised by the UUP leader Jim Molyneaux who said there should be no move towards talks with Sinn Féin until the word 'permanent' appeared in an IRA ceasefire statement. The DUP leader, Ian Paisley, rejected the IRA statement because there was 'no expression of regret'.[24]

There was much suspicion in unionist communities of behind-the-scenes negotiating and a feeling that the UK government had done a secret deal with the IRA. John Major insisted that no such agreement had been made. He tried to reassure unionists that they should accept his word and he repeated his view that Northern Ireland's place in the union was safe and that it would not change without the consent of a majority of people in Northern Ireland. In Dublin, speaking in the Dáil, the taoiseach, Albert Reynolds, praised the role of John Hume in helping to secure the IRA ceasefire.

Days later, he got the chance to speak to him in person when both Hume and Adams visited the Irish capital for a meeting. The three men talked about the IRA ceasefire and discussed what political opportunities could now open up. The main item for discussion was the establishment of a Forum for Peace and Reconciliation. It was quite a relaxed encounter and the three leaders enjoyed tea and buns. The waiting media naturally wanted to capture the occasion, and outside Government Buildings, Reynolds, Adams and Hume stood together and posed for a photograph where they joined hands. It became an iconic image of life post-ceasefire and captured a coming together of nationalist Ireland.

Focus now shifted to the loyalist paramilitaries to see if they would follow suit and call a ceasefire – 1994 had been a particularly bloody and gruesome year with attacks from the UVF and the UFF across Northern Ireland. One of the most horrific atrocities happened in June when UVF gunmen burst into a pub in Loughinisland and shot six Catholics dead as they watched the Republic of Ireland play Italy in the World Cup. One of those who died was Barney Green who was aged 87.

By late summer, discussions were going on in loyalist circles about a cessation of violence and what form it might take. The Combined Loyalist Military Command (CLMC), which was the umbrella body for the UFF, UVF and Red Hand Commando, met in September and set out what was needed for them to follow the IRA's move. On 13 October, at a press conference in Belfast, Gusty Spence, a UVF veteran, read out a statement announcing a ceasefire and declared that loyalist paramilitaries had 'abject and true remorse' for the killing of 'innocent' victims.[25]

This was all new territory. The loyalist ceasefire added to the sense of hope in Northern Ireland that life was about to change for the better. It was no longer a case of the peace process simply being a Hume–Adams initiative, or the work of the two governments. Now loyalists were part of the conversation and had a part to play. Politically, change was in the air elsewhere. In Westminster, Tony Blair was finding his feet as the new Labour leader. He had replaced John Smith, who had died suddenly of a heart attack in May. Seen as a moderniser, Blair had served in the shadow cabinet in the 1980s and early 1990s when he took on different roles in energy, employment and home affairs. Charismatic and telegenic, he became the youngest ever Labour leader after he defeated John Prescott and Margaret Beckett in the party ballot in July. He was viewed by many political commentators in Britain as the UK's next premier and he started to receive very good opinion poll ratings.

Blair and Hume knew each other. They had both arrived in the House of Commons as new MPs back in 1983. In an interview for this book, Blair recalls his impression of the SDLP leader: 'John was a very friendly, avuncular figure, particularly for the younger Labour MPs. He was very popular in the Labour Party. And you know, we would talk less about Northern Ireland in those days in the 80s when I was an MP first. We talked less about Northern Ireland. We talked about politics in general, democratic socialist and social democratic politics and, of course, he had an enormous influence and sway in Europe.'[26]

When Blair and Hume did talk about Northern Ireland, it is clear that the Foyle MP did not hold back:

> John had this habit. He would, if you were in the division lobby, he would sidle up to you in a very conspiratorial way, then he would just say, 'Can I have a quick word with you?' And, to be honest, it wasn't often a quick word, but he would explain the situation and he would explain the pressures that were on him, pressures from within his own party. A lot of people within his own party were actually quite irritated with what he was doing. In fact, angry about what he was doing, because they thought it was validating Sinn Féin without forcing them to change. So that again is where his own … the bigness of this character was very important. I mean, I never thought of him as an SDLP

figure. I thought of him as John Hume, you know, as I say he was a figure in his own right.[27]

After becoming Labour leader, Blair told BBC Radio 4's *Today* programme he strongly backed the Downing Street Declaration and that he would not be a persuader for Irish unity. It was a significant move away from the party's original position of Irish unity by consent. Other changes were afoot.

He appointed Mo Mowlam, the MP for Redcar, as shadow Northern Ireland secretary. She had similar views to Blair and had helped to organise his leadership bid. Mowlam succeeded Kevin McNamara, who was on the 'green wing' of the Labour Party and politically and personally close to Hume. McNamara's demotion was welcomed by unionists who felt his views had coloured the Labour leadership's view on Northern Ireland and they hoped this marked a change in direction.

However, Mowlam's appointment raised some eyebrows in the conservative male-dominated world of Northern Ireland politics. She was a blunt, plain speaker who was personable and fun and engaging and did not stand on ceremony. She was seen by some commentators as a 'breath of fresh air' who threw herself into the new job. Like Blair, she made it clear she would not act as a persuader for a united Ireland but wanted a political settlement all sides could support.

Hume knew Mowlam well and got on with her. He was well used to her larger-than-life personality, her quirky sense of humour and her regular use of salty language. Mark Durkan recalls one occasion when he was taking her for the first time to the Humes's holiday home in Donegal. Durkan was driving her to Greencastle on the Inishowen peninsula and en route she told him to stop the car outside a shop. She then asked him what colour the Humes's bathroom was. Durkan seemed puzzled by the question and said he thought it was white.

Mowlam then disappeared into the shop and a few minutes later asked him for some help. Durkan remembers it clearly:

> She came out and she said, 'Can you carry that out? It's too much for me.' And essentially, I was carrying a whole big pack of toilet rolls. There must have been five or six dozen toilet rolls. So Mo explained to me, 'I know friends, friends of mine, who have weekend homes, holiday homes. The thing that is a good gift for them is toilet roll because it is always an issue.' So she basically came with what she estimated would be at least a year's supply of toilet rolls for the house.[28]

Durkan recalls how Mowlam then presented her hosts with their bumper supply of dozens of loo rolls. The Humes seemed quite bemused by the unusual gift, but they would soon get used to her unique style. Both Pat and John got on well with her, and she relaxed in their company. The Labour MP did ruffle a few feathers with her use of swear words and profanities and often had nicknames for other politicians.

Durkan remembers how she would often refer to Hume during meetings:

> If John was going into tutorial mode with her, she would go, 'Yes, Daddy, Yes Daddy, I understand that Daddy.' And at times she would call him shitface. This was not just to focus attention but also the attention of the room. She would also call Seamus [Mallon] shitface occasionally as well.[29]

Hume's relationship with Mowlam and Blair would prove to be crucial in the months after the ceasefire. He was given a rousing reception at the Labour Party conference in 1994 when he spoke in front of delegates. Neil, now Lord Kinnock, was on the platform that day. He recalls how Hume was received and remembers it as 'a moment of real satisfaction'.[30]

As the weeks passed, the SDLP leader was understandably keen to keep the pressure on the administrations in London and Dublin and was genuinely worried that the political process would slow or get bogged down in petty arguments or word games. There was much debate over whether the IRA's ceasefire was permanent – and endless discussions in the media over what the word meant. Aside from the linguistic arguments, there were obvious signs of change in Northern Ireland. John Major visited Belfast and said talks involving Sinn Féin could commence soon. For the first time in 25 years, soldiers stopped patrolling the streets of Derry, and RUC officers dispensed with their flak jackets when they went out on patrol. Barriers on unapproved border roads were removed and an investment conference was planned for December. To misquote W.B. Yeats, it seemed peace was coming, but dropping slowly.

As ever, unpredictable events dictated the mood and direction of the process. The IRA carried out a robbery in Newry and killed Frank Kerr, a postman. The awful news sent shockwaves through political circles and many politicians and political commentators started to question if the IRA was genuine and if the ceasefire was now in fact over.

The killing and the robbery of £131,000 placed a question mark against the credibility of the republican movement and as a consequence posed big questions for the administrations in London and Dublin. The IRA issued a statement to say that the robbery had not been sanctioned and apologised for what had happened. The Irish government reacted quickly and halted the release of a number of republican prisoners. The peace process was rocked and there was more instability to come.

In Dublin, Albert Reynolds dramatically resigned as taoiseach over a controversy surrounding the extradition of a paedophile priest from Belfast called Father Brendan Smyth. Smyth was accused of abusing children in Northern Ireland and there were allegations that his extradition had not been handled properly. The story grew bigger by the day and Albert Reynolds was in the line of fire. The tánaiste, Dick Spring, withdrew his support from the coalition government and the pressure on Reynolds intensified. His premiership was over and he resigned on 17 November, prompting much speculation about what his departure would mean for the peace process.

For republicans, it was a worrying development. After all, in their TUAS document, written before the ceasefire, activists spoke about Reynolds being a key influencer and described the Fianna Fáil coalition as 'the strongest government in 25 years or more'.[31]

With Reynolds gone, others were catapulted into the top tier of the political world. The Fine Gael leader, John Bruton, became taoiseach, heading a coalition government with Labour and the Democratic Left. Bertie Ahern was elected as leader of Fianna Fáil. The peace process now had two new faces. Hume knew them both well and hoped as political leaders they could work together and present a united front to John Major. His main concern was the speed of political change. He found things frustratingly slow and felt the two governments needed to be more proactive. He insisted that crucial time was being wasted.

As he travelled across Europe and the United States, Hume was prepared to say that to anyone who would listen.

17

PRESIDENT HUME

'I don't think he would have made a very good president.'
John Hume Junior

Neil Kinnock paid attention to the words of his old friend. They were talking about a familiar subject – Northern Ireland. For years he had been schooled in the intricacies of Irish politics by the SDLP leader. Now he and Hume had a new venue for their late-night discussions over several bottles of wine.

After leaving the House of Commons in 1995, Kinnock had become the European commissioner for transport and he and his MEP wife, Glenys, often found themselves in Strasbourg or Brussels on EU business. They would dine with John Hume and would quickly discover if the peace process was in a good place or dire straits. Kinnock says Hume's mood was linked to political progress and he recalls seeing him at times when he was clearly depressed:

> I did encounter him assailed by that private doubt. Things were manifestly bleak. People were doing and saying stupid things that could undo hours and hours and weeks and weeks of painful discussion and exchange, understanding. That is when he really got down. He would come out with phrases like 'These bastards, will they never, ever learn?' and then you knew he was hitting the bottom of any glass of optimism. And then you would encounter him two days later and a little bit of a nudge forward had been achieved. And he would say 'Not all the bastards are stupid.'[1]

For Hume, 1995 was a mixture of setbacks and forward moves. In February, the British government and the new John Bruton administration in Dublin published the Framework Document. The publication confirmed that the talks process would follow Hume's template and there would be three strands to the initiative. Strand one would examine relations within Northern Ireland, with the other two strands looking at London–Dublin arrangements and the North–South axis. The plans also included the establishment of a 90-seat assembly at Stormont with elections conducted by proportional representation. There would be a new North–South body and there were commitments from the Irish and British governments to amend legislation relating to Northern Ireland.

Consent was at the heart of the document, and it was based on getting the agreement of the local parties. Elements of the document were leaked to *The Times* newspaper in advance, which claimed the agreement brought 'a united Ireland closer'.[2] There was strong criticism of the publication from unionists who saw it as too nationalist, and Hume appealed to them to remain calm and cool. He hoped the document would open the door for all-party talks but he would be bitterly disappointed. Much of 1995 was spent discussing the issue of decommissioning.

The British government and the unionist parties wanted evidence that the IRA were genuine and that meant clear evidence that their weapons had been decommissioned. Sinn Féin and the SDLP saw things differently. The debate threatened to stall the entire peace process, and as the months slipped by, Hume became more and more exasperated by the political log-jam. There were now real fears in Irish government circles and in the nationalist and republican communities that the demand for prior decommissioning could derail the entire process. Over the summer, the debate continued and there was little sign of a resolution. July was dominated by a dispute at Drumcree in County Armagh after Orangemen were prevented from parading along the Garvaghy Road in Portadown. The standoff resulted in roadblocks and violence across Northern Ireland. Despite opposition from nationalists, a number of Orangemen were eventually allowed to make the journey into Portadown. On 11 July, in front of cheering supporters, Ian Paisley and David Trimble finished the parade holding their arms aloft.

It was a crowning moment for Trimble, who had become the MP for Upper Bann in 1990 and was seen by some observers as the coming man in unionism. In August, when Jim Molyneaux announced his resignation as UUP leader, the former academic from Queen's University joined the list of candidates. John Taylor, a veteran from the days of Sunningdale and a former MEP, was seen as the favourite and many thought Trimble would be beaten.

However, he defied the sceptics and the bookies, winning the contest and pushing Taylor into second place. His surprise victory triggered alarm bells in London and Dublin and within nationalism. Trimble was viewed by some as a sash-wearing hardliner who was battle-scarred from street protests. His past association with the right-wing Vanguard group in the 1970s and his stance over Drumcree led many political observers to conclude that the chances of a political deal were low. Hume and Trimble did not have a great relationship at this point. Trimble had been very critical of the Hume–Adams talks and he and the SDLP leader had regularly clashed in debates in the House of Commons. Trimble had been an opponent of the Sunningdale executive back in 1974 and worked behind the scenes in the campaign that finally toppled power-sharing. It was a time that Hume remembered as a missed opportunity.

Republicans took to the streets of Belfast in mid-August and repeated their demands for all-party talks. At the City Hall, a man in the crowd shouted: 'Bring back the IRA,' to which the Sinn Féin president Gerry Adams replied: 'They haven't gone away, you know.'[3] His off-the-cuff remark angered unionists, and inevitably it was raised with Hume in interviews with journalists. He replied that the most important thing was the fact that the violence was over. Not for the first time, Hume was having to explain Sinn Féin thinking. After a difficult summer and with the ceasefire over a year old and still no sign of all-party talks, Hume felt the prognosis for political progress looked bleak. As he took his annual holiday to France he was depressed. He saw the past 12 months as a year of wasted opportunities.

His gloom was spectacularly lifted in November with the visit of

President Clinton to Northern Ireland. Wherever he and the First Lady went they were given a rousing reception with massive crowds. In Derry, Hume shared the stage with the Clintons at Guildhall Square. It was a magical moment for the city and its MP, who felt thrilled at the prospect of having the most powerful man in the world in his hometown. In front of thousands of well-wishers, Clinton praised the SDLP leader. He told the crowd that he was 'proud to be here in the home of Ireland's most tireless champion for civil rights and its most eloquent voice for non-violence, John Hume'.[4]

Clinton was the first American president to visit Northern Ireland, and to Hume, it was an example of what a peace process could deliver. His trip included Belfast where he was watched by thousands of people under the Christmas lights at the City Hall and he also met Gerry Adams on the Falls Road. The presidential trip came hours after an Anglo-Irish summit that was aimed at breaking the log-jam over decommissioning. John Major and John Bruton established a three-person international body which would study how decommissioning could be brought about and how talks could commence. George Mitchell, who was a former US senator, was appointed chairman of the commission and he was joined by General John de Chastelain from Canada and the former Finnish prime minister Harri Holkeri.

The three men produced their findings in January 1996 after taking evidence from local parties, representatives from Dublin and London and church leaders. They concluded that the paramilitary groupings would not decommission their weapons before talks and recommended that talking and decommissioning should happen in tandem. In a sense, this was a 'twin-track' approach and the hope was it could uncork the political bottleneck which had lasted since the ceasefires of 1994. John Major took a different approach and said that the way forward was either prior decommissioning or an election.

The plan for an election later in the year was greeted warmly by unionists but was heavily criticised by Hume, Adams and the Dublin government. The Major plan was to elect a pool of representatives to a 110-strong body called the Northern Ireland Forum. After the election, the teams of party negotiators would emerge from that body. The hope from London was that smaller parties would end up as part of the negotiations, which would make the discussions as inclusive as possible.

Ninety seats were to be allocated using the traditional constituencies and a further twenty would be allocated to ten parties with the most votes overall. Major's plan could be characterised as elections first and talks afterwards.

Hume was angry with the prime minister's decision. He wanted all-party talks to happen immediately and saw the election to a fresh body as unnecessary and time-consuming. He knew it would take many weeks to organise and an election campaign would delay the start of all-party negotiations. The Foyle MP's arguments were in vain because the UK government began to put the election plan in place. Republicans felt Major had mishandled the situation and was pandering to unionists, whose votes at Westminster were proving crucial. Gerry Adams and John Hume had both warned London that the peace process was in crisis and within days those fears became real.

On Friday 9 February, the IRA detonated a massive bomb at Canary Wharf in London which killed two people, injured dozens of people and destroyed many buildings. The cost of the damage was put at around £100 million and that night the television images of destruction went around the world. The political establishments in the UK, Ireland and the United States reacted with horror and shock. Hume was heartbroken when he heard the news. He was in Dublin at a birthday party for Garret FitzGerald and the reports emerging from London's Docklands upset him. The 17-month ceasefire was shattered and to many political observers it looked like the peace process was dead and buried. Hume did not agree. He gathered his thoughts and, in the days that followed, argued that this was not a time to despair and politicians should redouble their efforts for peace.

Inevitably, unionists seized on his association with Adams and his talks with the Sinn Féin president and they called on Hume to disassociate himself from republicans. He ignored their advice and met Adams in an attempt to discover why the ceasefire had collapsed and how it could be restored.

In May, both men led their respective parties into the Forum elections. When the results were declared, the main parties dominated as ever. The UUP with new leader David Trimble was the largest party, securing 30 seats, with the DUP at 24, the SDLP with 21, Sinn Féin with 17 seats and the Alliance Party with 7. Sinn Féin polled its highest share of the vote for over a decade and the SDLP vote slipped marginally. The smaller parties, UKUP, PUP, UDP, Labour and the NI Women's Coalition, all gained seats as well, mainly from the regional list. It meant they could have a place in the talks process.

Hume had little enthusiasm for the new body and saw it as a distraction from his goal of all-party talks. He continued to meet and have discussions with Gerry Adams, in the hope that a second IRA ceasefire could be delivered which would open the door for substantive negotiations. As the talks continued behind the scenes, the SDLP made changes to the party structure and new people were brought in to help with organisation. After the Forum elections, a young political activist, Conall McDevitt, was appointed to look after the media operation. McDevitt, who was in his early 20s, had a background in the Irish Labour Party and had been a huge Hume admirer from afar. He had grown up in Spain and had previously met the SDLP leader at a conference of European socialists in Barcelona.

McDevitt found himself with Hume regularly, and as well as doing the traditional press officer work of writing news releases and organising interviews, he remembers being at meetings with the SDLP leader: 'I was getting invited to join John on escapades and little trips. I ended up in houses in Belfast and Derry and elsewhere, where I met Gerry Adams. So I was aware of what was going on.'[5]

McDevitt says Hume was determined to get a second IRA ceasefire, but the press coverage and criticism of his previous relationship with Adams had left him bruised:

I think he was carrying the scars of the criticism from the early 1990s, from the way that the *Sunday Independent* particularly had behaved in that period. I think he carried the hurt and the sense of betrayal by fellow Irish people. You know, a small majority of Irish people failed to support the bleedingly obvious endeavour he was engaged in. I think he carried that with great sadness and with a heavy burden, but by '96 I suspect he could see the end.[6]

As McDevitt began working for John Hume, another young man was starting a similar political apprenticeship. Law graduate David Kerr had been taken on by the UUP leader, David Trimble, to work as his personal assistant and adviser. Trimble needed someone to help with legislation and policy issues and Kerr was very keen to take on the role. He remembers the day of the job interview when his father, Bertie, said to him: 'You never know what might happen in the next year or two. You never know, there might even be a deal.'[7] David's father, Bertie, was a UUP councillor, and his prediction in the spring of 1996 would turn out to be prescient.

Like Conall McDevitt's relationship with Hume, David Kerr's role with Trimble took many forms. There were policies to research and documents to write; he briefed journalists and organised Trimble's schedule. Like McDevitt, he witnessed some important meetings, including one of the encounters in 1996 involving the SDLP and the UUP. He recalls Hume speaking to Trimble and remembers what he said. In a room on the Stormont estate, Hume sat down with his party colleagues and Trimble and his team and looked over at the UUP leader. Kerr recalls Hume explaining that they were all there to make an agreement – the UUP wanted an assembly and the SDLP wanted a North–South element in the agreement to recognise their Irish identity and give balance to the overall political equation. Kerr remembers Hume saying 'I don't really care what it is called. If we can get agreement on how that works and we can get a deal on power-sharing then you know we will have a deal.' According to Kerr, Trimble replied: 'Look, if the North–South element is not a threat to unionism then we are up for that, basically. We are up for a deal.'[8]

Kerr remembers that the meeting was conducted in a good atmosphere:

> It was very pleasant. It was very cordial. I genuinely thought when I got up from the meeting – I mean there was a bit of small talk and a bit of toing and froing but that didn't last very long – when I got up from the meeting, I thought, 'My God we will have this deal done in no time.'[9]

David Kerr shared his father's optimism that there could be a political agreement soon.

However, other leading UUP figures urged caution and claimed a deal was far from certain and Hume was unreliable. Kerr was told by party veterans that they held the Foyle MP responsible for scuppering a previous talks deal:

> The issue with John was that there was this legacy hangover issue from 1991/92. So I had it drummed into me by our talks team that they blamed him for the failure of the 1991/92 process. Because Reg said – and Reg Empey was our main guy across all the detail – and Reg said, 'Look, we thought we had a deal with John in the previous talks process, but when push came to shove, he didn't want to do a deal without Sinn Féin being party to it.'[10]

Mark Durkan has repeatedly rejected the suggestion that Hume was the reason there was no talks agreement in 1992. He insists his party leader was committed to talking and making an agreement, but back then unionists took a very different view. In the mid-1990s, it was part of the unionist mindset that Hume was a deal breaker and had to be watched. Unionists felt Hume was fixated with Adams and the IRA and wanted to put his discussions with republicans ahead of any talks with other parties.

David Kerr says the Hume–Adams process made unionists uneasy:

> Did that create a level of mistrust? It probably did. It certainly didn't make us feel overly confident about the chances of success. And so you know you had to work through the process and it was extremely slow. Then you had the IRA stuff going on in the background.[11]

The issue of decommissioning and the lack of an IRA ceasefire dominated the political process in 1996. The SDLP stayed away from the Northern Ireland Forum but continued to contribute to the talks under the chairmanship of Senator George Mitchell. Multi-party discussions continued in October without Sinn Féin but the pace was slow and progress was limited.

In the background, discussions were going on at many levels about the possibility of restoring the IRA ceasefire. Hume and Adams continued to talk, and there were internal discussions amongst republicans. Officials in Dublin and Washington also kept a dialogue going behind the scenes in an attempt to move the process forward. Hume felt he was making some headway with Adams and thought he had a formula that could change the atmosphere. He was working on a text that looked at a timeframe when Sinn Féin could enter the talks and included a list of measures the British government would take. As the year moved to an end, Hume presented John Major with new ceasefire proposals from the IRA.

The prime minister was sceptical and insisted that any fresh cessation would have to be assessed, and the IRA would have to prove it was not merely a tactic. Major used a statement in the House of Commons to make it clear that another ceasefire would not guarantee Sinn Féin immediate entry to the talks. Hume was deflated and angry with the response and felt political games were being played by Major and that he was trying to keep unionists sweet. Hume often went into Downing Street on his own and did not normally invite any other SDLP MPs to join him. That sometimes annoyed his colleagues, who felt they were being excluded. Joe Hendron who was MP for West Belfast remembers the mood in the party: 'Seamus was annoyed that he wasn't asked to go in too and Eddie McGrady was annoyed and so was I.'[12]

In the final days of 1996, John Major's premiership was living on borrowed time. At this stage, his parliamentary majority was evaporating and he was becoming reliant on David Trimble's UUP MPs. A general election was just months away and, if the polls were right, Tony Blair would soon be in Downing Street. Hume did not want to wait for the changing of the guard at Westminster.

The new year arrived the same way as the old had ended for Hume. He was depressed with the lack of political progress and was becoming deeply frustrated in his dealings with the Conservative administration in London. There were also other matters troubling the SDLP leader, and in January 1997 he held a meeting with Sir John Chilcott, the top civil servant in the Northern Ireland Office. The conversation was essentially to discuss the peace process but Hume took Chilcott by surprise when he began to discuss allegations that were being talked about privately by the media.

Unprompted and without warning, Hume said that on at least two occasions in recent months he had been told of stories circulating amongst journalists about his private life. The stories were suggesting he was conducting an affair or affairs in London and elsewhere. There had been a recent article about an unnamed politician, and after this appeared, Hume told Chilcott he had contacted the political editor of a tabloid newspaper to discuss the stories that were circulating about him. The journalist, according to Hume, told him he was aware of what was being said in media circles but his newspaper did not have any evidence and was not planning to publish such a story.

Hume was exercised about this, and in his meeting said that he and Pat would 'dismiss such stories out of hand'. Hinting at potential legal action if a story appeared, he said if anything was published he 'would expect to be richer in consequence'. He said that there were other suggestions that the 'IRA were blackmailing him' which he described as 'absurd nonsense'. Hume insisted that recent disputes with Sinn Féin on electoral matters 'gave it the obvious lie'.[13]

A detailed note of this conversation was written up by Sir John Chilcott and sent to the cabinet secretary who was Sir Robin Butler. He made the information available to the then prime minister, John Major. Today the document rests in the National Archives in London and it was made public in 2020 as part of the regular disclosure of cabinet and government papers. Both RTÉ and the current affairs magazine *Village* reported on the Chilcott document in December 2020.

Like many politicians, Hume found that his personal life was often the subject of gossip and rumour, and he knew tabloid journalists, in particular, had been asking questions. He was also conscious that he could be the target of 'dirty tricks' from either political opponents or state agencies. He was used to being in the public eye and knew that his movements were often being watched.

Sometimes the monitoring was official and legitimate, and other times it was covert and sinister. He had experienced his privacy being invaded after his home telephone in Derry was bugged by republicans and recordings were later discovered by the police involving conversations with family members. By the early spring of 1997, Hume had a great deal on his mind, and he felt under pressure. Many within his party wondered if his association with Sinn Féin would damage its electoral prospects in the forthcoming election. He continued to face criticism in the press and the chances of a second IRA ceasefire looked bleak.

Denis Bradley remembers the strain the SDLP leader was under:

> Hume came to this house most days, every second day. And he was under pressure from his party. I remember that period when people were wondering what was happening. And he was smoking a lot. People's memory of that time was how much John was smoking. He was chain-smoking. And the pressure was great. And [he] talked about the pressure and talked about everything. And it was difficult to watch because he was under enormous pressure and the Provos, I think, handled him very badly.[14]

All the local parties were now getting ready for the general election, and the issue of an electoral pact between the SDLP and Sinn Féin once again raised its head. Hume made it clear that there would have to be an IRA ceasefire and Sinn Féin would have to take their seats at Westminster before such an arrangement might be possible.

Without another IRA cessation, Hume was pretty explicit on how his party should respond: 'To make an electoral pact with Sinn Féin without an IRA ceasefire would be the equivalent of asking our voters to support the killing of innocent human beings by the IRA. The electorate should be aware that in voting for Sinn Féin, that is what they are voting for.'[15]

Hume's criticism was stark:

> This cannot go on. There must be a ceasefire so that we can begin to put the pieces together again, difficult though that might be. We can begin to rebuild a viable strategy for achieving a democratic settlement. Without a ceasefire, we are going to have to look elsewhere for a means of making progress.[16]

Hume's warning to the republican movement was blunt, and his frustration was laid bare in his threat to 'look elsewhere' if a cessation was not forthcoming. Politically things were on hold until after the general election, and it made sense to pause discussions since there was little chance of any movement during the campaign.

May brought political change on a massive scale. Tony Blair swept into power with a landslide victory and a thumping majority of 179 seats. John Major resigned as Conservative Party leader and the era of 'New Labour' began in earnest. Sinn Féin had a good election and took back the West Belfast seat from Joe Hendron. Martin McGuinness became the new MP for Mid Ulster. Despite losing West Belfast, the SDLP had its best-ever vote, securing 190,000 votes and 24 per cent of the poll. Hume, Mallon and McGrady all retained their seats but the defeat of Hendron to Adams left a sour taste with SDLP members.

The arrival of Tony Blair in Downing Street changed the political dynamic and there was a feeling that the peace process might just be given a new lease of life. Mo Mowlam landed in Belfast as the new Northern Ireland secretary, declaring that a fresh ceasefire was her priority. She and Hume quickly developed a good rapport, as Aidan Hume recalled: 'Mo Mowlam would be someone Dad had an enormous respect for. He saw her as one who had a lot of personal courage.'[17]

As promised, talks began again in June, but once more Sinn Féin was absent from the discussions. Blair made it clear how republicans could enter the talks process and made it clear that there had to be a fresh IRA ceasefire that was lasting and permanent. In July, Hume and Adams met, and after their discussions, the two men issued a joint statement. It was quite an upbeat assessment which praised the new British government and the new Irish administration headed by Fianna Fáil's Bertie Ahern. The new taoiseach had taken office just weeks after Blair had come to power in the UK.

Blair says Hume had the ability to outline in precise terms exactly what was happening. In an interview for this book, Blair said Hume spoke clearly with authority:

> He was an incredibly useful explainer of what was really going on. Because part of the trouble you get into in the politics of Northern Ireland, for very obvious reasons, is you can never be quite sure what people are really saying to you. And it is very difficult if you are an outsider, and you know you are an outsider – even if you are British prime minister you are still an outsider, in one sense. And it's very hard at times to comprehend whether what people are telling you is what they are really telling you.[18]

By now, both Hume and Adams had high hopes that the new leaders in Dublin and London would give the peace process a fresh dimension. After their discussions, they said there was now a huge onus on both governments to respond 'positively and imaginatively'.[19]

In a statement to the media, they said 'considerable progress' had been made. This naturally pre-empted speculation that a ceasefire was on the cards. The two men knew exactly what was about to happen. Two days later, the IRA said it had ended its campaign of violence. It was announced that there would be 'a complete cessation of military operations' from midday on Sunday 20 July.[20]

Hume was relieved and delighted. He felt vindicated at continuing his discussions with republicans and believed that at last political progress could be made. However, he was well aware that an IRA ceasefire was only part of the equation, as the issue of decommissioning remained unresolved. Hume knew that convincing unionists to begin talks without it would be difficult but he insisted the issue could be tackled during the discussions. As expected, the DUP withdrew from the talks but the UUP said it would remain in the process. However, the party asked Tony Blair for clarification on the issue of decommissioning.[21]

David Trimble made it clear the UUP was prepared to take part in talks if the conditions were right. In order to deal with decommissioning, both the British and Irish governments agreed to set up an international body aimed at securing the removal of weapons. It was to be in place by September, a few days after the multi-party talks at Stormont were to recommence.

As Hume prepared for a summer break in France, he found himself the subject of more media scrutiny. Earlier in the year, Mary Robinson had announced that she would not be standing for a second term of office as Irish president. She decided to take a job with the United Nations and her departure resulted in speculation that Hume might be a candidate for Áras an Uachtaráin. It was reported that if the SDLP leader was nominated he would get the backing of several parties in the Dáil and would easily win the contest. He was seen as a 'shoo-in' and the idea of a Hume presidency started to gain a lot of traction. Mary McAleese, who ultimately became the Irish president in 1997, remembers the speculation about the SDLP leader:

> When Mary Robinson decided that she was not going to remain as president, if you remember, she left a little bit early to take on the job of UN High Commissioner and my immediate reaction on hearing that was John Hume will be the next president of Ireland. It was his for the taking, without a shadow of doubt. All he had to do was to say he was interested and John Hume would have been president. And a number of people including Alec [Reid] asked me to consider it ... and my reaction was, this is John Hume's. This is John Hume's moment and I thought he would have made a great president.[22]

As Hume holidayed in France, at a house near La Rochelle on the Atlantic coast, the speculation over his presidential nomination continued. He met up with his old friend from home Maurice Hayes, and the subject of the Irish presidency was discussed. Hume's son John recalls those days: 'I remember there were various sorts of emissaries, sorts of phone calls. I think he was very flattered to be asked, extremely flattered, to be honest.'[23]

The stories about a Hume candidacy continued throughout August and into early September and it was clear he would get the support of major parties in the Dáil if he decided to run. Letters and cards started to arrive at the office asking Hume to consider the nomination.

The SDLP's head of press, Conall McDevitt, remembers the weekend in early September 1997, when Hume made his intentions public and declared he was not interested. McDevitt was on a weekend away with his fiancée at a hotel in County Cavan. The pair were just weeks away from their wedding and needed a break from the hustle and bustle of life in Belfast. The Sunday papers were keen to determine whether or not Hume was a serious contender and McDevitt was taking calls from journalists. Looking back, he says it was not the right time for Hume to leave the political fray in Northern Ireland: 'I think had the presidential election come around in the summer of '98, my personal hunch is that John would have accepted the nomination and become president of

Ireland.' McDevitt insists that Hume wanted to see a political settlement and 'was not leaving Northern Ireland until the job was done'.[24]

Hume issued a statement saying it would have been an honour to become president of Ireland as an agreed candidate and he thanked those who had supported him and encouraged him to stand. However, he insisted the peace process was at 'a very crucial stage' and he wanted to stay with his colleagues in the SDLP and work towards achieving 'a new and agreed Ireland based on a lasting settlement and a lasting peace'. He said he would remain in his present position and said it had been 'a very difficult decision'.[25]

His son John insists that his father was never going to run for the presidency: 'I don't think it was ever under serious consideration. I don't think he would have been a very good president.'[26] Jokingly, John thinks some aspects of the role would never have suited him: 'Could you see him sitting through rugby matches?' He thinks his father would have found the role constraining: 'Dad would just go wandering, I mean they would not have been able to keep an eye on him.'[27]

Aidan Hume agrees with his brother and thinks his father would have found the role difficult: 'I don't think being president was something that would have really appealed to him. I think he would have been a prisoner to Phoenix Park in many ways.'[28]

With the speculation about his future put to bed, Hume and his colleagues settled down to a series of political discussions in September. Sinn Féin signed up to the Mitchell Principles of non-violence and formally joined the talks process. Likewise, after long meetings behind closed doors, the UUP decided to participate in the inter-party negotiations despite concerns over decommissioning. The DUP stayed away but the smaller loyalist parties, the UDP and the PUP, both took part.

Bertie Ahern and Tony Blair knew it was key to keep David Trimble at the table, so the two premiers issued a statement on decommissioning and consent in the hope it would reassure wavering unionists. The early stages of discussions under the chairmanship of George Mitchell were slow and at times tortuous. Hume used his annual address to party activists in November to appeal to unionists to take the opportunity that the talks presented. The hope was that by December party delegations could have agreed key issues and made substantial progress, but that did not happen, so George Mitchell adjourned the talks until the new year. Some political commentators who were optimistic suggested it was good that the parties were still engaged. Other observers, well used to the failure of past initiatives, predicted it was only a matter of time before the process ended without agreement.

As 1998 began, the talks process faced enormous pressure on several fronts. The Continuity IRA, a dissident republican group which opposed the peace process, carried out a series of bomb attacks and the INLA murdered a leading loyalist. UDA and UFF inmates in the Maze prison withdrew their support for the talks. That prompted politicians, including Mo Mowlam, to visit the jail in an attempt to get them to change their minds. On the streets, the breakaway Loyalist Volunteer Force carried out a series of shootings.

There was strong political opposition to the talks process from Ian Paisley's DUP and Bob McCartney's UK Unionist Party. By mid-January, the bones of a possible deal began to take shape when a 'Heads of Agreement' document was drawn up by the British and Irish governments. It was a piece of educated guesswork on the part of London and Dublin on what might be acceptable to the parties. The document talked about an assembly, a new British–Irish agreement and a North–South ministerial council. There were also suggested changes to Articles 2 and 3 of the Irish Constitution and to the Government of Ireland Act at Westminster.

It was a bold move by Tony Blair and Bertie Ahern. The two premiers were trying to find common ground to keep the process alive. The initiative was described by Mo Mowlam as a 'breakthrough' but her upbeat assessment was somewhat optimistic.[29]

The mood soured in the weeks that followed and there was a series of complaints, spats and changes to who sat at the talks table. Sinn Féin criticised the 'Heads of Agreement' saying it made concessions to loyalist violence. In turn, the UUP had issues with a further talks paper that was produced on North–South links. The UDP, which had its origins in the loyalist paramilitary group the UDA, voluntarily left the talks process.

The UDP exit came after it was ruled that the loyalist paramilitary group the UFF (a cover name for the UDA) had been involved in a killing and had therefore breached the Mitchell Principles of non-violence. In late February, there was another exit from the talks table when Sinn Féin was expelled after the RUC declared that the IRA had been involved in two recent murders. There were other moments when private discord became public. John Hume took aim at Sinn Féin, saying its opposition to an assembly was not helpful.

The UUP MP Jeffrey Donaldson, who would later defect to Ian Paisley's DUP, also claimed that relations with Mo Mowlam were bad and claimed she was showing favouritism to Sinn Féin. The mood music was not good. It seemed everyone had grievances and there was little sign of trust or goodwill. By late February, inter-party relations were poor, nothing had been agreed and the prospect of a deal looked slim.

18

DOWN AT THE WATERFRONT

'I am not going to negotiate with a fucking fax machine.'
John Hume

On the last day of March, 1998, John Hume walked up the most famous street in London. It was a familiar journey. He arrived at the polished black door that he had knocked on a hundred times before and within seconds he was ushered inside. He crossed the black-and-white floor, passed the portraits and made his way along the labyrinth of corridors. The SDLP leader was angry and there was a lot he wanted to say.

Primarily, he was cross with Tony Blair for the way he was treating the talks process. He did not think he was handling the negotiations properly. He was exasperated by the lack of progress and frustrated by the way the discussions were going. Hume had seen too many political initiatives come and go over the decades. He was battle-hardened and very anxious, and he did not want to see this latest initiative fail. He felt the new occupant of Number 10 had shown leadership since coming into power but had misjudged the moment. When the two men met there was little time for niceties or diplomacy.

Hume looked at the prime minister: 'I am not going to negotiate with a fucking fax machine.' Hume told Blair that he and Ahern needed to get personally involved in the talks. He insisted the talks were an 'inclusive process' and they could not be conducted remotely.[1]

Hume's rage had been prompted by a fax from Downing Street to the offices of the SDLP in Belfast outlining the government's latest ideas on a multi-party agreement. He had read the document and had not been impressed. After discussing it with his colleagues he then boarded a plane to London to see Tony Blair in person.

By early April 1998, the chances of a political deal looked remote. Days before, the UUP MP John Taylor, often seen as a barometer of party thinking, put the odds of success as low as 5 per cent. In his role as talks chairperson, George Mitchell had stated that 9 April was the deadline for agreement. The significance of that day was not lost on some who had a keen eye on the calendar. It was Holy Thursday. Mitchell remained hopeful that there was a chance an agreement could be made but he knew very well that the underlying mood was still not positive. With the Easter holidays fast approaching, the feeling was that this moment could well pass by without a breakthrough.

With the deadline hours away, Tony Blair and Bertie Ahern arrived in Northern Ireland in the hope that they could narrow the differences between the parties and make a historic deal. The presence of the two premiers gave the discussions a sense of urgency and increased speculation that a deal was imminent, but behind the scenes, there was still a lot of work to do. For hours, the parties met and various texts were discussed. The atmosphere altered all the time. Sometimes it seemed an agreement was possible, and at other moments the discussions looked like they were on the brink of collapse.

The talks were detailed and complex and the text was constantly changing. Even battle-hardened negotiators sometimes had to be reminded about what plans were up for discussion and what ideas were not. During endless conversations, there was one amusing moment when Hume was caught out by the detail.

SDLP General Secretary Gerry Cosgrove recalls being in a meeting with him: 'So John sat down in the middle of the room and the [Irish] Department of Foreign Affairs representatives went through whatever was happening and I was standing there and I said to myself, "I must be really stupid because I haven't a clue what they are talking about. I don't know what that means." I was standing there thinking. So they finished what they had to say and then they went out.'[2] Gerry Cosgrove remembers Hume's reaction: 'He looked up then and said, "Can someone tell me what they are talking about because I don't know." And I went, Thank you, God, I am not the only one that did not understand.'[3]

As Good Friday approached, dozens of journalists had gathered outside the Castle Buildings complex on the Stormont estate, their focus on the unremarkable brick building that was playing host to the talks. Such was the media interest that by now there was rolling television and radio coverage. There were press photographers and camera staff from across the world, all reporting on what had become an international news story. Every arrival and departure was filmed and when talks negotiators crept outside for a smoke or a break their every move was captured.

There were big issues to solve: power-sharing, policing, decommissioning, prisoners and future political relationships. There were serious rows and disagreements. At times it seemed like the process was on the verge of collapse.

However, on other occasions, the atmosphere was positive, as Hume recalled in an unpublished interview he gave in 2003:

> I remember at one stage looking out of a window with some of my colleagues at the press outside and saying God, if those boys were in here, they would not believe it. Because of the normality of the relationship that had developed between the negotiators from the different parties. Because we were together so long and so often.[4]

Using the three-stranded approach to the talks process, which had been Hume's original idea, the agreement started to take shape. The UUP leader, David Trimble, was having difficulty convincing some of his colleagues that the deal was worth backing and, in particular, there was strong opposition from leading figures including Jeffrey Donaldson and Arlene Foster. They had major objections to the release of paramilitary prisoners and the reform of the RUC. Foster and Donaldson would later join, and subsequently lead, the DUP. Despite the internal dissent, Trimble felt there was more in the deal to support than oppose and he signalled his intent to make an agreement. Bríd Rodgers remembers the moment when Seamus Mallon came into the SDLP room at Castle Buildings to give her the good news.

As Seamus Mallon returned very late to the SDLP room, Rodgers was unaware at that time that the building was being filmed by a TV crew standing outside the perimeter:

> Seamus came down that night and said that we had reached agreement with the unionists on the Northern Ireland thing (Strand One). So the relief was huge. So I just gave Seamus a big hug, but obviously, the cameras were on us, which I did not know. Anyway, it was a relief. It was just the emotion was unbelievable that we had actually got it.[5]

The silhouette image of a joyful Mallon and Rodgers embracing told the story. It was an iconic moment – confirmation that a deal appeared to be coming. Yet in reality, it was not completely signed and sealed, and when Good Friday arrived, President Clinton wanted to speak to John Hume.

Conall McDevitt remembers the call:

> The phone rings. It is the White House, but for whatever reason they put the president straight through. So I hear this voice on the end of the phone going, 'John, John?' And I am like 'Mr President, it's not John, it's Conall McDevitt.' 'I thought I was going to speak to John?' 'I am his press officer.' 'Is he there?' 'Ok, well,' I said, 'yes, he is. Let me get him for you.' So I had a brief exchange with Clinton. The only time I have ever answered the phone and found the president on the end of it. And then they went away and then they talked.[6]

Hume's influence was clear. Clinton was taking his lead from the man who had been lobbying US presidents for decades and whose judgement he trusted. There were other conversations that Hume had, as George

Mitchell's new deadline approached. There were some last-minute discussions involving Tony Blair and Bertie Ahern and Hume was nervous about getting a deal over the line. Margaret Ritchie says there were telltale signs of Hume's state of mind: 'You could always tell when John was around because there would have been ashtrays with cigarettes packed in them, three-quarters smoked. And that was always John.'[7]

The other issue on Good Friday morning was the lack of food. The party negotiators had had little sleep and were desperate for something to eat. Mo Mowlam got the canteen staff to come in early, and bacon rolls and croissants were provided which were warmly received. Conall McDevitt remembers one thoughtful staff member providing John Hume with his favourite breakfast of scrambled eggs and smoked salmon. As the day wore on Mark Durkan remembers casually remarking to Mo Mowlam that the hunger levels were rising: 'I remember saying, Mo, look, Good Friday or not, there is going to be an outbreak of cannibalism in the SDLP rooms if we don't get something.'[8]

With the negotiators from all sides suitably fed and watered there was the small matter of forging a deal. The mood in the talks was changeable – one minute it seemed like a deal was coming, the next it looked like the hours of discussions would lead to nothing. There was particular unease in unionist ranks over the release of prisoners and the lack of guarantees over paramilitary decommissioning. The UUP met with Tony Blair to seek a precondition that there must be decommissioning before Sinn Féin could hold ministerial office. Jeffrey Donaldson made it clear he could not support the release of prisoners and there were rumours he was about to walk out.

Tony Blair produced a side letter for the UUP which was hand-delivered to the UUP's office in Castle Buildings. The letter made it clear that if the provisions for decommissioning were shown to be ineffective in the first six months of the shadow assembly, his government would support 'changes to these provisions to enable them to be made properly effective in preventing such people from holding office'.[9]

The letter made an impact, and after David Trimble and John Taylor read it they believed the deal was worth backing. The UUP had further discussions amongst themselves and David Trimble took a call from President Clinton. The UUP leader then made one of the most important calls of his political career. He rang Senator Mitchell and told him plainly: 'I am ready to do business.'[10]

It was not good enough for Jeffrey Donaldson, who left the talks building. He became a critic of the Good Friday Agreement and ultimately joined the DUP in 2004.

When the agreement was revealed on air by BBC Northern Ireland's political editor, Stephen Grimason, there were many familiar parts to it. There would be a power-sharing Assembly with an Executive made up of ministers. New cross-border institutions would be established and a British-Irish Council would be set up involving politicians from across the UK, the Channel Islands and the Isle of Man. An independent commission would examine policing and controversially there would be the early release of paramilitary prisoners. The deal would be put to a referendum which would be held on the same day on both sides of the border. The referendum plan was a key argument put forward by Hume, who believed any agreement had to have the endorsement of the public. He also insisted that it had to have a mandate across the island of Ireland.

After George Mitchell called the parties together for a plenary session the parties went outside and spoke to the world's press who had been waiting patiently for days. The SDLP team appeared in front of the cameras wearing red roses in their lapels. It was a surreal atmosphere. There was a sense of occasion mixed with understandable nervousness. For so long, politicians in Northern Ireland had talked at each other and played a blame game. So-called political solutions came and went in the 1970s, '80s and '90s and peace seemed like a concept rather than a possibility. Now there was agreement and a sense of hope. Seamus Mallon instantly saw the parallels with history and famously described the Good Friday Agreement as 'Sunningdale for slow learners'.

As the news broke of a deal and the bulletins were filled with the sound bites of politicians, the inevitable questions began to be asked by commentators and journalists who had tracked the history of the Troubles. Was this the moment when decades of differences were being put aside? Or was this a false dawn? Was it 1974 all over again?

In front of cameras and arc lights, there was a procession of suited politicians holding impromptu press conferences, all hurriedly conducted under a moody and changeable sky. The weather was indecisive and hard to read – one minute the sun was shining, and the next it was sleeting.

The UUP official, David Kerr, recalls watching Hume as he spoke to the media. He thought the SDLP leader had got an easier deal to sell, compared to the task that David Trimble was about to face:

> And I remember forlornly looking at Hume. As I think the sun shone on him and when we went out to do ours it snowed and rained. And goodness me, I thought, if that isn't a metaphor for what is ahead of me I don't know what is.[11]

Kerr knew how bitterly unionism was divided on the agreement. He had watched colleagues leave the negotiations in protest and he was well aware that the forthcoming referendum campaign would be a brutal battle. For John Hume, the events of Good Friday marked a high point in his career. Eamonn McCann says the agreement was a personal and political triumph for the SDLP leader:

> You look at the Good Friday Agreement. Look at it. What is it? It is John Hume's speeches from the 1970s. There it is codified into an agreement. All of it, John Hume was saying. North–South bodies, East–West bodies, power-sharing within the North, the three strands of it. John Hume was explicitly advocating all of those things in 1973 and 1974.[12]

Hume had every reason to feel vindicated. After suffering years of personal and political attacks for his talks with Gerry Adams, the process eventually delivered a multi-party agreement. The deal was based on three sets of relationships which Hume had identified and repeatedly stressed as needing to form part of any solution. He was also aware that the deal struck in Castle Buildings involved compromise and this was a chance for a fresh start:

> Only once in a generation does an opportunity like this come along, an opportunity to resolve our deep and tragic conflict. No one should diminish the difficulties we face. No one should deny the tough decisions that have been made and tough choices that have to be made. We must draw assurances that our agreement today reflects the firmest wish of all our people. Once before we came very close, only to have our hopes dashed.[13]

Hume's reference to the past was not just a political point. He had been a minister for 148 days when Northern Ireland had last experienced power-sharing in 1974 – a deal that collapsed after loyalist opposition. It was a time that promised so much but caused hurt and despair. Since then he had developed networks and contacts and experienced a remarkable political journey. His life in the public eye had taken him from the streets of Derry to Strasbourg, Brussels, Washington, Westminster and Dublin. He had the ear of presidents and prime ministers and now he hoped he could convince the people of Ireland – north and south – that this was the best chance for peace. When Lord Eames caught sight of what was contained in the agreement he could instantly see the fingerprints of his old friend from Derry: 'It was John Hume in print. It was John Hume's vision in print. It was John Hume's hopes and philosophy in print.'[14]

As the images of the Good Friday deal went global, Hume's family were in different parts of the world. His daughter Mo was in rural Guatemala with a friend from Downpatrick. They were employed as development workers and were in Coban, an area known for its coffee production. Away from home and off the beaten track, they were feeling disconnected as they heard the dramatic news from Belfast: 'My memory is of staring at each other a bit incredulous and feeling we were living through something significant, but not knowing how to respond.' Mo and her friend were staying in budget accommodation: 'We both sat out in the corridor and said, "What should we do to celebrate this? This is a big thing." I think we went and had a piece of chocolate cake.'[15]

Mo's brother John was living in Brussels at the time and had gone to Alicante for a few days. He found a pub to watch the news reports in English and soon saw television images of his father: 'It was completely surreal, you know, just to see the sort of sheer joy and relief on Dad's face.' Looking back at what was agreed at Castle Buildings in 1998, John Hume Junior says the Good Friday Agreement was a culmination of his father's 'lifetime's work'.[16]

Plaudits arrived in the shape of letters and cards to Hume's office and home. George Mitchell sent Hume a note to the party offices on the Ormeau Road in Belfast. He told the SDLP leader that his 'commitment and perseverance prevailed'. The letter was typed but in a hand-written addition at the bottom of the letter the senator wrote, 'History will rightly judge you to be the architect of peace.'[17]

For the SDLP leader, making the deal was just the first stage of this process. Now the legally binding accord had to be voted on and there was a referendum campaign to win. The date was set for 22 May and the poll would be held, as agreed, on both sides of the border. The battle lines were clear and the arguments were all too obvious.

Unionism was divided over the agreement, with Trimble supporters in the Yes camp and Ian Paisley's DUP and Bob McCartney (leader of the UK Unionist Party) in the No camp. For many unionists, the planned release of paramilitary prisoners and the reform of the RUC made the deal completely unpalatable and the No camp made these moves a central plank of its campaign. The issue of decommissioning was another area anti-agreement unionists were keen to target. As the days went by, it became clear that the No camp was campaigning well and its message was resonating with many unionists.

As a close aide of Trimble, David Kerr was firmly in the Yes camp and felt the deal was the best way to take Northern Ireland forward. He knew the arguments well, having listened to sceptical unionists in party meetings voice their concerns. He felt the positive parts of the Good Friday deal were being lost in the criticism coming from the anti-agreement lobby: 'We had all the prisoner releases, the Balcombe Street stuff. We had Michael Stone parading at the Ulster Hall. We had all the hysteria about the RUC reform, everything that was negative for unionism. And of course, that was very deliberate.'[18]

Kerr says the anti-agreement unionists appeared to be winning the argument and it looked like a majority of unionists would vote No:

> They were having a field day because they were picking on the three most sensitive areas of the agreement. Peter Robinson had honed in on that and it was relentless criticism. So it was very, very difficult for us to shift the media away from a discussion of unionism infighting to actually see the big picture.[19]

With time running out, Tim Attwood of the SDLP, who was helping to coordinate a Yes vote, was also starting to get worried. He felt there needed to be a big moment in the final days of the campaign to galvanise voters. He recalls the problems: 'There was a lot of interference and noise and antagonism within unionism and it was very difficult. John Hume was saying "How do we energise and create a picture that is more positive?"'[20]

Attwood began to think of ideas that could give the campaign a lift and show that the Good Friday Agreement was about the future and offered hope. He started to think of photo opportunities with celebrities who could endorse the Yes campaign. He remembered Hume's friendship with Bono. The lead singer of U2 had been friends with Hume for years and the musician had a great deal of respect for the SDLP leader.

The musician had invited him to his concerts and the pair had often met socially and, as Attwood acknowledges, there was a bond between the two men: 'Hume and Bono are just kindred spirits, very different you know. But their mindset, their thinking, their inspiration is very, very similar. Anytime they met there was something. They should really have been son and grandfather but there was something special about their relationship.'[21]

John Hume Junior also recalls how Bono had rung the family home in Derry to speak to his father. He says it was clear that his dad enjoyed the rock star's company: 'Dad would go to Slane for example, if U2 were playing, and he would hang out backstage.'[22]

Tim Attwood managed to obtain Bono's mobile phone number and one afternoon, as he stood outside a Belfast hotel, he dialled the Dubliner's number:

> I rang Bono. And he explained, 'Look, Tim, I will do anything for John Hume that he wants me to do. But I don't want to do anything that will cause difficulties for David Trimble.' I said, 'Well, you know at some stage we have to symbolise unionism and nationalism coming together to represent what the Good Friday Agreement means for everyone.' I said, 'Trimble is in trouble so we have to change the dynamic.' He said, 'Put it this way, I'll do whatever John wants me to do.'[23]

With Bono on board, Tim Attwood knew if he could bring the singer, Hume and Trimble together it would be a wonderful image. There was a discussion about getting the three men to pose for a photo call but Attwood thought that was a missed opportunity: 'I said that is pretty damp. That is not going to excite people, especially when you have someone like Bono who can sing a decent song, so I said, "Why don't we try to go for some sort of musical event around this?"'[24]

The next call Attwood made was to the music promoter Eamonn McCann, a namesake of the Derry politician, and he told him that this event was needed to get the Yes campaign over the line and get the right imagery. McCann agreed and loved the idea. He did not hang about and very quickly booked the Waterfront Hall in Belfast, which was one of the city's iconic venues. The local band Ash was contacted and soon the idea of a concert featuring an appearance by Bono, Trimble and Hume gathered pace. Attwood still had other people to speak to and he soon encountered Jonathan Stephenson, the chair of the SDLP.

He informed him of the plans and said the event had to happen and it had the blessing of John Hume. Stephenson's response was blunt: 'Tim, if this doesn't come off you are fucked. If it does come off you are a hero.'[25]

Attwood and his colleague Conall McDevitt then had to make contact with David Trimble's team to see if he would participate in the event. They arranged to meet David Kerr in Belfast's Europa Hotel and explained to him that Bono had agreed to appear with Trimble and Hume at the Waterfront Hall and sing a few songs and the local band Ash would also appear. They told Kerr that Hume was completely on board with the idea and thought a joint photo call with Trimble would prove effective.

Kerr did not need any convincing. He instantly got the idea and was a big U2 fan himself. He sensed this was exactly the right kind of image that the Yes campaign needed. He felt a concert and the image of Trimble and Hume together could send out a message of 'the centre ground of unionism and nationalism coming together, locking hands, to say we will forge a new political future for Northern Ireland'.[26]

Kerr spoke to Trimble and encouraged him to take part, telling him it could engage people who had no interest in politics. Trimble was a music fan but would not have had an intimate knowledge of Bono's work. He was an opera lover and also liked Elvis Presley but he immediately understood the importance of the idea. He instantly agreed, although other unionists in the Yes camp were not convinced. The UUP leader knew he was fighting for the hearts and minds of unionism and sensed this event could sway people who were undecided.

With the UUP leader on board it was full steam ahead and in the days that followed tickets were distributed to students and young people and the event began to gather the media's attention both nationally and internationally. Other bands expressed an interest in participating and The Corrs' management team made contact with Tim Attwood and said they would happily perform. However, after a discussion, it was decided to keep the original lineup to Bono and Ash. David Kerr remembers hearing Ian Paisley on BBC Radio Ulster denounce Bono's decision to appear with Trimble and Hume: 'I remember thinking at the time, He knows this is a master stroke by us. He knows it. He knows that if this works we are going to prevail here and we are going to come out on top.'[27]

Paisley was not the only one who was critical of the Bono intervention. For different reasons, the SDLP deputy leader, Seamus Mallon, was not convinced the involvement of the U2 frontman was a good idea. The Newry and Armagh MP had other plans for the evening, as Conall McDevitt recalled: 'Seamus was not happy and so, because he didn't agree with doing this, he called an executive meeting to coincide with the concert.'[28]

He was now double-booked and put party before pleasure. Hume's right-hand man would probably have preferred to listen to Bono and Ash but instead he spent his evening discussing strategy and opinion polls, whilst his close friend and party leader was being feted alongside David Trimble.

By early evening, there were crowds of people mingling inside and outside the Waterfront Hall. There was an air of excitement and expectation and much nervousness in the Trimble and Hume camps. There were worries that it might not go as planned and protestors might try to disrupt the event. There were some last-minute discussions to consider how the two men would be presented to the crowd. It was agreed they would appear in shirts and ties without jackets to look more informal than normal. They would be called onto the stage for a photograph by Bono, who would stand between them and raise their arms aloft. There would be no speeches – just music.

For the two politicians, this was new territory – they were out of their natural comfort zone. Both leaders could sometimes be awkward on social occasions, but David Kerr says the personal chemistry between the two men that night was good: 'John Hume that night – I thought he was very good with David. And I thought even though both of them were very nervous, I think Hume helped. I think Hume helped calm David more than the other way round.'[29]

As befitting their global rock star status, U2 arrived on a private jet at Belfast International Airport and Tim Attwood met them there and briefed them on what to expect when they arrived at the concert venue. Ash was the first to entertain the excited crowd. Playing for around 40 minutes, they managed to get the crowd of schoolchildren and young students into a party mood very quickly. After a noisy set, when they played a number of their hits, the Downpatrick band then left the stage, lending their equipment to Bono and his bandmates, who kept the atmosphere in a similar vein. The Waterfront Hall was now rocking to a packed audience of two and a half thousand, as the leaders of unionism and nationalism waited in the wings.

When the moment came, Bono called Trimble and Hume to the stage and the crowd cheered as the two men came in from opposite sides. They looked happy and, as agreed, had taken their jackets off. Hume was smiling in his tie and yellow shirt with Trimble looking content and laughing in a blue shirt. They shook hands and then, as planned, Bono held their arms aloft. It was the image the photographers and camera crews had come to capture and within seconds it was over. For the organisers, it was mission complete.

Afterwards, Hume, Trimble and Bono all gathered at a reception in the Waterfront Hall complex which was attended by some families who had lost relatives in the Troubles. Tim Attwood felt it was important the family members were given an opportunity to talk to the band and the politicians. Bono came into the gathering and met Sarah Conlon, the widow of Giuseppe, who was the victim of a miscarriage of justice. He had been wrongly convicted after the IRA bombed Guildford in 1974 and died in prison. The U2 frontman hugged Sarah and asked her what she thought of the performance. She gave him quite a candid response: 'You were very good but you were very loud.'[30]

Afterwards, when he made his way back to his dressing room, Bono caught sight of the BBC news on a television screen. Not surprisingly his appearance in Belfast with Hume and Trimble was being replayed and analysed and the image of the three men on stage was now going around the world. Bono knew the significance of what had just happened and would later tell a music journalist: 'We are here to try to convince those who have real fears to vote Yes. To vote No is to play into the hands of the extremists. Their day is over.'[31]

Tim Attwood was delighted with the way the evening went and felt the imagery of the three men on stage, the music and the excited crowd was exactly what was needed: 'That was the moment that changed the campaign.'[32] McDevitt had the same analysis: 'I absolutely believe that was the turning point of the campaign. We needed to create an image that was the future of Northern Ireland, that was about power-sharing, that was about a new Ireland, an international place, an outward-looking place.'[33]

If the idea was to convince wavering voters that they should vote Yes, David Kerr thinks that evening at the Waterfront Hall did the trick. He believes the event was a game changer:

> Nobody will ever tell me anything different. That for me was the defining moment of the campaign. And despite everything else that had happened, all the negative stuff, all the emotive stuff with that campaign, when you saw the two of them standing there you knew they embodied the centre ground of Northern Ireland politics. The moderate unionists and the moderate nationalists, and they spoke for that.[34]

When this author asked David Kerr how many votes he thought the Waterfront Hall event delivered he replied: 'It was worth certainly more than 100,000 votes.'[35] It is impossible to quantify precisely what impact the event may have had electorally, but what is clear is that, when the votes were finally counted later that week, David Kerr had every reason to be happy. He watched the ballot boxes being emptied at the King's Hall in Belfast and, in one of the highest turnouts in electoral history, 71.1 per cent backed the Good Friday Agreement with 28.9 per cent voting against it. In the Republic, the figures were even starker with a staggering 94 per cent voting in favour and 6 per cent against.

For Hume and Trimble it was a mixture of happiness and relief. The SDLP leader told RTÉ's Miriam O'Callaghan that people had not just voted for themselves, but they had voted for 'their children and grandchildren and future generations'.[36] It was a result that exceeded expectations in the Yes camp, but it was only a job half done. What was clear was that, even though the Yes camp had triumphed, the anti-agreement unionists had fought an effective campaign and, at times, Trimble thought they could sway a majority of unionists. The two party leaders had just fought one campaign and within days had another to organise – this time for the Northern Ireland Assembly, which was a centrepiece of April's agreement.

The battle for Stormont was very familiar and was in many ways like a replay of the referendum campaign, particularly amongst the unionist parties. Hume was involved in the campaigning but also continued to travel to fulfil his other political commitments in London and Brussels.

For Hume, the poll was a personal triumph as the SDLP knocked the UUP into second place and topped the poll, securing 24 seats in the new Assembly. Trimble's party secured fewer votes but returned more members and remained the largest party with 28 seats. The DUP took 20 seats and Sinn Féin secured 18, with Alliance on 6. The nationalist and republican parties had polled well and the arrival of Jane Morrice and Monica McWilliams, as members of the Women's Coalition, and Billy Hutchinson and David Ervine of the PUP brought new faces to the benches of Stormont. The votes of the June poll meant that David Trimble was in line to become first minister, with the SDLP in position to nominate a deputy first minster. If Hume wanted this role it was there for the taking. As party leader and architect of the Good Friday Agreement, no one would have stood in his way if he wanted to take the job.

Like the opportunity of becoming Irish president, this was another key moment. Hume had a decision to make. He had achieved much in the last few years. The violence had largely stopped. He had helped to deliver an IRA ceasefire on two occasions. His party negotiators had secured a multi-party agreement, power-sharing was back, there was an Irish dimension and the referendum had been successful. Was this the time to be in the Executive as deputy first minister? Was this the moment to finish a job that was cut short way back in 1974?

19

A NIGHT IN OSLO

'Bloody hell. He is going to be on that wall.'
Mo Hume, on her father's Nobel Peace Prize

With a sense of urgency, Seamus Mallon drove to the Wellington Park Hotel in South Belfast. It was a June day in 1998 and he was late. He had mistakenly gone to Parliament Buildings on the Stormont estate, thinking that was where his party was meeting. Ironically, it was an old political rival, the UUP deputy leader John Taylor, who spotted his mistake and casually informed him that he was in the wrong place.

Mallon hopped in his car and quickly made his way from east Belfast to the Malone Road. When he finally arrived at the hotel, the meeting was already underway. As he recalled in his memoirs, when he entered the room, John Hume pulled him aside for a quick word. Hume had something important to say. He told Mallon that he was not going to take a position in the new Executive: 'This Deputy First Minister thing – you're going to have to do it because the doctors have told me I shouldn't.'[1]

Hume did not want the job, even though it was there for the taking, in the same way he had opted out of running to be president of Ireland, a year earlier. He had concluded that this position in the new Executive was not right for him. He felt it was not a good fit.

Mark Durkan remembers conversations with Hume about the job and he was clearly concerned about his health: 'He was starting to worry about his own levels of concentration at that stage. It was as far back as during the Brooke or the Mayhew talks that I remember John saying to me in the car one day that he thought he had Alzheimer's. This was because we were listening to the radio – the Pat Kenny show on RTÉ – and they had a doctor on and the doctor was talking about Alzheimer's.'[2]

The conversation in the car was typical, as Hume often talked about his health. It was a favourite topic of conversation. Aside from any medical worries he might have had, Durkan also thinks Hume recognised that his particular talents lay elsewhere and he felt that his skills 'were not what they were for this new patch'.[3]

Seamus Mallon also felt Hume was better suited for other jobs: 'I think John probably realised that when it came to the detail of day-to-day political engagement and horse-trading, especially with unionists, I was a better operator than him. He was the vision man; I was the negotiator.'[4]

Conall McDevitt says Hume was deeply scarred by his experience in the 1974 power-sharing Executive and concluded that he was not the person for this new role:

> Do I think that he felt at that moment in time he was the best person for the job? Actually, I think he understood he probably wasn't. It was that Seamus would do a much better job grinding out the nuts and bolts.[5]

Lord Empey says Hume's decision was probably based on his experience of Sunningdale, the Ulster workers' strike and the ultimate end of his tenure as commerce minister: 'I think he had his fingers burnt and he did not want to go back in there – because he could have. He could have, at the click of a finger. He could have been straight in there as Deputy First Minister.'[6]

What is clear is that Hume was content with his current parliamentary roles and did not feel he had to have a position in the new Executive. John Alderdice says Hume did not completely feel at home at Stormont, in the way he felt about the European Parliament, so he was not surprised when he turned down the prospect of a job as a minister:

> He didn't like Stormont very much. He didn't like the cut and thrust of the political chamber very much. He would

make speeches. He would be good at making speeches, but the whole way the process operates is within the chamber itself and outside the chamber itself. I don't think he ever really had a big appetite for that, but politically he was very much a European.[7]

Seamus Mallon became the SDLP's nominee for the post of deputy first minister. On 1 July 1998, in the new Assembly, the UUP Leader David Trimble was elected first minister and Seamus Mallon stood opposite him, smiling and shaking his hand. Under the watchful gaze of John Alderdice, the Speaker, Mallon formally took on the role of deputy first minister.

Trimble, keen to play down the occasion, said it was not a historic day but simply another step. Mallon believed the UUP leader's decision to embrace power-sharing before decommissioning was 'brave'.[8]

There appeared to be genuine warmth between the two men. As Northern Ireland's marching season reached its peak some days later, Trimble and Mallon had little time to find their political feet. A standoff was continuing at a church at Drumcree in County Armagh where members of the Orange Order were being prevented from marching along Portadown's Garvaghy Road. Police and protestors had clashed, and across Northern Ireland, there had been a series of disturbances. It was a worrying and tense time when political leadership was badly needed.

On 12 July three Catholic boys were killed in Ballymoney when their house was petrol-bombed by loyalists. Their deaths threw Northern Ireland into despair and sparked outrage and condemnation. The killings put the spotlight on the ongoing protests at Drumcree and prompted the Reverend William Bingham, an Orange Order chaplain, to say that: 'No road is worth a life.'[9] The deaths of the Quinn boys and the Drumcree protest placed great strains on the political process. A month later there was horror on an unprecedented scale.

On 15 August, the Real IRA, a dissident group which split from the Provisional IRA, planted a bomb in Omagh. It killed 29 people, including a woman pregnant with twins. It was the biggest loss of life in a single

A NIGHT IN OSLO

incident in the Troubles. The hopes of Good Friday seemed a world away as the world's press reported once again on the bloody carnage of a bomb attack. Another caught up in the bomb would die some days later and Omagh now joined the long list of Northern Irish towns and villages forever associated with bloodshed.

The Real IRA attack on that Saturday afternoon changed the political atmosphere and there would be a series of high-profile visits in the weeks that followed. There were events in Omagh and Armagh, and Assembly members gathered in Belfast to hear President Clinton speak at the Waterfront Hall – where Hume and Trimble had joined Bono on stage some months earlier. Clinton praised the work of the power-sharing Executive and urged the local parties to work together and secure lasting reconciliation. He told the crowd that peace needed to be seized upon and stressed, 'It will not come again in our lifetime.'[10]

Away from the presidential diplomacy and the VIP meetings, the issue of decommissioning still dogged the political process. Hume and Trimble took different stances. The UUP leader argued that Sinn Féin could not be part of the Executive without IRA decommissioning. The SDLP leader made it clear that decommissioning was not a precondition of the Good Friday Agreement. The argument seemed circular and never-ending.

It was a difficult time but Hume was often reminded that, despite the setbacks and the political spats, Northern Ireland had changed. In September, Mo Mowlam felt compelled to send him a letter:

> In all the carry-on of the last weeks and months, the hard slog of years of work was down to you. We still, as you know, have many hurdles to climb over – it won't be easy. People the world over know who struggled to get us to where we are – thank you.[11]

There was much still to finalise, as Mo Mowlam referred to, and talks continued between the parties over when an Executive could be formed and how the North–South bodies could work. The mechanics of the

Good Friday Agreement were a work in progress. The outline structures had been agreed in April but by October much of the detail still had to be formally agreed.

Despite the obvious differences and the ongoing arguments, to the outside world Hume and Trimble were seen as politicians who had taken risks and been courageous. They were viewed as peacemakers who had secured the Good Friday Agreement and helped to solve one of the world's seemingly intractable problems – the Northern Ireland Troubles. The two men were now being talked about as potential Nobel Peace Prize winners and speculation started to appear in the press that they would be jointly awarded the honour. Hume had experienced such speculation before when his name was linked to the prize. In 1995 he was nominated unsuccessfully by a series of American politicians including Senator Ted Kennedy. However, this time it seemed different. Both Hume and Trimble were being tipped as joint winners and the press speculation appeared to have some credibility.

One October morning, Conall McDevitt got up early and after breakfast made the familiar journey from Belfast to Hume's Derry home. As he pulled up at West End Park his mobile phone rang and it was a friendly Norwegian journalist whom he had been talking to in recent days. She had the inside track on what was about to happen and told Conall: 'You are going to get some very good news.'[12] He thanked the reporter for the tip-off and they agreed to talk later in the day. Pat Hume ushered McDevitt into her house and they went into the parlour where John was sitting on a soft chair, close to the stove.

McDevitt informed his boss that he was going to get a phone call about the Nobel Peace Prize. Hume wanted to know how he knew. McDevitt replied that he had been reliably informed by a Norwegian journalist. The SDLP leader had been down this road before and told McDevitt, 'You had better be right.'[13]

They all waited for the phone call. Hume was often poor at small talk and McDevitt remembers that the delay was agonising: 'We stood there for what seemed like an age for that bloody phone to ring.' Finally, at the appointed time the phone rang and John Hume took the call, which lasted about five minutes. He did not say much and ended the conversation, and Pat asked him what was said. He confirmed that he was being awarded the Nobel Peace Prize and added: 'Trimble is getting it too.'[14] They celebrated the news with hugs and cups of tea.

Across the Atlantic in a hotel bedroom in Denver, Colorado, David Trimble was in bed. Seamus Mallon was in his own room in the same hotel. The two men were in the United States on a promotional tour of major cities aimed at drumming up inward investment for Northern Ireland. As a key adviser to Trimble, David Kerr was on the trip as well. He says many in the UUP were worried that the Nobel Peace Prize would be split three ways between Trimble, Hume and Adams. He remembers how the conversations went: 'The big fear was what if Gerry Adams gets it as well? Are they stupid or crazy enough to give it to all three of them? Because if they do, we are always going to have to pull out of it.'[15]

The UUP's fears did not come to pass. In the small hours of the morning, Mallon was woken up by a phone call from home informing him that his party leader and David Trimble had jointly been awarded the prize by the Nobel organising committee. Tucked up in bed, Trimble was oblivious to the breaking news. His wife, Daphne, was back home in Northern Ireland: 'I found out later that he had given out strict instructions that he was not to be disturbed because it was the middle of the night in Denver and he wanted his sleep.'[16]

Seamus Mallon decided that this news would not wait for the morning, so he decided to tell the first minister in person. Dressed in his pyjamas, he walked down to Trimble's room and knocked on the door. The UUP leader was in no mood for guests and shouted: 'Too late, too late.' Mallon persisted. 'Open up – I've got a piece of news for you that you'd probably like to hear.' The rather bleary-eyed first minister was then told of his honour and he immediately went red with embarrassment. He turned to Mallon and said, 'Thank you, thank you. Leave it with me.' With that, he closed the door and went back to bed.[17]

As the details of the award became public, reporters and political correspondents all wanted a reaction from Hume and Trimble. The UUP leader was now asleep in his hotel room and at home Daphne Trimble was fielding dozens of inquiries: 'David could not be contacted. I was getting all the calls and saying all the things that I thought David would want me to say.'[18]

David Kerr says Trimble was 'absolutely delighted' with the news. He says the joint honour made sense and when he heard his boss and the SDLP leader were being recognised he thought back to the concert with Bono: 'When it was just John and David it was perfect because it vindicated both men. And again for me, it goes back to that image on the stage. It's about the two of them.'[19]

Trimble was interviewed on BBC Radio Ulster's *Good Morning Ulster*, just hours after the announcement was made official. He was somewhat understated in his reaction to the award and said he hoped it 'did not turn out to be premature'.[20]

When Bono heard about the award he invited Pat and John Hume to his Dublin home for a celebratory brunch. When the Humes arrived at the entrance to the rock star's Killiney home there were a number of tourists outside taking pictures – which is a regular occurrence. Tim Attwood was in the car:

> We arrived at the big black gates and Bono said beep the horn three times. There were about 40 French students there, mainly 14-year-olds. John wound down the window and as the gates opened John turned to me and said, 'How did they know I was coming?' I said, John, they aren't here for you. They are here for Bono.[21]

The brunch was an enjoyable affair and gave Hume a chance to thank Bono for his work during the referendum campaign. Attwood remembers that Hume was feeling poorly and quite worried about what to say. He recalls that when the time came Hume delivered a short one-minute speech: 'I am always worried in these situations when John is not well. Will he even know who U2 are?' Yet Hume did and told Bono, 'Most people think pop bands and movie stars have their heads in the clouds most of the time and don't live in the real world. You and your band are different.' Hume continued: 'U2 are different because you won the Good Friday Agreement. You brought young people out to a concert. You got them to tell their parents to vote YES. You won the Good Friday Agreement. Thank you, Bono.'[22]

Attwood was stunned:

> It was only a minute. It was a wow moment. He was brilliant. And Bono, for once, was speechless. It was not like him, it was just wow. There were tears in people's eyes and John just recognised how important that moment in the Waterfront Hall actually was and captured it brilliantly.[23]

Others took time to contact Hume to congratulate him on the Nobel award. Seamus Heaney was planning to be in Japan when the ceremony was taking place and wrote to him and wished him well:

> The political achievement is the good works part of your life, the unshakeable history, but the prize is like a grace streaming in. We'll be with you and Pat in spirit on 10 December, even though our bodies will be on the go in Japan. Try to enjoy it utterly – try to let the sheer celebration enter you both. It is totally deserved.[24]

In truth, the news about the Nobel ceremony provided some relief for the UUP and the SDLP, as relations between the parties over decommissioning and cross-border bodies were not good. The negotiations over the North–South institutions had become fraught and in late November it looked like the entire Good Friday project could collapse. Relations were so bad that Tony Blair came to Belfast to try and shore up a deal.

In December, Hume and Trimble left their inter-party troubles at home when they first travelled to Washington to receive another award and then they were flown to Oslo in time for the Nobel Peace Prize ceremony. A large group had travelled from Derry including the Hume family, close friends and SDLP colleagues.

Hume's son John remembers arriving in the city: 'It was that beautiful sort of cold Scandinavian sort of weather. There was no rain, just that crisp, sunny sky. It got dark at four o'clock every day, but it was just brilliant.'[25]

David Trimble made the journey with his wife, Daphne, and their four children, and his brother and sister were also with him. A series of UUP figures also arrived in Norway, as well as Trimble's adviser David Kerr. He was impressed by the way Hume and Trimble were received by the public and the press: 'The first night we arrived in Oslo and we went into the hotel, the two men came out onto the balcony of the hotel to wave to onlookers and they had celebrity status. There is no other way of describing it. So the world's media was chasing them for interviews. I remember CNN doing a set piece with David at the time. It was a global story, so it was a huge deal for both of them.'[26]

Recalling the events of Oslo, Kerr says Hume seemed more relaxed than his UUP counterpart:

> I think Hume was a lot more comfortable with it than David if I am being absolutely honest about it. Because he kind of revelled in it; because he liked talking about home. He liked talking about the journey that they had taken.[27]

Before they received their awards, there was a rehearsal of events and, as is tradition, both Hume and Trimble met King Harald and Queen Sonja at the royal palace and then spent some time with local schoolchildren. The ceremony itself was naturally full of glamour, with celebrities, politicians and diplomats from around the world in attendance. In his acceptance speech, Hume reverted to many of his traditional themes including the need for reconciliation and partnership government. He said the community he and Trimble represented had long been divided 'by the forces of a terrible history'. He said he would 'humbly accept this honour on behalf of a people who, after many years of strife, have finally made a commitment to a better future in harmony together'. He ended his address with the words 'we shall overcome', a phrase he and many others had sung on those civil rights marches back in the 1960s.[28]

Hume's speech had been typed up as usual by Gerry Cosgrove, who had travelled from Northern Ireland with other party members to Oslo. She looked on with great pride as Hume delivered his acceptance address. Even though she knew exactly what he was going to say, she found the occasion incredibly emotional: 'It was just electrifying. He got up and spoke those words. You just felt this is a person who has given his life for doing the right thing and it was so well deserved.'[29]

For Hume, being in Norway marked the culmination of years of work. From the streets of Derry to the Nobel Peace Prize – it had been quite a journey for the former teacher. Trimble's transition from being a shy academic to becoming an internationally acclaimed peacemaker had been equally remarkable – from protesting against power-sharing in the 1970s to being elected first minister in the 1990s. Like Hume, the UUP leader used his address to talk about the ills of the past and say that he looked forward to a better future together. His was at times an academic address and he quoted the writers Edmund Burke, Amos Oz and George Keenan. He talked of the current political difficulties back home:

> There are hills in Northern Ireland and there are mountains. The hills are decommissioning and policing. But the mountain, if we could but see it clearly, is not in front of us but behind us, in history. The dark shadow we seem to see in the distance is not really a mountain ahead, but the shadow of the mountain behind – a shadow from the past thrown forward into our future.[30]

Trimble also talked about the fear that had been created in the unionist community by nationalists and how unionists had done the same to the nationalist community. He admitted that Ulster Unionists had created 'a cold house for Catholics. And Northern nationalists, although they had a roof over their heads, seemed to us as if they meant to burn the house down.' He added that: 'None of us is entirely innocent.' At the end of his address, he made reference to the events of Good Friday some eight months earlier: 'That agreement showed that the people of Northern

Ireland are no petty people. They did good work that day. And tomorrow is now another day.'[31]

Trimble's use of the words 'petty people' was deliberate and pointed. They were a reference to comments made by John Hume in 1983 when he said that unionists had become 'a petty people'. [32]

Trimble had waited a long time to publicly respond to Hume's 'petty people' jibe and 15 years after it was said he proved that unionists have long memories. The inclusion of the remark by Trimble drew criticism from some media commentators when his speech was analysed. Many viewed his address as too political and contrasted it to Hume's, which was seen by some political writers as more diplomatic and appropriate. Yet Trimble's supporters would later stand by the tone and content of his speech. They argued that it was necessary to define the position of modern-day unionism and explain where it had come from. Trimble loyalists would also say that he did criticise the behaviour of unionists. They would point to the admission that unionists had created a 'cold house for Catholics' as a very public acknowledgement of unionism's failings.

With the speeches and formalities nearly over, the prize winners smiled and posed for photographs as they held their Nobel medals aloft. It was a poignant moment for the leaders of unionism and nationalism, not unlike the evening they shared when they stood together with Bono at the Waterfront Hall. Seven months on, they were centre stage again. Under the glare of the television lights, they looked happy, smiling and waving – two men representing different traditions, who were promoting one message.

The night after the ceremony, there was a musical celebration, again in the presence of the Norwegian king and queen. Two artists from Northern Ireland were on the bill. Family friend Phil Coulter from Derry was joined by flautist Sir James Galway, who, like Coulter, was known across the globe. The son of a Belfast shipyard worker, Galway left school at 14 and played in Orange bands. He had a Protestant upbringing whereas Coulter, like Hume, was raised a Catholic.

On the evening of the concert, the two Ulstermen shared a dressing room, and as they waited in the wings getting ready to perform they chatted about the occasion. Galway told Coulter that their presence might be seen by some people as rather 'appropriate'. Coulter looked at his friend: 'What do you mean appropriate?' 'Well,' said Galway, 'you could say, we are a sort of a musical version of Hume and Trimble.' Coulter laughed heartily.[33]

Minutes later it was show time, and the two musicians made their way to the stage to entertain the crowd. It was the first of many performances for Coulter in Oslo. After the public side was over, the Hume and Trimble parties made their way back to their hotel and, away from the cameras, a private celebration unfolded. Naturally, a piano was located and inevitably John Hume got up to sing.

Phil Coulter says everybody mixed together and the atmosphere was fantastic: 'There was no question of them and us. It wasn't like a Trimble faction and the unionists over there and our crowd over there. It was a party.'[34]

Over the decades, Coulter and Hume had performed many times together, often singing 'The Town I Love So Well' – their homage to their home city. They had performed their duet in places like Washington, London, Donegal, Dublin and Derry. Now they could add Oslo to that list. Phil Coulter says the trip to Norway was a surreal experience: 'I thought this was way beyond my wildest dreams. I just felt privileged to be part of it in any capacity and particularly because it was two guys from home who got the award, especially because one of the guys happened to be a family friend.'[35]

Coulter and Galway were not the only performers at the Nobel concert and shared the bill with a list of household names including the Irish band The Cranberries and the singer Alanis Morissette. During a break in proceedings, both Trimble and Hume were brought onto the stage and interviewed briefly. It was broadcast live on TV and both men explained what the prize meant to them. Hume's family and invited guests were watching on. At one stage the female presenter asked Hume, 'How do you feel?' It prompted a member of Hume's party to remark, 'Fuck, she's taking a risk.' To which Bishop Daly, who was sitting nearby, replied, 'Isn't she just.'[36]

For John Hume, it was important that he shared this time in Norway with those who meant the most to him. Pat Hume had travelled over with her husband, and she took the opportunity to get to know Daphne Trimble – who would later become Lady Trimble. The two women got on well together, so much so that they agreed to jointly assist the Northern Ireland Memorial Fund, which was set up to help those who suffered injury or bereavement in the Troubles. Lady Trimble says the two wives had a smoother relationship than their husbands: 'I got on better with Pat than David got on with John. They had business to do. We had the luxury of being able to get on as friends.' Lady Trimble also says the two leaders sometimes came across as brusque with each other and she observed at times they 'had their moments'.[37]

It is clear the two men often found each other frustrating, and at times there was a lack of trust. Hume was wary of Trimble and, in turn, the UUP leader used to complain about the SDLP leader when he met British ministers. On one occasion when Trimble held private talks with Northern Ireland Office Minister Michael Ancram in 1997, he accused Hume of behaving in a 'duplicitous' way with relation to decommissioning.[38]

There was no sign of any friction in Oslo between the two men or their families. They all mixed well and, according to Lady Trimble, both groups 'were relaxed and enjoyed themselves'.[39] The Hume group included Pat and John's grown-up children and lifelong friends like Bishop Edward Daly. John Hume had also invited his Aunty Bella along, who was the youngest of his aunts. For Hume's grown-up children the trip to Norway was exciting and understandably they were full of pride. Aidan Hume says the trip to Oslo was 'an incredible few days' and one of his abiding memories was how his family and the Trimble party got on. He says people just intermingled and 'everybody was friendly'.

Mo Hume recalled seeing framed pictures of previous Nobel Peace Prize winners at the Grand Hotel in Oslo. She was thinking of her dad when she spotted a portrait of Nelson Mandela and thought: 'Bloody hell, he is going to be on that wall.'[40] Hume was now a statesman of international standing, and with it came recognition and reward.

The Nobel Peace Prize came with a sizeable financial award and Hume decided that two of the beneficiaries would be the Salvation Army and the Society of St Vincent de Paul. He was very familiar with both groups, which worked in the community helping vulnerable people. Trimble used some of his prize money for a family holiday and later set up a think tank with part of the award. Hume's son Aidan says his father was always going to donate the cash to charity: 'He would not have considered for one second keeping it.' He says when money was made available for events or prizes his dad insisted that it was given away to a good cause: 'If he was giving a speech that came with a stipend that all went, too. It would not have gone to the party, it would have gone to charity ... He wasn't that interested in material things or money. The house in Donegal was all he ever wanted.'[41]

After the excitement of Oslo, Hume was soon back in his beloved retreat in Inishowen. As 1998 ended he could reflect on one of the most dramatic years of his life. He had played a crucial role in the signing of the Good Friday Agreement, helped to win the referendum and travelled to Norway to receive the world's greatest accolade for peace-making. When he and Trimble got back to Northern Ireland there was still a great deal of work to be done in trying to establish an Executive. After intensive talks an agreement was reached on the departments the Executive would have and the areas of North–South cooperation, but the issue of decommissioning still dogged the process. Politically the year had been a triumph for Hume. He had achieved much of what his working life had been about. In contrast, 1999 would bring very different emotions.

20

DOCTOR'S ORDERS

*'I have become heavily overloaded with work,
and I have serious health problems.'*
John Hume

In the noise of Amsterdam Airport John Hume spotted a familiar face from home. He and Monica McWillams were going in different directions but had time to spare before their connecting flights. Hume was heading to a meeting in Austria whilst McWilliams was off to the United States for an awards ceremony featuring Hillary Clinton and Mikhail Gorbachev.

The two seasoned travellers had known each other for decades and amidst the busy shops and packed cafes they soon found a place for a coffee and a catch up. McWilliams had first encountered Hume in January 1972, when on the beach at Magilligan Strand he famously led an anti-internment protest. As a young girl she had watched in awe as he challenged the authority of a British Army officer under the gaze of television cameras. In the years since, their paths had crossed many times. As a member of the Women's Coalition, McWilliams had observed Hume at close quarters during the Good Friday Agreement talks and rated him highly. The pair were now both elected to the Northern Ireland Assembly, albeit for different parties. Comfortable in each other's company, they chatted about the latest news from home and Hume, as he would often do, started to talk about his health. As Monica McWilliams recalled:

> He complained of being really unwell and he did look really unwell. And I advised him not to go on the flight

if he was that unwell. And I said, come to think of it, I am not feeling great myself. Turned out what I had was minor. Mine was threatened appendicitis and I had an appendectomy the minute I hit the States.[1]

It was August 1999 and Hume and McWilliams went their separate ways, unaware that each would face a serious health crisis in the hours ahead. The SDLP leader travelled to the village of Alpbach in Austria for a conference, where he was joined by Pat. Hume was clearly stressed and tired by the time he arrived at the venue.

Before he left Northern Ireland he had attended a media training session in Derry organised by the party. Gerry Cosgrove remembers him coming into the event and having a conversation with him:

> John came in at the end and talked to the people who were there and again I said, 'John, how are you doing?' 'Oh, Gerry, I don't feel well. I have got this and that and the other wrong.' And we were saying he is not well again. But that was the time he actually went away the next day and that's when he took seriously ill, and I must admit we did all feel very guilty at the time.[2]

Ronan McCay, who worked for Hume, had also started to notice a change in his demeanour in the weeks leading up to his trip to Alpbach. 'In the build-up to going to Austria, he had said, "I really don't feel well." He was sweating a lot and he was feeling terrible anxiety and said, "There is something happening."'[3]

After he arrived in Alpbach, Hume started to feel particularly unwell and was taken to a hospital in Kufstein in the Austrian state of Tyrol. He was examined by medical staff and it became clear that he had a ruptured diverticulum and was in a lot of pain and he needed surgery. He had three laparotomies over a series of days and after the surgery he was then moved into intensive care and was put on a ventilator to ease his breathing. The situation was serious. Hume's daughter Áine, who is a GP, says her father was seriously ill: 'I think inevitably he had sepsis, there were problems with oxygen. His memory was just not quite right after that. That was the beginning really.'[4]

Áine and her brother John joined their mum at the hospital in Kufstein whilst their dad was receiving care. Hume's son John travelled to Austria from his base in Brussels and was quickly told what had happened. He recalls being given the news at the hospital: 'He was in a very, very bad way.' He says that his father may also have had 'a number of strokes which may have hastened the dementia. But he was very sick in Austria.'[5]

The news of Hume's admission to hospital and subsequent surgery soon reached home and it was reported by broadcasters and print journalists. His party colleagues and political rivals sent messages of support to the family and when he was able to take phone calls from his hospital bed, one of those who rang was Mo Mowlam, the Secretary of State. Hume wasted little time in telling her exactly what had happened and giving her the full details on his condition. Mowlam was delighted to hear that he was recovering. She would later jokingly remark to an official that she had regretted making the call because he gave her 'chapter and verse on his woes'.[6]

The illness and subsequent operation in Austria would change Hume's life. He was flown home to Northern Ireland and transferred to Altnagelvin Hospital in Derry. There was further treatment after he returned, as Áine, his daughter, recalled: 'He had another operation about three months later. He had a colostomy, which was reversed, and then he went straight back to work.'[7]

Hume was not the only politician to get news coverage for their health problems. Journalists also reported that Monica McWilliams's trip to America ended up with her having to have an appendectomy. Hume read the coverage of her trip and hospital stay and then sent McWilliams a letter. She recalled that he joked that she was stealing his limelight yesterday getting press coverage of her medical issues: 'It was tongue in cheek and funny given that he had just had a life-threatening crisis. So that endeared him to me.'[8] As Áine recalls, her father was desperate to return to frontline politics after weeks of being off work: 'He didn't want to rest and he wanted to dive back to work, and so that was when things started to get more difficult for him.'[9]

It was clear to his friends and family that after his collapse in Austria he was starting to become a little forgetful and struggle with tasks that previously he would have taken in his stride. He wanted to resume his life as before but it was clear adjustments would have to be made. He spoke at the party's annual conference in November 1999 on what would be his twentieth time as leader. It was a milestone – a moment to savour – yet when he was in his hospital bed in Austria it must have looked near impossible.

Hume rose to speak at the Wellington Park Hotel in Belfast in front of SDLP members and watching journalists. There was a lot of media interest, as this was his first set-piece occasion since his surgery and recuperation. Political correspondents watched on, wondering if his performance would be any different from the many other occasions he had spoken to the party faithful. He began by addressing his colleagues and visitors with a simple greeting: 'It's good to be back.' He explained how difficult the past few months had been and said he was 'determined that nothing would stop me from being here today'. Hume was back in person, the oratory skills were still there and in many ways it seemed that nothing had changed – but in reality he was a different man.[10]

Ronan McCay says after the trauma of surgery and the stays in hospital in Derry and Austria, Hume's appearance had changed dramatically:

> He looked gaunt. He had lost a huge amount of weight and he never fully recovered from that. But eventually, you know, he got back again and came around physically and was active again. Thank God it did not cost him his life, although I am pretty sure it was really definitive in shaping John's health for the rest of his life.[11]

McCay was not the only colleague to see a change in Hume's demeanour. Others, like Conall McDevitt, thought Hume was different: 'He began to withdraw a bit into himself.' He also feels Hume's temperament changed:

'For me there was a slight change in personality, you know – he had lost that *joie de vivre*.'[12]

When Hume was hospitalised, he missed many important political meetings and discussions. In his absence his colleagues had worked to try and install some life into Northern Ireland's stop-start peace process. For much of 1999 the same old subjects dominated the news agenda and the inter-party talks. Decommissioning, policing, power-sharing and the ongoing dispute at Drumcree occupied political minds.

David Trimble had two goals – to achieve devolution and decommissioning. He had an original policy of 'no guns, no government', making it clear that unless the paramilitaries officially destroyed their weapons there could be no power-sharing Executive. However, that policy started to change and the year was dominated by endless rounds of discussions aimed at coming up with a formula that could see power-sharing fully restored but also see demands over decommissioning met.

In July there was an attempt to establish an Executive, but it became farcical after the SDLP and Sinn Féin nominated ministers but the Alliance Party and the UUP stayed away. The move failed to garner cross-community support and ministers were in place for just minutes. Seamus Mallon announced his resignation as deputy first minister and urged David Trimble to follow suit, but the UUP leader ignored the suggestion.

This was not what a government for all looked or sounded like. The optics were bad and the prospects for power-sharing in the future looked bleak. However, a few months later the atmosphere had changed. On 29 November, a full Executive took shape with the UUP, SDLP, DUP and Sinn Féin all having ministers. The DUP however made it clear they would be boycotting Executive meetings though the party would take up ministerial positions.

Seamus Mallon was once again back in his familiar office. He and David Trimble became the public face of power-sharing and were quickly dubbed 'The Odd Couple'. After many years of political work in the 1970s without a salary, and decades in Hume's shadow, for Mallon this was now the pivotal moment of his career. With Hume's health under the spotlight there was some speculation that he might stand down from the party leadership. If he did step aside, then it seemed there was really only one person who would get the role – Seamus Mallon. The Newry and Armagh MP had been Hume's deputy for two decades and was well-equipped for the position. Mallon knew the party inside out, was articulate, a formidable debater and campaigner and was well-connected in London and Dublin. If there was a vacancy no one would beat him. It was Mallon's job for the taking. Except that the post was not going to be available.

Even though Hume was not well and had previously told Mallon he had no intention of seeking the deputy first minister's job on the advice of his GP, he had no immediate plans to quit as party leader. It was a decision that caused some friction with Seamus Mallon. He thought the Deputy First Minister should be the party leader. He argued that if Hume had ruled himself out of being at Stormont then he should step aside as leader. He firmly believed that it made practical and political sense if the same person did both jobs:

> When the Executive was set up at the end of 1999 would have been the optimum time for him to stand down as leader for several reasons. Number one, because of his health. Number two, because his continuing leadership of the SDLP made it difficult for me as Deputy First Minister. In that job, I had key decisions to make, but out of courtesy to John as party leader, I had to go back before I made them to consult with him. I had the power of appointing Ministers to the Executive, but John continued to insist that it was his call who should be appointed from the SDLP. I had to tell him that any such decisions would be constitutionally invalid.[13]

Writing in his memoirs, Mallon says it would have been in Northern Ireland's interest and that of his party if the Deputy First Minster's position and the SDLP leader's post were held by the same person. However, he added that, 'I was never going to make the SDLP leadership an issue.'

Mallon goes on: 'I had far too much respect for John. Friends who were closer to him knew only too well it was time to step down and should have put the question to him.'[14]

Was Mallon right and should Hume's close circle of friends have asked him to step away from the party leadership in 1999? What is clear is that some of Hume's family believed that it was time to think about a life away from politics. They reminded him that he had been a public figure for over 30 years, party leader for over 20; he had been a minister, an MP and an MEP. He had spent much of his working life travelling, jet-setting to Washington, Brussels, Strasbourg and London. His wife, Pat, and his children could see that he was tired and that the job had taken its toll.

Many commentators said the Good Friday Agreement marked Hume's finest political achievement and suggested that since his lifetime's work was now recognised globally it was time to leave the stage. Pat Hume was deeply worried about her husband and sensed he needed a slower lifestyle. Áine says her mother encouraged him to take it easy: 'I think Mum wanted him to rest. She just wanted him to stop for a while and give himself some breathing space ... Dad had not done anything but work for so long, so that even to imagine not working was very difficult for him.'[15]

Getting John Hume to rest and step off the political treadmill was difficult for his family. He was not a man who could easily relax, and he did not have any regular hobbies. He used to enjoy reading for pleasure but in later years lost his love of books. However, his lifelong desire to sing and entertain remained undiminished. Barry White, who worked for the Ulster Unionists at Westminster, remembers Hume in his company late one evening when the SDLP leader was in full voice: 'I was sitting in the sports and social club bar with Roy Beggs [UUP MP] and a sing-song developed. Beggs sang an Irish ballad and then Hume sang "The Sash" [an Orange ballad]. He was in tune and word perfect, and it went down a storm with whoops and cheers.'[16]

Hume's other passion, aside from singing, was Derry City – a club he adored. His love for 'The Candystripes' remained throughout his adult life and he was very familiar with their Brandywell ground, which was very close to his family home. Hume was a regular at home games and the club made him president in 1999 – it was a position he loved.

Hume enjoyed reminiscing about the trials and tribulations of being a lifelong fan. Ruairí O'Kane recalls conversations with him:

> He loved Derry City. One of the last times he was in my car we were going to something and Derry had been playing the night before. It came on the radio on the news that Derry had drawn and he started talking nearly the whole journey to Belfast about the match. I think they didn't play well or whatever and he just loved the Brandywell.[17]

Hume was now well aware that mentally he was not as sharp as he used to be and there were lapses in his memory. Mark Durkan remembers having conversations with him: 'John was getting very conscious of his memory and his concentration and all the rest of it. This was starting to worry him and he was talking to a lot of people about it.'[18]

Eamonn McCann, his old political sparring partner, can recall sitting talking with Hume in a bar in Derry when he began to notice that John's memory was failing him:

> I realised that there was something wrong. John said something to me. I forgot what we were talking about and about 30 seconds later he said exactly the same thing again, exactly the same thing. I suddenly realised, there is something wrong. There is something wrong.[19]

Political correspondents who dealt with Hume regularly started to notice that the once sharp mind was not what it was. One lobby journalist recalls an occasion on the terrace at Westminster when Hume mistook the reporter for someone else and repeated himself several times. The Humes began to talk about the possibility of John cutting down on his political commitments. By 2000 he was an Assembly member, MP, MEP and, of course, party leader. For a fit and healthy person that involved an enormous workload coupled with much travel. For an individual who had been through a number of operations and had been hospitalised, it was almost impossible.

The idea of a phased retirement was mooted privately, which would mean Hume giving up his various positions over a period of time. It began in August 2000, a year after he underwent emergency surgery in Austria, when he informed party colleagues that he would quit the Assembly. He made it clear in a statement to journalists that his working commitments had become too much: 'I have become heavily overloaded with work, and I have serious health problems over the past year. I am leaving now because I have every confidence in the SDLP team in the assembly and I feel now the new institutions are on a secure footing.'[20]

In December 2000 he set his resignation in motion when he wrote to the Assembly Speaker, Lord Alderdice, informing him that he was giving up his seat at Stormont. It was the first stage of his retirement plan, and there was more news to follow in 2001. There was speculation that after leaving Stormont Hume was now considering giving up the party leadership. Despite such talk, he remained at the helm for the general election on 7 June.

Behind the scenes, all was not well within the SDLP family. There was private criticism that Hume was out of touch and spent too much time away from Northern Ireland. One experienced party member told this author:

> I think he was naïve. Some of us would have taken the view that John was too often at thirty thousand feet travelling backwards and forwards relating to popes and princes. And at various times that he was not sufficiently attuned to the way thinking was going on in the community around the street.[21]

As the general election loomed in 2001, Hume was adamant that the voters would not forget his work for peace and the efforts the SDLP had made, and he was convinced his party would stay ahead of Sinn Féin.

He was challenged by some colleagues that Sinn Féin were on the cusp of leapfrogging the party. Some leading party figures had previously argued that the Hume–Adams initiative would ultimately give Sinn Féin an electoral advantage.

Other colleagues had concerns that too little planning had gone into the groundwork needed in key constituencies. Hume was not interested in party structures and had not given the organisation of the party much attention. Eamon Hanna, who was SDLP general secretary, says that it was one of Hume's failings: 'I think he should have kept his eye on the organisation more and made sure the party was in good health all over, organisationally, which we weren't. It meant we were swept aside in constituencies like Mid Ulster and Fermanagh and South Tyrone.'[22]

There was real change happening across the electoral landscape in nationalist and republican areas, and Sinn Féin were seen as more proactive on the ground. The party was more organised and had more resources, and particularly for many young nationalists, the party had become their preferred choice. Sinn Féin had an edge in a way the SDLP did not. Hume's party seemed old-fashioned and dated whereas Sinn Féin seemed more modern and purposeful.

When the results emerged the SDLP returned three MPs to Westminster. Not surprisingly Hume retained his seat in Foyle as did Seamus Mallon in Newry and Armagh and Eddie McGrady in South Down. However, it was Sinn Féin's big moment and the party eclipsed the SDLP for the first time and polled 175,392 votes compared to the SDLP tally of 169,865. It was a small difference but of massive significance. Sinn Féin now had four MPs in the constituencies of West Belfast, Fermanagh and South Tyrone, Mid Ulster and West Tyrone – although they refused to take their seats in parliament.

It was a watershed moment in the battle for the hearts and minds of nationalists. Hume's pre-poll optimism seemed misplaced and the election results raised more questions about his leadership of the party and its future direction. In the 1998 Assembly election the party had gained the largest share of the vote but it had now been pushed into fourth place. Tom Kelly, a member of the SDLP's back room team, wrote in the *Irish*

News that the party had been given a 'bloody nose' and that it was now time for 'invigorated leadership'. He wrote that: 'The SDLP to a large degree tried to lead the electorate to a new type of politics which has been loosely described as post-nationalist. The bald reality is that the nationalist electorate is not ready for that message.'[23]

The council election results also made difficult reading for the SDLP. Sinn Féin again outpolled the party by around 10,000 votes, although the SDLP ended up with more councillors. Over the summer, behind closed doors, the discussions continued in SDLP meetings about what the party should do and where it needed to improve. John Hume's family had been having their own conversations and in September he announced that he would be stepping down as party leader. In his statement he said he had been 'thinking about it for some time now'.[24]

The news of Hume's impending resignation meant that the focus now shifted to Seamus Mallon. Was this his time to become leader? He had been deputy leader for decades and was often talked about as the natural successor to Hume. Mallon had a decision to make and after some thought decided, like his colleague, that he too would step down from his leadership role.

There were other factors to consider. His wife, Gertrude, was ill and Mallon had a choice to make: 'So I had to decide – which was my greater responsibility, to lead the SDLP or to look after my very sick wife? and I decided it was to look after her.'[25]

On 19 September, Seamus Mallon called a press conference to announce he would be resigning as deputy leader and would not be contesting the party leadership. It signalled the end of his political career. His decision brought to an end a partnership that had dominated the SDLP for a generation. Mallon and Hume were the party's building blocks through the political darkness of the 1980s and through the tortuous days of talks and endless negotiations of the 1990s. It was not an easy relationship, and there were arguments and moments of great tension. They were, in the words of one observer, like 'an old married couple, who fought and argued but who ultimately came back together'. In the autumn of 2001, they both got ready to say farewell.

21

STEPPING DOWN

'You could read from the phone book, and they will clap.'
Seamus Mallon on John Hume's final leader's speech

In the bar of the Slieve Donard Hotel, dozens of SDLP activists were enjoying a few drinks. The room was busy and there was a buzz about the place. For some members the trip to party conference was like an annual pilgrimage, an opportunity to catch up with old friends, hear the latest political gossip and refresh their ideas and thoughts. It was also a chance to plan the latest campaign and come away feeling energised. Party conferences generally have two audiences. One is the watching public and the media, for whom it's important to transmit a professional image that shows the party is relevant and making a difference. The other audience is the internal one – the membership. For leaders, the purpose of the event is to send those grass-roots activists home happy.

However, this gathering in Newcastle, in the shadow of the Mournes, was no routine affair. This was a very different occasion. Change was on the agenda. Party veterans and new recruits had all come together to see history happening. Amongst the drinkers that November evening were Ronan McCay, who was helping to draft Hume's final address as party leader. He was sitting alongside his friend Colum Eastwood, who, like McCay, had been interested in politics since his mid-teens. At age 18, Eastwood was seen by some in the party and in the media as a rising star. He had joined the SDLP at the time of the Good Friday Agreement and was being tipped to become a party representative in the near future.

Eastwood and McCay quickly spotted Seamus Mallon in the bar and joined their deputy leader for a drink. Soon, others arrived, including John Hume, and a crowd built up around the two veterans. Pints of stout were deposited on the table and champagne was also produced.

It had the air of a party and Eastwood recalls how everyone wanted to see what was happening: 'Within half an hour, the bar was packed and the two of them were competing with each other for sing-songs.'[1]

Ronan McCay watched as Hume and Mallon seemed at ease in each other's company: 'Seamus stood up and sang and then John stood up and sang. You just felt you were in a moment of real history and these two immense figures were saying goodbye to themselves and to their role as leaders, and saying goodbye to their party. And it was just a great privilege.'[2] Eastwood recalled that the singing lasted many hours: 'The two of them were singing all night together, it was just unbelievable. And some of us said, "Have you not got a speech tomorrow?" and he said, "Sure it will be grand."'[3]

Mallon was not the only one with a farewell speech to make. Ronan McCay recalled how after hours of performing his favourite songs, Hume said he had to get some rest before his big day: 'And in the wee small hours, John said, "I have to go to bed, I have a very major speech to give tomorrow." And Seamus just turned and said to John, "You could read from the phone book and they will clap."'[4]

Mallon's cheeky jibe had a degree of truth. He knew that such was the devotion of the party faithful that Hume would get a rousing reception in the hours ahead and that is exactly what happened. His final address as party leader was a classic Hume affair. He talked of the importance of Europe and the role of the United States in the peace process. He quoted two of his political heroes, Martin Luther King and his long-term friend Ted Kennedy. He had high praise for other political leaders such as Tony Blair, Bertie Ahern, John Bruton, Charlie Haughey, Garret FitzGerald and Albert Reynolds, and talked about their work towards political reconciliation. He also had warm words for Seamus Mallon as he stood down as deputy leader, and he described him as an 'inspirational figure' who 'deserves our sincere thanks and praise today for his immense contribution to Irish politics'.[5]

Traditionally Hume ended his speech with a rallying call he had been using for over three decades. His final words to the conference as leader were 'we shall overcome'.[6] Hume's political life had come full circle and his leadership ended as it began – with applause. As Mallon predicted, the conference audience cheered every word and he was given a rousing send-off.

The party was now under new stewardship, and he was succeeded as party leader by fellow Derry man Mark Durkan, his protégé and confidante whom Hume described as, 'the most gifted political figure of the new young generation'. Hume insisted his successor was the best choice because he had the 'calibre, integrity and the vision to lead this party into the twenty-first century'.[7]

As 2001 came to a close the SDLP began life in a post-Hume world. With Mark Durkan and Bríd Rodgers now in the roles of leader and deputy leader, it was new territory, as Mallon and Hume became the elder statesmen of the party rather than the power brokers. Hume's retirement plan was now in full swing. He had quit the Assembly and the party leadership, leaving in place his roles of MP and MEP.

There were plans afoot to relinquish those positions in the years ahead, but in the meantime, Hume continued to travel to Brussels and Strasbourg and London. He also regularly went abroad to speak at conferences and he received international honours. In 1999, before his retirement as party leader, he had been awarded the Martin Luther King Jr Nonviolent Peace Prize in Atlanta. It was a particularly important award to Hume since King was a political hero of his, who inspired his philosophy and commitment to non-violence. In February 2002 he was awarded the Gandhi Peace Prize and he travelled to India to pick up the award. Like the Martin Luther King Jr prize, the Gandhi prize meant a lot to Hume personally. He was keen that his honour would be reported back in Derry and when he was in India he rang his office to see if the news had been picked up by the local press.

Ronan McCay recalled the conversation with Hume, who wanted to know if the *Derry Journal* had covered the news. The old habits of a media-savvy politician were still very much evident. Hume also told McCay he was ringing from his hotel swimming pool, which in itself was quite unusual, as he famously found relaxing difficult. McCay told the MP that the news had been reported in the Derry paper but not on the front page. McCay could not resist teasing his boss by inquiring if the award had been carried by the *Delhi Journal*. The joke appeared to be lost on Hume. McCay thought it was interesting that even though Hume was in the twilight of his political career and was not going to fight another election he was still thinking like a politician and wondering about news coverage.

Hume remains the only person to receive the Nobel Peace Prize, the Martin Luther King Jr Nonviolent Peace Prize and the Gandhi Peace Prize. He was proud to have all three honours and he enjoyed showing the awards to people when he was invited to give talks. On one occasion he was invited to talk to pupils at Thornhill College in Derry and McCay dutifully collected him from his home. As he got into the car Hume handed him a plastic carrier bag from Wellworths. When they arrived at the school the two men were given a tumultuous reception and were greeted by hundreds of schoolchildren lined up in the playground. Hume then told McCay to bring the rather incongruous-looking bag inside but did not tell him what it contained.

During the talk, Hume turned to McCay and asked for his Nobel medal. Hume's assistant was confused. What was he talking about? He had not said he was bringing the medal and McCay had certainly not seen it. Hume then explained that he kept it in the Wellworths bag. McCay was taken aback momentarily but not completely surprised. He thinks the story of the medal says a lot about Hume: 'I just think it captures him beautifully: the highs of winning a prestigious prize, the honour, and then the everydayness of a Wellworths bag. I just think that sums him up.'[8]

Away from politics, Hume had more time to indulge in his love for Derry City Football Club. His son John says this was a godsend and a great distraction: 'When the dementia was starting to kick in, I mean Derry City became a real outlet for him. He would go to the Brandywell and he would be so well looked after and so respected and they treated him like he was God. It was brilliant.'[9]

As club president, Hume had an ambassadorial role, which he loved, and his experience of networking would often prove quite useful. Off the pitch, Derry's path was not always a smooth one, and like many other clubs they ran into financial trouble when an unpaid bill from the Inland Revenue threatened their very existence. There were real fears that without a sudden and dramatic influx of cash, the team would have to stop playing senior football for a second time. Club officials turned to John Hume for help. They wondered if he could use his political contacts to secure a glamour fixture with a top European side that could generate enough cash to stop any financial threat to the club.

Hume was happy to oblige and after a series of conversations it was agreed that several high-profile friendlies should be arranged. Using personal contacts he had made over years of public life, he was instrumental in getting Real Madrid and Barcelona to travel to the Brandywell. His powers of persuasion reached into the boardrooms of Europe's footballing elite, but he could not have done it on his own.

His daughter Mo, who could speak Spanish, was also asked to help, and she made phone calls on behalf of the club to help with arrangements. The trips to the Brandywell were a success and the much-needed revenue helped Derry City's balance sheet. Hume's links to different corners of the world were legendary and if he wanted help or assistance for a particular project he was never shy in reaching out and asking for support. A phone call or a personal visit would often do the trick and he would be blunt and straight to the point. A Hume request always proved hard to turn down. He was a professional persuader.

Mo Hume recalls a time when she was organising a fundraising concert in Derry for humanitarian work in El Salvador. Her father knew that the Irish folk band The Dubliners were in the city getting ready to play a concert that evening, and he thought they could help his daughter's fundraising efforts. So, with his daughter in tow, Hume made his way to a local hotel and arrived at the reception desk. Hume told the receptionist that he was there to see Ronnie Drew, the band's enigmatic lead vocalist. Drew was called on the phone and told the receptionist that Hume should make his way up to his room.

Moments later, Hume and his daughter knocked on Drew's bedroom. The singer, thinking he was just meeting the politician, had just come out of the bath, so he opened the door wearing just a towel to cover his modesty. He was shocked to see Hume standing there with his daughter. Caught unawares, he declared: 'Jesus, John, I didn't realise you had somebody with you.'[10]

The half-naked Drew quickly retreated inside his room and told his visitors that they should talk in the hotel lobby. Minutes later, the fully dressed musician arrived on the ground floor and soon got chatting. Hume asked the singer if he could plug his daughter's fundraising event when he was performing his own gig in a few hours time. Drew thought he could do more than that.

That night, after they had performed their own concert, three of The Dubliners made their way across the city. Colum Eastwood was helping out at the door when he saw them arrive : 'I just remember Ronnie Drew turning up with other band members. And I thought, bloody hell – is this for real?' The surprise guests played an impromptu gig with borrowed instruments and they brought the house down.

After stepping down from the party leadership and the Assembly, the second part of Hume's retirement plan soon came into play. With the European elections on the horizon in 2004 it made sense for Hume to declare that he would not be a candidate.

After quitting the leadership this was expected, but it meant a lot to Hume, who had been involved with European politics for half his life. Leaving this political stage would prove to be a hard decision, as he felt at home in the European Parliament and hugely enjoyed being in Brussels and Strasbourg. Hume always saw himself as a committed European and he knew it would be a wrench to give up his MEP seat.

Aidan Hume insists that during the Troubles and the tortuous days of talks and negotiations, his father always found a trip to the European Parliament liberating: 'Europe was like a mental break for him.' Aidan Hume also insists that things could have been different: 'I think if his health had been better he might have done another five years in Strasbourg. He loved the European Parliament.'[11]

His departure from Europe came in May 2004 when he made his final speech that ended his 25-year career as an MEP. In his closing address, he returned to many of the themes that he had regularly discussed during his time as one of Northern Ireland's three representatives. He talked about reconciliation, respecting difference, and he praised the role of the European Union in helping to secure peace in Northern Ireland. It was hard for Hume to step away from a parliament and an institution that he genuinely adored and saw as a force for good. He saw the European Union as the best example of conflict resolution across the world. He believed the member states could offer moral, political and financial support to peace-making efforts in Ireland and he saw the EU as a way to assist human rights and social justice.

The SDLP wanted to protect what they saw as Hume's European legacy and felt the best way to do that was to elect Martin Morgan as his successor. An activist from his teens, Morgan was a Belfast City councillor and one of a number of fresh faces on the campaign trail. Ultimately, two new MEPs were elected when the ballots were finally counted but Morgan was not one of them. Ian Paisley, like Hume, had decided to retire, which resulted in the DUP's Jim Allister topping the poll. The UUP's Jim Nicholson held onto his seat and Sinn Féin made history when Bairbre de Brún won the party's first seat in Northern Ireland at the expense of the SDLP. Hume had hoped Morgan would retain the seat for the party and carry on his work but De Brún's victory simply underlined the gap that had opened up now electorally between Sinn Féin and the SDLP.

Morgan was seen as a new-generation candidate and he had run for office before, but he could not attract the support Hume had traditionally received. It was a big challenge to follow in the footsteps of a political giant who traditionally was elected on the first count. Morgan witnessed the party vote slump from 28 per cent to around 16 per cent of the vote. There was a great sense of disappointment in SDLP ranks that the party could not hold onto Hume's seat. Hume nearly topped the poll in 1999 when he got 190,000 votes. Morgan's tally in 2004 of just under 90,000 showed how far the party had fallen.

Hume's resignation from Europe was followed by the news that he would not contest the 2005 Westminster election. His obvious successor as Foyle MP was Mark Durkan, who had succeeded him as party leader back in 2001. Durkan, as expected, took the seat in the general election but the SDLP got mixed results across Northern Ireland. Seamus Mallon stood down in Newry and Armagh and Sinn Féin's Conor Murphy took his seat. A split in the unionist vote in South Belfast helped Alasdair McDonnell become the party's first MP in that constituency, so the party went back to Westminster with three seats. The SDLP won in Foyle, South Belfast and South Down, where Eddie McGrady retained his seat. However, it was clear Sinn Féin was now the leading voice for nationalism and it seemed the SDLP would continue to be outflanked by them.

Away from the corridors of Westminster, the party meetings and the endless flights to Brussels, life for John Hume was now very different. He no longer had the pressures of a political job but he was still in demand for speeches and talks. He remained keen to discuss the peace process and his role in it. His work over the decades did not go unrecognised.

In retirement, he was the recipient of numerous honorary degrees from universities and colleges across the UK and Ireland. A multi-million-pound research centre at the National University of Ireland at Maynooth was named in his honour and was opened by President Mary McAleese. He was no stranger to visiting colleges and received more academic awards than any other Irish politician. He continued his bond with the University of Ulster campus at Magee, the building which was right on his doorstep. It was a place that meant much to him as he'd started his political apprenticeship in the 1960s campaigning for the city to host Northern Ireland's second university. Magee was part of Hume's DNA and he felt he belonged there.

Amongst the staff there he was highly thought of, and he was given the honorary role of the Tip O'Neill Chair in Peace Studies at the university, a position named in honour of his late friend. Hume helped to bring speakers to the institution to discuss peace-building and reconciliation and he was a regular face around the campus.

As he got used to retirement, two of his political rivals, Ian Paisley and Martin McGuinness, were about to experience the pinnacle of their careers. The duo made world headlines in May 2007, in a move that many thought they would never see. The DUP and Sinn Féin agreed to share power, and in a ceremony at Stormont in front of visiting dignitaries, the two men became first and deputy first ministers. It was a show-stopping moment – a time to pause and consider how history had changed.

Paisley, at nearly 80 years of age, who had spent his entire political career vowing to smash Sinn Féin and never to share power with republicans, was now standing alongside an IRA commander. Paisley's language was now about a shared future and he was beginning to make speeches that years earlier would have been unthinkable.

Journalist Denis Murray who observed the Northern Ireland political scene for decades says it is clear Hume had an influence on the DUP leader. He recalled a moment some years earlier when the two MEPs gave speeches at a Belfast hotel about European funding. Hume had told Murray to pay close attention to Paisley's speech and Murray could not believe what he was hearing:

> When Paisley came to speak, it took me a minute or two to grasp what I was hearing. After a few preliminaries he started to talk about this 'piece of earth' and 'our divided people' and how we had to 'share our future' – it was like listening to what even John called Hume's single transferable speech. I realised I was sitting there with my mouth open. I couldn't believe it. I had seen this man turn a peaceful crowd into a rampaging mob. Unbelievable. Hume was sitting behind Paisley, facing the audience. I caught his eye and he grinned and did that universal hands out, palms up shrug which says 'See? Told you.' I was convinced from that moment, and I remain convinced, that whether it was Hume alone or his general European experience, Paisley became convinced there were peaceful and compromising ways forward.[12]

Looking back, Ian Paisley Junior says his father and Hume had a long-standing relationship of over 40 years and, having served in the same parliaments at Westminster and Strasbourg, had respect for each other. He says the two leaders took a different view on many social issues and the constitution but his father regarded his fellow MEP as 'an intellectual' and he 'fully understood where Hume was coming from'. He says his dealings with the SDLP politician were 'much deeper and more extensive than his dealings with Martin McGuinness and were at the outset based on respecting democratic principles'.[13]

Hume's conversations and encounters over the years with Martin McGuinness were very different. Even though they lived close to each other, it is obvious that at times he had a strained relationship with his fellow Derry man. This may stem from Hume's personal experience, when he would have held McGuinness personally responsible for the trouble and violence inflicted on his home city. As one person close to Hume made clear, forging a relationship with McGuinness would have been challenging 'if you knew what went on in Derry during the 1970s and 80s'.[14]

Hume's main point of contact with Sinn Féin had always been Gerry Adams, so he had little reason to cultivate a relationship with McGuinness. What is clear is that there are numerous instances when Hume's dislike of McGuinness was on show. During the second visit of President Clinton to Derry in 2014, the US politician walked over the peace bridge with John and Pat Hume. Martin McGuinness then appeared and, according to Ruairí O'Kane, Hume made his feelings known: 'Obviously Martin was Deputy First Minister and John turned round and said to him, "What the fuck are you doing here? What the fuck did you ever do for the peace process?"'[15]

Even allowing for Hume's condition at the time, there are other occasions when his dislike of McGuinness was apparent and public. The former Irish diplomat Seán Donlon noticed that the personal chemistry between Hume and the Sinn Féin politician was poor: 'For some reason, he didn't like McGuinness, maybe because he was a fellow competitor in Derry.' Donlon recalls being at a function in Derry when the republican approached Hume: 'We were in a drinks reception afterwards and I was with John and McGuinness came over to greet us. John literally turned his back on him and left me shaking hands with him. He just had no time for McGuinness.'[16]

As the months passed, retirement meant more time in Donegal and Derry and there were greater opportunities to see his children and grandchildren. However, it became increasingly clear that he was not able to operate in the same way he did during the height of his career. His recollection of events and names and places and his concentration were declining. His condition prompted Mark Durkan to famously remark: 'What John could no longer remember we should never forget.'[17]

John would get invited to dinners and social occasions, but friends and family would keep an eye on him. It was often hard work. Phil Coulter recalls being with him at events during this time: 'Those were not comfortable days.'[18] Understandably, Pat and the Hume family were very protective of him, and Áine Abbott recalls how they all noticed the change: 'It was a really gradual process. And he was just needing more support really. It became clear that his memory was becoming less good.'[19]

Hume began to spend more time at home in Derry. He became a creature of habit and he and Pat would try and go out every day. Hume enjoyed walking and most days would leave the house, as Áine recalled:

> So, Dad, he really was an independent soul. He did not want any of us following him around. He really wanted to be able to go out the front door and go for a walk by himself. And that was a huge worry, you know, but he did it every day pretty much. So he had a routine with Mum where they would go to mass in the morning. They would walk over and walk back except that Dad usually hitched a lift back because he did not want to walk.[20]

The former Foyle MP also enjoyed walking into the city and having a drink. Aidan says his father would often be inundated with offers of lifts home from strangers: 'They would look after him. Taxis would stop and just pick him up so it was nice. I was back once and we went to a Derry City game with him and walking out he probably had about five or six offers of a lift home. It was nice – people really looked after him.'[21]

It is clear from the way he was treated that the people of Derry regarded Hume as one of their own. There was a warmth towards him on the streets and, in his retirement, it seemed there was an unofficial pact between his former constituents and his family. It was payback time. After years of service as their MP, now it was their turn to look after him. Such generosity and kindness helped the Hume family deal with his condition. Hume's son John says they felt that even when their father was out walking alone they knew he would be safe: 'It was a great sort of comfort and relief to Mum. She would always know if he got confused or whatever, which did happen quite often, you know, there would be somebody that would make sure he got home.'[22]

Mo says her father was constantly being dropped home by strangers and had perfected the ability to hitch a ride: 'He would almost stare the person down until they stopped and offered him a lift. Again, he was the great persuader.'[23]

After a lifetime of political activity, Hume was also keen to keep up with the friendships and relationships he had forged and enjoyed whilst he was on the frontline. He loved going to Dublin and was a regular visitor to the city, often going to see Bertie Ahern, who had become a good friend. Hume would visit the Dáil where there would be no shortage of people keen to see him for a coffee and a chat. He may have retired, but his thoughts were still sought by politicians across the board. Hume would also go to see Ahern at his office in Drumcondra and would travel there on the bus from Derry. Occasionally he would get a return lift home, as Ahern recalled: 'I had to watch him to make sure he was okay. And then, once or twice, I had my drivers bring him home all the way to Derry.'[24]

The former taoiseach kept a close eye on his friend and would sometimes help to organise Hume's Dublin itinerary. The two men would often go for a drink together and, conscious of Hume's legendary sweet tooth, Ahern's office staff would often organise some apple pie for him if they knew he was visiting. On one occasion, Ahern was contacted by Aengus Fanning, the former editor of the *Sunday Independent*, the Dublin-based newspaper which had heavily criticised Hume's talks with Adams. Their coverage had angered Hume and Fanning wanted to chat with him about it, so Ahern brought the two men together. Ahern says it was a chance for Fanning to build bridges with the former SDLP leader: 'John was beginning to drift at this stage but we still met up and we had a good conversation ... It wasn't heavy because he was not able but it was a good one, just to make peace.'[25]

Whether Hume completely understood the significance of Fanning's approach is not clear. Amongst Hume's loyal friends and family, there was little love for the *Sunday Independent* and to this day some SDLP supporters still refuse to buy the paper. Mary McAleese thinks the *Sunday Independent*'s olive branch, which came years after its coverage, was too little too late: 'He was long gone in the mind before they bothered to apologise.'[26]

In 2009 the SDLP tried to wrestle back Hume's European seat and he was called upon to campaign for the party. His involvement was limited and carefully managed by SDLP officials who felt the Hume brand and his history in Europe could woo some voters. Alban Maginness, who was the first nationalist to be elected mayor of Belfast, was selected to run for the seat. A lawyer by profession, he was an MLA for North Belfast and had been chair of the party.

The hope was that rather than fielding a younger candidate, as the party did in 2004, a more established campaigner might yield better results. Hume was asked to do some work close to his home and, as he had done dozens of times before, he helped to canvass in Derry. As expected on the campaign trail he got quite a lot of attention – sometimes more interest than the actual candidate.

Whilst canvassing close to the Long Tower Church, Ruairí O'Kane recalled how Hume was stopped by local people and tourists who wanted photographs with him and he remembered that Hume was in great form. Although the former MP's memory was failing, it was clear he still retained his ability to remember certain stories and in particular songs that he had sung for decades. At one stage Hume held court with a group of American visitors and the subject of emigration arose. He pointed out the role that Derry had played in the story of emigration and made them aware that nearby was a place where boats took emigrants across the Atlantic to the United States. O'Kane says what happened next was remarkable:

> Whoever was with me at the time nudged me and said here wait for this, because they had obviously heard it before. And he says there is a song about this. And the next thing 'Danny Boy' was getting belted out by John in the middle of the afternoon in the churchyard of the Long Tower Church.[27]

Hume's impromptu rendition of the emotional ballad moved his audience, as O'Kane recalled: 'They were in tears. They were crying proper tears as John sang "Danny Boy" from start to finish.'[28] Hume had difficulty remembering names and places, but his ability to recall song lyrics was impressive, and he could switch between songs in Irish, English and French. He was no longer a politician, but there was still huge interest in him and he was often treated like a celebrity.

Despite the party's best efforts, the attempt to win back Hume's seat failed. Even though the SDLP vote went up, Sinn Féin maintained their electoral superiority with Bairbre de Brún taking a seat along with Diane Dodds of the DUP and Jim Nicholson of the Ulster Unionists. The days of an SDLP voice in Europe were well and truly over. Traditionally Northern Ireland elected 2 MEPs from the unionist tradition and one came with nationalist support. Now Sinn Féin was the voice of Northern nationalism in the European Parliament, just as it was in councils across Northern Ireland.

The result was another disappointment for Mark Durkan and a reminder that the party was not the political force it used to be. Whilst SDLP officials could take heart that their vote had increased slightly, it was clear that without Hume on the ballot paper electoral success was proving elusive. Hume's European votes would never be bettered by the party.

As 2010 arrived he had now been away from active politics for nearly five years. He had received numerous awards for his peace-building work and apart from the occasional interview and documentary programme he had largely slipped away from public view. However, one more honour was about to come John Hume's way and for a few brief weeks his life and legacy would be back in the media spotlight.

22

IRELAND'S GREATEST

'Pat, do you hear this? ... I am Ireland's Greatest.'
John Hume

The RTÉ presenter Miriam O'Callaghan was standing in a Derry street learning her lines. She was getting ready to deliver another piece to the camera. It was her stock-in-trade, something she had done thousands of times before during her long television career. After taking a few moments to compose herself, she was confident she knew exactly what to say. Filming outside in a busy city centre always posed challenges. Sometimes there was a battle to be heard above the noise of passing traffic; occasionally there could be barking dogs or overhead planes. Passersby often wanted to chat and take a selfie and the unpredictable Irish weather meant proceedings regularly got delayed. Interruptions were part and parcel of the job and O'Callaghan and her crew were well versed in the stop-start nature of their work.

After a while everyone was ready to start filming and the conditions seemed perfect. The shot was framed, the background noise was deemed acceptable and the crew were getting ready to record. Suddenly, Gerry Hoban, the producer of the film, caught sight of a familiar couple. He quickly alerted Miriam that John and Pat Hume were right behind her. It was perfect timing. The broadcaster immediately turned around and saw the Humes. They were all on friendly terms and had known each other for many years. O'Callaghan, who had reported extensively on Northern Ireland for both RTÉ and the BBC, had interviewed both John and Pat on numerous occasions for various television and radio programmes.

From talking to Pat recently she was well aware of John's condition. As she smiled at him, she could sense that he seemed confused. Pat intervened and reminded her husband who she was: 'It's Miriam and she is up doing a story.'[1]

'Why are you not interviewing me?' asked Hume. He persisted: 'You are in my home city; why are you not interviewing me?'[2] O'Callaghan was on a special project that she did not want to share with the city's former MP. Pat Hume knew exactly why Miriam O'Callaghan had travelled to Derry to carry out some filming but had not told her husband. The journalist, one of the best-known faces in Irish television, was making a film about John Hume's life and legacy for an RTÉ series called 'Ireland's Greatest'. The idea was a simple one. Several journalists and presenters had been asked to compile short films extolling the virtues of living or dead historical figures. The presenters then went on air to argue for their particular subject and using the films they tried to persuade the voting public that their candidate should be awarded the accolade of 'Ireland's Greatest'.

O'Callaghan had been asked if she would do a film about Hume and champion his work. It was an unusual situation for the presenter as she normally grilled politicians. It was strange for her to become an advocate for the former SDLP leader's legacy. However, she and the RTÉ management felt that, since Hume was retired, 'he was beyond politics now'.[3]

The format for the RTÉ programme had been successfully used previously in the UK when the BBC broadcast a series and Winston Churchill was deemed by the voting public to be the greatest Briton in history. O'Callaghan had interviewed Hume many times during the days of the peace process and had scrutinised his moves and methods. They had often clashed as she questioned his statements and analysis, but the pair had always remained on good terms. She recalled their times together in the studio: 'He was impossible to interview because no matter how much you challenged him, he had such a strong conviction that what he was doing was correct.'[4]

O'Callaghan was convinced that it was Hume's personality that helped to maintain the peace process and secure ceasefires in Northern Ireland, personality traits that in her words could be 'irritating and annoying' but helped to get 'peace over the line'. She felt he should be awarded his place in history and believed that 'his brain had been worn down by all the stress'.[5] She wanted Hume to win the honour but felt he had little chance of taking the accolade. The other nominees were the Irish revolutionary leader Michael Collins, the former Irish president Mary Robinson, the socialist and trade union leader James Connolly, who was a key figure in the 1916 Easter Rising, and the rock star Bono. Before filming got underway, O'Callaghan remembers what she thought: 'He so deserves it but he'll never win. Because in the Republic people, especially at that time, still turned off their television when there was anything on the North. It was almost like they didn't want to know. It was too painful.'[6]

O'Callaghan put together a film that traced Hume's life story and viewers were encouraged to vote in a telephone poll for which person deserved the honour. The documentary was only part of the selection process and Miriam O'Callaghan also appeared live on RTÉ's *Late, Late Show* with Ryan Tubridy. There she made her pitch for Hume to be given the honour by the voting public. After the votes were finally tallied, Hume was declared 'Ireland's Greatest' much to Miriam O'Callaghan's delight: 'I could not believe it. I was so happy. I jumped up. I was just so happy.' The presenter says the decision was overwhelming: 'It's my proudest career moment, without a doubt.'[7]

In the green room after the broadcast, Miriam O'Callaghan was phoned by Pat Hume who was delighted:

> She was quite emotional and said, 'Miriam, we are all here watching it. And John says he isn't well enough to talk to you, Miriam, but he's so happy and so touched and he was very emotional.' So I actually shed a tear. I was so happy. I felt – work done. I felt happy and made up for all the times I gave him hell.[8]

The next day everybody wanted to get a reaction from the Humes. Ruairí O'Kane remembers his mobile phone buzzing constantly as journalists wanted a quote from Hume: 'My phone was going ballistic. Oh, where is John? Where can we get him? I said as soon as I can find him I will let you know.'⁹

O'Kane jumped in his car and drove to the Hume family home in Derry and recalls informing John what had happened the night before: 'So I had to go and tell John what had gone on. And he said, "I am what?" I said, "You are Ireland's Greatest." "Who says?" I said, "There was a vote." He said, "Was there?" I said, "Yes." He says, "What do I get?"' Hume's question brought a response of laughter. Then O'Kane explained: 'You don't get anything, John, but we will go and do some pictures.' Hume seemed very content with the news: 'Grand, no problem. Pat, do you hear this? I am going to do pictures. I am Ireland's Greatest.' Pat Hume smiled: 'Sure, we always knew that, John.'¹⁰

Five years after his retirement, the RTÉ award was a reminder to Hume and to his family of the esteem in which he was held. Life was not easy for Pat, as she worked hard to make sure John got the right care and help. Inevitably he had days when his memory was good and there were other occasions when he was unable to remember names and events. One senior party figure said John was like a mobile phone: 'There were days when there was a full network and there were other days when there was no coverage.'¹¹

The political landscape was almost unrecognisable from the time Hume stepped away from public life in 2005. There had been a changing of the political guard at Westminster and history was made at Stormont as Paisley and McGuinness embarked on power-sharing. Meanwhile, Hume's former colleagues in the SDLP were once again encountering tough times. In February 2010, his friend Mark Durkan stood down as leader. He had made the surprise announcement some months earlier during an interview with the *Inside Politics* programme on BBC Radio Ulster, saying he wanted to step aside from the leadership to concentrate on his role at Westminster. He had served eight years at the helm and, like Hume, had to deal with his fair share of internal party critics. It had been a difficult time to be party leader and it was clear there were times he did not enjoy the role.

Durkan had learned so much from his years with Hume and it showed. He was extremely able and well-read; he had inherited Hume's logical approach to problem-solving and had an encyclopaedic knowledge of legislation. He was funny, and his one-liners were legendary amongst colleagues and journalists. Yet, somehow, the role of leadership appeared at times to weigh him down and he felt it was time for change. The party had been unable to close the electoral gap with Sinn Féin and the loss of the European seat was a bitter blow. If Durkan looked and sounded tired, so too did his party, whilst Sinn Féin came across as sharper, brighter and better organised. Margaret Ritchie became the party's first female leader after she defeated her sole rival, Alasdair McDonnell. She was minister for social development in the Executive and had become the South Down MP in May 2010 when Eddie McGrady retired. She joined Mark Durkan in the House of Commons. He retained his seat in Foyle and Alasdair McDonnell maintained the party's hold in South Belfast.

Aside from the general election, the other major political news story of the year that concerned Hume was the publication of the Bloody Sunday Inquiry, set up under the chairmanship of Lord Saville to establish exactly what happened on the streets of Derry in January 1972. In June, Hume joined hundreds of others in the city's Guildhall Square to hear an official announcement that those shot on Bloody Sunday were innocent. It was the end of a remarkable campaign for the families, as Hume watched the prime minister, David Cameron, apologise for the 'unjustified and unjustifiable deaths'.[12]

His apology prompted remarkable scenes, as the crowd cheered the words of a British Conservative premier – something that years earlier would have been unimaginable. The British establishment had, at last, acknowledged the decades of hurt and suffering felt in the city and accepted that the original official version of events had been wrong and had caused great anguish and pain. For Hume, it was an emotional and poignant day. It was a moment when he declared: 'The truth has won out.'[13]

Bloody Sunday had been a running sore in Derry for decades and Hume had raised the desire of relatives for a fresh inquiry countless times with different prime ministers. The announcement in June 2010 marked the end of a long and tortuous road. Saville's inquiry had commenced back in March 2000, with the final witness being called almost five years later in January 2005. Set up because the initial investigation by Lord Widgery was regarded by the relatives and campaigners as a whitewash, it became the longest inquiry in British legal history. Hume shared the joy and relief of the people in Derry when Lord Saville overturned the original report, discredited the actions of the soldiers and said the killings were unjustified. After decades of being at the centre of events, Hume was now an observer of the twists and turns of political life.

His story, from the streets of Derry, via Maynooth, to the offices of presidents and prime ministers, still fascinated programme makers. BBC Northern Ireland commissioned a film about his life and legacy. With an impressive list of contributors, the documentary charted his achievements and work and gave a glimpse of his life post-politics. In one scene Hume is filmed walking on the city's walls when he encounters a group of tourists and he asks them where they are from. The visitors tell him they have travelled from Canada. Hume speaks to them in French. It illustrated that on his good days, he was able to converse and carry on as normal – not just in one language but two.

It was also an example that, despite being away from the world of television doorsteps and recorded interviews, he was still able to perform for the camera. In 2010 he was asked to do a televised tribute to Mark Durkan and, after reading the prepared script, he was able to deliver it in one take. Hume's thoughts were regularly in demand by journalists, but family members and party officials limited his appearances and controlled what media he used. They were conscious that some days he could perform well and other days it was a struggle.

Hume's role in the history of Irish political life continued to be chronicled by academics and writers and former party colleagues. Seán Farren and Denis Haughey produced a book in 2015 that examined his legacy through a series of essays. Pat wrote a piece about what life was like being married to John and to promote the book she gave an interview to Miriam O'Callaghan. She explained that he would not be travelling to Dublin for the launch as he 'does not like being away from home now. He loves Derry'.[14] She candidly talked about his health and said caring for John can be 'very tough', but she praised her neighbours and friends and said the beauty of Derry is that it is 'a very dementia-friendly city'.[15]

Seán Farren also produced another book that told Hume's life story through his speeches, articles and comments, and the writer and documentary maker Maurice Fitzpatrick made a film and wrote a book about Hume's links to the United States. In the broadcast, former US president Bill Clinton described Hume as 'the Martin Luther King of the Irish conflict'. Although interest in Hume remained high, his public appearances became fewer and fewer.

Family and friends noticed that his condition was worsening as he struggled more and more with his memory. Much rested on the shoulders of Pat. She was his main carer and organised his meals and medicine and encouraged him to be independent, which he wanted. She encouraged him to go for walks and remain active and when they were invited to events she always accompanied him. In political life, Pat had supported her husband and helped him function. For decades she was the behind-the-scenes organiser, his first port of call for advice or help. Now in his retirement she was now doing a similar role, and whilst the pressures were very different, they were still very demanding.

Hume's grown-up children were now all living independent lives in different parts of the world with their own families, but on their visits back home to Derry and at family gatherings they could see how their father was changing. His son John noticed differences: 'I think as he got older and the dementia really sort of kicked in, he changed, you know, because he stopped wanting to go out. He didn't want to socialise anymore. He sort of preferred to stay at home. And then once a week, every Saturday, they were going to Kealy's in Greencastle to have their dinner and that was their night out.'[16]

Life for the Hume family was tough but, despite the obvious difficulties, there were still many moments of fun and laughter at family occasions and celebrations. Mo Hume says her dad's love of music never left him and his ability to break into song was at times breathtaking:

So we would play music or he would sing. I remember my mum's 80th birthday. We were in Rossnowlagh to celebrate and he went from 'The Town I Love So Well' to 'Tráthnóna Beag Aréir' – so he went from English to Irish and then sang 'La Mer' in French seamlessly.[17]

In April 2018 there was considerable media focus on the twentieth anniversary of the Good Friday Agreement, yet John Hume had little recollection of the role he played in its creation. Pat spoke publicly about her husband's dementia: 'It is very sad, his memory has just gone. John does not remember very much about the agreement of 1998, or about the Anglo-Irish Agreement or Sunningdale or anything else. Yet he gave his entire life to the achievement of them. But he is in a good place, he is content, he is very happy.'[18]

By the middle of 2018, there were ongoing worries in the Hume household over John's health. He had a fall, which was most unlike him, and he was hospitalised for a number of weeks. He was seriously ill and suffering from headaches. Some family members feared the worst and thought he would die in hospital. After a series of tests, he was diagnosed with temporal arteritis, which explained the head pains, and, more worryingly, there were concerns about his eyesight as the condition can result in serious vision problems.

Hume's condition of temporal arteritis was severe. His daughter Áine, with years of medical experience, knew what her father was going through:

> He had a very aggressive form of it. So he lost his sight literally over the course of a week. It normally responded to steroids and it didn't respond. So he lost his sight. He had a little bit of the sight left but partly because of the dementia and partly because of his personality he had such self-belief. He kind of just filled in the gaps and he was convinced he could see, which was kind.[19]

Hume's younger daughter Mo says this new diagnosis, and particularly his loss of mobility, changed things:

> So he could not walk very well and at that point that was when we had to get extra care because obviously Mum had been caring for him at home, which was really hard for us. Because there was no way she could continue to care for him because she had her own health conditions and we could not find a way to make it work at home.[20]

By this stage, Pat and John Hume had moved out of the family home in West End Park, the house they had shared for decades. They moved a short distance to an apartment. That obviously resulted in their space being reduced and also meant that there was not much room for carers to come in and look after John. The family concluded that this new diagnosis, coupled with his dementia, meant he could not stay at home. They knew it would be hard on Pat not to have her husband at home but felt it would give her a break from her role as his full-time carer. Aidan Hume says it was obvious his mother could not look after their father at home: 'She couldn't possibly care for him. And that was very hard for her mentally initially.'[21]

Away from the difficulties of caring for John, there were moments of joy for Pat. Her own work during the Troubles and throughout the peace process was honoured by the Irish Red Cross, which presented her with a Lifetime Achievement Award. She was described as a 'perpetual tonic' and was given the honour at a gala evening in Dublin. It was a night to savour and enjoy.[22]

However, back in Derry there were some big decisions that needed to be taken. After decades of married life together, Pat knew that her husband needed support and care and they would have to be apart. It was a tough call but the Hume family felt it was the only course of action. Thoughts then turned to securing a place at a suitable care home. A room was available at a home which was a short drive from Derry city centre and had great views over the River Foyle. The complex, which was close to the border with the Republic, seemed absolutely perfect. It catered for people with dementia and the family were impressed with the facilities and the kindness of the staff.

In September 2018, John Hume began his new life. He was given an en suite room on the ground floor which was decorated in dementia-friendly colours with a cream carpet and blue curtains. His family and staff made it comfortable for him and he was surrounded with memories of his home life and political achievements. There were photographs of Pat and his children and a picture of his parents, Annie and Sam. There was also a picture from 1998 when he was awarded the Nobel Peace Prize and there was a collection of books about politics and Derry. Hume's room had views of the Foyle and visitors and staff would often describe the activities on the water, as boats made their way to and from Derry. Hume could not visibly make out what was taking place in the distance but enjoyed hearing about the happenings outside. As his eyesight was very poor, staff recall how he often wanted to sit close to the window as he could still see shadows.

Amy McCloskey, who was a carer, remembers meeting John Hume on his second day in the home. Over time, she got to know him well and says he was always immaculately turned out in a shirt and tie and was well-mannered and very funny. She found him great company and they spent time together often, talking about the people he met in his life and the events he was involved in. A book about his career was kept in his room and that helped spark memories of his political work.

In an interview for this book, Amy recalled how the conversations would often go:

> If I had the chance I would have sat down and spoken to John because he loved to talk. I would open the book and read out wee parts of the book. Everything came back to his memory. He was able to tell me. If I asked him a question about the book, he was able to rhyme it off and talk about the Nobel Peace Prize. And he said making peace was one of the best days of his life. Happiest days, best days.[23]

His son John said his father never lost his desire to find out what was going on: 'Dad loved talking to people. You know, being in a place like that where there are lots of comings and goings and lots of families coming to visit their relatives whatever – so Dad was in his element.'[24]

The care home staff quickly became aware of Hume's likes and dislikes. They were told of his lifelong sweet tooth and in particular his love of Cadbury's Crunchie bars. Even though John was a diabetic and on medication, supplies of the bar regularly ended up in his room. Amy McCloskey recalls going off to purchase them:

> At this stage he was allowed to eat, you know, whatever he wanted, and we gave it to him, especially the Crunchie bars. I used to go up to the shop next door to work and buy his Crunchie bars or a Crunchie ice pop. And that would have made his day, even though he shouldn't have had it.[25]

Amy McCloskey also recalls how he always wanted to sing for fellow residents:

> We would have had a music day in work for two hours. I would have walked John over to it. He never really liked a big crowd or the noise but whenever he knew it was music he would have got up and he would come with me. He always wanted the mic at the end for the wee music session and he always sang 'The Town I Loved So Well' and 'Danny Boy'.[26]

Whilst John Hume struggled with dates and names from his long career, his recollection of his favourite songs remained in place, ballads that he had sung the world over. Hume the politician had long gone, but Hume the performer was still very much alive.

23

THANK YOU JOHN

'There are people alive today who would not be alive had it not been for John's vision.'
Father Paul Farren

John Hume's world had shrunk. He was no longer the international traveller or the statesman on the global stage. He had moved away from the familiar streets of his boyhood and his life now revolved around the comings and goings of the care home. He was in the capable hands of professional carers who clearly adored him, and his day-to-day living was well-organised and comfortable.

Each day Pat Hume made her way to the home where she would sit with John. They would chat and reminisce, discuss the day's events and sometimes play music. She had heart problems, yet despite her own health issues, she was determined to see her husband every day and offer him support and love, just as she had done for decades.

Their daughter Áine says the daily visits meant her mother could spend quality time with her father without worrying about his day-to-day care: 'Mum still was there every day. The time they spent there they were chatting, they were relaxing and it wasn't about getting dressed and, you know, it wasn't about tasks. She was able to spend time with him. So, that was great.'[1]

Hume loved to chat, not just with family members but with the care-home workers and other residents. It is clear he had a great relationship with the staff, and although his dementia was now very pronounced, parts of his personality and life story were always on show, as Áine remembers:

> The young carers were just fantastic with him. He would ask them the same twenty questions over and over again and invite them to Donegal and say, 'I have a house. You must come and stay in my house and tell your mother and father to come. We will go out for a meal together.'[2]

However, his loss of sight coupled with his dementia meant he often was unable to recognise family members and close friends although he continued to acknowledge Pat and used her name regularly. Mo Hume remembers visiting her father:

> If he saw you he probably would have known he knew you from somewhere. 'Remind me, who are you again?' But after that he could not see us and did not hear our voices every day. So he would wonder who we were. That recognition was compromised. He would say things like, 'Can you turn the lights on, I can't see properly.' And we would say 'The lights are on, Dad,' and he would say, 'No they are not, because I can't see.' So I think that was really challenging.[3]

However, in 2020, the routine of everyday life was completely shattered with the arrival of Covid. The Coronavirus pandemic caused disruption, the world over, to lives and livelihoods and changed the daily habits of millions of people. In March 2020, Northern Ireland recorded its first death from the virus and in the same month the UK government ordered that non-essential contact should cease, as should travel. Prime Minister Boris Johnson announced lockdown measures and ordered people to 'stay at home'. The Northern Ireland Executive met and put lockdown measures in place in a bid to keep the virus under control.

Care homes and their vulnerable residents found themselves in the front line. In an attempt to keep them free of the virus and stop it spreading, visiting was restricted so residents found themselves increasingly shut off from the outside world. Staff wore protective aprons and masks and residents were placed in lockdown. For John Hume and others in the home it was a tough time. John's son Aidan, who was living in the United States, says the new regime hit his father hard: 'Dad to the very end was a very social character. He loved company. He loved visitors. And from the last March to August he didn't really have any visitors because nobody was really allowed to go in.'[4]

In the summer of 2020, John Hume's health deteriorated, and he became seriously ill. The family had a lot of experience dealing with his different medical conditions as he had been in and out of hospital over the years. Sometimes they would fear the worst but such was his strength of character that he often had an ability to pull through just as things seemed bad. However, on this occasion it became clear that things were very different. Hume's son John was away from Ireland when he got the news about his father's condition: 'I was on holidays in France at the time. It was early, sort of maybe days before he died. It was clear he was not going to recover from this.'[5]

By August, Hume was in bed in the home as his condition worsened and before he died his family were able to see him. Amy McCloskey remembers that time:

> In the final two or three days the family were allowed to come in because we got the go-ahead for people to come in. And I was actually the last person John had his eyes open for. I was going off shift then Áine let me know then whenever I was at home that her Daddy's eyes were no longer open. I was the last person he looked up and smiled at.[6]

In the early hours of Monday 3 August, aged 83, John Hume died. His family issued a statement announcing that he had passed away peacefully after a short illness. They thanked the staff at the nursing home and said the care they had shown John in the last few months of his life had been 'exceptional.' They remarked, 'As a family we are unfailingly inspired by the professionalism, compassion and love they have shown John and all under their care. We can never adequately show them our thanks for looking after John at a time when we could not. The family drew great comfort in being with John again in the last days of his life.' The Humes also thanked the people of Derry and Moville and Greencastle, 'who have looked after John and shown us much kindness as his dementia has progressed. Celebrating community in all its diversity went to the heart of John's political ethos and we are very appreciative that our communities supported, respected and protected John.'

They added: 'John was a husband, a father, a grandfather, a great grandfather and a brother. He was very much loved and his loss will be deeply felt by all his extended family.' There was an acknowledgement of how the Covid restrictions to meeting in public would affect John's funeral and the family stated that it would take place 'according to current government regulations with very strict rules on numbers'.[7]

As the news of his death became public, the tributes to Hume's life and legacy came from all parts of the world. The former US president Bill Clinton said he had 'fought his long war for peace in Northern Ireland'. He added that Hume's chosen weapons were 'an unshakeable commitment to non-violence, persistence, kindness and love'.[8] Tony Blair, the former prime minister, described the former SDLP leader as, 'a visionary who refused to believe the future had to be the same as the past'.[9]

Likewise, Hume's friend Bertie Ahern said he would 'stand tall in our history alongside giants like Parnell and O'Connell always'.[10] Fellow Nobel Laureate Lord Trimble also acknowledged that Hume's contribution to public life would be remembered for many years: 'He was a major contributor to politics in Northern Ireland, particularly to the process that gave us an agreement that we are still working our way through.'[11]

The former Sinn Féin president Gerry Adams said he felt a great sense of loss and praised Hume's tenacity: 'When others talked endlessly about peace, John grasped the challenge and helped make peace happen.'[12]

There was a real sense that Hume's passing marked a seismic moment in Irish politics and, for his contemporaries, it was a time to mourn and reflect. Austin Currie, who had known Hume since the 1960s, described him as 'the greatest Irishman since Parnell'.[13] The DUP leader Arlene

Foster acknowledged his commitment to non-violence throughout the Troubles and called him 'a giant in Irish nationalism'.[14]

As prominent figures came forward to pay tribute, the list of contributors read like an A to Z of Irish politics over the past 40 years. There was a real warmth to the tributes and a sense amongst commentators and historians that Hume's passing marked the death of someone who had changed the narrative of Ireland and altered the course of Anglo-Irish relations. Naturally, in Derry there was an acute sense of grief. The city had lost one of its most famous sons who had championed their particular corner of Ireland.

The Hume family was overwhelmed by the reaction to John's death. They were genuinely touched by the many messages of support they received. Preparations were now being put in place for the funeral which, under normal circumstances, would have been a public occasion with crowds of mourners. The family asked people to respect the Covid restrictions and stay at home on the day of the funeral. It was suggested that people could light a candle at home to honour John Hume's work if they so wished and thousands of people did – including the prime minister Boris Johnson, who marked Hume's passing with a candle in Downing Street.

On Wednesday 5 August, a drizzly day in Derry, around 120 mourners gathered at St Eugene's Cathedral to say a final farewell to John Hume. Covid restrictions also meant Aidan Hume was unable to fly home from the United States. It was a cruel and unfortunate consequence of the pandemic and on the day of the funeral his absence was felt acutely by his mother and brother and sisters. Holding umbrellas and sporting red roses in their lapels, Aidan's siblings and their mother Pat dodged the rain on their way into the cathedral. Inside, wearing face masks, Áine, John, Therese and Mo sat in the front pew beside Pat. To their right was their father's wicker coffin and to their left, behind a collection of candles, was a black-framed portrait of their father resting on an easel. The church may have been half empty, but the world was watching.

Socially distanced, and sprinkled across different rows, sat close friends, a small selection of party colleagues and dignitaries. Across the aisle from the Hume family was the president of Ireland, Michael D.

Higgins. Nearby, with face coverings and wearing black, sat Northern Ireland's first minster, Arlene Foster, and deputy first minister, Michelle O'Neill. In other rows were the leading politicians from across the island, including the taoiseach, Micheál Martin, the foreign minister, Simon Coveney, and the Northern Ireland secretary, Brandon Lewis.

Party veterans were there too, including Mark Durkan, Bríd Rodgers, Joe Hendron, Austin Currie, Seán Farren, Alasdair McDonnell and Denis Haughey. The party's new generation was also represented with Nichola Mallon and Claire Hanna attending, along with current SDLP leader Colum Eastwood. The Humes had also invited Amy McCloskey and other colleagues from the care home who had all formed a close bond with John in his final months. It was an indication of how much the family valued the care he had been given.

The congregation heard messages from the pope, the Dalai Lama, the prime minister, Boris Johnson, and the former US president Bill Clinton. There was also a statement from Bono, who famously appeared with Hume and Trimble during the 1998 referendum campaign. The U2 singer summed up his friend by declaring: 'We were looking for a giant and found a man whose life made all our lives bigger.'[15]

Father Paul Farren told the congregation that they had come to give thanks to God for 'the gift of John Hume'. He said: 'Make no mistake about it there are people alive today who would not be alive had it not been for John's vision and work.' He said Hume had made 'peace visible for others'.[16] And he also praised the work of Pat Hume for her role behind the scenes. Father Farren was not the only priest who officiated and he was joined in the cathedral by Father Danny McGettigan, Pat Hume's cousin, who was from Donegal. They were joined by Archbishop Eamon Martin and Bishop Donal McKeown, who presided at the mass.

Even though there was an element of official protocol to the service, it still had the personal stamp of the Hume family. John's grandchildren read prayers and Mo Hume read a poem written by her brother Aidan. His poem talked about his dad's work and how he approached life. Mo's brother John delivered a tribute to his father. It was a funny and moving address that captured his dad's values, personality and character traits.

There was talk of his love of music and singing, his relationship with Pat, his political optimism and his dogged determination to change society. There was even a nod to his father's reputation for always delivering a 'single transferable speech'.[17]

There were many references to the famous Hume sweet tooth. His love of crème brûlée raised a smile and there was mention of his liking for sweet wine, and John Junior also talked about his dad's obsession with chocolate. The funeral mass ended with John Hume's coffin being taken out of the cathedral. As his remains were being removed, Phil Coulter, his lifetime friend, played 'The Town I Loved So Well'. It was a fitting finale. Outside in the August drizzle, John Hume's coffin was lifted into a black Volvo hearse.

Then, spontaneously, pockets of mourners broke into applause, and someone shouted, 'Thank you John'.[18] It was a moment of raw emotion. Derry was saying goodbye. Minutes later, the funeral cortège slowly made its way out of the cathedral grounds and headed towards the City Cemetery for a private burial. As the line of cars drove through the streets, small groups of people stood and watched. Some clapped and many blessed themselves as the hearse passed by. Others simply stood in silence and bowed their heads. They were witnessing a political giant take his leave from a city that he loved – a place that in turn loved him.

At the City Cemetery in a plot overlooking the familiar buildings of his childhood, John Hume was laid to rest. By chance, his grave had a great view of the Bogside and the Brandywell – two places that were cornerstones of his life. As a Derry City fan his view of the stadium could not have been more appropriate. As his family sang 'We Shall Overcome', the civil rights anthem that had been a soundtrack to his life, John Hume's journey came to an end. The short ceremony marked special moments for Pat, her children and grandchildren.

For the extended Hume family, the private time in the graveyard was much needed. It was a chance to say farewell away from the cameras and a watching crowd. Áine Abbott says it was important to have some privacy and it was 'really nice to have had a level of intimacy'.[19]

John Hume Junior insists that his father would have cared little about his own particular funeral arrangements. He also thinks the restrictions on numbers actually helped the family's grief: 'It was a more intimate affair. I think it was much better for my mother.'[20]

Mo agrees with her brother and also feels that the public safety guidelines indirectly helped the family experience a more personal occasion:

> It was about saying goodbye to our dad, or Mum's husband. And I think because of the pandemic ironically we were able to do that in a way we probably wouldn't have been if it had not been pandemic conditions because protocol would have taken over.[21]

In the end, the Covid regulations did not disrupt the sense of occasion. Therese Hume says there was a 'privacy and calmness' to her father's wake and despite the obvious feelings of grief it was 'a nice passing'.[22] Phil Coulter believes the service was conducted in a way that John Hume would have approved of. As the musician played 'The Town I Love So Well', his lifetime friend was carried from St Eugene's Cathedral one last time. Coulter says during the service he reflected on the adventures he and Hume had experienced as young men and in older life. He had watched his pal go from being a Derry schoolboy to becoming a statesman on the international stage. They had travelled the world together and entertained presidents and prime ministers, but Derry was always home: 'What it was, was a hometown send-off to a hometown hero, and that is what it was. That is what John would have wanted, never mind the bells and whistles.'[23]

In the weeks that followed the funeral, well-wishers regularly made their way to his grave to pay their respects. It was like a pilgrimage, as visitors brought flowers and sometimes prayed. Others would come and take photographs of the spot which was now marked by a simple wooden cross which bore his name and date of death. That would just be a temporary memorial, as the family had other plans. The Hume family commissioned a headstone to be crafted in stone from John's beloved

Inishowen which was put in place in the summer of 2021. It was erected in time for the first anniversary of his death and bore his name and an oak leaf – the symbol of Derry. The grave also included a kneeling stone with the word 'Síocháin', which means 'peace' in Irish.

With the backing and support of the family, a charitable foundation was established to honour the work of the Humes. Entitled the John and Pat Hume Foundation it was launched in 2020 and began to organise lectures and events around leadership and peace-building. Mo Hume and her brother John became board members, alongside a broad range of people from different backgrounds including the former Ulster Unionist leader Mike Nesbitt and Dawn Purvis, who once led the Progressive Unionist Party. The patrons of the group include Senator George Mitchell and the former Irish president Mary McAleese. Covid prevented the group from doing many public events, but as the pandemic eased their activities became more open and widespread.

The relaxation of restrictions also meant Aidan Hume could at last return home from America to see his mother and siblings in Derry and Donegal. After the heartbreak of missing his father's funeral, he wanted to catch up with his family and in particular spend time with his mother. He spent a week working from the family holiday home in Donegal and then he took a week off. He says the family had a great time together but he noticed that his mother had declined: 'I could see her health wasn't what it was.'[24]

In the months after John's passing, Pat Hume's health deteriorated, and around a year after his death she was hospitalised. Then on 2 September 2021, she died after a short illness. It all happened very quickly. The family was devastated and issued a statement to the media: 'We are heartbroken to announce the death of Pat Hume at home in Derry this afternoon after a short illness. Pat died as she lived – surrounded by family, peacefully and generous to the end.' The statement continued: 'Pat spent some days in the hospital in the days preceding her death and she saw first-hand the outstanding work that health care workers do and the pressures they are facing due to Covid. She would prioritise public health at all times.'[25]

Tributes came in from dignitaries across the world. Hillary Clinton, the former US Secretary of State, said 'she made the world a better place'.[26] Her husband, President Bill Clinton, who met the Humes on his visits to Derry, praised her work in achieving peace in Northern Ireland and said she advanced her cause with 'grace, courage and good humour'.[27]

The former Irish president Mary McAleese, who had spent time recently with Pat, praised her 'huge wisdom' and described her as the 'perfect partner' for John.[28] There were tributes too from all the local political parties and the DUP first minister Paul Givan spoke for many when he said her passing marked 'a real sense of loss'.[29] Mark Durkan, who had known her for decades, described her as 'truly special but in a very natural way' and Baroness Paisley, the wife of the late Ian Paisley, told BBC Radio Ulster that John Hume 'would have been lost without her'.[30]

They were sentiments that no one could disagree with. For the Hume children, having to prepare for their mother's funeral so soon after their father's was hard. Just as they had done some 13 months earlier, they now had to organise a service in line with Covid guidelines in the same venue.

On 6 September 2022, the family gathered in the familiar surroundings of St Eugene's Cathedral. In many ways it was like John Hume's funeral mass – a mixture of the private and the political. There were representatives from the British and Irish governments in attendance and President Michael D. Higgins travelled north just as he done for John Hume's funeral. Lord Trimble, the former Ulster Unionist leader and fellow Nobel Laureate, came to pay his respects as did many from other parties.

Father Paul Farren, who gave the homily, told mourners: 'If John brought the brilliant mind to peace-making then Pat brought the pure heart.' He said, 'She was an example to us all.'[31] This time Aidan Hume was able to attend and he paid tributes to his mother, describing her as 'unflappable' and said she 'sustained us when the world was full of uncertainties'. He said his father would not mind admitting that she 'was the more glamorous side of the partnership'.[32]

There were also contributions from John Junior and Pat's grandchildren. Like John's funeral it had the personal touch of the Hume family.

THANK YOU JOHN

After the service the cortège made its way to the City Cemetery and, en route, applause echoed through the streets, as Derry's citizens paid their own tribute. Down by the path in the lower part of cemetery, overlooking Brandywell stadium, the family gathered once more.

Husband and wife were reunited again.

24

THE PERSUADER

'He was a priest. He was a pastor. He was a prophet.'
Mary McAleese

John Hume is pictured fixing his gaze. It is something he has done a thousand times before. His finger rests on the top of his glasses and his thumb is squeezed under his left lens. He is squinting slightly and it looks like he is concentrating. It is a characteristic pose and it is captured perfectly in oil paint on a large canvas.

Colin Davidson's portrait of the politician hangs in Portcullis House in Westminster as a reminder of the Derry man's 22 years as an MP. For a few hours back in 2016, the two men spent time together in Hume's home in Greencastle as the artist made a series of sketches of the Nobel Laureate. Using a pen, he drew on a sketchpad, as Hume chatted and ate custard creams.

Hume sat with his back to the window which meant, as Davidson looked at him, he got a fantastic view of Lough Foyle in the background. As he looked at Hume he suddenly saw the image he wanted to recreate: 'I saw him adjusting his glasses. I realised that is the moment I want to paint. It captured something of the spirit of the John Hume I admired and respected.'[1]

After Hume died, the South Belfast MP Claire Hanna suggested that the former SDLP leader should feature in the parliamentary art collection, and with the blessing of the Commons Speaker a portrait was commissioned. Davidson was a natural choice for the work, having previously painted a series of striking portraits of Troubles victims in association with the charity WAVE Trauma Centre, an organisation which helps people bereaved or injured during the Northern Ireland conflict. The County Down artist had an impressive back catalogue that included portraits of the queen, Ian Paisley and Martin McGuinness and he was critically acclaimed with a worldwide reputation. By the late summer, the portrait was complete and the large painting was finally unveiled in November, in front of MPs and members of the Hume family.

Earlier in the year, other parliamentarians organised similar tributes. In March 2022 Taoiseach Micheál Martin unveiled a bust of Hume in Washington in front of family members and US politicians. It was another reminder of how the former SDLP leader was viewed across the Atlantic.

In June, another tribute was put on display, this time by the authorities in Strasbourg. The sculpture of the Nobel Laureate was created by the Irish artist Liz O'Kane and was again unveiled by Taoiseach Micheál Martin and the European Parliament President Roberta Metsola. Back home in Ireland, the story of the Humes continues to fascinate the public and there is an ongoing appetite for insights into their lives and legacy. Pat and John Hume are Derry royalty. They are part of the city's story.

A musical drama entitled *Beyond Belief* was performed at the Playhouse Theatre in March and April 2023. An exhibition of letters and photographs chronicling their story also went on public display, as did John Hume's three major awards – the Gandhi Peace Prize, the Martin Luther King Jr Nonviolent Peace Prize and the Nobel Peace Prize. He remains the only person to be awarded all three. They are tangible reminders of his efforts to end violence. Hume is the most decorated Irish politician in recent times, in terms of his awards and honorary degrees. His name is synonymous with peace and he is spoken of in the same breath as Charles Stewart Parnell and Daniel O'Connell. He had an ability to change minds and he ultimately altered the course of history. Even his opponents would agree that he had extraordinary powers of persuasion.

So how should we assess his contribution to political life and Irish history? What did Hume get right and what were his weaknesses as a politician? Like all political leaders, his actions are not immune from criticism and analysis. Within unionism, there are mixed feelings about him. Lord Trimble, who passed away in July 2022, said that without his fellow Nobel Laureate there would have been no peace process. He insisted that Hume deserved his place in history and worked hard to secure a political accommodation.

However, he found his political rival deeply frustrating at times. Although Trimble also had a reputation for being difficult, he often complained about Hume. On one occasion he spoke to John Major about the SDLP leader. Trimble contrasted Hume's manner with that of his deputy, Seamus Mallon: 'His style was adversarial but at least straight. Dealing with Hume is like grappling with fog.'[2]

Whilst recognising Hume's role in history, Lord Empey has questions over his dialogue with Gerry Adams. He insists the context of talking to Sinn Féin in principle 'is not wrong or was not wrong because we did it ourselves' but he has concerns over the timing. He believes Hume reached out to republicans at a time when their campaign of violence was showing signs of slowing:

> Many of us felt that he probably saved Adams' bacon because we felt that they were really backs-to-the-wall at that stage. The IRA were getting hammered by the security forces. And in many cases, we felt he had rescued Adams and Sinn Féin. Others said he took a huge risk which ultimately led to agreement.[3]

Sir Jeffrey Donaldson shares much of Lord Empey's analysis over the Hume–Adams talks. The DUP leader thinks the discussions gave Sinn Féin a status at the time that they should not have been afforded:

> I believe that the dialogue accorded a degree of legitimacy to Sinn Féin that their ongoing support for violence at that time did not merit. In retrospect, did the dialogue influence the PIRA on the path to calling a ceasefire in 1994? It is difficult to say. Perhaps Gerry Adams used the

dialogue as cover to help persuade some of the republican hardliners that there was value in developing their party's political strategy and engagement with others.[4]

Looking back, Lord Empey says he understands why Hume sat down with Gerry Adams, but says he was 'very angry at the time' over the ongoing dialogue between the SDLP leader and the Sinn Féin president. On a personal level, Empey says Hume was pleasant to deal with but found him 'very hard to pin down'.[5]

A veteran of many inter-party negotiations, there were other SDLP politicians whom he preferred to deal with:

> You could get Seamus Mallon and you could say, 'Right Seamus, what are we doing with this? This is how it works and what way do you want that to work?' You couldn't do that with John ... He wasn't interested in the mechanics to that extent. We found him much more difficult to engage with in the detailed stuff. But on the wider issues you could certainly engage with him. But not on detail.[6]

Seamus Mallon claimed that some unionists were put off by the way Hume spoke to them:

> It was the one reason John Hume had such a problem with unionists: they never knew what to make of him. His 'Humespeak' frightened them; they couldn't translate it into their own black and white language. They felt its cleverness and ambiguity represented a threat to them.[7]

Others say Hume was often a figurehead during inter-party discussions and he let his colleagues do the day-to-day negotiating. UUP official David Kerr, who worked for David Trimble, says during the 1998 talks process Hume was 'sub-contracting and delegating' to others. He says the SDLP leader let his colleagues deal with the minutiae: 'Very often with entrepreneurs and visionary people, they will convene the right people around that table but ultimately they will let others execute the detail. And this is exactly how that happened.'[8]

Kerr says Hume was a big picture politician:

> I don't ever recall him being up to his neck in the detail of the text. The people who we were doing the arguing with were Seamus Mallon, Mark Durkan and Seán Farren all the time, and the Irish government and of course British government delegates. They were the people doing all the arguing; they were the people we were fighting with. Like on the Wednesday evening of that final week when Bertie Ahern came back from burying his mother. It was the Irish government and the SDLP and the British government we were fighting with over North–South. But John was not in there.[9]

David Kerr says Hume's legacy is 'complex'. He accepts Hume's behind-the-scenes work saved countless lives but says his judgement does need to be examined. He feels Hume spent too much time trying to bring Adams into the political process to the detriment of other parties. He thinks his approach bordered on an 'obsession' and ultimately gave Sinn Féin an undue influence. He contends: 'The legitimatisation of them through the process has arguably strengthened them politically and weakened the SDLP, and that itself has changed the dynamic of politics not just in Northern Ireland but also on the island of Ireland.'[10]

He insists had Hume taken a stronger line with republicans during the Good Friday Agreement, particularly by tying prisoner releases to decommissioning, 'from our perspective we would have had a more stable agreement and a better outcome'. Not surprisingly, David Kerr's boss at the time, David Trimble, agrees. He thinks Hume and the SDLP should have been tougher with republicans and been a 'a bit more robust in reminding Sinn Féin about who had actually done the positive work in creating the new institutions'.[11]

Sir Richard Needham, who was the longest-serving minister in the Northern Ireland Office, is an admirer of Hume's skills as a politician. They spent much time together, particularly in the United States seeking inward investment. Such was their friendship that Needham even carried a political endorsement from Hume in his election literature. It must have seemed rather strange to the voters of Wiltshire to read about the local Conservative candidate being supported by an Irish nationalist from Derry. Needham believes Hume was a conviction politician and he backed his efforts to secure peace, but feels that sometimes he could have done more to engage with unionists: 'I just felt he could have gone further than he did in admitting to the problems facing the unionist community. He could have done more outreach. He could have been more sympathetic.'[12]

So did Hume really understand unionists? Seamus Mallon, who lived in the rural area of Markethill in County Armagh, insists that Hume's city background in Derry gave him a view of unionists very different to his own. Mallon says it was a cultural difference based on their upbringing. Mallon's view is noted in a previous chapter, and he insists John Hume's analysis often 'frightened' unionists and they did not know what to make of his approach.[13]

Mallon insisted that he spoke in a more direct way to unionists in contrast to Hume. His party colleague Denis Haughey believes geography played a part in Hume's attitude to unionists: 'His view of unionists was coloured by his experience of growing up in Derry and the way in which the sheer unfairness of gerrymandering left 65 to 70 per cent of a nationalist city in the hands of a cabal of unionists.'[14]

Lord Trimble was also convinced that Hume's background influenced him: 'Part of the problem of John's view of unionism is that it is based on the fact of his coming from the west bank of the Foyle. He probably had very little contact with unionists.'[15] Yet, Hume did grow up in a mixed religious area and had plenty of personal contact and friendships with unionists throughout his life.

However, it is clear there was a deep distrust of Hume within the unionist parties that stretched back decades. According to some who knew him, that opposition may contain an element of jealousy. Mary McAleese picked that up during her time at Queen's University: 'They were sceptical of John mainly on account of some kind of envy of his ability.' McAleese also detected that there was a high level of hostility from unionists towards Hume: 'He was despised by people I knew, people who I had a lot of time for.'[16]

At various stages of his career Hume became a hate figure for some unionists who felt his brand of politics threatened the status quo. Irish diplomat Seán Ó hUiginn, who knew Hume well, thinks some unionists were suspicious of his motives and saw him as 'a more cunning version of the nationalist bogeyman piggybacking on the IRA'.[17] Loyalist paramilitaries wanted to kill him and regarded him as a key member of the 'pan-nationalist front', which was a loaded term often used by loyalist terror groups when they carried out murders of Catholics.

Dan Keenan, who worked for the SDLP and later as a journalist, says Hume's description of unionists is worthy of examination. Keenan argues earlier in this book that some of Hume's public utterances about unionists did little to endear him to those who supported the union. Keenan highlights phrases which could be seen as inflammatory terms. Hume described unionists as 'a petty people', a remark David Trimble responded to in his Oslo speech in 1998. Hume also told the *Observer* newspaper that 'the Protestant boil had to be lanced'.[18]

Both these remarks, according to Keenan, simply added to unionist fears. Trimble did not like Hume often referring to unionists as having a siege mentality – something that obviously stemmed from the SDLP leader's Derry roots. As a unionist he did not take kindly to Hume making comparisons between his political identity and the Afrikaners in South Africa.

In an unpublished interview he gave to Frank D'Arcy in September 2002, Hume repeated the point: 'Their [unionists] mindset was what I called the Afrikaner mindset – they want to protect their identity and their ethos.' Hume went on to say: 'My challenge was to their method, which was to hold power in their own hands which meant widespread discrimination – the Afrikaner mindset. And the challenge to their mindset was that because of their geography and their numbers the problem could not be solved without them. Therefore, they should come to the table and reach an agreement that would protect their identity forever.'[19]

It was a political point that David Trimble challenged and found odd: 'John Hume kept saying unionists were similar to Afrikaners, which was a weird view. The only similarity is that Afrikaners were Dutch Calvinists.'[20] A critique of Hume's approach to unionism was carried out by Professor Arthur Aughey when he contributed to a series of essays about Hume's life back in 2015. Aughey has repeatedly criticised Hume's use of language and, like Trimble, thinks his attempts to link unionists to Afrikaners were 'particularly crass and insulting and simply replayed the traditional Irish practice of defining one's political opponents according to its worst elements'.[21]

For 15 years Jim Nicholson was a UUP MEP and worked alongside Hume in Strasbourg and Brussels. He says he had a great working relationship with Hume and they worked together to bring jobs and investment into Northern Ireland. He had many private conversations with him and says the SDLP leader did have 'a good understanding' of unionism although he says at times his analysis could perhaps be 'over-simplistic'.[22]

Others who had dealings with Hume say his relationship with unionists evolved over the years and went through strained times. Sir Jeffrey Donaldson got to know him when he was in the UUP. He later joined the DUP and became party leader in 2021. Donaldson thinks history will be kind to Hume but he says the young John Hume did not endear himself to unionists: 'I think that he failed to fully understand the unionist psyche and his approach in those times was marked by a willingness to go over the heads of the unionist community and to contrive with governments to find solutions that lacked inclusivity or consensus. Latterly, I think he did develop a better understanding of unionism and drew upon the lessons of the failings of Sunningdale and the Anglo-Irish Agreements.'[23] Donaldson believes Hume's approach to unionists altered over the years and as it moved, so did his own view of Hume: 'As his attitude and approach to unionism changed along that journey, so too did my opinion of him. In the end I believe that he genuinely wanted to see cross-community consensus in this place.'[24]

Lord Bew, who was an adviser to David Trimble, takes a similar view on Hume's attitude to unionism: 'He frequently did not understand unionists but then they frequently did not get it right either.' Bew believes Hume was the most important politician of the Troubles and a man of 'real substance'.[25]

Close friends of Hume and family members insist that he could take on board personal criticism, provided it came from quarters that he respected, otherwise he ignored much of it. Sometimes the attacks really hurt, as they did when newspapers repeatedly questioned him over his talks with Gerry Adams.

Yet, in a sense, Hume would ultimately have the last word on that. Days after Hume's death in 2020, the editor of the *Sunday Independent*, Alan English, spent some time reviewing his newspaper's coverage of the Hume–Adams era. He concluded that the paper was entitled to question the dialogue the two men were involved in but accepted mistakes were made in refusing the SDLP an opportunity to explain their position. English stated that Hume is 'widely regarded now as the man who did more than anyone alive or dead to deliver peace in Ireland. For that, we are all in his debt'.[26]

In party-political terms, Hume was not a traditional leader. His critics suggest he cared little for organisation and party structures and largely left that to others. His leadership style often appeared selfish and he kept much of his work private and secret. He shared information about meetings and initiatives when he felt it necessary but often only with a select gathering of individuals. Denis Bradley says Hume preferred working on his own: 'His weakness was that he wasn't necessarily a team player. He wasn't a natural leader of his party. He was too individualistic. He had his own views.'[27]

As this book has extensively documented, Hume's reluctance to share information brought him into conflict with other party figures and, particularly during the Hume–Adams era, there were severe tensions with colleagues. Many within the SDLP hierarchy felt excluded, particularly

Seamus Mallon and Eddie McGrady. Looking back at the 1990s, Hume supporters argue that the discussions with Gerry Adams were so secretive and important that he could not share contents widely.

Hume argued that it was about saving lives, but it is clear he was quite possessive of his discussions with Adams. Austin Currie, who died in November 2021, believed Hume should have shared more details, particularly with his deputy, Seamus Mallon: 'John didn't provide information and intelligence to him that he should have.' In an interview for this book in January 2021, he also maintained that Hume was quite territorial and protective of his discussions with Adams: 'I suppose he kept things to himself. I don't know why.'[28]

Austin Currie's observations are shared by other party figures who worked with Hume over decades. Joe Hendron knew Hume for over fifty years and says he had 'a brilliant mind' and had an ability to think years ahead. Hendron made his political power base in West Belfast and dramatically took the Westminster seat off Gerry Adams in 1992. He backed Hume's talks with Sinn Féin and saw the discussions as bigger than party politics, but he felt Hume could have told him he was meeting Adams – particularly since some of the talks were happening in his constituency: 'I thought he could have given me more information. I felt a wee bit hurt.'[29]

Sir Richard Needham says it was clear to him that Hume kept many of his colleagues deliberately in the dark: 'He left others out. He really needed to involve his own people. And he didn't always do that.'[30]

Within the SDLP he had his fair share of critics who questioned his leadership style and tactics. Such was the level of internal criticism that he was on the verge of resigning in 1992, as Mark Durkan details in the prologue to this book. Party colleagues repeatedly warned him that the political result of talking to Gerry Adams and bringing Sinn Féin into the talks process would mean that republicans would overtake the SDLP in the polls. Hume maintained that the voting public would not forget his role and that of his party in securing peace. Bríd Rodgers remembers those conversations:

When we said Sinn Féin are going to take advantage of this and John would say, 'No, no, the people know what we stood for. The people know what we have done. The people will never do that.' But, you know, that probably was a bit naïve.[31]

So did Hume sacrifice his party in the wider interest of securing peace? Paul Arthur, who was a close friend of Hume's, says he was right to talk to Adams. Arthur says, if there were party-political consequences for the SDLP, then that was the price for peace: 'My point would be that what he [Hume] did was absolutely right. And if it meant sacrificing the party, so be it.'[32]

Hume had to make a judgement call. He felt that political progress could only be achieved if the violence stopped, and that became his starting point and ultimately the most important point. But did he consider what the political consequences were of his engagement with Sinn Féin? Lord Alderdice, the former Assembly Speaker, says Hume underestimated Sinn Féin's growing popularity and misjudged the mood of the electorate: 'I personally believe it was naïve. And it was naïve on two fronts. First of all, it was naïve to not believe that there would be this profound threat, particularly if Sinn Féin moved away from violence. Because then the question would be very much, you know, who should we vote for?'[33]

In correspondence with this author, Sir John Major praised Hume for his talks with Gerry Adams and suggested that the SDLP leader must have been aware of what the party-political consequences would be: 'I much admire John Hume for his initiative in talking with Gerry Adams, not least because he must have known that, by doing so, it could adversely affect his own political party, the SDLP, which in due course, it did.'[34]

Lord Alderdice says there are historical lessons in assuming that voters will reward those who secure peace and change history: 'There is no bigger example of that than Winston Churchill who, after the war, gets dumped. And there is no point in saying to people "But look what I have done." Because people vote on the basis not of what you have done for them but what they think you will do for them. The electorate is not grateful, in that sense, in any way.'[35]

During the late 1980s and into the 1990s Sinn Féin started to become a polished party machine and tapped into the changing political mood in a way that the SDLP was unable to. In the 1997 election under John Hume, the SDLP outpolled Sinn Féin by some 60,000 votes but by 2010 the figures were the other way around. Sinn Féin was seen as sharper, better organised and seemed more in touch with the nationalist electorate and had a greater appeal to younger voters. In contrast the SDLP seemed outdated and out of touch, and later research commissioned by the party supported that view.

Hume's lack of interest in the party structures frustrated those charged with building the SDLP and making it fit for elections and keeping it financially sound. Dan Keenan, who was an SDLP press officer, says Hume did not see the running of the party as his job:

> I think Hume was in many respects an unparalleled political leader. In many respects, he was a dreadful party leader because he did nothing to deepen the roots of the party. He did nothing to build structures. He did nothing to encourage legions of people coming up behind him because he, the political leader, was so far in front.[36]

Even though he was party leader, Hume saw himself apart from the day-to-day operation of the SDLP. Eamon Hanna, who was SDLP general secretary, accepts that looking after the internal party processes was not Hume's forte: 'He had a view that the non-elected people did the organisation, and the elected people did the politics, and that really didn't work because the elected people have to do the organisation as well.' Hanna says Hume should have given the party organisation more consideration: 'I think he should have seen to it that the party was in better heart.' Both Eamon and his wife Carmel, who joined the party in the 1970s, believe Hume was right to 'put peace before party'.[37]

Sir Richard Needham wonders if Hume's desire to secure peace took precedence over everything else. He questions whether his involvement in the Hume–Adams dialogue meant that party politics seemed irrelevant and inconsequential: 'If you were in the SDLP, and you were a loyal foot soldier of the SDLP, you would ask yourself whether you will be sacrificed on the altar of John's determination to get peace. Almost any price, I mean. I mean, I think I am not sure the extent to which he really had the concerns of and beliefs of his party at heart. Did he really care about the SDLP?'[38]

Needham's observation may be borne out by comments that were attributed to Hume at the early stages of the peace process. When party members were expressing disquiet to Hume about his dialogue with Adams he is reported to have said: 'If it is a choice between the party and peace, do you think I give a fuck about the party?'[39]

Others who observed Hume in action agree that he had little time for or interest in the internal workings of the SDLP and how it should be run. Margaret Ritchie, who would serve as South Down MP and party leader, says Hume cared little for party business: 'John was not into meetings about organisation or the party or internal meetings about fundraising or membership collections. He left that to other people to do that job. John's pursuit was peace, with justice and equality.'[40]

It was apparent that Hume was more interested in the wider political picture. Yet the modern world dictates that leaders have to play many roles. They are public representatives, legislators, media performers and the figureheads for their particular parties. It was obvious Hume was not keen on the requirements of being in charge of a political organisation that needed much careful attention and support, particularly as it began to lose votes and influence.

Ruairí O'Kane, who worked as the SDLP director of communications, accepts Hume neglected his party work: 'I think some of the charges he faced about sacrificing the SDLP at the expense of the greater good, there probably is some merit in that. He was not that fussed on party organisation.'[41]

In deconstructing his leadership, it is impossible to separate Hume the politician from Hume the person. Like all human beings, he was flawed. As this book has detailed, his predictions were sometimes wrong and misplaced and he could be wildly over-optimistic at times. Like all politicians, he made remarks he should not have made, and in the harsh landscape of public life, some of his contemporaries found him difficult and impatient. His critics, including those in his own party, thought he was too secretive and not sufficiently collegiate.

However, there are many examples of where he cared and showed compassion to his colleagues. Patsy McGlone, who served as the SDLP general secretary and later became an MLA, recalls the time when his pregnant wife, Geraldine, was in hospital and was seriously ill suffering from pre-eclampsia. She recovered but the couple had lost the baby and were distraught. When he returned home he noticed on his caller display that someone had been repeatedly ringing the home from an international number. He did not recognise the number and assumed they were cold calls.

The nine missed calls had come from Hume who was away on MEP business. The SDLP leader had spent all day trying to track his colleague down so he could pass on his sympathy. Hume's actions touched Patsy McGlone: 'Here was a man on the international stage, a busy man, and yet he found the time to make the call nine times. He tried again and finally got us. That meant a lot to us.'[42] Margaret Ritchie tells a similar story of Hume speaking to her after the death of her father, and then again when her mother passed away. She was touched by the way Hume spoke to her. He clearly had great personal skills and knew the importance of offering words of comfort.

No one doubts Hume's ability to communicate and even his political opponents accept that it was perhaps one of his greatest qualities. His use of the same phrases came to dominate the public debate and seep into people's consciousness. He had an ability to find the right words and sum up events and occasions perfectly. His political actions and his desire for an end to violence had unintended consequences.

For example, was he naïve in his assessment of what the peace process would mean for Sinn Féin's electoral chances? Professor Arthur

Aughey thinks the peace process ultimately benefitted Sinn Féin politically to the detriment of the SDLP. He accepts that Hume had difficult decisions to make:

> Maybe his room for manoeuvre was limited, but it is also possible that his vision was equally limited. The remarkable legacy has been a republican re-writing of history in which Hume's and the SDLP's contribution to peace is being systematically marginalised.[43]

So was the SDLP hierarchy slow to see the electoral mood change? Ruairí O'Kane says a number of people need to bear some responsibility: 'John went and Seamus went as well at the same time. It was almost like trying to turn the *Titanic*. They could not move quick enough. The Shinners were like a speed boat in comparison.'[44]

In politics, timing is everything. The Hume leadership of the SDLP ended in 2001, but did he stay too long as party leader and should he have stepped aside sooner? Seamus Mallon thought so. He believed those close to Hume should have encouraged him to resign earlier than he did.

As discussed earlier in this book, Mallon felt the person who was the SDLP leader should also be the party's nominee for deputy first minister. He felt that since Hume had ruled himself out as deputy first minister for health reasons, he should have then stepped aside as leader. It would have given Mallon an opportunity to take on a role he had been waiting to do for decades. As Mallon makes clear, his position was that, having one individual as party leader and another as deputy first minister proved difficult and blurred the lines of authority.

Colum Eastwood, who became SDLP leader in 2015, thinks it would have been beneficial to the party if Mallon had assumed the leadership after John Hume: 'It would have been nice if Mallon had got a couple of years out of it. And to steady the ship and all that. But Gertrude [Seamus Mallon's wife] was too sick at that point.'[45]

Alban Maginness, who was party chair and later an MLA, says there was never any suggestion or move within the party to ask Hume to stand down. However, he agrees with Colum Eastwood and feels Hume should have stepped away from the leadership sooner: 'He never lost the affection of the party. There was never a time he lost that. He probably overstayed his time as leader and should have allowed Seamus [Mallon] to take over. I think that would have been better.'[46]

Since the departure of Hume and Mallon, the party has seen a series of leaders at the helm. Mark Durkan, who took over in 2001, was followed by Margaret Ritchie, who only lasted a year and was succeeded by Alasdair McDonnell in 2011. After a series of poor results and unease in the party, he was challenged in a leadership election by Colum Eastwood, who beat him in a vote amongst members in 2015.

Much has rested on the shoulders of Eastwood, a former councillor in Derry and the youngest ever leader of the SDLP. Youthful, articulate and energetic, there were high hopes amongst the party faithful that he could turn their fortunes around. However, like his predecessors, he has learned that changing the leader does not necessarily guarantee success and he has had his fair share of setbacks. In 2017 the party lost its three seats in the general election. It was a bombshell moment and the first time since Hume's election in 1983 that the SDLP was not represented at Westminster. Mark Durkan was particularly upset at having lost Hume's seat in Foyle which his party had held for over 30 years.

The loss of all three MPs posed fundamental questions about the SDLP's existence. What did the party represent? What was it for? Should it carry on or think of a merger or disbandment? Colum Eastwood began a political arrangement with Fianna Fáil, although a full-blown merger was ruled out and ultimately the discussions did not lead to anything of substance.

In the 2019 Westminster poll, there was some relief when the party regained two parliamentary seats. In Hume's old constituency of Foyle, Eastwood was elected with a large majority and retook the seat from Sinn Féin, while in South Belfast, Claire Hanna, the former MLA, triumphed.

However, the electoral success was short-lived, Colum Eastwood's woes continued in the 2022 assembly election when Sinn Féin became the largest party and the SDLP took a battering when they lost four seats and ended up with a vote share of just 9 per cent. It was far cry from the elections to Stormont after the Good Friday Agreement in 1998 when, under Hume, the party polled the most votes and secured 22 per cent of the vote – a defining moment for a party that he helped to set up.

Hume's legacy is more than just winning elections. His record shows that he contributed intellectually and politically to Anglo-Irish relations for over 40 years. His approach at a European level and in the United States widened the debate about Northern Ireland and put the issue on a much bigger stage.

Hume sensed, more than any other politician of his generation, that the answer to Northern Ireland's problems lay beyond the shores of his home place. He knew that any solution had to be arrived at with international help and assistance. In that area of political lobbying, he was light years ahead of his political rivals. His ideas and clarity created a political template at Stormont, which is not perfect by any means, but it has endured. Bertie Ahern says Hume had an ability to see a problem and then diagnose the solution: 'I think he gave the vision for the next generation, and it is not everyone in politics that can do that.'[47]

That ability to challenge conventional wisdom was one of Hume's strengths. In an interview for this book, John Bruton argued that Hume's philosophy of trying to unite people rather than obsessing over land and borders put him in a different place to other leaders: 'He was able to draw from the richness of the European Union and put that into Irish politics. I think he is much more an original thinker in Irish nationalism than John Redmond or De Valera or any of the others who thought in terms of territory.'[48]

That analysis is shared by Senator George Mitchell, who believes Hume's contribution to political life was immense: 'He reframed the conflict to be one of addressing relationships rather than territory. It was the people who were divided, not the territory.'[49]

It was that approach which defined Hume's assessment of Irish nationalism. He wanted a united Ireland but, in his words, it had to be an agreed Ireland. He challenged those who simply believed that the existence of partition was the sole problem and argued that agreement amongst all the people of the entire island was key. He constantly rejected the traditional analysis of the IRA that an armed struggle would lead to a British withdrawal in Northern Ireland and somehow unionists and loyalists would be won over. He argued that the British identity in Northern Ireland could not be dismissed and any new settlement had to be consensual. That principle looms large over Hume's career and can be traced back to his early writings in the *Irish Times* in 1964. Hume envisaged a new Ireland that was consensual and pluralist. That consent was key to his insistence that the Good Friday Agreement was put to referenda on both parts of the island.

Using his European experience, where people of different backgrounds work together, Hume consistently argued that any new political settlement in Ireland had to similarly be all-encompassing and include different identities. Hume may not have lived to see a united Ireland, but he changed much of traditional nationalist thinking across the island. He was one of the first politicians from a nationalist party to sit in a power-sharing administration at Stormont. He was regarded as the leading nationalist voice in Northern Ireland for decades and he had the ear of Irish, British and American administrations. When it came to talking about Northern Ireland, many leaders waited for Hume's analysis before they made their public comments.

Hume changed the narrative and political vocabulary of Northern Ireland. Phrases that were once considered to be part of 'Humespeak' were quickly adopted by all parties, and many of his ideas became common political parlance. The peace process came to be built on Hume's words. He understood the critical importance of relations between London, Dublin and Belfast and it was his analysis that led to the three-stranded talks process. He was one of the first politicians to call for a new police service – an argument he made in the early 1970s.

On the big calls of making political agreements, mapping an agreed way forward and securing paramilitary ceasefires, his efforts excelled. There were casualties in all of that, some personal and some political. Peace was the biggest prize of all, but it came with a price – most notably his health. Hume's staying power, according to Mark Durkan, was one of his greatest attributes: 'Stickability was probably John's favourite word about himself. But it applies in spades to Pat. You know, John's stickability could sometimes be grumpy – Pat's stickability was always graceful.'[50]

Outside his family, Mark Durkan probably witnessed Hume's mood swings more than anyone else. He was often consumed with anxiety and at times could be blunt and at other times unresponsive. Michael Lillis, who worked for the Irish Department of Foreign Affairs and helped to negotiate the Anglo-Irish Agreement, spent many hours with Hume and found him at times to be hard work: 'An extremely nice generous man. And you know he had many reasons to be arrogant. And I think in his dealings in politics he was sometimes obliged to be a bit difficult. Not impossible but a bit difficult.'[51]

Other civil servants found Hume reluctant to talk at times, and they recall conversation could be hard work. Seán Donlon, who, like Michael Lillis, worked for the Irish Department of Foreign Affairs, was frequently in his company: 'He wasn't an easy person to talk to. I am not the only one, for example, who drove John from Dublin to Derry and couldn't get a word out of him. He would have long silences. Sometimes I would go to Derry for the weekend and he would be very ... reticent is the wrong word ... moody could be a better description. Sometimes he wasn't in the mood to talk.'[52]

In chronicling Hume's life, you quickly get a picture of how much personal courage he showed in the face of violence and intimidation. You can trace that from his early days on Derry's streets, to marching on Magilligan beach, to the times when his house was routinely attacked by republicans and the threats from loyalist paramilitaries. His tenacity and bravery, particularly during the Hume–Adams talks, proved to be one of his enduring characteristics. Lord Eames, who first encountered John Hume in Derry in the 1970s, thinks that determination to bring peace will be his lasting legacy: 'He managed to achieve things that would have shattered the efforts of another human being.'[53]

From a young age, he valued the power of money and how it could transform people's lives. His work with the credit union movement was ground-breaking and it is telling that he regarded that endeavour as his finest achievement in life. He became the youngest-ever president of the organisation and established himself very quickly as its most passionate and articulate advocate. As an island-wide body, it is still operational today, which is a physical reminder of Hume's efforts in the 1960s.

As the MP for Foyle, he brought jobs to areas that were ravaged by unemployment, and he constantly encouraged investors to consider Northern Ireland as a location for business. His involvement in operations like the Derry–Boston ventures, and his work in lobbying companies like Seagate and Fruit of the Loom to operate in Northern Ireland, was evidence of his commitment to creating work. He applied the same tenacity in Europe when he and his fellow MEPs from Northern Ireland successfully campaigned for grant aid and peace money to support communities that had been blighted by the Troubles.

Hume understood deprivation and the misery of being without work. He had witnessed economic hardship in his home city for decades, including his own father's joblessness, and he observed his mother's struggles to keep the family afloat. Although he knew how money could transform people's circumstances he was not motivated by the financial trappings of office and he was not materialistic. He donated his Nobel Peace Prize winnings and all other prize money to charitable organisations. Trust funds and scholarships have also been given to students across the UK and Ireland and set up under the name of Pat and John Hume. His generosity was well-known. He would routinely empty his pockets of coins and notes when he encountered homeless people on the streets. When he was driving he constantly offered lifts to hitchhikers and there are numerous stories of Hume going out of his way to get people to their final destinations.

Friends, colleagues and complete strangers were often invited to join him at his holiday home in Donegal. He loved to host guests but, as ever, the practicalities of sourcing beds and food were often left to Pat. On trips abroad, he would rarely waste an opportunity to promote Derry as a place for companies to invest in. He developed an impressive network of business contacts that would rival many industrialists. He was very persuasive. An invitation from Hume was hard to turn down and that applied equally to leaders in the fields of business, sport and music.

Dementia robbed him of precious memories at the end of his life. He deserved a longer time to enjoy his legacy, and in his final years, he could not recall the key political moments he had been involved in. His retirement was not the one he had planned, but he retained his inquisitive nature and remained sociable in his final days. He was surrounded by a great network of friends, family and carers and he was much loved. His grown-up children marked the first anniversary of his death with a warm tribute and recalled their father as a paradox, someone who was an 'unapologetic, grounded, lofty, demanding, generous, compassionate, gregarious, deeply serious personality'.[54]

When assessing the life and achievements of John Hume, historians and journalists will naturally focus on his political achievements, and he will be best remembered as a peacemaker. Dick Spring says that is Hume's ultimate achievement. However, he offers this rather chilling assessment: 'If John Hume had not been in Northern Ireland politics, we probably would still be in the middle of conflict.'[55]

Mary McAleese, who first encountered John Hume in a cold Belfast church hall in the 1960s, believes the Nobel Laureate should be given three titles: 'He was a priest. He was a pastor. He was a prophet.'[56]

John Hume deserves one more accolade. He was also a persuader.

ACKNOWLEDGEMENTS

Writing this book has at times been a very solitary experience but without the help of many individuals my efforts would never have made it into print. Over the past three years, I been assisted by dozens of people including interviewees, fellow journalists, staff at Gill Books and, of course, my family and friends. Right at the beginning of this project the Hume family showed me enormous kindness. Without their contribution this publication would lack real insight and context.

I am particularly grateful to Therese, Áine, Aidan, John and Mo Hume for sharing personal moments with a wider audience and for their patience in answering endless questions. For the first time they have all jointly told the story of their parents and have spoken with love and honesty.

I would also like to thank those who were able to talk about John Hume's days at St Columb's and his time at Maynooth. His former colleagues in the SDLP were most gracious with their time, as were current and retired politicians from other parties.

I was also assisted greatly by the recollections of former British and Irish diplomats, fellow reporters and family friends. I am particularly grateful to Amy McCloskey who has spoken for the first time about the care and love shown to John Hume during his final months.

I first interviewed John Hume in November 1990, when I was a journalist with BBC Radio Leeds and he came to Yorkshire to deliver a lecture about Ireland and Europe. As a reporter with BBC Northern Ireland our paths crossed many times. In Belfast, London and Dublin I covered the endless twists of the peace process and John Hume was naturally at the heart of the story.

When he died in 2020, I was struck by the life he had lived and by the tributes that were paid to him. He had shaped the history of the last 50 years and transformed the political landscape. Yet, how much did we really know about the man away from the public gaze? What, I wondered, would his legacy be?

This book is based on 100 interviews, including 25 unpublished conversations with John, Pat and Patsy Hume conducted by Frank D'Arcy back in 2002 and 2003. I am particularly grateful to Seán Hayes at Gill Books for making those transcripts available.

From the word go Seán has been an enthusiastic advocate of this book and I am indebted to him for his support and to his colleagues Margaret Farrelly, Anne Sophie Blytmann, Fiona Murphy, Cormac Kinsella and Laura King. For Gill Books, this is about finishing a project first considered twenty years ago. I am also grateful to David Headley, who was involved in the early stages of this book.

My close friend Mark Carruthers has watched this biography grow from start to finish and, as with my previous books, he has offered sound advice, wise counsel and grammatical observations!

Dan Keenan, Mark Devenport, Martin Cowley, Freya McClements, Alex Kane, Sam McBride and Hugh Jordan all read versions of this book and made helpful suggestions to improve the text.

In Derry, Enda McClafferty and Keiron Tourish were great hosts and my former comrades in BBC Northern Ireland have been most supportive, amongst them Gareth Gordon, Jayne McCormack and Raymona Crozier. I have also benefitted from the photographic talents of Charles McQuillan and John Morrissey.

My family have had to live with my preoccupation with John Hume for a number of years now and I am thankful for the support of my father, my brothers, Matthew and Geoff, and my sister Kate.

Writing involves lots of time and many sacrifices. It is felt most at home. So thank you Katrin, Grace, Jack and Gabriel.

My name is on the front cover, but this book carries your fingerprints.

Stephen Walker, County Down, 1 July 2023.

SOURCES

1. *Interviews conducted by Stephen Walker for this book*

Lord Alderdice, 3 October 2020
Lord Empey, 4 October 2020
Colum Eastwood, 6 October 2020
Bertie Ahern, 13 October 2020
Lord Eames, 16 October 2020
Lord Kinnock, 17 October 2020
Richard Needham, 18 October 2020
Mary McAleese, 7 December 2020
Michael Lillis, 15 December 2020
Tim Attwood, 18 December 2020
Nancy Soderberg, 31 December 2020
Conall McDevitt, 5 January 2021
Eamonn McCann, 5 January 2021
Bríd Rodgers, 5 January 2021
Baroness Paisley, 19 January 2021
Ruairí O'Kane, 21 January 2021
Dáithí Ó Ceallaigh, 22 January 2021
Seán Donlon (1), 22 January 2021
Seán Ó hUiginn, 22 January 2021
Ronan McCay, 23 January 2021
Baroness Ritchie, 23 January 2021
Denis Bradley, 23 January 2021
Austin Currie, 23 January 2021
David Kerr, 26 January 2021
John Bruton, 30 January 2021
Mark Durkan (1), 19 March 2021
Gerry Cosgrove, 23 March 2021
Mark Durkan (2), 23 March 2021
Phil Coulter, 23 March 2021
John Hume Junior, 7 May 2021
Sir Tony Blair, 7 May 2021

Mo Hume, 15 May 2021
Gerry Adams, 7 September 2021
Áine Abbott, 22 October 2021
Miriam O'Callaghan, 29 March 2022
Aidan Hume, 2 April 2022
Carmel Hanna, 1 May 2022
Eamon Hanna, 1 May 2022
Seán Farren, 2 May 2022
Dan Keenan, 2 May 2022
Denis Haughey, 2 May 2022
Dick Spring, 4 May 2022
Paul Arthur, 14 May 2022
Mons. Brendan Devlin, 1 June 2022
Seán Donlon (2), 30 July 2022
Jim McGonagle, 30 July 2022
Seán McCool, 11 August 2022
Tony Johnston, 11 August 2022
Martin Cowley, 16 August 2022
Rosemary Logue, 17 August 2022
Jimmy Logue, 17 August 2022
Don McCrea, 22 August 2022
Jim Hendron, 25 August 2022
Robert Ramsay, 5 September 2022
Monica McWilliams, 8 October 2022
Aidan McKinney, 8 October 2022
Amy McCloskey, 1 November 2022
Therese Hume, 1 February 2023
Colin Davidson, 7 February 2023
Joe Hendron, 22 February 2023
Alasdair McDonnell, 25 February 2023
Jim Nicholson, 31 March 2023
Barry White (former UUP aide), 1 April 2023
Patsy McGlone, 21 April 2023
Ian Paisley Junior, 25 April 2023

Lady Trimble, 25 April 2023
Lord Bew, 1 May 2023
Hugh Logue, 2 May 2023
Alban Maginness, 8 June 2023

2. *Interviews conducted by Frank D'Arcy*

John Hume, 27 April 2002
John Hume, 3 May 2002
John Hume, 11 May 2002
John Hume, 17 May 2002
John Hume, 30 September 2002
John Hume, 1 October 2002
John Hume, 3 October 2002
John Hume, 5 October 2002
John Hume, 14 October 2002
John Hume, 30 October 2002
John Hume, 9 November 2002
John Hume, 10 November 2002
John Hume, 11 January 2003
John Hume, 13 February 2003
John Hume, 24 February 2003
John Hume, 11 March 2003
John Hume, 22 March 2003
Patsy Hume, 24 March 2003
Pat Hume, 26 March 2003
John Hume, 28 March 2003
John Hume, 15 April 2003
John Hume, 16 April 2003
John Hume, 23 April 2003
John Hume, 29 May 2003

3. *Author's correspondence*
Bríd Rodgers
Sir Jeffrey Donaldson

Mike Nesbitt
Sir John Major
Senator George Mitchell
Denis Murray
Danny Morrison
John Cushnahan

4. *Author's personal notes*

5. *Official records*
National Archives, London
Public Record Office of Northern Ireland
Hansard, House of Commons
Hansard, Northern Ireland Assembly
New Ireland Forum Public Sessions
Dáil Proceedings

6. *Publications*
The Christian Science Monitor
Derry Journal
Irish Times
Irish Examiner
Belfast Telegraph
Irish News
NewsLetter
Irish Independent
The Journal.ie
Sunday Independent
The Guardian
The Times
The Sunday Times
The Observer
The Independent
Sunday Life

Sunday World
Daily Telegraph
Sunday Telegraph
Washington Post
New York Times

7. *Films, documentaries, television and radio*
BBC Northern Ireland
BBC Radio Ulster
BBC Radio Foyle
RTÉ
UTV
ITV

A City Solitary. BBC and RTÉ film, 1963. Terry McDonald and John Hume.

Hume. BBC Northern Ireland documentary, produced by Below The Radar, 2011. Broadcast 19 September 2011.

In the Name of Peace: John Hume in America. RTÉ documentary produced by Maurice Fitzpatrick, 2017. Broadcast on 25 July 2018.

BIBLIOGRAPHY

Adams, Gerry, *A Farther Shore* (Random House, 2003)

Adams, Gerry, *Before the Dawn* (Mandarin, 1997)

Adams, Gerry, *Hope and History: Making Peace in Ireland* (Brandon, 2003)

Aitken, Jonathan, *Margaret Thatcher: Power and Personality* (Bloomsbury, 2013)

Anderson, Don, *14 May Days* (Gill and Macmillan, 1994)

Arthur, Paul, *The People's Democracy 1968–73* (The Blackstaff Press, 1974)

Bardon, Jonathan, *A History of Ulster* (The Blackstaff Press, 1992)

Beresford, David, *Ten Men Dead* (Grafton Books, 1987)

Bew, Paul and Gordon Gillespie, *Northern Ireland: A Chronology of the Troubles 1968–1993* (Gill and Macmillan, 1993)

Blair, Tony, *A Journey* (Hutchinson, 2010)

Bloomfield, Ken, *Stormont in Crisis: A Memoir* (The Blackstaff Press, 1994)

Campbell, Alastair, *The Blair Years* (Hutchinson, 2007)

Carruthers, Mark, *Alternative Ulsters* (Liberties Press, 2013)

Currie, Austin, *All Hell Will Break Loose* (The O'Brien Press, 2004)

Devenport, Mark, *Flash Frames* (The Blackstaff Press, 2000)

Devlin, Paddy, *Straight Left: An Autobiography* (The Blackstaff Press, 1993)

Donoghue, David, *One Good Day* (Gill Books, 2022)

Drower, George, *John Hume, Man of Peace* (Victor Gollancz, 1995)

Duffy, Joe and Freya McClements, *Children of the Troubles* (Hachette Books Ireland, 2019)

Eames, Robin, *Unfinished Peace* (Columba Press, 2017)

Elliott, Sydney and W. D. Flackes, *Northern Ireland: A Political Directory, 1968–1999* (Blackstaff Press, 1999)

BIBLIOGRAPHY

Farren, Seán, *John Hume: In His Own Words* (Four Courts Press, 2018)

Farren, Seán and Denis Haughey, *John Hume, Irish Peacemaker* (Four Courts Press, 2015)

Faulkner, Brian, *Memoirs of a Statesman* (Weidenfeld and Nicolson, 1978)

Fitzpatrick, Maurice, *John Hume in America: From Derry to DC* (Irish Academic Press, 2017)

Gillespie, Gordon, *Years of Darkness* (Gill and Macmillan, 2008)

Hayes, Maurice, *Minority Verdict* (The Blackstaff Press, 1995)

Hennessey, Thomas, *Hunger Strike* (Irish Academic Press, 2014)

Hume, John, *A New Ireland: Peace, Politics and Reconciliation* (Roberts Rinehart Publishers, 1996)

Hume, John, *Derry Beyond the Walls* (Ulster Historical Foundation, 2002)

Keenan, Dan, *John Hume: Origins of a Derry Icon 1960–74*, PhD Thesis (University of St Andrews, 2019)

Kelters, Seamus, *Belfast Aurora* (Merrion Press, 2021)

Lacey, Brian, *Discover Derry* (Guildhall Press, 2016)

Lynn, Brendan, *Holding the Ground: The Nationalist Party in Northern Ireland 1945–72* (Routledge, 1997)

Mallie, Eamonn and David McKittrick, *The Fight for Peace* (Heinemann, 1996)

Mallon, Seamus with Andy Pollak, *A Shared Home Place* (The Lilliput Press, 2019)

McCann, Eamonn with Maureen Shiels and Bridie Hannigan, *Bloody Sunday in Derry: What Really Happened* (Brandon, 1992)

McDonald, Henry, *Trimble* (Bloomsbury, 2000)

McKittrick, David, Seamus Kelters, Brian Feeney and Chris Thornton, *Lost Lives* (Mainstream Publishing, 1999)

McKittrick, David, *Despatches from Belfast* (The Blackstaff Press, 1989)

McLoughlin, Peter John, *John Hume and the Revision of Irish Nationalism* (Manchester University Press, 2010)

Mowlam, Mo, *Momentum* (Hodder and Stoughton, 2002)
Moloney, Ed, *Voices from the Grave* (Faber and Faber, 2010)
Murphy, Gary, *Haughey* (Gill, 2021)
Murray Gerard, *John Hume and the SDLP* (Irish Academic Press, 1998)
Needham, Richard, *Battling for Peace* (The Blackstaff Press, 1998)
Needham, Richard, *One Man, Two Worlds* (The Blackstaff Press, 2021)
O'Doherty, Malachi, *The Trouble with Guns* (The Blackstaff Press, 1998)
Purdy, Martina, *Room 21* (Brehon Press, 2005)
Routledge, Paul, *John Hume, A Biography* (HarperCollins, 1997)
Ryder, Chris, *The RUC 1922–1997* (Mandarin, 1997)
Ryder, Chris, *Fighting Fitt* (Brehon Press, 2006)
Sharrock, David and Mark Devenport, *Man of War, Man of Peace? The Unauthorised Biography of Gerry Adams* (Macmillan, 1997)
White, Barry, *John Hume: Statesman of the Troubles* (The Blackstaff Press, 1984)

ENDNOTES

Prologue

1 Durkan, Mark. Interview conducted by Stephen Walker. 19 March 2021.

1: Wee Johnny Hume

1 Hume, John. Interview conducted by Frank D'Arcy. 11 January 2003.
2 Hume, Aidan. Interview conducted by Stephen Walker. 2 April 2022.
3 Hume, John. Interview conducted by Frank D'Arcy. 11 January 2003.
4 Hume, John. Interview conducted by Frank D'Arcy. 11 January 2003.
5 Hume, John. Interview conducted by Frank D'Arcy. 11 January 2003.
6 Hume, John. *A New Ireland: Politics, Peace, and Reconciliation*, Roberts Rinehart Publishers, 1996.
7 Farren, Seán. *John Hume: In His Own Words*, Four Courts Press, 2018.
8 Hume, John. Interview conducted by Frank D'Arcy. 11 January 2003.
9 Hume, John. Interview conducted by Frank D'Arcy. 11 January 2003.
10 Hume, John. Interview conducted by Frank D'Arcy. 11 January 2003.
11 Hume, John. *A New Ireland: Politics, Peace, and Reconciliation*, Roberts Rinehart Publishers, 1996.
12 Hume, John. Interview conducted by Frank D'Arcy. 11 January 2003.
13 *Irish Times*, 17 October 1998
14 Hume, John. Interview conducted by Frank D'Arcy. 11 January 2003.
15 Farren, Seán. *John Hume: In His Own Words*, Four Courts Press, 2018.
16 Farren, Seán. *John Hume: In His Own Words*, Four Courts Press, 2018.
17 Hume, John. Interview conducted by Frank D'Arcy. 11 January 2003.
18 Hume, John. Interview conducted by Frank D'Arcy. 11 January 2003.
19 Hume, John. Interview conducted by Frank D'Arcy. 11 January 2003.
20 Hume, John. Interview conducted by Frank D'Arcy. 11 January 2003.
21 Hume, John. Interview conducted by Frank D'Arcy. 11 January 2003.
22 Hume, John. Interview conducted by Frank D'Arcy. 11 January 2003.
23 McCool, Sean. Interview conducted by Stephen Walker. 11 August 2022.

24 McGonagle, Jim. Interview conducted by Stephen Walker. 30 July 2022.
25 Hume, John. Interview conducted by Frank D'Arcy. 11 January 2003.
26 *Irish Times*, 17 October 1998.
27 Hume, John. Interview conducted by Frank D'Arcy. 11 January 2003.
28 Hume, John. Interview conducted by Frank D'Arcy. 11 January 2003.
29 Coulter, Phil. Interview conducted by Stephen Walker. 23 March 2021.
30 Coulter, Phil. Interview conducted by Stephen Walker. 23 March 2021.
31 Mitchell, Senator George. Correspondence with Stephen Walker. 30 September 2021.

2: *Maynooth man*

1 Hume, John. Interview conducted by Frank D'Arcy. 11 January 2003.
2 Devlin, Brendan. Interview conducted by Stephen Walker. 1 June 2022.
3 Donlon, Seán. Interview conducted by Stephen Walker. 22 January 2021.
4 Donlon, Seán. Interview conducted by Stephen Walker. 22 January 2021.
5 Hume, John. Interview conducted by Stephen Walker. 11 January 2003.
6 Devlin, Brendan. Interview conducted by Stephen Walker. 1 June 2022.
7 Donlon, Seán. Interview conducted by Stephen Walker. 22 January 2021.
8 Donlon, Seán. Interview conducted by Stephen Walker. 22 January 2021.
9 Devlin, Brendan. Interview conducted by Stephen Walker. 1 June 2022.
10 Donlon, Seán. Interview conducted by Stephen Walker. 22 January 2021.
11 Hume, John. Interview conducted by Frank D'Arcy. 11 January 2003.
12 Keenan, Dan. Interview conducted by Stephen Walker. 2 May 2022.
13 Devlin, Brendan. Interview conducted by Stephen Walker. 1 June 2022.
14 Devlin, Brendan. Interview conducted by Stephen Walker. 1 June 2022.
15 Hume, John. Interview conducted by Frank D'Arcy. 11 January 2003.
16 Hume, John. Interview conducted by Frank D'Arcy. 11 January 2003.
17 McCool, Seán. Interview conducted by Stephen Walker. 11 August 2022.
18 Routledge, Paul. *John Hume, A Biography*, HarperCollins, 1997.
19 White, Barry. *John Hume: Statesman of the Troubles*, The Blackstaff Press, 1984.

ENDNOTES

20 Hume, Aidan. Interview conducted by Stephen Walker. 2 April 2022.

21 McGonagle, Jim. Interview conducted by Stephen Walker. 30 July 2022.

22 McCool, Seán. Interview conducted by Stephen Walker. 11 August 2022.

23 Johnston, Tony. Interview conducted by Stephen Walker. 11 August 2022.

24 Donlon, Seán. Interview conducted by Stephen Walker. 22 January 2021.

3: *Pat and parcel*

1 McCrea, Don. Interview conducted by Stephen Walker. 22 August 2022.

2 McCrea, Don. Interview conducted by Stephen Walker. 22 August 2022.

3 Devlin, Brendan. Interview conducted by Stephen Walker. 1 June 2022.

4 Farren, Seán and Denis Haughey. *John Hume, Irish Peacemaker*, Four Courts Press, 2015.

5 Logue, Rosemary. Interview conducted by Stephen Walker. 17 August 2022.

6 Abbott, Áine. Interview conducted by Stephen Walker. 22 October 2021.

7 Hume, Aidan. Interview conducted by Stephen Walker. 2 April 2022.

8 Coulter, Phil. Interview conducted by Stephen Walker. 23 March 2021.

9 Devlin, Brendan. Interview conducted by Stephen Walker. 1 June 2022.

10 TheJournal.ie. 5 August 2020.

11 McAleese, Mary. Interview conducted by Stephen Walker. 7 December 2020.

12 Bradley, Denis. Interview conducted by Stephen Walker. 23 January 2021.

13 Bradley, Denis. Interview conducted by Stephen Walker. 23 January 2021.

14 White, Barry. *John Hume: Statesman of the Troubles*, Blackstaff Press, 1984.

15 Arthur, Paul. Interview conducted by Stephen Walker. 14 May 2022.

16 Cowley, Martin. Interview conducted by Stephen Walker. 16 August 2022.

17 *Irish Times*, 8 August 2020.

18 *Irish Times*, 8 August 2020.

19 *Irish Times*, 18 and 19 May 1964.

20 *Irish Times*, 18 and 19 May 1964.

21 *Irish Times*, 18 and 19 May 1964.

22 *Irish Times*, 18 and 19 May 1964.

23 *Irish Times*, 18 and 19 May 1964.

24 Hume, John. Interview conducted by Frank D'Arcy. 3 May 2002.

4: *The faceless men*

1 McCann, Eamonn. Interview conducted by Stephen Walker. 5 January 2021.

2 McCann, Eamonn. Interview conducted by Stephen Walker. 5 January 2021.

3 Currie, Austin. Interview conducted by Stephen Walker. 23 January 2021.

4 White, Barry. *John Hume: Statesman of the Troubles*, Blackstaff Press, 1984.

5 Routledge, Paul. *John Hume, A Biography*, HarperCollins, 1997.

6 Arthur, Paul. Interview conducted by Stephen Walker. 14 May 2022.

7 Hume, John. Fulham speech, June 1965.

8 Hume, John. Fulham speech, June 1965.

9 Hume, John. Fulham speech, June 1965.

10 *Derry Journal*, May 1965.

11 Keenan, Dan. *John Hume: Origins of a Derry Icon 1960 - 74*. PhD Thesis, University of St Andrews, 2019.

12 Hume, John. Fulham speech, June 1965.

13 Minutes of BBC appointment board, 13 July 1965.

14 Hume, Pat. Interview conducted by Frank D'Arcy. 26 March 2003.

15 Hume, Pat. Interview conducted by Frank D'Arcy. 26 March 2003.

16 Hume, John. Interview conducted by Frank D'Arcy. 3 May 2002.

17 Hume, John. Interview conducted by Frank D'Arcy. 3 May 2002.

18 Hume, Pat. Interview conducted by Frank D'Arcy. 26 March 2003.

19 Hume, Aidan. Interview conducted by Stephen Walker. 2 April 2022.

20 Hume, John. Interview conducted by Frank D'Arcy. 3 May 2002.

21 Coulter, Phil. Interview conducted by Stephen Walker. 23 March 2021.

22 Coulter, Phil. Interview conducted by Stephen Walker. 23 March 2021.

5: Ulster at the crossroads

1. McCann, Eamonn. Interview conducted by Stephen Walker. 5 January 2021.
2. McCann, Eamonn. Interview conducted by Stephen Walker. 5 January 2021.
3. Cowley, Martin. Interview conducted by Stephen Walker. 16 August 2022.
4. RTÉ, 5 October 1968.
5. RTÉ, Report by Kevin O'Kelly, 1972.
6. RTÉ, 5 October 1968.
7. RTÉ, 5 October 1968.
8. Cowley, Martin. Interview conducted by Stephen Walker. 16 August 2022.
9. Cowley, Martin. Interview conducted by Stephen Walker. 16 August 2022.
10. Cowley, Martin. Interview conducted by Stephen Walker. 16 August 2022.
11. Hume, John. Interview conducted by Frank D'Arcy. 3 May 2002.
12. Routledge, Paul. *John Hume, A Biography*, HarperCollins, 1997.
13. Currie, Austin. Interview conducted by Stephen Walker. 23 January 2021.
14. Logue, Rosemary. Interview conducted by Stephen Walker. 17 August 2022.
15. McCann, Eamonn. Interview conducted by Stephen Walker. 5 January 2021.
16. Hume, John. Interview conducted by Frank D'Arcy. 3 May 2002.
17. McCann, Eamonn. Interview conducted by Stephen Walker. 5 January 2021.
18. Hume, John. Interview conducted by Frank D'Arcy. 3 May 2002.
19. BBC television address, 9 December, 1968.
20. Hume, John. Interview conducted by Frank D'Arcy. 11 May 2002.
21. ITV, *World in Action*, 20 January, 1969.
22. Routledge, Paul. *John Hume, A Biography*, HarperCollins, 1997.
23. Haughey, Denis. Interview conducted by Stephen Walker. 2 May 2022.
24. Hume, John. Interview conducted by Frank D'Arcy. 11 May 2002.
25. Hanna, Eamon. Interview conducted by Stephen Walker. 1 May 2022.

26 Hanna, Eamon. Interview conducted by Stephen Walker. 1 May 2022.
27 Durkan, Mark. Interview conducted by Stephen Walker. 19 March 2021.
28 Coulter, Phil. Interview conducted by Stephen Walker. 23 March 2021.
29 Hume, John. Interview conducted by Frank D'Arcy. 11 May 2002.
30 McCann, Eamonn. Interview conducted by Stephen Walker. 5 January 2021.
31 Lynn, Brendan. *Holding the Ground: The Nationalist Party in Northern Ireland. 1945–72* Routledge, 1997.
32 Bradley, Denis. Interview conducted by Stephen Walker. 23 January 2021.
33 McCann, Eamonn. Interview conducted by Stephen Walker. 5 January 2021.

6: We shall overcome

1 Stormont proceedings, 5 March 1969.
2 Hume, John. Interview conducted by Frank D'Arcy. 11 May 2002.
3 Hume, John. Interview conducted by Frank D'Arcy. 11 May 2002.
4 Arthur, Paul. Interview conducted by Stephen Walker. 14 May 2022.
5 Cameron Commission report, 1969.
6 Hume, John. Interview conducted by Frank D'Arcy. 11 May 2002.
7 BBC News website, On This Day, Archive.
8 *Irish Times*, 3 January 2000.
9 Hume, John. Interview conducted by Frank D'Arcy. 11 May 2002.
10 RTÉ, 13 August 1969.
11 RTÉ, 13 August 1969.
12 Stormont proceedings, 14 August 1969.
13 Stormont proceedings, 14 August 1969.
14 RTÉ, 28 August 1969.
15 RTÉ, 28 August 1969.
16 RTÉ, 28 August 1969.
17 RTÉ, 28 August 1969.

7: *Party time*

1. Rodgers, Bríd. Interview conducted by Stephen Walker. 5 January 2021.
2. Hume, Mo. Interview conducted by Stephen Walker. 15 May 2021.
3. Donlon, Seán. Interview conducted by Stephen Walker. 22 January 2021.
4. Hume, John Junior. Interview conducted by Stephen Walker. 7 May 2021.
5. Hume, Therese. Interview conducted by Stephen Walker. 1 February 2023.
6. Rodgers, Bríd. Interview conducted by Stephen Walker. 5 January 2021.
7. Currie, Austin. Interview conducted by Stephen Walker. 23 January 2021.
8. McCann, Eamonn. Interview conducted by Stephen Walker. 5 January 2021.
9. Devlin, Paddy. *Straight Left: An Autobiography*, The Blackstaff Press, 1993.
10. Hendron, Jim. Interview conducted by Stephen Walker. 25 August 2022.
11. Hendron, Joe. Interview conducted by Stephen Walker. 22 February 2023.
12. Hendron, Jim. Interview conducted by Stephen Walker. 25 August 2022.
13. Hendron, Jim. Interview conducted by Stephen Walker. 25 August 2022.
14. Hendron, Jim. Interview conducted by Stephen Walker. 25 August 2022.
15. Hume, John. Interview conducted by Frank D'Arcy. 17 May 2002.
16. Hume, John. Interview conducted by Frank D'Arcy. 17 May 2002.
17. Hume, John. Interview conducted by Frank D'Arcy. 17 May 2002.
18. Hume, John. Interview conducted by Frank D'Arcy . 17 May 2002.
19. Haughey, Denis. Interview conducted by Stephen Walker. 2 May 2022.
20. Haughey, Denis. Interview conducted by Stephen Walker. 2 May 2022.
21. Haughey, Denis. Interview conducted by Stephen Walker. 2 May 2022.
22. Bew, Lord. Interview conducted by Stephen Walker. 1 May 2023.
23. Currie, Austin. Interview conducted by Stephen Walker. 23 January 2021.
24. Haughey, Denis. Interview conducted by Stephen Walker. 2 May 2022.
25. Haughey, Denis. Interview conducted by Stephen Walker. 2 May 2022.
26. *New York Times*, 21 March 1971.
27. Stormont proceedings, 22 June 1971.
28. Faulkner, Brian. *Memoirs of a Statesman*, Weidenfeld and Nicolson, 1978.

29 Devlin, Paddy. *Straight Left: An Autobiography*, The Blackstaff Press, 1993.

30 Faulkner, Brian. *Memoirs of a Statesman*, Weidenfeld and Nicolson, 1978.

31 *Irish Times*, 20 August 1971.

32 Devlin, Paddy. *Straight Left: An Autobiography*, The Blackstaff Press, 1993.

33 Devlin, Paddy. *Straight Left: An Autobiography*, The Blackstaff Press, 1993.

34 Haughey, Denis. Interview conducted by Stephen Walker. 2 May 2022.

35 Logue, Hugh. Interview conducted by Stephen Walker. 2 May 2023.

8: Bloody Sunday

1 BBC, 22 January 1972.

2 BBC, 22 January 1972.

3 CAIN Archive – Conflict and Politics in Northern Ireland.

4 Hume, John. Interview conducted by Frank D'Arcy. 30 October 2002.

5 McWilliams, Monica. Interview conducted by Stephen Walker. 8 October 2022.

6 McWilliams, Monica. Interview conducted by Stephen Walker. 8 October 2022.

7 Hume, John. Interview conducted by Frank D'Arcy. 30 October 2002.

8 Hume, Therese. Interview conducted by Stephen Walker. 1 February 2023.

9 Hume, John. Interview conducted by Frank D'Arcy. 30 October 2002.

10 Hume, Therese. Interview conducted by Stephen Walker. 1 February 2023.

11 Devlin, Paddy. *Straight Left: An Autobiography*, The Blackstaff Press, 1993.

12 Devlin, Paddy. *Straight Left: An Autobiography*, The Blackstaff Press, 1993.

13 Bloody Sunday Inquiry, 15 June, 2010.

14 Hume, John. Interview conducted by Frank D'Arcy. 30 October 2002.

15 Donlon, Seán. Interview conducted by Stephen Walker. 22 January 2021.

16 Donlon, Seán. Interview conducted by Stephen Walker. 22 January 2021.

17 *Irish Times*, 31 January 1972.

18 RTÉ, 31 January 1972.

19 Faulkner, Brian. *Memoirs of a Statesman*, Weidenfeld and Nicolson, 1978.

20 McCann, Eamonn. Interview conducted by Stephen Walker. 5 January 2021.
21 Bradley, Denis. Interview conducted by Stephen Walker. 23 January 2021.
22 *Irish Press*, 31 January 1972.
23 Hume, John. Interview conducted by Frank D'Arcy. 30 October 2002.
24 Widgery Report into Bloody Sunday, April 1972.
25 BBC TV, 31 July 1972.
26 Hanna, Eamon and Carmel. 1 May 2022.
27 Hanna, Eamon and Carmel. 1 May 2022.
28 'Towards a New Ireland', SDLP document, September 1972.
29 Faulkner, Brian. *Memoirs of a Statesman*, Weidenfeld and Nicolson, 1978.
30 Hume, John. Interview conducted by Frank D'Arcy. 30 September 2002.
31 Farren, Seán and Denis Haughey, *John Hume, Irish Peacemaker*, Four Courts Press, 2015.
32 US Senate, Autumn 1971.

9: *Writing on the wall*

1 Hume, Therese. Interview conducted by Stephen Walker. 1 February 2023.
2 Abbott, Áine, Interview conducted by Stephen Walker. 22 October 2021.
3 Abbott, Áine. Interview conducted by Stephen Walker. 22 October 2021.
4 McCann, Eamonn. Interview conducted by Stephen Walker. 5 January 2021.
5 McCann, Eamonn. Interview conducted by Stephen Walker. 5 January 2021.
6 Hume, Aidan. Interview conducted by Stephen Walker. 2 April 2022.
7 Hume, Therese. Interview conducted by Stephen Walker. 1 February 2023.
8 Abbott, Áine. Interview conducted by Stephen Walker. 22 October 2021.
9 Hume, Mo. Interview conducted by Stephen Walker. 15 May 2021.
10 Cosgrove, Gerry. Interview conducted by Stephen Walker. 23 March 2021.
11 Devlin, Paddy. *Straight Left: An Autobiography*, The Blackstaff Press, 1993.

12 Irish National Archives. Meeting between John Hume and Irish officials, 3 March 1973.
13 Haughey, Denis. Interview conducted by Stephen Walker. 2 May 2022.
14 Mallon, Seamus. *A Shared Home Place*, The Lilliput Press, 2019.
15 Haughey, Denis. Interview conducted by Stephen Walker. 2 May 2022.
16 Faulkner, Brian. *Memoirs of a Statesman*, Weidenfeld and Nicolson, 1978.
17 Ramsay, Robert. Interview conducted by Stephen Walker. 5 September 2022.
18 Ramsay, Robert. Interview conducted by Stephen Walker. 5 September 2022.
19 Lillis, Michael. Interview conducted by Stephen Walker. 15 December 2020.
20 Hume, John Junior. Interview conducted by Stephen Walker. 7 May 2021.
21 Hume, John Junior. Interview conducted by Stephen Walker. 7 May 2021.
22 Cosgrove, Gerry. Interview conducted by Stephen Walker. 23 March 2021.
23 Attwood, Tim. Interview conducted by Stephen Walker. 18 December 2020.
24 Ahern, Bertie. Interview conducted by Stephen Walker. 13 October 2020.
25 Donlon, Seán. Interview conducted by Stephen Walker. 30 July 2022.
26 Currie, Austin. Interview conducted by Stephen Walker. 23 January 2021.
27 Faulkner, Brian. *Memoirs of a Statesman*, Weidenfeld and Nicolson, 1978.
28 Faulkner, Brian. *Memoirs of a Statesman*, Weidenfeld and Nicholson, 1978.

10: Yes Minister

1 Faulkner, Brian. *Memoirs of a Statesman*, Weidenfeld and Nicolson, 1978.
2 Faulkner, Brian. *Memoirs of a Statesman*, Weidenfeld and Nicolson, 1978.
3 Faulkner, Brian. *Memoirs of a Statesman*, Weidenfeld and Nicolson, 1978.
4 Speech by Hugh Logue, issued to journalists, January 1974.
5 Logue, Hugh. Interview conducted by Stephen Walker. 2 May 2023.
6 Detail contained in the Sunningdale Agreement, December 1973.
7 Faulkner, Brian. *Memoirs of a Statesman*, Weidenfeld and Nicolson, 1978.
8 Bloomfield, Ken. *Stormont in Crisis: A Memoir,* The Blackstaff Press. 1994.

ENDNOTES

9. Ramsay, Robert. Interview conducted by Stephen Walker. 5 September 2022.
10. Faulkner, Brian. *Memoirs of a Statesman*, Weidenfeld and Nicolson, 1978.
11. BBC, 7 February 1974.
12. Devlin, Paddy. *Straight Left: An Autobiography*, The Blackstaff Press, 1993.
13. Hume, John, Interview conducted by Frank D'Arcy. 23 April 2003.
14. Farren, Seán and Denis Haughey, *John Hume, Irish Peacemaker*. Four Courts Press, 2015.
15. Bloomfield, Ken. *Stormont in Crisis: A Memoir*, The Blackstaff Press, 1994.
16. Bloomfield, Ken. *Stormont in Crisis: A Memoir*, The Blackstaff Press, 1994.
17. Bloomfield, Ken. *Stormont in Crisis: A Memoir*, The Blackstaff Press, 1994.
18. BBC, 25 May 1974.
19. Devlin, Paddy. *Straight Left: An Autobiography*, The Blackstaff Press, 1993.
20. Bloomfield, Ken. *Stormont in Crisis: A Memoir*, The Blackstaff Press, 1994.
21. Mallon, Seamus. *A Shared Home Place*, The Lilliput Press, 2019.
22. Mallon, Seamus. *A Shared Home Place*, The Lilliput Press, 2019.
23. Anderson, Don. *14 May Days*, Gill and Macmillan, 1994.
24. Ryder, Chris. *Fighting Fitt*, Brehon Press, 2006.
25. Hume, John. Interview conducted by Frank D'Arcy. 11 March 2003.
26. Hume, John. Interview conducted by Frank D'Arcy. 11 March 2003.
27. Ryder, Chris. *Fighting Fitt*, Brehon Press, 2006.
28. Ryder, Chris. *Fighting Fitt*, Brehon Press, 2006.
29. Ramsay, Robert. Interview conducted by Stephen Walker. 5 September 2022.
30. Hume, John. Interview conducted by Frank D'Arcy. 9 November 2002.
31. Farren, Seán and Denis Haughey, *John Hume, Irish Peacemaker*. Four Courts Press, 2015.
32. Hume, Aidan. Interview conducted by Stephen Walker. 2 April 2022.
33. Empey, Lord. Interview conducted by Stephen Walker. 4 October 2020.
34. Hume, John. Interview conducted by Frank D'Arcy. 22 March 2003.

11: *Follow the leader*

1. Eames, Lord. Interview conducted by Stephen Walker. 16 October 2020.
2. Eames, Lord. Interview conducted by Stephen Walker. 16 October 2020.
3. Eames, Lord. Interview conducted by Stephen Walker. 16 October 2020.
4. Hume, John. Interview conducted by Frank D'Arcy. 11 March 2003.
5. Currie, Austin. Interview conducted by Stephen Walker. 23 January 2021.
6. Hume, John. Interview conducted by Frank D'Arcy. 11 March 2003.
7. Donlon, Seán. Interview conducted by Stephen Walker. 22 January 2021.
8. Lillis, Michael. Interview conducted by Stephen Walker. 15 December 2020.
9. Lillis, Michael. Interview conducted by Stephen Walker. 15 December 2020.
10. Lillis, Michael. Interview conducted by Stephen Walker. 15 December 2020.
11. Statement from President Carter, 30 August 1977.
12. Ó hUiginn, Seán. Interview conducted by Stephen Walker. 22 January 2021.
13. Ó hUiginn, Seán. Interview conducted by Stephen Walker. 22 January 2021.
14. Hume, John. Interview conducted by Frank D'Arcy. 30 September 2002.
15. Mallon, Seamus. *A Shared Home Place*, The Lilliput Press, 2019.
16. Devlin, Paddy. *Straight Left: An Autobiography*, The Blackstaff Press, 1993.
17. Ryder, Chris. *Fighting Fitt*, Brehon Press, 2006.
18. Ryder, Chris. *Fighting Fitt*, Brehon Press, 2006.
19. Durkan, Mark. Interview conducted by Stephen Walker. 19 March 2021.
20. Paisley, Ian Junior. Interview conducted by Stephen Walker. 25 April 2023.
21. McCrea, Don. Interview conducted by Stephen Walker. 22 August 2022.
22. Paisley, Baroness. Interview conducted by Stephen Walker. 19 January 2021.
23. *Belfast Telegraph*, 22 November 1978.
24. Rodgers, Bríd. Interview conducted by Stephen Walker. 5 January 2021.

25 Hume, Aidan. Interview conducted by Stephen Walker. 2 April 2022.
26 Cosgrove, Gerry. Interview conducted by Stephen Walker. 23 March 2021.

12: Ourselves alone

1 Ó Ceallaigh, Dáithí. Interview conducted by Stephen Walker. 22 January 2021.
2 Ó Ceallaigh, Dáithí. Interview conducted by Stephen Walker. 22 January 2021.
3 Rodgers, Bríd. Interview conducted by Stephen Walker. 5 January 2021.
4 Moloney, Ed. *Voices from the Grave*, Faber and Faber, 2010.
5 Hennessey, Thomas. *Hunger Strike: Margaret Thatcher's Battle with the IRA,* Irish Academic Press, 2014.
6 Hennessey, Thomas. *Hunger Strike: Margaret Thatcher's Battle with the IRA,* Irish Academic Press, 2014.
7 Hennessey, Thomas. *Hunger Strike: Margaret Thatcher's Battle with the IRA,* Irish Academic Press, 2014.
8 Routledge, Paul. *John Hume, A Biography*, HarperCollins, 1997.
9 Cushnahan, John. Correspondence with Stephen Walker. 1 June 2023.
10 Maginness, Alban. Interview conducted by Stephen Walker. 8 June 2023.
11 Cushnahan, John. Correspondence with Stephen Walker. 1 June 2023.
12 *Belfast Telegraph*, 6 August 1981.
13 Ahern, Bertie. Interview conducted by Stephen Walker. 13 October 2020.
14 Farren, Seán. *John Hume: In His Own Words,* Four Courts Press, 2018.
15 Farren, Seán. *John Hume: In His Own Words*, Four Courts Press, 2018.
16 Farren, Seán. Interview conducted by Stephen Walker. 2 May 2022.
17 Farren, Seán. Interview conducted by Stephen Walker. 2 May 2022.
18 *Belfast Telegraph*, 29 January 1983.
19 Keenan, Dan. Interview conducted by Stephen Walker. 2 May 2022.
20 Keenan, Dan. Interview conducted by Stephen Walker. 2 May 2022.
21 New Ireland Forum proceedings, 30 May 1983.
22 New Ireland Forum proceedings, 30 May 1983.

23 Cushnahan, John. Correspondence with Stephen Walker. 1 June 2023.
24 Hansard, 28 June 1983.
25 Hansard, 28 June 1983.

13: *The monkey and the organ grinder*

1 Durkan, Mark. Interview conducted by Stephen Walker. 19 March 2021.
2 Durkan, Mark. Interview conducted by Stephen Walker. 19 March 2021.
3 Durkan, Mark. Interview conducted by Stephen Walker. 19 March 2021.
4 Durkan, Mark. Interview conducted by Stephen Walker. 19 March 2021.
5 Durkan, Mark. Interview conducted by Stephen Walker. 19 March 2021.
6 Spring, Dick. Interview conducted by Stephen Walker. 4 May 2022.
7 Hanna, Eamon. Interview conducted by Stephen Walker. 1 May 2022.
8 New Ireland Forum Report, 2 May 1984.
9 Morrison, Danny. Correspondence with Stephen Walker. 21 April 2023.
10 Bew, Paul and Gordon Gillespie, *Northern Ireland: A Chronology of the Troubles 1968–1993*, Gill and Macmillan, 1993.
11 UPI (United Press International) Report, 21 November 1984.
12 Drower, George. *John Hume, Man of Peace*, Victor Gollancz, 1995.
13 Lillis, Michael. Interview conducted by Stephen Walker. 15 December 2020.
14 Donlon, Seán. Interview conducted by Stephen Walker. 22 January 2021.
15 Fitzpatrick, Maurice. *John Hume in America: From Derry to DC*, Irish Academic Press, 2017.
16 Bradley, Denis. Interview conducted by Stephen Walker. 23 January 2021.
17 Hume, John. Interview conducted by Frank D'Arcy. 1 October 2002.
18 Bradley, Denis. Interview conducted by Stephen Walker. 23 January 2021.
19 Adams, Gerry. Interview with Stephen Walker. 7 September 2021.
20 Speech by Peter Robinson, 16 November 1985.
21 Hume, John. Interview conducted by Frank D'Arcy. 30 September 2002.
22 *The Guardian*, 21 January 1986.
23 Dáil Proceedings, 21 November 1985.

24 Durkan, Mark. Interview conducted by Stephen Walker. 19 March 2021.
25 Spring, Dick. Interview conducted by Stephen Walker. May 2022.
26 *The Observer*, 27 April 1986.
27 Keenan, Dan. Interview conducted by Stephen Walker. 2 May 2022.
28 Keenan, Dan. Interview conducted by Stephen Walker. 2 May 2022.
29 Durkan, Mark. Interview conducted by Stephen Walker. 19 March 2021.
30 Empey, Lord. Interview conducted by Stephen Walker. 4 October 2020.

14: Let's talk

1 Adams, Gerry. Interview conducted by Stephen Walker. 7 September 2021.
2 Adams, Gerry. Interview conducted by Stephen Walker. 7 September 2021.
3 Adams, Gerry. Interview conducted by Stephen Walker. 7 September 2021.
4 Mallon, Seamus. *A Shared Home Place*, The Lilliput Press, 2019.
5 Adams, Gerry. *Hope and History: Making Peace in Ireland*, Brandon, 2003.
6 Letter courtesy of Pat Hume and BBC NI *Spotlight on the Troubles: A Secret History*, 2019.
7 Letter courtesy of Pat Hume and BBC NI *Spotlight on the Troubles: A Secret History*, 2019.
8 Letter courtesy of Pat Hume and BBC NI *Spotlight on the Troubles: A Secret History*, 2019.
9 Letter courtesy of Pat Hume and BBC NI *Spotlight on the Troubles: A Secret History*, 2019.
10 Durkan, Mark. Interview conducted by Stephen Walker. 19 March 2021.
11 Adams, Gerry. *Hope and History: Making Peace in Ireland*, Brandon, 2003.
12 Hume, Mo. Interview conducted by Stephen Walker. 15 May 2021.
13 Cowley, Martin. Interview conducted by Stephen Walker. 16 August 2022.
14 Hume, Mo. Interview conducted by Stephen Walker. 15 May 2021.
15 *Irish Times*, 9 May 1987.
16 Hume, Mo. Interview conducted by Stephen Walker. 15 May 2021.
17 Arthur, Paul. Interview conducted by Stephen Walker. 14 May 2022.
18 McWilliams, Monica. Interview conducted by Stephen Walker. 8 October 2022.

19 Spring, Dick. Interview conducted by Stephen Walker. 4 May 2022.
20 *Hume*, BBC Northern Ireland documentary, 2011.
21 Adams, Gerry. *Hope and History: Making Peace in Ireland*, Brandon, 2003.
22 Farren, Seán. Interview conducted by Stephen Walker. 2 May 2022.
23 Keenan, Dan. Interview conducted by Stephen Walker. 2 May 2022.
24 Adams, Gerry. Interview conducted by Stephen Walker. 7 September 2021.
25 Keenan, Dan. Interview conducted by Stephen Walker. 2 May 2022.
26 *Belfast Telegraph*, 2 November 1981.
27 Farren, Seán. Interview conducted by Stephen Walker. 2 May 2022.
28 Adams, Gerry. Interview conducted by Stephen Walker. 7 September 2021.
29 Farren, Seán. Interview conducted by Stephen Walker. 2 May 2022.
30 Morrison, Danny. Correspondence with Stephen Walker. 21 April 2023.
31 Hume, Mo. Interview conducted by Stephen Walker. 15 May 2021.
32 Hume, Mo. Interview conducted by Stephen Walker. 15 May 2021.
33 Keenan, Dan. Interview conducted by Stephen Walker. 2 May 2022.
34 Hendron, Joe. Interview conducted by Stephen Walker. 22 February 2023.
35 Keenan, Dan. Interview conducted by Stephen Walker. 2 May 2022.
36 Ritchie, Baroness. Interview conducted by Stephen Walker. 23 January 2021.
37 Mallon, Seamus. *A Shared Home Place*, The Lilliput Press, 2019.
38 Haughey, Denis. Interview conducted by Stephen Walker. 2 May 2022.
39 Alderdice, Lord. Interview conducted by Stephen Walker. 3 October 2020.
40 SDLP Conference speech, 25–27 November 1988.
41 SDLP Conference speech, 25–27 November 1988.
42 Hume, John. Interview conducted by Frank D'Arcy. 3 October 2002.
43 *Sunday Tribune*, 11 November 1990.
44 Needham, Sir Richard. Interview conducted by Stephen Walker. 18 October 2020.
45 Needham, Sir Richard. Interview conducted by Stephen Walker. 18 October 2020.
46 RTÉ, 17 December 1997.

47 RTÉ, 17 December 1997.

48 RTÉ, 17 December 1997.

49 Kinnock, Lord. Interview conducted by Stephen Walker. 17 October 2020.

50 Alderdice, Lord. Interview conducted by Stephen Walker. 3 October 2020.

51 Alderdice, Lord. Interview conducted by Stephen Walker. 3 October 2020.

15: *Peace in a week*

1 Rodgers, Bríd. Interview conducted by Stephen Walker. 5 January 2021.

2 Rodgers, Bríd. Interview conducted by Stephen Walker. 5 January 2021.

3 McDonnell, Alasdair. Interview conducted by Stephen Walker. 25 February 2023.

4 McDonnell, Alasdair. Interview conducted by Stephen Walker. 25 February 2023.

5 Adams, Gerry. Interview conducted by Stephen Walker. 7 September 2021.

6 Hume, John. Interview conducted by Frank D'Arcy. 3 October 2002.

7 Empey, Lord. Interview conducted by Stephen Walker. 4 October 2020.

8 Durkan, Mark. Interview conducted by Stephen Walker. 19 March 2021.

9 Bew, Paul and Gordon Gillespie. *Northern Ireland: A Chronology of the Troubles 1968–1993*, Gill and Macmillan, 1993.

10 Abbott, Áine. Interview conducted by Stephen Walker. 22 October 2021.

11 Hume, Aidan. Interview conducted by Stephen Walker. 2 April 2022.

12 Durkan, Mark. Interview conducted by Stephen Walker. 19 March 2021.

13 Coulter, Phil. Interview conducted by Stephen Walker. 23 March 2021.

14 Ó Ceallaigh, Dáithí. Interview conducted by Stephen Walker. 22 January 2021.

15 Durkan, Mark. Interview conducted by Stephen Walker. 19 March 2021.

16 Durkan, Mark. Interview conducted by Stephen Walker. 19 March 2021.

17 Hume, John Junior. Interview conducted by Stephen Walker. 7 May 2021.

18 Durkan, Mark. Interview conducted by Stephen Walker. 19 March 2021.

19 *Irish Independent*, 18 September 1993.

20 *Sunday Tribune*, 26 September 1993.

21 BBC Radio Ulster interview, 30 October 2013.

22 Durkan, Mark. Interview conducted by Stephen Walker. 19 March 2021.

23 Hume, Pat. SDLP video, 2015.

24 Logue, Hugh. Interview conducted by Stephen Walker. 2 May 2023.

25 BBC Northern Ireland website, 30 October 2013 (20-year anniversary)

26 Abbott, Áine, Interview conducted by Stephen Walker. 22 October 2021.

27 Mallie, Eamonn and David McKittrick. *The Fight for Peace*, Heinemann, 1996.

28 Hume, Aidan. Interview conducted by Stephen Walker. 2 April 2022.

29 BBC Northern Ireland website, 30 October 2013 (20-year anniversary).

30 BBC Northern Ireland website, 30 October 2013 (20-year anniversary).

31 BBC Radio Ulster interview, 30 October 2013.

32 BBC Radio Ulster interview, 30 October 2013.

33 BBC Radio Ulster interview, 30 October 2013.

34 BBC Radio Ulster interview, 30 October 2013.

35 Major, Sir John. Correspondence with Stephen Walker. February 2021.

36 Major, Sir John. Correspondence with Stephen Walker. February 2021.

37 *Irish Independent*, 9 November 1993.

38 Abbott, Áine, Interview conducted by Stephen Walker. 22 October 2021.

39 Hansard, 1 November 1993.

40 *Hume*, BBC Northern Ireland documentary, 2011.

41 Bradley, Denis. Interview conducted by Stephen Walker. 23 January 2021.

42 Bradley, Denis. Interview conducted by Stephen Walker. 23 January 2021.

43 Adams, Gerry. *Hope and History: Making Peace in Ireland*, Brandon, 2003.

44 *The Independent*, 29 November 1993.

45 *Irish Independent*, 11 December 1993.

16: *Thumbs up*

1 Downing Street Declaration, 15 December 1993.

2 Downing Street Declaration, 15 December 1993.

3 Major, Sir John. Correspondence with Stephen Walker. February 2021.

ENDNOTES

4 Major, Sir John. Correspondence with Stephen Walker. February 2021.
5 Downing Street Declaration, 15 December 1993.
6 The Journal.ie. 29 December 2021.
7 The Journal.ie. 29 December 2021.
8 The Miller Center, *Oral Histories*, 16 May 2016.
9 Hume, Aidan. Interview conducted by Stephen Walker. 2 April 2022.
10 Soderberg, Nancy. Interview conducted by Stephen Walker. 31 December 2020.
11 Soderberg, Nancy. Interview conducted by Stephen Walker. 31 December 2020.
12 BBC NI website, Release of state papers, 28 December 2018.
13 Soderberg, Nancy. Interview conducted by Stephen Walker. 31 December 2020.
14 Soderberg, Nancy. Interview conducted by Stephen Walker. 31 December 2020.
15 Major, Sir John. Correspondence with Stephen Walker. February 2021.
16 Fitzpatrick, Maurice. *John Hume in America: From Derry to DC*, Irish Academic Press, 2017.
17 UPI, 1 February 1994.
18 Nesbitt, Mike. Correspondence with Stephen Walker. 27 February 2023
19 *Sunday Tribune*, 23 April 1995.
20 *Sunday Tribune*, 23 April 1995.
21 *Irish Times*, 29 August 2019.
22 Hume, John and Gerry Adams. Joint statement. 28 August 1994.
23 BBC Radio Ulster, 31 August 1994.
24 BBC Radio Ulster, 31 August 1994.
25 CLMC statement, 13 October 1994.
26 Blair, Tony. Interview conducted by Stephen Walker. 7 May 2021.
27 Blair, Tony. Interview conducted by Stephen Walker. 7 May 2021.
28 Durkan, Mark. Interview conducted by Stephen Walker. 19 March 2021.
29 Durkan, Mark. Interview conducted by Stephen Walker. 19 March 2021.

30 Kinnock, Lord. Interview conducted by Stephen Walker. 17 October 2020.
31 *Sunday Tribune*, 23 April 1995.

17: President Hume

1 Kinnock, Lord. Interview conducted by Stephen Walker. 17 October 2020.
2 *The Times*, 2 February 1995.
3 *The Independent*, 14 August 1995.
4 CAIN Archive – Conflict and Politics in Northern Ireland.
5 McDevitt, Conall. Interview conducted by Stephen Walker. 5 January 2021.
6 McDevitt, Conall. Interview conducted by Stephen Walker. 5 January 2021.
7 Kerr, David. Interview conducted by Stephen Walker. 26 January 2021.
8 Kerr, David. Interview conducted by Stephen Walker. 26 January 2021.
9 Kerr, David. Interview conducted by Stephen Walker. 26 January 2021.
10 Kerr, David. Interview conducted by Stephen Walker. 26 January 2021.
11 Kerr, David. Interview conducted by Stephen Walker. 26 January 2021.
12 Hendron, Joe. Interview conducted by Stephen Walker. 22 February 2023.
13 PREM 19/6147 Ireland part 130 19. UK National Archives, Kew, London. *Village* Magazine, 27 December 2020 and RTÉ 30 December 2020.
14 Bradley, Denis. Interview conducted by Stephen Walker. 23 January 2021.
15 *Irish News*, 20 February 1997.
16 *Irish News*, 20 February 1997.
17 Hume, Aidan. Interview conducted by Stephen Walker. 2 April 2022.
18 Blair, Sir Tony. Interview conducted by Stephen Walker. 7 May 2021.
19 Joint statement from John Hume and Gerry Adams, 17 July 1997.
20 IRA statement, 19 July 1997.
21 BBC, 19 July 1997.
22 McAleese, Mary. Interview conducted by Stephen Walker. 7 December 2020.
23 Hume, John Junior. Interview conducted by Stephen Walker. 7 May 2021.

ENDNOTES

24 McDevitt, Conall. Interview conducted by Stephen Walker. 5 January 2021.
25 *Irish News*, 7 September 1997.
26 Hume, John Junior. Interview conducted by Stephen Walker. 7 May 2021.
27 Hume, John Junior. Interview conducted by Stephen Walker. 7 May 2021.
28 Hume, Aidan. Interview conducted by Stephen Walker. 2 April 2022.
29 *Christian Science Monitor*, 14 January 1998.

18: *Down at the Waterfront*

1 Durkan, Mark. Interview conducted by Stephen Walker. 19 March 2021.
2 Cosgrove, Gerry. Interview conducted by Stephen Walker. 23 March 2021.
3 Cosgrove, Gerry. Interview conducted by Stephen Walker. 23 March 2021.
4 Hume, John. Interview conducted by Frank D'Arcy. 23 April 2003.
5 Rodgers, Bríd. Interview conducted by Stephen Walker. 5 January 2021.
6 McDevitt, Conall. Interview conducted by Stephen Walker. 5 January 2021.
7 Ritchie, Baroness. Interview conducted by Stephen Walker. 23 January 2021.
8 Durkan, Mark. Interview conducted by Stephen Walker. 19 March 2021.
9 Donoghue, David. *One Good Day: My Journey to the Good Friday Agreement*, Gill Books, 2022.
10 Donoghue, David. *One Good Day: My Journey to the Good Friday Agreement*, Gill Books, 2022.
11 Kerr, David. Interview conducted by Stephen Walker. 26 January 2021.
12 McCann, Eamonn. Interview conducted by Stephen Walker. 5 January 2021.
13 *Irish News*, 11 April 1998.
14 Eames, Lord. Interview conducted by Stephen Walker. 16 October 2020.
15 Hume, Mo. Interview conducted by Stephen Walker, 15 May 2021.
16 Hume, John Junior. Interview conducted by Stephen Walker. 7 May 2021.
17 Letter from Senator Mitchell to John Hume. 30 April 1998.
18 Kerr, David. Interview conducted by Stephen Walker. 26 January 2021.

19 Kerr, David. Interview conducted by Stephen Walker. 26 January 2021.

20 Attwood, Tim. Interview conducted by Stephen Walker. 18 December 2020.

21 Attwood, Tim. Interview conducted by Stephen Walker. 18 December 2020.

22 Hume, John Junior. Interview conducted by Stephen Walker. 7 May 2021.

23 Attwood, Tim. Interview conducted by Stephen Walker. 18 December 2020.

24 Attwood, Tim. Interview conducted by Stephen Walker. 18 December 2020.

25 Attwood, Tim. Interview conducted by Stephen Walker. 18 December 2020.

26 Kerr, David. Interview conducted by Stephen Walker. 26 January 2021.

27 Kerr, David. Interview conducted by Stephen Walker. 26 January 2021.

28 McDevitt, Conall. Interview conducted by Stephen Walker. 5 January 2021.

29 Kerr, David. Interview conducted by Stephen Walker. 26 January 2021.

30 Attwood, Tim. Interview conducted by Stephen Walker. 18 December 2020.

31 *Washington Post*, 20 May 1998.

32 Attwood, Tim. Interview conducted by Stephen Walker. 18 December 2020.

33 McDevitt, Conall. Interview conducted by Stephen Walker. 5 January 2021.

34 Kerr, David. Interview conducted by Stephen Walker. 26 January 2021.

35 Kerr, David. Interview conducted by Stephen Walker. 26 January 2021.

36 RTÉ, 23 May 1998.

19: *A night in Oslo*

1 Mallon, Seamus. *A Shared Home Place*, Lilliput Press, 2019.

2 Durkan, Mark. Interview conducted by Stephen Walker. 19 March 2021.

3 Durkan, Mark. Interview conducted by Stephen Walker. 19 March 2021.

ENDNOTES

4   Mallon, Seamus. *A Shared Home Place*, Lilliput Press, 2019.
5   McDevitt, Conall. Interview conducted by Stephen Walker. 5 January 2021.
6   Empey, Lord. Interview conducted by Stephen Walker. 4 October 2020.
7   Alderdice, Lord. Interview conducted by Stephen Walker. 3 October 2020.
8   Mallon, Seamus. *A Shared Home Place*, Lilliput Press, 2019.
9   BBC NI website, 12 July 1998.
10 President Clinton address, Waterfront Hall, Belfast, 3 September 1998.
11 Letter from Mo Mowlam to John Hume, September 1998.
12 McDevitt, Conall. Interview conducted by Stephen Walker. 5 January 2021.
13 McDevitt, Conall. Interview conducted by Stephen Walker. 5 January 2021.
14 McDevitt, Conall. Interview conducted by Stephen Walker. 5 January 2021.
15 Kerr, David. Interview conducted by Stephen Walker. 26 January 2021.
16 Trimble. Lady. Interview conducted by Stephen Walker. 25 April 2023.
17 Mallon, Seamus. *A Shared Home Place*, Lilliput Press, 2019.
18 Trimble, Lady. Interview conducted by Stephen Walker. 25 April 2023.
19 Kerr, David. Interview conducted by Stephen Walker. 26 January 2021.
20 BBC Radio Ulster, 16 October 1998.
21 Attwood, Tim. Interview conducted by Stephen Walker. 18 December 2020.
22 Attwood, Tim. Interview conducted by Stephen Walker. 18 December 2020.
23 Attwood, Tim. Interview conducted by Stephen Walker. 18 December 2020.
24 Letter from Seamus Heaney to John Hume, 30 November 1998.
25 Hume, John Junior. Interview conducted by Stephen Walker. 7 May 2021.
26 Kerr, David. Interview conducted by Stephen Walker. 26 January 2021.
27 Kerr, David. Interview conducted by Stephen Walker. 26 January 2021.
28 Speech at Nobel Peace Prize, 10 December 1998.

29 Cosgrove, Gerry. Interview conducted by Stephen Walker. 23 March 2021.
30 Speech at Nobel Peace Prize, 10 December 1998.
31 Speech at Nobel Peace Prize, 10 December 1998.
32 *Belfast Telegraph*, 29 January 1983.
33 Coulter, Phil. Interview conducted by Stephen Walker. 23 March 2021.
34 Coulter, Phil. Interview conducted by Stephen Walker. 23 March 2021.
35 Coulter, Phil. Interview conducted by Stephen Walker. 23 March 2021.
36 Durkan, Mark. Interview conducted by Stephen Walker. 19 March 2021.
37 Trimble, Lady. Interview conducted by Stephen Walker. 25 April 2023.
38 *Irish Times*, 30 December 2020 (release of British State Papers).
39 Trimble, Lady. Interview conducted by Stephen Walker. 25 April 2023.
40 Hume, Mo. Interview conducted by Stephen Walker. 15 May 2021.
41 Hume, Aidan. Interview conducted by Stephen Walker. 2 April 2022.

20: Doctor's orders

1 McWilliams, Monica. Interview conducted by Stephen Walker. 8 October 2022.
2 Cosgrove, Gerry. Interview conducted by Stephen Walker. 23 March 2021.
3 McCay, Ronan. Interview conducted by Stephen Walker. 23 January 2021.
4 Abbott, Áine. Interview conducted by Stephen Walker. 22 October 2021.
5 Hume, John Junior. Interview conducted by Stephen Walker. 7 May 2021.
6 Conversation with unnamed source.
7 Abbott, Áine. Interview conducted by Stephen Walker. 22 October 2021.
8 McWilliams, Monica. Interview conducted by Stephen Walker. 8 October 2022.
9 Abbott, Áine. Interview conducted by Stephen Walker. 22 October 2021.
10 SDLP annual conference speech, November 1999.
11 McCay, Ronan. Interview conducted by Stephen Walker. 23 January 2021.
12 McDevitt, Conall. Interview conducted by Stephen Walker. 5 January 2021.
13 Mallon, Seamus. *A Shared Home Place*, Lilliput Press, 2019.

14 Mallon, Seamus. *A Shared Home Place*, Lilliput Press, 2019.

15 Abbott, Áine. Interview conducted by Stephen Walker. 22 October 2021.

16 White, Barry. Interview conducted by Stephen Walker. 1 April 2023.

17 O'Kane, Ruairí. Interview conducted by Stephen Walker. 21 January 2021.

18 Durkan, Mark. Interview conducted by Stephen Walker. 19 March 2021.

19 McCann, Eamonn. Interview conducted by Stephen Walker. 5 January 2021.

20 *The Guardian*, 31 August 2000.

21 Conversation with unnamed source.

22 Hanna, Eamon. Interview conducted by Stephen Walker. 1 May 2022.

23 *Irish News*, 11 June 2001.

24 *The Guardian*, 17 September 2001.

25 Mallon, Seamus. *A Shared Home Place*, The Lilliput Press, 2019.

21: Stepping down

1 Eastwood, Colum. Interview conducted by Stephen Walker. 6 October 2020.

2 McCay, Ronan. Interview conducted by Stephen Walker. 23 January 2021.

3 Eastwood, Colum. Interview conducted by Stephen Walker. 6 October 2020.

4 McCay, Ronan. Interview conducted by Stephen Walker. 23 January 2021.

5 Speech to SDLP Conference, 10 November 2001.

6 Speech to SDLP Conference, 10 November 2001.

7 Speech to SDLP Conference, 10 November 2001.

8 McCay, Ronan. Interview conducted by Stephen Walker. 23 January 2021.

9 Hume, John Junior. Interview conducted by Stephen Walker. 7 May 2021.

10 Hume, Mo. Interview conducted by Stephen Walker. 15 May 2021.

11 Hume, Aidan. Interview conducted by Stephen Walker. 2 April 2022.

12 Murray, Denis. Correspondence with Stephen Walker. 19 April 2023.

13 Paisley, Ian Junior. Interview conducted by Stephen Walker. 25 April 2023.

14 Conversation with unnamed source.

15 O'Kane, Ruairí. Interview conducted by Stephen Walker. 21 January 2021.
16 Donlon, Séan. Interview conducted by Stephen Walker. 22 January 2021.
17 Durkan, Mark. Interview conducted by Stephen Walker. 19 March 2021.
18 Coulter, Phil. Interview conducted by Stephen Walker. 23 March 2021.
19 Abbott, Áine. Interview conducted by Stephen Walker. 22 October 2021.
20 Abbott, Áine. Interview conducted by Stephen Walker. 22 October 2021.
21 Hume, Aidan. Interview conducted by Stephen Walker. 2 April 2022.
22 Hume, John Junior. Interview conducted by Stephen Walker. 7 May 2021.
23 Hume, Mo. Interview conducted by Stephen Walker. 15 May 2021.
24 Ahern, Bertie. Interview conducted by Stephen Walker. 13 October 2020.
25 Ahern, Bertie. Interview conducted by Stephen Walker. 13 October 2020.
26 McAleese, Mary. Interview conducted by Stephen Walker. 7 December 2020.
27 O'Kane, Ruairí. Interview conducted by Stephen Walker. 21 January 2021.
28 O'Kane, Ruairí. Interview conducted by Stephen Walker. 21 January 2021.

22: *Ireland's greatest*

1 O'Callaghan, Miriam. Interview conducted by Stephen Walker. 29 March 2022.
2 O'Callaghan, Miriam. Interview conducted by Stephen Walker. 29 March 2022.
3 O'Callaghan, Miriam. Interview conducted by Stephen Walker. 29 March 2022.
4 O'Callaghan, Miriam. Interview conducted by Stephen Walker. 29 March 2022.
5 O'Callaghan, Miriam. Interview conducted by Stephen Walker. 29 March 2022.
6 O'Callaghan, Miriam. Interview conducted by Stephen Walker. 29 March 2022.
7 O'Callaghan, Miriam. Interview conducted by Stephen Walker. 29 March 2022.

ENDNOTES

8 O'Callaghan, Miriam. Interview conducted by Stephen Walker. 29 March 2022.

9 O'Kane, Ruairí. Interview conducted by Stephen Walker. 21 January 2021.

10 O'Kane, Ruairí. Interview conducted by Stephen Walker. 21 January 2021.

11 Conversation with unnamed source.

12 Hansard, 15 June 2010.

13 *The Guardian*, 15 June 2010.

14 RTÉ, 23 November 2015.

15 RTÉ, 23 November 2015.

16 Hume, John Junior. Interview conducted by Stephen Walker. 7 May 2021.

17 Hume, Mo. Interview conducted by Stephen Walker. 15 May 2021.

18 RTÉ, 23 November 2015.

19 Abbott, Áine. Interview conducted by Stephen Walker. 22 October 2021.

20 Hume, Mo. Interview conducted by Stephen Walker. 15 May 2021.

21 Hume, Aidan. Interview conducted by Stephen Walker. 2 April 2022.

22 *Irish News*, 26 November 2018.

23 McCloskey, Amy. Interview conducted by Stephen Walker. 1 November 2022.

24 Hume, John Junior. Interview conducted by Stephen Walker. 7 May 2021.

25 McCloskey, Amy. Interview conducted by Stephen Walker. 1 November 2022.

26 McCloskey, Amy. Interview conducted by Stephen Walker. 1 November 2022.

23: *Thank you John*

1 Abbott, Áine. Interview conducted by Stephen Walker. 22 October 2021.

2 Abbott, Áine. Interview conducted by Stephen Walker. 22 October 2021.

3 Hume, Mo. Interview conducted by Stephen Walker. 15 May 2021.

4 Hume, Aidan. Interview conducted by Stephen Walker. 2 April 2022.

5 Hume, John Junior. Interview conducted by Stephen Walker. 7 May 2021.

6 McCloskey, Amy. Interview conducted by Stephen Walker. 1 November 2022.

7 *The Guardian*, 3 August 2020.

8 *The Guardian*, 3 August 2020.

9 BBC News NI, 3 August 2020.

10 *Irish Independent*, 3 August 2020.

11 BBC News NI, 3 August 2020.

12 *Irish Independent*, 3 August 2020.

13 BBC News NI, 3 August 2020.

14 *Belfast Telegraph*, 3 August 2020.

15 RTÉ, 5 August 2020.

16 RTÉ, 5 August 2020.

17 RTÉ, 5 August 2020.

18 *Irish Times*, 6 August 2020.

19 Abbott, Áine. Interview conducted by Stephen Walker. 22 October 2021.

20 Hume, John Junior. Interview conducted by Stephen Walker. 7 May 2021.

21 Hume, Mo. Interview conducted by Stephen Walker. 15 May 2021.

22 Hume, Therese. Interview conducted by Stephen Walker. 1 February 2023.

23 Coulter, Phil. Interview conducted by Stephen Walker. 23 March 2021.

24 Hume, Aidan. Interview conducted by Stephen Walker. 2 April 2022.

25 BBC News NI, 2 September 2021.

26 *Derry Journal*, 5 September 2021.

27 *Derry Journal*, 5 September 2021.

28 BBC News NI, 3 September 2021.

29 *Belfast Telegraph*, 3 September 2021.

30 BBC News NI, 6 September 2021.

31 BBC News NI, 6 September 2021.

32 BBC News NI, 6 September 2021.

24: *The persuader*

1 Davidson, Colin. Interview conducted by Stephen Walker. 7 February 2023.

2 *Irish News*, 30 December 2019.

ENDNOTES

3 Empey, Lord. Interview conducted by Stephen Walker. 4 October 2020.
4 Donaldson, Sir Jeffrey. Correspondence with Stephen Walker. 2 April 2023.
5 Empey, Lord. Interview conducted by Stephen Walker. 4 October 2020.
6 Empey, Lord. Interview conducted by Stephen Walker. 4 October 2020.
7 Mallon, Seamus. *A Shared Home Place*, The Lilliput Press, 2019.
8 Kerr, David. Interview conducted by Stephen Walker. 26 January 2021.
9 Kerr, David. Interview conducted by Stephen Walker. 26 January 2021.
10 Kerr, David. Interview conducted by Stephen Walker. 26 January 2021.
11 *Irish Times*, 3 August 2020.
12 Needham, Sir Richard. Interview conducted by Stephen Walker. 18 October 2020.
13 Mallon, Seamus. *A Shared Home Place*, The Lilliput Press, 2019.
14 Haughey, Denis. Interview conducted by Stephen Walker. May 2022.
15 *Irish Times*, 3 August 2020.
16 McAleese, Mary. Interview conducted by Stephen Walker. 7 December 2020.
17 Ó hUiginn, Seán. Interview conducted by Stephen Walker. 22 January 2021.
18 SDLP conference speech, 29 January 1986, and *The Observer*, 26 April 1986.
19 Hume, John. Interview conducted by Frank D'Arcy. 30 September 2002.
20 *Irish Times*, 3 August 2020.
21 Farren, Seán and Denis Haughey. *John Hume, Irish Peacemaker*, Four Courts Press, 2015.
22 Nicholson, Jim. Interview conducted by Stephen Walker. 31 March 2023.
23 Donaldson, Sir Jeffrey. Correspondence with Stephen Walker. 2 April 2023.
24 Donaldson, Sir Jeffrey. Correspondence with Stephen Walker. 2 April 2023.
25 Bew, Lord. Interview conducted by Stephen Walker. 1 May 2023.
26 *Irish News*, 10 August 2020.
27 Bradley, Denis. Interview conducted by Stephen Walker. 23 January 2021.
28 Currie, Austin. Interview conducted by Stephen Walker. 23 January 2021.

29 Hendron, Joe. Interview conducted by Stephen Walker. 22 February 2023.
30 Needham, Sir Richard. Interview conducted by Stephen Walker. 18 October 2020.
31 Rodgers, Bríd. Interview conducted by Stephen Walker. 5 January 2021.
32 Arthur, Paul. Interview conducted by Stephen Walker. 14 May 2022.
33 Alderdice, Lord. Interview conducted by Stephen Walker. 3 October 2020.
34 Major, Sir John. Correspondence with Stephen Walker. February 2021.
35 Alderdice, Lord. Interview conducted by Stephen Walker. 3 October 2020.
36 Keenan, Dan. Interview conducted by Stephen Walker. 2 May 2022.
37 Hanna, Eamon. Interview conducted by Stephen Walker. 1 May 2022.
38 Needham, Sir Richard. Interview conducted by Stephen Walker. 18 October 2020.
39 Farren, Seán and Denis Haughey. *John Hume, Irish Peacemaker*, Four Courts Press, 2015.
40 Ritchie, Baroness. Interview conducted by Stephen Walker. 23 January 2021.
41 O'Kane, Ruairí. Interview conducted by Stephen Walker. 21 January 2021.
42 McGlone, Patsy. Interview conducted by Stephen Walker. 21 April 2023.
43 Farren, Seán and Denis Haughey. *John Hume, Irish Peacemaker*, Four Courts Press, 2015.
44 O'Kane, Ruairí. Interview conducted by Stephen Walker. 21 January 2021.
45 Eastwood, Colum. Interview conducted by Stephen Walker. 6 October 2020.
46 Maginness, Alban. Interview conducted by Stephen Walker. 8 June 2023.
47 Ahern, Bertie. Interview conducted by Stephen Walker. 13 October 2020.
48 Bruton, John. Interview conducted by Stephen Walker. 30 January 2021.
49 Mitchell, Senator George. Correspondence with Stephen Walker. 30 September 2021.
50 Durkan, Mark. Interview conducted by Stephen Walker. 19 March 2021.
51 Lillis, Michael. Interview conducted by Stephen Walker. 15 December 2020.
52 Donlon, Seán. Interview conducted by Stephen Walker. 22 January 2021.
53 Eames, Lord. Interview conducted by Stephen Walker. 16 October 2020.

INDEX

A

Adams, Gerry x, 162, 165, 170, 194, 195, 229, 251
    General Elections and 174, 175, 199, 259
    Hume, meetings with 196, 200–1, 203, 206, 213–15, 214, 217, 218
    IRA bombings, reaction to 200, 222
    IRA funeral, pall bearer at 222
    US visa 234–5, 236, 238
    Whitelaw, talks with 109–10
    see also Hume–Adams talks; Sinn Féin

Ahern, Bertie 247, 260
    Good Friday talks 263, 264, 267
    Hume and 123–4, 169, 247, 266, 308, 318–19, 336, 360

Alderdice, John 205, 212, 238, 283–4, 304, 354–5

Aldershot bombing 106

Alliance Party of Northern Ireland 139, 166, 174, 205, 300
    Assembly and 121, 147, 170
    Convention elections (1975) 146, 147
    Council Elections (1973) 120
    Darlington conference 112
    Duisburg discussions 205–6
    formation of 84–6, 90
    Hume and 85, 86, 212
    New Ireland Forum and 173
    Sunningdale talks 125

Andrews, Irene 120, 121

Anglo-American relations 151, 236, 237

Anglo-Irish Agreement (1985) 187–90, 206, 362
    Hume and 188, 190, 200, 202, 208

Anglo-Irish relations 159, 168, 169, 183, 211, 221, 360

Anglo-Irish Summit (1995) 251

Anti H Block election candidates 166, 168

Apprentice Boys 2, 49, 70–2, 75

Armagh District Council 120

Arthur, Paul 30, 41, 59, 66, 69, 198, 354

Atkins, Humphrey, Secretary of State 154–5, 157, 159, 162

Atlantic Harvest, Hume and 45–6, 62, 65

Attwood, Tim 123, 275–7, 279, 280

Aughey, Arthur 351, 357–8

B

Ballymoney petrol-bombing 284

BBC Northern Ireland 31–2, 43–4, 220, 227, 271, 279, 327

BBC Radio 4, *Today* programme 244

BBC Radio Foyle 241

BBC Radio Ulster 185, 288, 325, 342

Beggs, Roy 302

Begley, Thomas 221, 222, 223

Belfast 76–7, 101, 120
    bombings 106, 110, 211, 221–2
    riots 70, 91, 92

Belfast Telegraph 7, 155, 172

Blair, Tony 121, 243, 257, 259, 260
    Good Friday Agreement 289
    Good Friday talks 263, 264, 267, 270
    Hume and 243, 243–4, 245, 260, 266–7, 308, 336

Bleakley, David 93

Bloody Friday (1972) 110, 162

Bloody Sunday (1972) 102–6, 108, 326–7

Bloomfield, Ken 132, 136–7, 138

Bogside
    Apprentice Boys parade 71–2
    Battle of the Bogside 73, 76
    Callaghan's visit to 77–8

civil rights protest 102
Free Derry Corner 78
Hume and 64, 68-9, 71
riots 72-3, 74, 75
RUC and 54, 68-9, 72-3
Boland, Kevin 131
Bono 275-80, 288-9, 324, 338
border poll (1973) 117-18
Bradley, Denis 29-30, 64, 105, 146, 227
Hume and 185-6, 228-9, 258, 352
secret meetings, IRA and 227-8
Brighton bombing 182
British Army 76, 92, 108, 110
Aldershot bombing 106
arrests 97, 107
Bloody Sunday 102, 103
Catholic community and 76, 91, 110
fatalities 92
Hume arrested by 97
Operation Demetrius 95
Operation Motorman 110, 126
Parachute Regiment 99, 100-1, 102, 106
protestors attacked by 98, 99-100
SAS 196-7
shootings by 91, 93-4, 101, 102, 103, 104, 108, 110
British Embassy, Dublin 106
British-Irish Council 271
Brooke, Peter, Secretary of State 207-8, 211, 212, 215, 228, 233
Brookeborough, Basil Brooke, 1st Viscount 31, 207
Bruton, John 247, 249, 251, 308, 360
Burke, Richard, EEC Commissioner 152, 154, 155
Burntollet Bridge 59, 67
by-elections 61, 165-6, 167, 168, 190

C

Cahill, Joe 240-1
Callaghan, Jim 71, 76, 77-8, 153, 154
Cameron Commission report (1969) 69
Cameron, David 326

Campaign for Democracy in Ulster 41
Campaign for Social Justice 37
Canary Wharf bombing 252
Canavan, Michael 28, 44-5, 46, 55, 57, 62, 146
Carey, Hugh 148-9, 183
Carron, Owen 168, 170
Carter, Jimmy 149, 150-2, 238
Catholic Church 8, 20, 165
Catholics 33, 34, 48, 78, 92, 107
Bloody Sunday, reaction to 105
British Army and 91, 95, 101
discrimination and 37, 49, 50, 76, 77-8
Irish identity and 119
Chichester-Clark, Major James 70, 75, 87, 92, 95
Chichester-Clark, Robin 46, 87
Chilcott, Sir John 257-8
Citizens' Defence Association 73
Civil Rights Association 50, 102
civil rights campaign 56, 57-8, 60, 63, 87, 88
RUC and 67-8
'We Shall Overcome' 55, 99
see also Derry march; Magilligan protest
Claudy car bombs 110
Clinton, Bill 235
Good Friday and 269, 271
Hume and 237-8, 251, 269-70, 328, 336, 338
Northern Ireland visits 251, 285, 316
tribute to Pat Hume 342
US visa for Adams 236, 237, 240
Clinton, Hillary 251, 296, 342
Clonard Monastery 193, 194, 195, 199
Coleraine 39, 40, 41, 42-3, 120
Combined Loyalist Military Command (CLMC) 242
Conlon, Giuseppe and Sarah 279
Conservative Party 154-5, 182, 259
Constitution of Ireland (1937) 216, 264

INDEX

Constitutional Conference (1980) 159
Continuity IRA 264
Convention (1975) 144, 145, 146–7, 148, 170
Cooper, Bob 85, 136
Cooper, Ivan 50, 65, 71–2, 77, 82, 97, 102, 138
    Derry Citizens Action Committee 54, 55
    Hume and 67, 83, 86
Cosgrave, Liam 118, 125, 131, 138
Cosgrove, Geraldine (Gerry) 116–17, 123, 158–9, 210, 267–8, 291, 297
Coulter, Phil 12, 13, 292–3
    Hume and 13, 46, 63, 155, 218, 293
    Pat Hume, perception of 24, 27
    'The Town I Loved So Well' 13, 293, 339
Council Elections 119–21, 207, 306
Council of Ireland 119, 125–6, 131, 140
    Faulkner and 126, 127–8, 134, 136
    Hume and 119, 124, 126, 127, 128, 136, 140–1
    SDLP and 134, 136, 140
    unionist opposition to 130, 131, 132
Council for a New Ireland 170–1, 172
    see also New Ireland Forum
COVID-19 pandemic 334–5, 336, 337, 340, 341
Cowley, Martin 30–1, 50, 51–2, 53, 197
Craig, Bill 49, 54, 56, 58, 92, 147
    Vanguard movement 107, 119, 132, 133, 147
Credit Union League of Ireland 29
credit unions, Hume and 27, 28–9, 40, 43, 363
Crossmaglen car bomb 92
Currie, Austin 39, 124, 147, 166, 178, 338
    Derry march and 49, 50, 51, 52–3
    Hume and 53, 88, 125, 336, 353
    Nationalist Party and 67, 82
    SDLP and 89–90
Cushnahan, John 166, 167, 174, 175

D

Daly, Edward, Bishop of Derry 146, 293, 294
Davidson, Colin (artist) 344–5
de Brún, Bairbre 313, 320
de Chastelain, General John 251
decommissioning 249, 251, 256, 261, 274, 295, 348
    Blair and 263, 270
    Hume's views on 285
    Trimble and 285, 300
Democratic Unionist Party (DUP) 121, 132, 146, 155, 300, 313
    Council Elections (1973) and 120
    Donaldson and 271
    Duisburg discussions 205–6
    GFA talks process 263, 264
    Paisley and 132, 133, 155, 212, 215
    Robinson and 188
    Sinn Féin and 315
    withdrawal from talks 261
Derry Citizens Action Committee 54–7, 58, 59, 71
Derry Citizens' Defence Association 71, 76, 78
Derry City Cemetery 339, 343
Derry City Football Club 302, 310–11, 318
Derry Credit Union 27, 28–9
Derry Housing Action Committee 55
Derry Housing Association 36, 37
Derry Journal 40, 50, 51, 53, 309
Derry march 47–54, 56
    Hume and 48, 52–4
    NICRA and 47–9
    RUC and 49, 50–1, 52
Derry/Londonderry 2, 6, 31–2, 42, 69
    anti-internment rally 101–2
    Bloody Sunday 102–6
    British Army shootings 102–6, 110
    civil rights protest 67
    Corporation 36, 49, 57
    Creggan 54, 108
    explosions in 91
    Free Derry Corner 6, 102

407

gerrymandering 31, 48
housing crisis 36
Hume and 1, 32, 69
mixed communities 8
riots 69, 70, 74–5
Rossville Street 72, 102, 103
royal charter and 2
RUC attack 68
segregation 8, 19, 36
siege (1688–9) 2, 49
social injustices 31, 32
unionists and 2, 43
university campaign 37–8, 39
'You Are Now Entering Free Derry' 59–60
see also Bogside
Devenney, Phyllis 68, 71
Devenney, Sam 68
Devlin, Bernadette 58–9, 73, 87, 106
Devlin, Brendan, Monsignor 15, 17, 18–19, 25, 28
Devlin, Paddy 124, 127, 134, 138, 155
Adams and 109–10
Bloody Sunday 102, 103
Hume and 67, 82, 83, 87–8
SDLP and 88, 94, 96, 117, 152–3
Dodds, Diane 320
Donaldson, Sir Jeffrey 351–2
DUP and 271, 351
Good Friday Agreement, criticism of 271
Hume–Adams talks, views on 346–7
UUP and 265, 268, 270, 271, 351
Donlon, Seán 15–16, 17, 22–3, 80–1, 184
Hume and 104, 125, 149, 184, 316–17, 362
Downing Street Declaration (1993) 212, 232, 233, 234, 239, 244
Drew, Ronnie 311–12
Drumcree, County Armagh 249–50, 284
Dublin Castle 173, 177–8, 230
Duddy, Brendan 185–6, 227–9

Duisberg, West Germany 205–6
Dungiven 70
Dungiven Castle 94, 96
Durkan, Mark x, 62, 189, 216, 220, 235, 338
Father Reid and 193, 199
Hume and x–xi, 156, 177–9, 191, 282–3, 317, 326, 327, 361–2
Hume–Adams document 218–19
Hume–Adams meeting, views on 195–6
Mowlam and 244–5
New Ireland Forum 177–8
resignation 325, 326
SDLP Leader 309, 314, 320, 359
Stormont election (1969) 63
tribute to Pat Hume 342

E

Eames, Robin, Bishop of Derry and Raphoe 145–6, 362
Eastwood, Colum 307–8, 312, 338, 358, 359–60
Education Act (Northern Ireland) (1947) 9
Empey, Reginald 142, 191, 215–16, 255, 346, 347
Enniskillen bombing 199–200
European Economic Community (EEC) 126, 152, 153, 154, 155
European Parliament
elections 207, 313, 319
Hume as MEP 155–6, 158–9, 176, 182, 207, 283, 309
Hume's retirement 312, 313, 314
MEPs from Northern Ireland 155, 182, 207, 313, 320, 351
European Union (EU) 313, 360

F

Farren, Neil, Bishop of Derry 8, 56
Farren, Revd Paul 333, 338, 342
Farren, Seán 171, 200, 201–2, 327, 328, 338, 348
Faulkner, Brian 56, 70, 121, 122, 131, 137

INDEX

Chief Executive 124, 130, 133, 139
Council of Ireland and 126, 127–8, 134
Heath and 95, 106, 107
Hume and 93, 105, 122, 130, 142
internment, views on 94–5
Prime Minister, election as 92–3
resignation 107, 139
SDLP and 111–12, 121–2
Sunningdale and 125, 126, 127, 134–5
UPNI and 145, 146, 147
UUP resignation 130–1
Fianna Fáil 118, 169, 171, 194, 247
Fianna Fáil-Labour coalition (1993–4) 246–7
Fianna Fáil-Progressive Democrats coalition (1997–2002) 260
Fine Gael-Labour coalition (1973–7) 118, 124
Fine Gael-Labour coalition (1982–7) 168, 196
Fine Gael-Labour-Democratic Left coalition (1994–7) 247
Fitt, Gerry 39, 82–3, 120, 122, 137, 174
attacks on 51, 52, 153
Deputy Chief Executive role 124
Derry march and 49, 50, 52–3
Executive and 133, 139–40
Hume and 53, 67, 82, 83, 88
IRA, criticism of 153
SDLP and 88, 89, 90, 94, 96, 122, 153, 154, 157–8
UWC strike 138, 140
Westminster elections 87, 145, 154, 155
FitzGerald, Garret 168, 171, 196
Anglo-Irish Agreement (1985) 188
Hume and 171, 180, 183, 185, 209, 252, 308
New Ireland Forum and 172, 173
Thatcher and 182, 187
Forum for Peace and Reconciliation 242
Foster, Arlene 268, 336–7, 338
'Four Horsemen' 149, 183, 189, 231

Frizzell, Desmond 221
Fruit of the Loom 208–9, 363

G

Galway, Sir James 292–3
Gandhi Peace Prize 309–10, 345
Garda Síochána, An, death of Garda Fallon 92
General Election (1979) (UK) 154–5
General Election (1981) (Irish) 168
General Election (1983) (UK) 173–6
General Election (1987) (UK) 199
General Election (1997) (Irish) 260
General Election (1997) (UK) 259
General Election (2001) (UK) 304, 305
General Election (2005) (UK) 314
General Election (2010) (UK) 326
General Election (2017) (UK) 359
General Election (2019) (UK) 359
General Election (February 1974) (UK) 133, 142–3
General Election (October 1974) (UK) 144–5
Good Friday Agreement (1998) 271, 286, 329, 360
anti-agreement unionists 274, 275, 281
Donaldson's criticism of 271
Framework Document 249
Hume and 272, 273, 274, 280–1
No campaign 274, 281
North-South institutions 289
referenda North and South 271, 280–1, 361
Trimble and 280–1
Yes campaign 274, 275–80, 281, 289
Good Friday Agreement talks 142, 267–8
DUP's opposition to 264
Heads of Agreement document 264
Hume and 267–8, 270
North-South ministerial council 264
plenary session 271
Sinn Féin and 264, 265

409

Strand One: Northern Ireland 211, 249, 269
Strand Two: North-South axis 211, 215, 249, 250, 254–5, 264
Strand Three: British-Irish relationship 211, 249, 264
three-stranded approach 42, 211, 212, 249, 268, 269, 272, 273, 361
UUP and 264
see also decommissioning
Government of Ireland Act (1920) 93, 264
Green, Barney 242
Green, Jackie 178–9, 218–19, 220
Greysteel massacre 224–5
Guildford bombing 279

H

Hanna, Carmel 110–11, 355
Hanna, Claire 338, 344, 359
Hanna, Eamon 62, 110–11, 180–1, 305, 355
Harvard University 148–9
Haughey, Charles J. 159, 168, 171, 193–4, 196, 205
    Anglo-Irish Agreement (1985) 188–9
    Hume and 180–1, 185, 308
    New Ireland Forum and 171–2, 173, 179–80
Haughey, Denis 61, 88, 90–1, 96, 119, 178, 327, 349
Hayes, Maurice 136, 141, 262
Heaney, Seamus 11–12, 289
Heath, Edward (Ted) 87, 92, 133
    Assembly, talks about 112
    Bloody Sunday tribunal 106
    border poll (1973) 112, 117–18
    Faulkner and 95, 106, 107
    General Election (1974) 133, 142
    Sunningdale talks 125
    three-day working week, UK and 131–2
    unionist politicians and 106–7
Hendron, Jim 84, 85, 86, 257

Hendron, Joe 84–5, 175, 199, 205, 222, 259, 338, 353
Higgins, Michael D. 337–8, 342
Holkeri, Harri 251
Hone, Mary and Patrick 26
Hone, Patricia *see* Hume, Patricia (Pat) (*née* Hone)
Hughes, Brendan (The Dark) 162, 164–5
Hughes, Francis 165
Hume, Agnes (sister) 4
Hume, Aidan (son) 4, 26, 27, 114, 116, 142, 158, 341
    Atlantic Harvest and 45–6
    European Parliament, Hume and 312
    Hume's reaction to criticism 217
    Hume's retirement 317–18, 330–1
    Nobel award, Hume and 295
    security measures 223–4
    tributes to his mother 342
    visa for Adams, Hume and 235
Hume, Áine (*later* Abbott) (daughter) 26, 27, 114, 116, 217
    concerns about Hume 114–15, 226
    dementia, Hume and 317, 333–4
    health issues, Hume 297–9, 302, 335
    Hume–Adams talks and 223
    IRA's attempt to kidnap 115
Hume, Annie (*née* Doherty) (mother) 2, 3–4, 6, 7, 11
Hume, Annie (sister) 4
Hume, Harry (brother) 4
Hume, Jim (brother) 4
Hume, John
    assessment/analysis of 345–59
    background 2–6, 7
    books and films about 327–8
    business ideas 43–5
    Catholic faith 8, 10, 11, 12
    charitable donations 295, 363
    childhood 1, 4–5, 6, 7
    children 26

INDEX

criticism of 41, 216–17, 218, 253–4, 352, 353–4, 357
death 335–7
dementia 303, 310, 317–19, 325, 328, 329–35, 336, 364
education 7–8, 9–10, 11–12, 16–20
France and 19, 250, 261, 262
friendships 12–13, 15
funeral 337–40
headstone 340–1
honorary degrees 314
hospitalisation 124, 131, 226, 297–8, 300, 329
ill health 74, 75, 123–4, 218, 258, 282–3, 288, 296, 296–301, 302
Irish language and 81–2
Irish Presidency and 261–3
kindness/generosity 8, 12, 357, 363
language skills 19–20, 25, 132, 329
leadership style 352, 356–7
legacy 348, 360–1, 362
office/car, attacks on 198
pacifism 73
peace prizes awarded to 309–10, 345
perception of 29, 37, 55, 122–3, 146, 150
personal appearance 209–10
personal courage 362
personality 12, 20, 122–3, 323–4, 362
portrait of 344–5
priesthood, vocation to 10, 11, 13, 14
private life, media allegations 257–8
retirement 304, 306, 308–9, 312, 314, 315, 317–21, 327–8, 330–5, 364
safety, concerns about 198–9
singing, love of 13, 302, 308, 320, 328–9, 332
'single transferable speech' 5, 191, 315, 339
sport and 9, 10–11, 25, 302–3, 310–11, 318
teaching posts 24, 25, 28

tributes paid to 336–7, 338
unemployment 113, 147–8
Westminster, maiden speech 175–6
'City Solitary, A' (script) 31
Irish Times articles 32, 34, 35, 87, 361
'Northern Catholic, The' 32
'Social and Economic Aspects of the Growth of Derry, 1825–50' 27–8, 31

Hume, John (son) 26, 81, 114, 123, 219, 263, 274
    ill health, Hume and 298, 310, 328
Hume, Mo (daughter) 26, 80, 114, 273–4, 311–12, 328–9
    Adams's visit to the house 203
    dementia, Hume and 330, 334
    Nobel Peace Prize, Hume and 282, 294
Hume, Patricia (Pat) (*née* Hone) x, xi, 24, 114, 197, 323
    children 26
    death 341–2
    dementia, Hume and 325, 327–8, 329–30, 333–5
    essay on Hume 327–8
    funeral 342–3
    Greysteel massacre, reaction to 224–5
    Hume–Adams talks, views on 223, 225
    Hume's Derry office 178
    Lifetime Achievement Award 330
    organisation of Hume's trips 113, 210
    perception of 24, 27, 157, 362
    personality 27
    press coverage, distressed by 217–18
    pro-Coleraine lobby, Hume and 42
    relationship with Hume 26–7
    as sole breadwinner 147
    tributes paid to 342
Hume, Patrick (Patsy) (brother) 4, 9
Hume family 328–9
    attack on family home 197–8

death of their mother 341–2
demonstrations at family home 116
Donegal and 80–2, 199, 218, 223–4, 244–5, 363
Hume's death and funeral 337–40
Hume, family, Hume's funeral 340
Hume family
    Nobel Peace Prize ceremony 294
    Provisional IRA's plan to kill 114, 115
    telephone, bugged by republicans 258
Hume, Sally (sister) 4
Hume, Samuel (Sam) (father) 2, 3–6, 14, 21–2
Hume, Therese (daughter) 26, 81, 101, 102, 116, 340
Hume, William (great-grandfather) 2–3
Hume–Adams document 218–19, 220–1, 225, 226, 229, 233
Hume–Adams joint statement 260
Hume–Adams talks 196, 201–5, 218–19, 220, 232, 233, 241, 362
    continuation after Greysteel 225
    criticism of 203, 250, 352
    Hume family and 223
    Major's views on 354
    SDLP team 201, 202
    SDLP's views on 203–5, 305, 352–3, 354, 356
    Sinn Féin team 201, 202
    unionist perception of 256, 346–7, 348
    vindication of 272
hunger strikes 161–7, 169
    decision to end 164–5
    Hume and 161–2, 163–4, 165
    nationalist perception of 167–8
    Thatcher's stance 161–2, 167–8
Hurd, Douglas, Secretary of State 182, 185

I

International Body on Arms Decommissioning 251
internment 92, 94–5, 101, 109
    Magilligan protest 98–100
    SDLP and 112, 124, 126, 127
Irish Department of Foreign Affairs 104, 122–3, 125, 184, 194, 267–8
Irish Independent 17, 230
Irish National Liberation Army (INLA) 164, 264
Irish News 305–6
Irish Red Cross 330
Irish Republican Army (IRA) 76–7, 79, 83, 140
    American supporters 148, 149, 151
    Army Council 186, 240
    attack on Hume planned by 114
    back channel 227, 228, 229
    Bloody Friday and 110
    bombings 110, 120, 182, 199–200, 211, 221–2, 252
    British soldiers killed by 92
    campaign of violence 165, 185, 199–200, 202, 206, 211, 215, 221, 236
    ceasefire collapse 252–3
    ceasefires 109, 211, 228, 239, 245–6, 256, 261
    cessation of military operations 240, 241, 261
    fatalities 92, 196–7
    hatred of Hume 115, 136
    Heathrow Airport, mortars fired at 239
    Hume and 78–9, 109, 177, 185–6, 206, 210, 240
    Hume's daughter, attempt to kidnap 115
    killings 120, 182, 199–200, 221, 246
    prisoners, dirty protest and 159–60
    recruits 105, 106
    robbery in Newry 246
    secret channel, UK government and 212, 226–7
    secret talks, Hume informed about 228–9
    Sinn Féin and 195
    supporters 78, 148, 149, 151
    TUAS document 239–40

INDEX

see also Continuity IRA; decommissioning; hunger strikes; Official IRA; Provisional IRA; Real IRA

Irish Times, Hume's articles 32, 34, 35, 61, 87, 361

Irish unity 111, 171, 179–80, 181, 232, 244
    Hume's views on 33–4, 61, 87, 118, 180, 181, 233, 360–1
    principle of consent, Hume and 33, 35, 61, 118

ITV, *World in Action* 60

J

John and Pat Hume Foundation 341, 363

Johnson, Boris 334, 337, 338

K

Keenan, Dan 18, 173, 190, 200, 201, 204, 350, 355

Kennedy, Edward (Ted) 112–13, 148–9, 183, 308
    Anglo-Irish Agreement (1985) 189
    Hume's meetings with 112–13, 134, 148, 231–2, 234–5
    visa for Adams, Hume and 234–5, 236

Kerr, David
    Good Friday Agreement 274–5
    Hume–Adams talks 256, 348
    Trimble and 254–5, 274, 287, 288, 347
    Waterfront Hall concert 277–8, 280
    Yes campaign 277–8, 280

Kerr, Frank 246

King, Sir Frank 138

King, Martin Luther 55, 308, 309

King, Tom, Secretary of State 201, 207

Kinnock, Neil 210–11, 245, 248

L

Labour Party (British) 41, 49, 133, 142, 154, 243, 244, 245

Lemass, Seán 38

Lenihan, Brian, Snr 189

Lewis, Brandon, Secretary of State 338

Lillis, Michael 122–3, 149–50, 184, 362

Lockwood, Sir John 38, 39, 40, 43

Logue, Hugh 97, 131, 146, 222–3

Logue, Rosemary 26, 53

Loughinisland killings 242

loyalist paramilitaries 91, 130, 206, 242
    hatred of Hume 116, 136, 221, 350
    killings 120, 223, 224, 242, 284
    Ulster Workers' Council and 134

loyalist strike (1977) 152

Loyalist Volunteer Force 264

Lynch, Jack 71, 74–5, 104

M

McAleese, Mary 261–2, 314, 319, 341, 342
    Hume and 29, 344, 350, 364

McAteer, Eddie 38, 39, 40, 41, 64, 71–2, 154
    Derry march and 49, 50, 51, 52–3
    Hume and 61–2, 87
    see also Nationalist Party

McBride, Sharon 221

McCann, Eamonn 36–7, 47, 83, 114, 115, 214
    Bloody Sunday and 105
    civil rights campaign and 55
    Derry march and 48, 51, 53–4
    Good Friday Agreement 272
    Hume and 37, 55, 303
    Northern Ireland Labour Party 61, 63
    Stormont election (1969) 63–4

McCartney, Bob 264, 274

McCay, Ronan 297, 299–300, 307–8, 309–10

McCloskey, Amy 331–2, 335, 338

McCloskey, Francis 70

McCluskey, Patricia and Conn 37

McCool, Seán 10, 20, 22

McCrea, Don 25, 156–7

McDaid, Michael 103

413

McDevitt, Conall 253–4, 262–3, 269, 278, 280, 286
McDonnell, Alasdair 90, 214, 326, 338, 359
McFeely, Tom 164
McGettigan, Revd Danny 338
McGimpsey, Christopher and Michael 179
McGimpsey, Ross, RUC District Inspector 52
McGlone, Patsy 357
McGonagle, Jim 10, 12, 22
McGrady, Eddie 90, 166, 190, 199, 259, 305, 314, 326
   Hume and 204–5, 353
   Hume–Adams talks, views on 203, 204, 205
McGrory, Paddy 199
McGuinness, Martin 109–10, 228–9, 259, 345
   Deputy First Minister 315, 316
   Hume's dislike of 316–17
   Paisley and 315, 316, 325
McKenna, Seán 164
McWilliams, Monica 100–1, 198, 281, 296–7, 298
Magilligan protest
   British Army and 98–9, 101
   Hume and 98–100, 126, 296
Maginness, Alban 167, 319, 358–9
Maguire, Frank 145, 155, 165, 166
Major, Sir John 208, 215, 219, 246, 251, 256
   Downing Street Declaration 232, 233
   Hume and 220, 225, 225–6, 232, 233, 256–7, 354–5
   IRA, secret communication with 212, 227
   Mayhew and 229
   Northern Ireland Forum 251–2
   resignation 259
   Reynolds and 229–30, 239
   Ulster Unionist MPs, reliance on 233, 257
   unionists, attempt to reassure 241–2
   US visa for Adams, objection to 237
Mallon, Gertrude 306, 358
Mallon, Seamus 120, 184, 190, 194, 259, 305
   Deputy First Minister 282, 284, 300, 301
   Deputy Leader, SDLP 158, 159, 163, 301
   Good Friday Agreement 269, 271
   Hume and 138–9, 144, 158–9, 306, 308, 353, 358
   Hume–Adams talks 201, 205
   New Ireland Forum 180
   Prior's 'rolling devolution' and 169
   resignation as Deputy First Minister 300
   resignation as SDLP Deputy Leader 306
   retirement as MP 314
   SDLP and 119–20, 152–3, 154, 282, 358
   Trimble and 284
   unionists, Hume and 347, 349
Mansergh, Martin 194
Martin Luther King Jr Nonviolent Peace Prize 309, 310, 345
Martin, Micheál 338, 345
Mason, Roy, Secretary of State 152, 153
Maudling, Reginald 106
Mayhew, Sir Patrick, Secretary of State 227, 229, 236
Mayhew talks (1992) 215–16
Maynooth University 314
Maze Prison 159–62, 163–4, 186, 264
   see also hunger strikes
Meharg, William, RUC Inspector 50, 53
miners' strike (UK) 131–2, 134, 135
Mitchell, George 13, 251, 256, 264, 271, 341
   deadline for agreement 267, 270
   Hume and 274, 360
Mitchell Principles 263, 265
Moloney, Ed 213, 214

INDEX

Molyneaux, Jim 201, 212, 215, 241, 250
Moore, James 225
Morgan, Martin 313
Morrison, Danny 181–2, 201, 202–3
Mowlam, Mo, Secretary of State 244–5, 260, 264, 265, 270, 285, 298
Moynihan, Daniel Patrick 148–9, 183, 236
Mulvey, Revd Anthony 28, 36, 37, 69
Murray, Denis 193, 201, 206, 315

N

Napier, Oliver 85, 137
National Democratic Party (NDP) 90, 117
Nationalist Party 37, 40–1, 82, 86, 90, 154
    Hume's critique of 32–3, 34, 63
    McAteer and 40–1, 62, 63, 64, 169–70
    Stormont Election (1969) 65, 67
Needham, Sir Richard 208–9, 349, 353, 356
Nesbitt, Mike 238–9, 341
New Ireland Forum
    Haughey and 171–2, 173, 179–81
    Hume and 171–2, 176, 180–2, 183
    Protestant churches and 179
    Report 179–80, 181, 182
    Spring and 172, 173, 180
    Thatcher and 173, 182
New Ulster Movement 84
Newry protest march 60
Nicholson, Jim 190, 207, 313, 320, 351
Nobel Peace Prize (1998) 286–95
    Hume and 13, 282, 286–7, 290–1, 295, 310, 331, 345, 363
    Trimble and 286, 287–8, 291–2
Northern Ireland 16, 31, 32, 38, 112
    British identity in 361
    Direct Rule 106, 107, 143
    discrimination 37
    education in 9, 10, 37
    fiftieth anniversary 93, 94
    first cross-community government 125
    gerrymandering 1, 19, 31, 48, 54, 349
    housing crisis 36, 49, 57, 77–8
    Hume and 30, 34, 42, 128, 176
    Hume's promotion of 132, 134, 208–9, 349, 351, 363–4
    joint sovereignty, SDLP and 111–12
    nationalists 32–3
    President Carter's comments 149
    Protestant tradition in 33
    reform, need for 56
    status of 131, 187
    strikes 107, 135–40, 152
    unemployment 208
Northern Ireland Assembly 119, 126
    British troops, announcement 76
    demonstration, Hume and 67
    emergency session 75
    fall of (1974) 139–40, 141
    first power-sharing government 129–30
    Hume and 37, 40, 66, 82, 84, 93
    prorogued 143
    Public Order Bill, debate on 66–7
    SDLP boycott of 95–6, 108
    SDLP walk-out 94
    Sunningdale Agreement and 134–5
    unionists 66, 67
    University for Derry campaign 39–40
    Whitelaw's proposal 111, 118
    see also power-sharing
Northern Ireland Assembly (1982) 169, 170, 179
Northern Ireland Assembly (1998) 281
Northern Ireland Assembly elections (2022) 359–60
Northern Ireland Civil Rights Association (NICRA) 47–9, 52, 59, 101–2
Northern Ireland Executive 124–5, 134, 145
    Devlin and 121–2
    Faulkner's resignation 139–40

Hume and 121–2
inter-party discussions 121–2
Joint Ministerial Steering Group 136–7
Minister for Commerce, Hume as 124, 125, 132, 135, 139–40, 142
opposition to 132
power-sharing 121–2, 128, 129–30
power-sharing failure (1974) 139–40, 141–2, 143
unionists and 121
UWC strike and 136–7, 138–9
Northern Ireland Executive (1998) 285, 295, 300, 301
  Deputy First Minister, Mallon as 282, 284, 300, 301
  First Minister, Trimble as 281, 284, 300
  Hume and 281, 282–4
Northern Ireland Forum 251–2, 253, 256
Northern Ireland General Election (1969) 61–5
Northern Ireland Labour Party 50, 65, 93, 112, 117
  Devlin and 67, 82, 83, 90
  McCann and 61, 63
Northern Ireland Memorial Fund 294
Northern Ireland Office (NIO) 109, 136, 163, 164, 169, 189
  Hume and 163, 208, 257, 294, 349
  Provisionals, talks with 145
Northern Ireland Women's Coalition (NIWC) 100, 253, 281, 296

O

O'Callaghan, Miriam 280–1, 322–4, 327–8
Ó Ceallaigh, Dáithí 161, 218
Official IRA 79, 91, 106, 108
Official Unionist Party (OUP) 133, 145, 146, 155, 159, 166, 175, 190
Ó Fiaich, Tomás, Cardinal 16–18, 22–3, 28, 162, 165
O'Hanlon, Paddy 65, 67, 82, 83, 138
Ó hUiginn, Seán 151, 350

O'Kane, Liz (sculptor) 345
O'Kane, Ruairí 303, 316, 319–20, 324–5, 356, 358
Omagh bombing 284–5
O'Neill, Terence 31, 38, 56, 70
  election called by 40, 58, 60–1, 70
  Hume's criticism of 41–2
  reforms and 37, 57, 64
  resignation 70
  University for Derry campaigners and 39, 40
O'Neill, Thomas Patrick (Tip) 148–9, 150, 183, 231
Orange Order 2, 249–50, 284
Orme, Stan 136

P

Paisley, Eileen 157, 342
Paisley, Ian, Jnr 156, 315
Paisley, Revd Ian 112, 126, 135, 345
  Drumcree march and 249–50
  DUP and 132, 133
  First Minister 315
  Good Friday Agreement, opposition to 274
  Hume and 156–7, 159, 212, 315, 316
  Hume–Adams meeting, criticism of 201
  IRA statement, views on 241
  McGuinness and 315, 316, 325
  MEP for Northern Ireland 155, 159, 182, 207, 313, 315
  O'Neill, criticism of 38, 58
  power-sharing and 315, 325
  Stormont election (1969) 65
  Sunningdale, opposition to 130
  UUUC and 132, 143
  Westminster election (1970) 87
People's Democracy 58, 59, 89
Phoblacht, An 165
Plantation of Ulster 2
Police Authority 127
police reform 119, 126–7, 159, 274, 275
  see also Royal Irish Constabulary (RUC)

INDEX

Porter, Robert 67, 68, 76
Powell, Enoch 175, 190, 199
power-sharing 121–2, 128, 129–30, 191
    coalition against 145
    failure (1974) 139–40, 141–2, 143
    SDLP and 147
    unionist opposition to 146
    voluntary coalition proposal 147
Prior, Jim, Secretary of State 169, 208
prisoners
    IRA dirty protest 159–60
    release of 268, 271, 275, 348
    see also hunger strikes
Progressive Unionist Party (PUP) 253, 263, 281, 341
proportional representation 111, 118, 119
Protestant church leaders 145, 179
Protestants 48, 49, 76, 91, 92
    Hume, language used by 190–1
    SDLP and 86, 90–1
Provisional IRA 79, 91, 96, 205
    ceasefires 108–9, 109–10, 145
    Hume family, attempt to kill 115
    Hume's negotiations with 108–9
    killings 110
    NIO, discussions with 145
    Protestant church leaders and 145
    Whitelaw's secret talks with 109–10
Public Order Bill 66–7
Purvis, Dawn 341
Pym, Francis, Secretary of State 129, 133

Q

Queen's University Belfast 37, 58, 133, 177, 350
Quinn boys, deaths of 284

R

Raidió na Gaeltachta 82
Ramsay, Robert 122, 132, 141
Reagan, Ronald 183
Real IRA 284–5
Red Hand Commando 242

Rees, Merlyn, Secretary of State 133, 137, 139, 140, 145
Reid, Revd Alec 193–6, 199, 201, 206
Republican Labour 65, 67, 82, 86, 90
Reynolds, Albert 219, 227
    Adams and Hume, meeting with 242
    Downing Street Declaration 232, 233
    Hume and 221, 242, 308
    Major and 229–30, 239
    resignation 246–7
Reynolds, Revd Gerry 194, 195, 201
Ritchie, Margaret 204–5, 270, 326, 356, 357, 359
Robinson, Mary 261, 262, 324
Robinson, Peter 188, 275
Rodgers, Bríd 80, 158, 164, 268–9, 338
    Hume and 353–4
    Hume–Adams meetings, views on 213–14
    SDLP Deputy Leader 309
Routledge, Paul 20, 53, 166
Rowntree, Francis 108
Royal Ulster Constabulary (RUC) 59, 107, 126, 136, 196, 265
    assaults by 51–2, 68, 69, 70, 71
    B Specials and 75
    Bogside riots 72–3
    civil rights protestors and 49, 50–2, 60, 67–8
    fatalities 91–2
    Hume and 126–7, 139
    Loughgall RUC Station 196–7
    reform of 274
    Rosemount RUC Station 73–4
RTÉ, 'Ireland's Greatest' series 324–5

S

St Anne's Primary School 147
St Colman's High School, Strabane 25–6, 28
St Columb's College
    Hume's education at 9, 10, 11–13, 82

Hume's teaching post 20, 28, 29, 30–1, 43
St Eugene's Cathedral 8, 337, 342
St Eugene's Primary School 7
St Mary's College, Belfast 26
St Patrick's College, Maynooth 10
   discipline at 14–16, 21
   Hume and 13–23, 24, 28
   Ó Fiaich, Tomás and 16–17
Sands, Bobby 162, 164–6, 167
Saville Inquiry 103, 326, 327
SDLP (Social Democratic and Labour Party) 41, 87, 90, 152–3, 154, 253
   abstentionist policy 96, 157, 169–70, 179
   Acting Leader, Hume as 158
   annual conferences 154, 163, 206, 299, 308–10
   Assembly elections 170, 359–60
   boycotts and 95–6, 108, 112
   by-election 166
   candidates, training of 117
   Convention elections 146–7
   Council Elections 119–21
   Deputy Leader, Hume as 89, 90, 93, 96, 110–11, 122
   Deputy Leader, Mallon as 158, 159, 163, 194, 301
   Deputy Leader, Rodgers as 309
   Duisburg discussions 205–6
   Dungiven Castle assembly 94, 96
   electoral test (1973) 116–17, 119–21
   Faulkner and 94, 111–12
   Fitt and 153–4, 157–8
   formation, talks about 83, 86–7, 88–9
   General Election (1987) 199
   General Election (1997) 259
   General Election (2001) 304, 305
   General Election (2005) 314
   General Election (2017) 359
   General Election (2019) 359
   Hume's final address 308–9
   Leader, Durkan as 309, 314, 320, 359
   Leader, Eastwood as 358, 359
   Leader, Fitt as 88, 89, 90, 122
   Leader, Hume as 163, 301–2, 304, 355, 356, 358–9
   Leader, McDonnell as 359
   Leader, Ritchie as 326, 356, 359
   membership 90, 117
   North Belfast Branch 110–11
   Northern Ireland Executive 121–2
   Northern Ireland Forum 253
   party name, discussions about 89–90
   policy document 111–12, 119
   power-sharing and 147
   press officer 18
   Sinn Féin and 169, 170, 174, 185, 205, 214, 259, 305, 313, 314, 320, 326, 355
   sit-downs and demonstrations 96–7
   Stormont walk-out, Hume and 94
   Sunningdale Agreement and 134
   'Towards a New Ireland' 111–12, 119
   Ulster Unionists, talks with 93
Shankill Road bombing 221–2, 223, 224
Sinn Féin 173, 199, 229, 246, 256, 300
   abstentionist policy 167, 175, 196, 305
   Adams as President 185, 186, 222, 250
   Anglo-Irish Agreement (1985), views on 188
   Ard Fheis 196, 201
   Assembly seats (1982) 170
   Dáil Éireann and 196
   Downing Street Declaration and 239
   DUP and 315
   General Elections and 259, 305, 314
   Hume and x, 206, 257–8, 259, 265, 354
   Mitchell Principles and 263
   power-sharing 315
   rise of 169, 170, 187, 305, 355
   'Scenario for Peace, A' 196

INDEX

SDLP and 169, 170, 174, 185, 205, 214, 259, 305, 313, 314, 320, 326, 355
Smash H-Block campaign 163
Soderberg, Nancy 235–6, 237
Special Powers Act (1922) 57, 77
Spring, Dick 172, 173, 180, 189, 198–9, 221, 246
Stephenson, Jonathan 277
Sunday Independent, criticism of Hume 217, 218, 254, 319, 352
Sunningdale Agreement 130
    Hume and 140, 142
    negotiations 125–8, 130
    Northern Ireland Assembly and 134–5
    unionist opposition to 130, 131, 133, 142, 144, 146, 250

T

Taylor, John 75, 155, 182, 207, 250, 267, 270, 282
Thatcher, Margaret 154, 155, 157, 159, 160
    Anglo-Irish Agreement (1985) 187–8, 190
    Brighton bombing, IRA and 182
    FitzGerald and 182
    General Election (1983) 173–4
    Hume and 183–4
    hunger strikes and 161–2
    Irish diplomats and 187
    New Ireland Forum proposals, rejection of 182–3
    Northern Ireland, Britishness of 176
    'Out, Out, Out' speech 182
    Reagan and 183
    resignation 208
Thompson, Karen 224
Thornhill College, Derry 26, 310
Times 249
Tip O'Neill Chair in Peace Studies 314
Toner, Revd Tom 164
Trimble, Daphne 287–8, 294
Trimble, David 147, 254, 270, 342
    Clinton and 271
    Drumcree march and 249–50
    First Minister, role as 281, 284
    goals: devolution and decommissioning 300
    Good Friday Agreement 272, 274
    Hume and 250, 254–5, 294, 346, 349, 350
    inter-party talks 263, 268
    Major and 257
    Mallon and 284
    Nobel Peace Prize 286, 287
    Sunningdale, opposition to 250
    tribute to Hume 336
    UUP and 250, 253, 254, 257, 261
    Vanguard and 133, 147, 250
    Waterfront Hall concert 276, 277–8
Troubles 16, 30, 34, 47, 92, 162
    deaths 92, 94, 101, 113
    legacy of 146
TUAS document 239–40, 246–7
Tyndall, Charles, Bishop of Derry 56

U

UK Unionist Party (UKUP) 253, 264, 274
Ulster Army Council 130
Ulster Defence Association (UDA) 120, 130, 134, 221, 222, 224, 264, 265
Ulster Democratic Party (UDP) 120–1, 253, 263, 264–5
Ulster Freedom Fighters (UFF) 120, 223, 224, 242, 264, 265
Ulster Unionist Council 130
Ulster Unionist Party (UUP) 112, 142, 179, 191, 212, 215, 238
    domination of politics 31
    Donaldson and 265, 268, 270, 271
    Duisburg discussions 205–6
    Faulkner's resignation 130–1
    Good Friday Agreement 272
    Good Friday Agreement talks 261, 263, 270–1
    Hume and 34, 255
    leadership battle 92

Major and 233
Molyneaux's resignation 250
Northern Ireland Labour Party and 93
O'Neill, lack of support for 70
SDLP and 93, 254–5
Trimble and 250, 253, 254
Westminster election (1970) 87
Ulster University Magee Campus 314
Ulster Volunteer Force (UVF) 130, 134, 223, 242
Ulster Workers' Council (UWC) 133, 134
Ulster Workers' Council (UWC) strike 135–40, 143, 144, 152
    Hume's energy plan 136, 137, 138
Union of Students in Ireland (USI) 177, 178
Unionist Party of Northern Ireland (UPNI) 145, 146
unionist veto 188, 234
unionists 38
    Assembly and 121, 170
    civil rights campaign, views on 56
    Council of Ireland and 128
    Direct Rule and 107
    distrust of Hume 349–50
    Hume, language used by 172–3, 350, 351
    Hume, perception of 201, 347, 349
    Hume–Adams meetings, criticism of 201, 215
    Hume's appeal to 263–4
    Hume's attitude towards 349, 350–2
    Hume's critique of 172–3, 350
    Irish government and 215–16
    Major and 241–2
    mindset, Hume's perception of 350–1
    New Ireland Forum and 173, 181
    power-sharing, aversion to 141
    Sunningdale, opposition to 127, 130, 131, 133, 142, 144, 146

Sunningdale talks 125–6
two-day stoppage and 107
Westminster seats, resignation from 190
Whitelaw's proposals and 119
United Ulster Unionist Council (UUUC) 132, 133, 143, 146, 147
University College Dublin (UCD) 16, 23
University for Derry campaign 37–8, 39–40, 42–3
US visas
    Adams and 234–5, 238
    objection to 236, 240

V

Vanguard movement 107, 120, 121, 130, 142, 146
    Craig and 107, 119, 132, 133
Vanguard Unionist Progressive Party 119

W

Waldorf Astoria conference 238–9
Waterfront Hall concert 276–80
    Ash (local band) 276–7, 279
    Bono, Trimble and Hume on stage, imagery of 279–80, 288
    U2 and 276–9, 288–9
    Yes campaign and 276–80
WAVE Trauma Centre 344–5
West, Harry 132, 133, 145, 166, 167
White, Barry 21, 40, 302
White, John 120–1
White, Wilf 224
Whitelaw, Willie, Secretary of State 107, 108, 109–10, 112, 118–19
Widgery Report 108
Widgery Tribunal 106, 108, 327
Wilson, Harold 133, 142, 144–5
    Northern Ireland and 56, 57, 76, 137–8, 140
Wilson, Paddy 120, 121
Wyer, Finuala 225

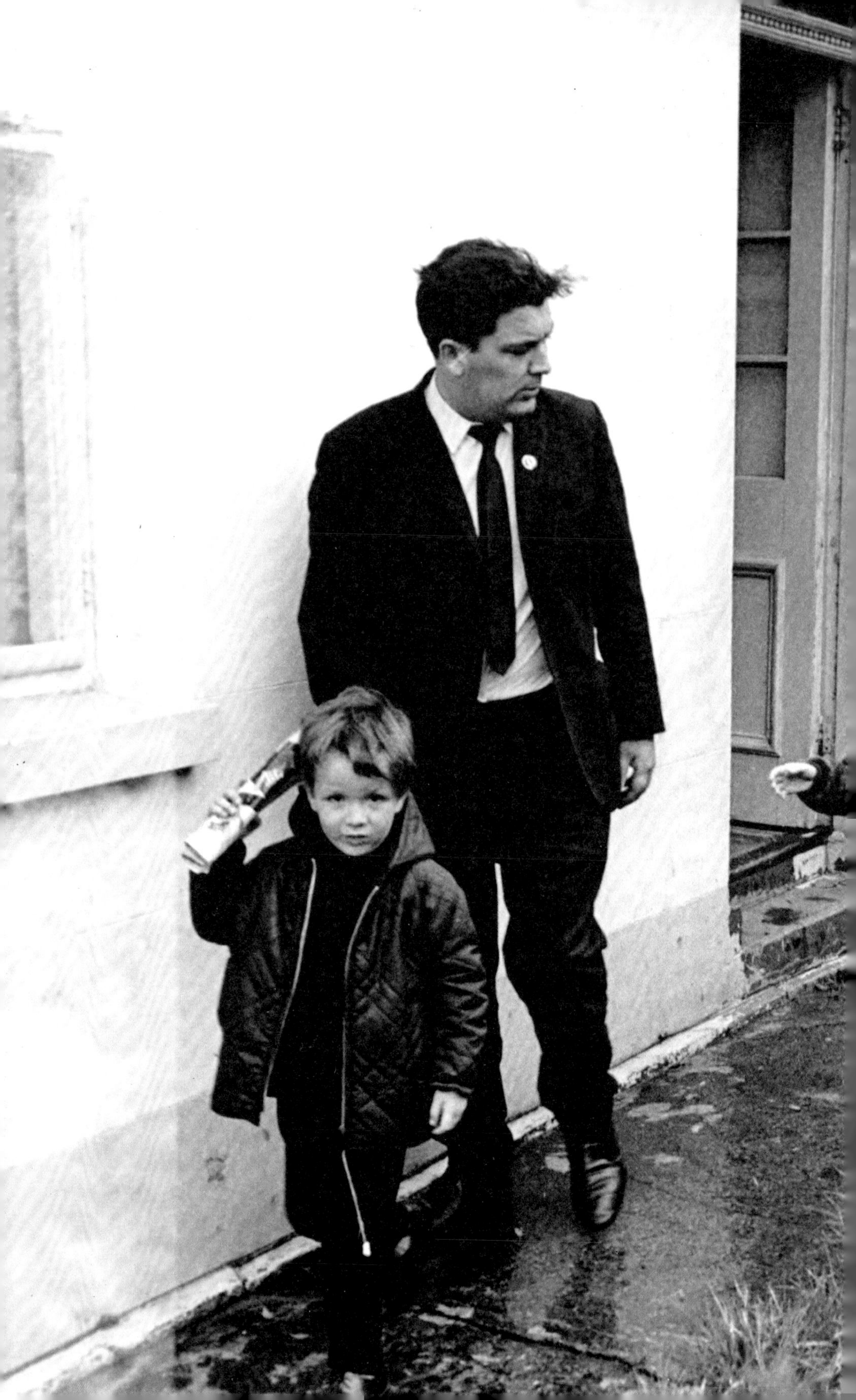